Science and Religion

Understanding the Issues

Nancy Morvillo

WILEY-BLACKWELL

A John Wiley & Sons, Ltd., Publication

This edition first published 2010
© 2010 Nancy Morvillo

Blackwell Publishing was acquired by John Wiley & Sons in February 2007. Blackwell's publishing program has been merged with Wiley's global Scientific, Technical, and Medical business to form Wiley-Blackwell.

Registered Office
John Wiley & Sons Ltd, The Atrium, Southern Gate, Chichester, West Sussex, PO19 8SQ, United Kingdom

Editorial Offices
350 Main Street, Malden, MA 02148-5020, USA
9600 Garsington Road, Oxford, OX4 2DQ, UK
The Atrium, Southern Gate, Chichester, West Sussex, PO19 8SQ, UK

For details of our global editorial offices, for customer services, and for information about how to apply for permission to reuse the copyright material in this book please see our website at www.wiley.com/wiley-blackwell.

The right of Nancy Morvillo to be identified as the author of this work has been asserted in accordance with the UK Copyright, Designs and Patents Act 1988.

Wiley also publishes its books in a variety of electronic formats. Some content that appears in print may not be available in electronic books.

Designations used by companies to distinguish their products are often claimed as trademarks. All brand names and product names used in this book are trade names, service marks, trademarks or registered trademarks of their respective owners. The publisher is not associated with any product or vendor mentioned in this book. This publication is designed to provide accurate and authoritative information in regard to the subject matter covered. It is sold on the understanding that the publisher is not engaged in rendering professional services. If professional advice or other expert assistance is required, the services of a competent professional should be sought.

Library of Congress Cataloging-in-Publication Data

Morvillo, Nancy.
  Science and religion : Understanding the Issues / Nancy Morvillo.
    p. cm.
  Includes bibliographical references and index.
  ISBN 978-1-4051-8966-8 (hardcover : alk. paper) – ISBN 978-1-4051-8965-1 (pbk. : alk. paper)
1. Religion and science.   I. Title.
  BL240.3.M68 2010
  215–dc22

                                                                                    2009045876

A catalogue record for this book is available from the British Library.

Set in 10.5/12.5pt Dante by Graphicraft Limited, Hong Kong.
Printed in Singapore by Ho Printing Singapore Pte Ltd

1   2010

Science and Religion

Contents

List of Figures

List of Tables

Acknowledgments

I wish to express my thanks to many people who made this book possible. To Rebecca Harkin at Wiley-Blackwell, and several anonymous reviewers, for helping me to shape and refine the manuscript, while keeping my intent and my passion intact. To Jackie Grennon Brooks, my long-time mentor and friend, for teaching me to make sure fun is always at the heart of the work. To the new friends and colleagues I have met in my recent quests, whose words of encouragement may not have seemed like much to them but meant the world to me. I particularly want to acknowledge Mary Kathleen Cunningham and Ted Peters in this regard. To the campus community at Florida Southern College: the administration, faculty, and students, who encouraged me and gave me room to explore new worlds. To two of the most brilliant men I know who have inspired me with their insights and knowledge in their respective fields of science and theology: Bob Baum and Waite Willis. And to my friend, colleague, and constant companion on my journey into and through this realm, Sara Fletcher Harding: none of this would have been possible without her. And finally to my family: my mother whose support and encouragement were unwavering, and my wonderful husband, Mike, and our beautiful children, Chris, Brian, and Matthew: they are my pillars, my home, my life.

Introduction

I was born and raised Catholic. I went to school and studied science, obtaining my Ph.D. in genetics. I joined the biology faculty at Florida Southern College, a United Methodist affiliated school. In recent years, I have explored the interplay and the relationship between science and religion, fascinated by the range of views in this interdisciplinary venture. I am the co-director for the Florida Center for Science and Religion, which was established through a grant from the Metanexus Institute on Religion and Science, itself funded by the Templeton Foundation. And I team-teach a course on science and religion. I am not a theologian. I am not a philosopher.

I found, through my teaching and research, that there are many good books addressing various aspects of science and religion. Notably, Ian Barbour and John Haught have written excellent guides for those interested in learning about the basic issues and views in the field. But none of these books addressed everything that I felt needed to be covered in an introductory course on science and religion. So, like any good academic, I decided to write one myself. In this venture, I hoped to accomplish several things.

First of all, I wanted basic coverage of the topics at the forefront of the dialogue. This includes methodology, cosmology, evolution, and ethical concerns. Throughout all, I also wanted to include some historical perspective, to help the reader understand how we got to where we are today.

Second, I wanted this book to be accessible to everyone. I didn't want to write a book on science for the theologian, or a book on theology for the scientist. I wanted a book that would provide an introduction to both fields, a book that someone interested in the dialogue but not very knowledgeable in one or both disciplines could have as a guide and resource. I hope this book will help faculty to feel comfortable teaching a course in science and religion, and students to explore questions from both perspectives. To accomplish this, I focus on addressing the science in more detail and presenting the theological concepts in a more basic fashion than other books in the field. My biggest disappointment in the science and religion books with which I am familiar is the lack of detail they provide with regard to science. Science has become a visual field: illustrations are essential in trying to understand topics and are included where appropriate. Theological ideas are often very difficult to grasp for those new to the field, so I have tried to present them at a basic level. Undoubtedly, this will be too basic for some. My goal is not to cover everything, but to provide some background and avenues for further exploration.

Third, I think students need to be acquainted with the major writings and thoughts of key figures in the dialogue. Textbooks summarize ideas, but this is no substitute for reading it yourself. From a teaching perspective, locating appropriate items can be a daunting and time-consuming task. I have tried to remove this barrier. Every chapter has a "Primary Literature" section. Several readings, from biblical passages to classical and contemporary works by scientists and theologians, are included. These readings are important supplements to each chapter, and I encourage you to utilize them. Students also need to reflect on the ideas presented in a text and be given a chance to consider their own positions. To address this, I have included questions at the end of each chapter to stimulate ideas and discussions.

An important issue that needs to be addressed is the overall focus of the book. I have discussed theological and religious viewpoints almost exclusively from Christian perspectives, and I have focused on viewpoints that examine where science and religion can dialogue. I do not spend much time on issues where science and religion conflict. This approach stems from my desire to comprehend how these two approaches help us understand the world, not how and why they may contradict each other. From my perspective, focusing on where the conflicts lie is limiting. So many more possibilities exist when we consider how the two disciplines can inform each other. Many religions have interesting views that relate to science, but I cannot cover all these views in such a limited space. Therefore, I have chosen to focus on Christianity as a place to start. The American Religious Identification Survey conducted by the Graduate Center of the City University of New York found that about 77 percent of people identified themselves as Christians in 2001. It seems logical, in an introduction to this field, to start from a Christian perspective. I hope this book will encourage you to explore other faith traditions, to gain a broader perspective.

Lastly, a few technical notes. All the biblical passages in this book are from the Revised Standard Version, unless otherwise noted. The companion website for this book will be a good resource: among other material it includes three chapters that were in the original manuscript of this book but had to be modified for the print version. There are extensive discussions of gender issues, biotechnology, and medicine in these chapters. Given the nature of science, some statistics and facts in this book will be outdated by the time you read them. I encourage you to find up-to-date information. It will be well worth your time and effort.

I hope you enjoy your time contemplating these topics as much as I do.

Part I

Systems of Thought

1

Learning from the Past

Overview

For most of human history, there was no distinction between the disciplines of science and religion. Our knowledge of ancient civilizations reveals that cultures ascribed the workings of the natural world to deities. The Greeks formulated philosophies that explained natural phenomena as having been caused by natural forces. These ideas were in some ways rejected by early Christian theologians, but the power of the pagan philosophies could not be ignored, and ways were found to incorporate these understandings into Christian theology. During much of the Middle Ages, the handmaiden formula allowed for investigations into the natural world as long as they helped to support scripture and further the understanding of God. By the end of the Middle Ages, it was becoming more acceptable to investigate natural philosophy apart from religious studies. In the fourteenth and fifteenth centuries a movement of rationalism and empiricism emerged from a period of political and social turmoil and crises regarding church authority. This new approach led not only to the birth of modern science, but to a transformation of society known as the Enlightenment. Reactions to the Enlightenment emphasized a return to personal experience, imagination, and emotion. In this era can be seen the beginnings of the division between science and religion that exists today.

Introduction

For some of us, acquiring knowledge of the past is an engaging, interesting enterprise that stimulates us intellectually and has implications for our understanding of present-day events and attitudes. For others, the pursuit of history appears to be a fruitless survey of endless dates and names. Although our fast-paced, ever-changing world may require all of our efforts just to keep up with current advancements, history does play an important role in our lives. If we simply examine our world today and exclude the past, we deny ourselves the understandings our ancestors worked so hard to achieve. Our culture, our current questions, and our current answers may be ones which inspired, angered, or even outraged our forebears. Did they possess some wisdom that we can adapt? Did they have answers we haven't? How did they influence what we think and believe today?

The subject of history is not just an interesting study of long forgotten and irrelevant events and people in the past. By analyzing what came before us, we may come closer to understanding who we are and how we got to this point. And maybe some light will be shed on our current problems. Therefore, our journey into the entanglement of science and religion today will begin by taking a look at their relationship in the past. In the space of just a few pages, we will examine some of the most important people and concepts that shaped Western culture and Christianity. By no means is this an inclusive study: the events and individuals mentioned represent only a small portion of history. Linear and logical relationships are highlighted, but it must be understood that this is a very basic introduction, and the actual history is rich in diverse ideas and involves individuals and controversies well beyond the scope of this book. Rather, this chapter is intended as an all too brief introduction to some of the works and ideas that helped to shape both science and theology. It provides a setting, a stage if you will, that can be filled with various other characters and events of the period. With an understanding supplied by this stage and an appreciation of the ideas and events of the past, we can better comprehend what we have today.

The relationship between science and religion today is very different than what it has been in the past. As we shall see, for most of recorded history, there was no distinct separation between the two disciplines. This may come as a shock to many of us living in this modern society, for example in the United States, where the separation of church and state, and the notion that science is somehow the antithesis of religion, is the norm. But in the past science represented a way of glorifying and understanding God. Science was often done by religious clerics and, as knowledge was in the hands of the church for many centuries, the teaching of science was conducted with the approval of the Christian authorities. This did not mean the relationship was always smooth, but it is fascinating to examine the attitudes of the earliest scientists and theologians and their influences on religion, science, and culture.

We will begin our investigations in the pre-Christianity era with the ancient Greeks and see how they helped to shape Christian thought. We will then look at the Middle Ages, the Enlightenment, and the reactions to the Enlightenment. You may find it interesting to look at the development of modern science and the development of Christian theology as parallel pathways: both disciplines began and grew strong in the same tree, and then separated into the branches representing our present situation. We will discuss modern methodologies and notions of science and theology in chapter 2.

And What of the Greeks?

We begin our discussion at the dawn of civilization, with existing written records that reveal what our ancestors thought about science and religion. We find the first of these in Mesopotamia and ancient Egypt. Within these cultures, there are some stunning examples of truly good science, such as detailed astronomical observations and the creation of calendars. Therefore, we know these ancient peoples were not ignorant of natural phenomena. But why did they have such knowledge? Why was it important for them to study these phenomena? Stargazing for us today may be a leisurely activity, but for these early cultures it was a necessity. Observations of celestial movements provided information to create calendars, which in turn provided knowledge of the seasons, a necessity for successful agriculture. Other scientific notions at the time related to agriculture included the breeding of plants and animals. Additional natural observations focused on illnesses and diseases. Regardless of the scientific facts these cultures discovered, the observed phenomena were ascribed to the workings of the gods. It was the gods who moved the stars and planets, and who wept to make the rain. In many instances, nature itself was considered divine, and humans and other creatures as created by divine forces. Polytheism was the norm, and the earthly images of gods were often associated with animals. The world was not eternal, and sickness was due to divine displeasure (we will examine some of these notions further in chapter 5).

The ancient Greek philosophers are revered in history as they were the first to reject the notion that natural events are caused by supernatural forces. According to their philosophies, natural phenomena were not caused by vengeful and whimsical gods; rather, nature behaved in a constant and uniform fashion. Therefore, to the Greek philosophers, it was irrational to ascribe the workings of the natural world to gods. This does not mean they rejected the notion of one or more deities: as we shall see, both Plato and Aristotle argued for a type of divine being.

At this time, the study of nature – what we would call "science" – is referred to as natural philosophy. For the most part, the study of natural philosophy was undertaken no differently from any other philosophy. Logic and reasoning were applied to problems and questions surrounding the natural world, but there was no formal system of experimentation, such as we have today, to test ideas and gain more information. Hence, "natural philosophy" is a fitting term for the beginnings of science.

The first recorded use of natural explanations for natural events can be traced back to Thales (c.625–547 BCE), Anaximander (c.611–547 BCE), and Anaximenes (c.585–528 BCE). These philosophers focused on the basic material from which all things are made. For example, Thales believed that water was this basic material. He held that the Earth rested on water and that earthquakes were the result of the movement of the Earth on the water. Thales was not using supernatural forces or magic to account for earthquakes – he invoked natural causes. We also see the beginnings of careful observation and even some rudimentary experimentation with the Greeks, particularly in the area of medicine. Hippocrates of Cos (c.470–c.377 BCE) and his followers asked, "If diseases are not caused by the gods, then where do they come from?" The answer to this important question required the analytical skills that we recognize today as the root of science.

Socrates (c.470–399 BCE) used logic and reasoning to construct a rational system of ethics. He employed a method of questioning to help determine the knowledge and beliefs of others, which, in fact, helped the respondents to see the contradictions in their own philosophies. This approach is known as the Socratic Method. Plato (c.427–347 BCE) was a student of Socrates. He used the style of dialogues (Socratic dialogues, in which Socrates is often a character) in his written works, many of which survive. Plato's subjects included metaphysics (the nature of being and existence), epistemology (the nature of knowledge), human physiology, and politics. In his work *Timaeus* Plato presented a cosmology where a single deity created the world from a chaos that already existed. This monotheistic concept is a characteristic feature of many of the Greeks who studied natural philosophy. The deity, however, is abstract, impersonal, and out of reach (beyond the sky) and so, as we said before, natural events are not explained by invoking the supernatural.

Aristotle (384–322 BCE) was a student of Plato, and his philosophy impacted science and religion for over 2,000 years. Like Plato, he valued reasoning and wrote on a wide range of subjects. However, Aristotle also felt that observation, and the collection of facts and data, were important in studying the natural world. Among his works are writings that comment on the structure and operation of the universe, and provide detailed accounts of animals and human behavior. His ideas are sound and reasonable when he could study his subjects directly. For example, due to his observation and dissection of marine animals and reliance on the authority of the fishermen he interviewed, Aristotle's work in zoology is quite remarkable for his time. On the other hand, most of his notions of physics and cosmology were based on either common sense or his own assumptions, and therefore his conclusions were horribly flawed. Many of these fallacies could have been corrected had Aristotle done some simple experimentation. For example, his notion that larger, heavier objects fall faster than smaller, lighter ones could easily have been tested during his time. His writings about the natural world, many of which survive, were so complete and comprehensive that Aristotle became *the* authority regarding natural phenomena, and all knowledge was thought to be contained in his writings. For centuries, science (natural philosophy) consisted of commenting on Aristotle. His work was translated into Arabic and had a major impact on the development of Islamic philosophy. Aristotle's approach to studying nature made use of observation and logical deduction from facts; unfortunately, this aspect of his efforts was almost completely disregarded by his followers. It was not until the sixteenth and seventeenth centuries that his ideas were finally challenged and modern science emerged.

Some of Aristotle's ideas were very much in line with Christian theology. For example, he believed in teleology, the notion that there is a goal or purpose for everything (he called this the "final cause"). However, many of his concepts contradicted Christian doctrine and were threatening to the church:

- Aristotle believed that the world was eternal, that it had no beginning and no end. This was in direct opposition to the biblical accounts of *ex nihilo* creation of the Earth.
- Aristotle believed in a divine spirit he called the Unmoved Mover, who was not the creator of the world, and not even aware of its existence, but was the cause of the movement of the planets and orbs around the Earth. This was ultimately responsible for all motion in the world. This is in contrast to Plato's *Timaeus* and it also conflicts with the Christian notion of a living God personally involved with the world.
- Aristotle defined the soul as the source of life that could not be separated from the body. He identified three kinds of souls, and argued that souls could perish with the body. Christian doctrine identifies the soul as separate from the body and contends that it is immortal.

These and other problems caused the church to question the pagan ideas of the Greeks and to reject them. Early Christian theologians, such as Tertullian (c.160–c.220 CE), denounced Greek philosophy. Tertullian thought the Greeks were vain and trivial and, of course, heretical. He espoused simple faith above the reasoning of the Greek philosophers. And Paul (3–67 CE) warned the Colossian Christians not to be influenced by philosophy:

> See to it that no one makes a prey of you by philosophy and empty deceit, according to human tradition, according to the elemental spirits of the universe, and not according to Christ. (Colossians 2:8)

Based on these attitudes, one could conclude that the Greek philosophies would be disregarded in Christianity. However, the situation is much more complex. The early theologians were well versed in the Greek philosophies, having been educated extensively in the methodologies; the philosophical underpinnings were deeply engrained in them. Most theologians of this time were philosophers who later converted to Christianity and attempted to integrate the two belief systems. In addition, their defense of Christianity required them to engage in dialogue with non-Christians, and so these early theologians needed to be well versed in the Greek philosophies to communicate with those who did not accept the faith. And, ultimately, theologians who denied the usefulness of the philosophers and considered them to be heretics still employed the pagan arguments. Basically, they were not against all natural philosophy but only what was considered dangerous to the Christian faith.

Augustine (354–430), the bishop of Hippo in North Africa, was among these early Christian thinkers. His influence on the development of Christianity was enormous. Augustine stressed that reason could not answer all the questions about human existence. For him, faith needed to come first. Empirical knowledge, the knowledge we gain from our senses, was secondary to knowledge from revelation, what is revealed to us by God. But reason could be employed to further understand faith. Augustine did not fear the consequences of natural philosophy as his predecessors did. He believed all truth to be God's truth. However, he changed the tenor of its purpose. Augustine employed what is known as the handmaiden formula: the use of natural philosophy in the service of theology. Natural philosophy should not be pursued for the sake of knowledge alone. However, it could be valuable as a means to an end: if natural philosophy could help us to understand scripture, its study was legitimate and could be undertaken. The handmaiden formula became the prominent view in the Middle Ages. Some might argue that this ideology was detrimental to scientific progress, restricting the advancement of knowledge of the natural world. However, it was the church that provided a place for natural philosophy in the curriculum of the expanding educational systems. The church may not have encouraged science specifically, but it kept science alive.

The Middle Ages

After the barbarian conquest of the Western Roman Empire, intellectual pursuits had a low priority. In the early Middle Ages, from about 500 to 1000, the institutions of learning were the monasteries in Europe. Here, Greek writings were translated into Latin, and commentaries were written about them. Although there was not much advancement of science during this time, the preservation of the existing works is of great importance, and the inclusion of natural philosophy in the curriculum transmitted the ideas to succeeding generations.

In the eleventh and twelfth centuries, there was a renewal of culture in Europe, with revivals of the political, economic, and social systems. This resulted in an expansion of educational institutions into the university system in the major cities. There was still a commitment to religion, but other subjects were given prominence as well. There was more instruction in the classics (including Plato's *Timaeus*), the use of natural explanations for natural phenomena, and the application of reason to explain human activity. And more of the Greek classics, preserved in Arabic, were translated into Latin, among them the works of, and commentaries on, Aristotle. With greater access to the Greek philosophers and an increased emphasis on natural philosophy, the tensions between science and religion started to grow.

Anselm (1033–1109) lived just prior to the influx of Aristotelian ideas into Europe. He was a follower of Augustine, and put faith above reason. He believed, however, that reason could clarify faith and provide proof for faith. Anselm used an abstract argument to prove the existence of God. He contended that God is the ultimate being, and that we cannot conceive of a being greater than God. Therefore, God must exist not only in thought, but also in reality. For, if God is the greatest being who we can conceive, but exists only in contemplation, then one who actually exists would be greater. Therefore, God must exist in reality, not just in thought.

By the thirteenth century, the power of the knowledge assembled by the Greeks and the Arabs to explain nature was well understood, but the problem of contradiction with church dogma was growing. As we saw, Aristotle's ideas of an eternal world, his cosmology, and his concept of the nature of the soul, in conjunction with his reliance on reason (in other words, the exclusion of revelation as a source of truth), proved problematic for theology. How could the valuable philosophy of the Greeks be utilized without contradicting the teachings of the church? The handmaiden formula was certainly an option, but the issues were too complicated to argue simply for the application of natural philosophy to theology. More clarification, and a fuller integration, was needed. This was accomplished primarily by Thomas Aquinas (c.1225–74).

Aquinas was known from a young age for his amazing intellect and became a Dominican monk when he was 18. He was a prolific writer, his most famous work being the multivolume *Summa Theologica*, begun in 1265 and completed after his death by his secretary. *Summa Theologica* contains detailed discussions of God's nature, perhaps the best written in all of Christianity. Aquinas is often cited as the most important Christian theologian in the history of the church.

Aquinas argued that philosophy was constructed by human reason, and many truths regarding the nature of God can be known by reason alone. Thus, Aquinas ascribes to philosophy an authority it does not have in the works of Augustine or Anselm. One of his famous arguments is his proof of the existence of God. Aquinas's proof differed from Anselm's in that Aquinas took into account sensory experience (empirical observations) whereas Anselm used only intellectual concepts.

But the truths necessary for salvation, Aquinas argued, are beyond reason. Revelation, through God's grace, is the way God makes these truths known. This does not destroy or undermine natural knowledge, but instead complements it. There can be no contradiction between philosophy and revelation since both are from God. Philosophy and religion can each stand alone, but they converge when considering the nature of God. In this sense, reason must be perfected by divine revelation in scripture. Faith is a kind of knowledge, and we can gain more knowledge of God by grace than by natural reason.

With regard to Aristotle, Aquinas incorporated his ideas into church doctrine, and in some cases "corrected" his philosophy for being wrong. By the end of the thirteenth century, there was an integration of Aristotelian philosophy into the Christian church and a reliance on these ideas, especially regarding the workings of the natural world. Theology still prevailed, in that divine freedom and omnipotence could not be contradicted. In one sense, this actually helped to advance science: ideas in natural philosophy could now be considered that were not contained in Aristotle's works. For example, if God could do anything, then he could, if he desired, create a void, something which Aristotle did not believe in. If a void did exist, what would it be like? How would objects move inside this void? The exploration of these ideas, the speculations and the possibilities, allowed for advancement in natural philosophy.

The Scientific Revolution

From the thirteenth through the fifteenth centuries, Aristotelianism was deeply rooted in the university systems in Europe. It was the basis for the curriculum, and consequently the basis for intellectual thought. However, the tide was turning as to exactly what natural philosophy was and what it should be used for. Natural philosophy became an important undertaking in and of itself. It no longer had to be tied to Christian theology. But, as we shall see, it could not contradict theology, and it was still used to provide understanding of and evidence for God.

Europe in the fourteenth and fifteenth centuries experienced much turmoil, including the Hundred Years War (1337–1453) and the Black Death (1347–50), which killed approximately one-third of the population. The church was under stress during this time, due to the political problems of the Avignon Papacy (1305–79) and the Papal Schism of 1378–1417. Science did not progress much during this period. Recovery from these events led to a time of high art, including the works of Michelangelo (1475–1564), and an intertwinement of art and science, as seen in the works of Leonardo da Vinci (1452–1519). It was also during this time that the Gutenberg Bible was first published (1455), signaling the beginning of the use of the printing press, a technology that would make it possible for ideas to be spread throughout Europe much more quickly. This technology helped to popularize recent translations of Greek literature (including the works of Epicurus (341–270 BCE) and Lucretius (c.99–55 BCE)), and it helped to shape the Protestant Reformation.

The time was ripe for a renewal in spirituality in Christianity, and the events of the Protestant Reformation are tied in with the beginnings of modern science. The break from the Catholic Church instigated by Martin Luther (1483–1546) and John Calvin (1509–64) involved many issues. Two of these concerned the road to salvation (which, according to Protestants, comes only through the mercy of God and not through works or intrinsic merit, as the Catholic Church taught), and the precedence of the Bible over reason, tradition, and experience (new Protestant notions stressed that everyone can speak to God directly through prayer, and that the Bible can be understood and interpreted by individuals, that is, without the mediation of the clergy, as was held by the Catholic Church). The reaction to the Reformation by the Catholic Church (in addition to excommunications, inquisitions, and executions) was a series of reforms and decrees stemming from the Council of Trent (1545–63), known as the Counter-Reformation. At Trent, meetings of bishops, cardinals, and theologians took place to counter the Protestant challenges to papal authority and the theological disagreements regarding doctrines and other matters of faith. The Council also attempted to correct a lack of discipline within the Roman Catholic Church, and reaffirmed the faith with a more literal interpretation of the Bible. It is arguable whether science was helped by the Reformation. Whatever the answer, there certainly was an impact on both the methodology of science and the acceptance of what came out of scientific investigations.

This sets the stage for the first figure who would propel science into the modern age: Nicolaus Copernicus (1473–1543). Copernicus wrote *On the Revolutions of the Heavenly Spheres* (1543) where he proposed a heliocentric (Sun-centered) solar system (this issue will be explored in greater detail in chapter 4). The Catholic Church rejected this notion for the prevailing geocentric (Earth-centered) solar system. This opposition was probably due as much to the pressure on the church from the Reformation as well as theological, philosophical, and common sense arguments. Philosophically, Aristotle had said the Earth was at the center, and common sense tells us we are not moving. Theologically, the biblical texts provide several examples to support the notion of the Earth standing still while other bodies move around it, as in the story of Joshua:

> On the day the Lord gave the Israelites victory over the Amorites, Joshua prayed to the Lord in front of all the people of Israel. He said, "Let the sun stand still over Gibeon, and the moon over the valley of Aijalon." So the sun and moon stood still until the Israelites had defeated their enemies. Is this event not recorded in The Book of Jashar? The sun stopped in the middle of the sky, and it did not set as on a normal day. (Joshua 10:12–13)

In 1616, *On the Revolutions of the Heavenly Spheres* was placed on the *Index of Prohibited Books*, a listing of books the Catholic Church considered immoral or containing theological flaws that could corrupt the faithful. Galileo Galilei (1564–1642), a good Catholic, advocated the Copernican system, and took it upon himself to interpret the Bible. He was tried by the Roman Inquisition in 1633 and placed under house arrest for the remainder of his life. As we shall see in chapter 4, a new technological advancement, the telescope, provided the evidence Galileo used to support the Copernican theory. Johannes Kepler (1571–1630), on the other hand, was able to convince his fellow Protestants that Copernicanism could be reconciled with the Bible through the principle of accommodation. This notion, based on the work of Augustine and used by theologians and scientists, stressed a figurative interpretation of the Bible (the same argument Galileo used). Scripture clarifies purpose, they stated, and should not be taken as explaining scientific matters. By about 1700, most scientists had fully accepted the heliocentric universe.

Another aspect of science that was advancing during this time was mechanical philosophy, based on the recently translated works of Epicurus. Mechanical philosophy was the attempt to explain all natural phenomena in terms of matter, motion, and collision. This excluded any kind of action-at-a-distance (as with God) and denotes another example of a rejection of Aristotelianism. Mechanical philosophy worked very well for the new physics being developed at the time, but it posed several problems for the Catholic Church and resulted in much skepticism. Some of the main problems were divine providence, the soul, and transubstantiation.

- Providence is God's sovereignty over everything. If all events could be explained through the action of matter, then where is God, and what of miracles?
- The religious notion of the soul was difficult for theologians to explain in light of mechanical philosophy, specifically with regard to the origin of the soul and its nature and immortality.
- Transubstantiation refers to the belief that the bread and wine used in the Eucharist is changed into the actual body and blood of Jesus Christ.

Pierre Gassendi (1592–1655) and René Descartes (1596–1650) laid the foundations for how mechanical philosophy should be used, and how science should be done. Gassendi was a Catholic priest, and he tried to modify mechanical philosophy to make it acceptable to the church. He supported the notion that God created and endowed atoms with motion, and that atoms colliding in empty space constitutes our physical world. God has complete freedom and can violate the laws of nature at any time. Humans have free will and an immaterial and immortal soul. Gassendi advocated empiricism in scientific methodology; he thought that, if God could intervene anywhere at any time, then we need to engage in experimentation and gather data to understand the properties of matter. Reason could not inform us, if God can intervene.

In contrast, Descartes contended that God is not a deceiver, and we can use reason to gain knowledge about the created world. He argued that matter has geometric properties and the laws of motion show God's immutability. Descartes believed that matter fills all space and can be divisible; therefore there are no atoms and no void. Movement is a property of a body, and God created matter together with movement. God is immutable and does not interact further with the creation. Any change in movement was due not to God, but rather to the interactions of the created matter. Descartes contended that everything tends to be preserved in its state with regard to motion, the opposite of the Aristotelian notion that all bodies tend to rest. The world was independent of the creator, a concept that led to deism. Descartes's ideas were not favored by the church, and his book, *Principia Philosophiae*, published in 1644, was placed on the *Index of Prohibited Books* in 1663 because it attempted to explain transubstantiation in the Eucharist in mechanistic terms.

In practice, two figures represent how mechanical philosophy was used in the seventeenth century. As we shall see, both were not just focused on the theological implications of this methodology but actually used scientific methods to gain knowledge of the divine.

Robert Boyle (1627–91) employed mechanical philosophy to explain chemical phenomena. He argued that matter was composed of particles that moved and could combine. He used the newly fashioned air pump in experiments to understand the properties of air. Boyle believed God created matter, endowed it with motion, and created natural laws that God could violate. Like Gassendi, Boyle believed experimentation was necessary, as reason could not be used if God wished to violate these laws. For Boyle, souls were spiritual, not material. He saw his work of investigating nature as a way to gain greater knowledge of God and creation.

Isaac Newton (1642–1727) is widely known for his contributions to mathematics and science, but is not as well recognized for his theological ideas or his investigations into alchemy (which are discussed further in chapter 4). Newton accepted the premises of mechanical philosophy early in his career. He thought, however, that some things, such as gravity and the properties of light, could be explained not through matter, but through forces of attraction and repulsion, which ultimately led to the extensive use of mathematics in physics. Matter was passive and under the power of God. Gravity was not an innate property of matter, but instead came from God. Newton's interest in science grew from his desire to find evidence for God's activity in the world. He felt reason alone was not sufficient to understand either God or the natural world. For him, physics and his cosmology were to reveal the creator's work, to prove the existence of God.

One of the major problems of mechanical philosophy was deism, the theological notion that God does not act directly in the world. God created the universe and the natural laws, but is no longer involved in the creation. Deists accept the doctrine of creation, but not of redemption. Newton rejected deism. However, the notion took hold after his death. Newtonian physics provided great explanatory power for the movement of bodies on Earth and in the heavens. But Newton always left a place for God. He believed God intervened in the motion of the planets, as he could not explain through gravity how they could remain in their orbits around the Sun. Using Newtonian physics, Pierre Laplace (1749–1827) finally demonstrated that the solar system is a stable system.

The period beginning with Copernicus and ending with Newton is sometimes referred to as the Scientific Revolution. It denotes a period in Western culture when science stepped out of the shadow of philosophy to become its own discipline. It is the beginning of modern science, and, as we have seen, a great many factors influenced the birth of this new methodology. What is even more remarkable is that this new era had a major impact on theology. Let's consider where we've just been.

- From the end of the Middle Ages, the church went through some substantial challenges resulting from internal problems and the Protestant Reformation.
- In addition, much of Aristotelian philosophy had been rejected by newly emerging science, another blow to the Catholic Church, which had embraced this philosophy for so long.
- A new era of experimentation and empiricism, aided by new technologies, was being developed, which helped to establish the methodology of science. This rationalism was impacting theology as well.
- The fields of science and religion are still intimately tied together, with science being used to glorify and understand God and creation.

In all of this, there was an overwhelming sense that we can know things; we can use reason, experimentation, and empiricism to understand our world. There is order in the universe, and its laws can be understood. The world is amazing in its workings, and it is good. This attitude permeates religion, and brings us to the Enlightenment.

The Enlightenment and Beyond

Before continuing our discussion, we should make a quick note of clarification regarding terminology. The terms "Scientific Revolution," "Enlightenment," and "Age of Reason" can be used to describe essentially the same period of time (or, at least, overlapping and closely related periods). The differential use of these terms denotes more of a focus on particular issues and trends of the time in particular areas, rather than identifying unique and distinct eras.

The emphasis on empiricism in the sciences, and the resulting enthusiasm, caused a dramatic shift in society. The prevailing attitude was that we can know everything, and that reason would lead the way to this knowledge. We could discover laws, similar to natural laws, that would help us understand society. We would then be able to control how humans behaved, which would allow for the abandonment of governments. Human nature was seen as good, not as sinful as church doctrine claimed. Humans were corrupted by society and ignorance, and so, if we changed society and educated the people, we could indeed find perfection. Science would bring happiness, salvation, liberation. Evil would vanish. Justice would prevail.

This attitude has its roots in the sciences, as exemplified by Newton. He represented the way science should be done. We had uncovered a mechanistic universe that was deterministic. If we know all the forces acting on a particle, then we can predict its movement. Exact natural laws allow for cause and effect, and all future events are already determined, based on these laws. This was an approach known as reductionism, which was applied not only to science but to all human activities, including theology. The progression of ideas in theology parallels the rise of reason in science. Faith in God and an understanding of moral conduct based in Christianity was prevalent prior to the Enlightenment. Reason could be used to confirm our understanding, and design in nature (natural theology) showed the completeness of the universe. The emphasis on empirical data, however, led to skepticism about events in the Bible, and resulted in a reliance on natural theology, not revelation, to provide understanding of God. This led to deism, the notion that God was not actively involved in human existence. However, the view of God as impersonal left many people questioning the necessity of worship and prayer, and resulted in reduced commitment to and involvement in faith communities. Some rejected religion altogether.

The pendulum had swung far from revelation, far from tradition. It reached an apex at the end of the eighteenth century which could not be sustained. Some looked at the results of the Enlightenment (such as the horrors of the French Revolution) and rejected it. The tide was turning, and the reaction caused several important new movements. One of these reactions is Romanticism, which revitalized the characteristics that had been "lost," such as emotion and the imagination, amid the passion for reason and rationalism. Romanticism first found expression in literature, where we see a revival of these qualities, and a critique of the limits of science. The contrasts between the two world views are striking (see table 1.1). Romanticism, like the Enlightenment, had an impact on religion. God was no longer seen as a creator distanced from creation. Instead, God is seen as a spirit, a force that pervades nature and can be known through human experience. Pietism, which emphasized this individual experience, flourished in Germany.

Table 1.1 Contrasting emphases in Enlightenment and Romantic thinking

	Enlightenment	Romantic
Epistemology (ways of knowing)	Abstract rational principles	Concrete human experience
Metaphysics (the nature of things)	Atomism and reductionism	Organic wholes and unity – an entity is more than the sum of its parts
Focus	Unchanging laws; reliance on universal and general principles	Growth and development, dynamic processes, individuality and self-expression
Forces for change	Determinism	Freedom and creativity
Role of science	Technology and reason will result in happiness	Human misery brought about by technology shows the limits of society for salvation

It is not dogma or reason, but rather the gospel and personal devotion, that lead to an understanding of God. The Methodist movement in England focused on Christ as personal savior. Science was valued if it had practical application and demonstrated God's wisdom, but mere mortals could never know everything about God's design, as some scientists claimed they could. Although deism was popular in the United States (Thomas Jefferson and Benjamin Franklin were deists), the fervor died down in the nineteenth century, and the Bible and personal experience gained in popularity.

The Philosophers

We cannot discuss this history without focusing on the ideas of three additional philosophers: Bacon, Hume, and Kant. In this section, we will briefly examine some of their ideas and how they impacted the Scientific Revolution and the Enlightenment, and religion and science to this day.

Francis Bacon (1561–1626) practiced law and was a member of the courts of Elizabeth I and James I. Many cite Bacon as being influential in the Scientific Revolution: indeed, some consider him to have instigated the new method of investigation and regard him as the father of modern science. He did not develop a philosophy himself, but rather advocated methods to develop systems of thought. During this period, deductive reasoning was a common method of attempting to arrive at the truth. This method relies on incorporating new data into previously determined laws or ideas. It's not surprising that this methodology was well used: after all, science was regarded as whatever Aristotle said it was, and so any new discoveries were integrated into his existing principles. Bacon advocated inductive reasoning, whereby we first observe phenomena and gather facts, and then derive laws based on our observations (we will look at deductive and inductive reasoning further in the next chapter). Inductive reasoning could be employed in all aspects of philosophy, from natural philosophy (science) to religion. However, Bacon considered philosophy to be based on reason, and religion to be based on revelation, and therefore religion was irrational.

Many, if not most, interpretations of Bacon's writings have led to the popular conclusion that Bacon saw science as domination over nature. The methods he advocated for studying the natural world required a victimization of nature: nature was a slave or a woman to be conquered and subdued. Man is an invader, a conqueror of nature. Nature is to be utilized by man and is functional in its utility to us. This interpretation of his work may have influenced how we investigate the natural world and our attitude regarding our role in the universe and how we revere nature. However, the extensive history invoking this interpretation of Bacon's ideas has been challenged. Bacon also stressed patience in our observations of nature, and the necessity of viewing ourselves as servants and interpreters. Nature can be subdued, but only by submission on our part. Unveiling its secrets is a game of give and take, a way of playing that is subtle and coaxing. We need to understand, on a theoretical level, what the natural world is about. We rely on the utility of nature, but the truths and theories that are out there are also important and critical. Knowledge that cannot be used today to improve our comfort, Bacon said, would indeed be useful tomorrow. So we should study nature for utility and for theoretical understanding. Central to this is the understanding, so pervasive in the Enlightenment, that nature can be studied and understood.

David Hume (1711–76) emphasized the role of observation and empiricism in knowledge, but rejected the emphasis placed on reason by the Enlightenment. Hume concluded that all we know is based on the impressions we get from the natural world, and we have no innate ideas in our mind. Our brain interprets these impressions and, through repetition, we compare observations, see patterns, and make theories. Cause and effect are not evident: the cause of a certain incident cannot be reasoned; it can only be concluded from the repeated observations and experiences that allow us to associate an event with its consequence. Because of this association, we tend to see the world as predictable – we expect the future to resemble the past. The conclusions we arrive at from our observations and our associations lead to theories and laws in science. However, these are not universal or certain as they are based only on human experience and the mind's ability to organize and connect events.

Hume's notions of causation had an impact on theology, as a result of his attacks on deism and natural theology. As we are dependent on our senses, he argued, we cannot draw conclusions on what we have not experienced. Since we have no experience of the attributes and operations of God, we cannot understand God. The argument from design contends that we know that God exists because nature is ordered and organized, and humans would build the world in a similar fashion if they could. Therefore, God must have designed it. Hume claimed this reasoning is faulty: we have never observed God creating, and therefore we cannot use the analogy of human design. We can only infer from our own observations, and the works of a supernatural power are beyond our scope of observation. Hume also showed other flaws in the argument. For example, if we continue the analogy of God being similar to a human creator, then God's mind is finite, implying that error and imperfection exist in God. This is contrary to theological doctrine. Hume used natural examples to argue that order is an inherent biological process and does not have to come from a supernatural force. For example, a relatively simple seed produces, via growth and development, a complex plant. This does not

require an external force, but rather an internal inherent drive. Neither can our percep-
tions help us to determine first cause, so we cannot conclude that God plays this role.
We also cannot prove or disprove the existence of God, so therefore we must reserve
judgment on the issue.

Hume acknowledged the role of imagination in human thinking. He showed that
imagination is necessary in thinking about something when our minds are not receiving
a direct impression of it. Imagination is also necessary when we try to connect our
impressions to each other and to the world we already know. So we believe in things
we do not see at a particular moment in time and relate different impressions into a
"whole." If I park my car when I go to work, I know my car is in the parking lot, even
though, when I'm working at my desk, I cannot see the car (I'm receiving no impressions
from it). Likewise, my view (impression) of my car as I get out of it is different from
my view when I walk back to it, but I still know it's the same car. In addition, Hume
commented that imagination can help us to incorporate past impressions to formulate
general and abstract ideas, and imagination can help fill in the gaps in our knowledge.
Imagination allows us to extend our understanding beyond what our senses can perceive.
Adam Smith (1723–90) made use of Hume's ideas on the imagination and related them
to creativity in science. He emphasized the importance of the imagination on scientific
discovery. When we find something unexpected in nature, this gives rise to surprise and
wonder. The mind tries to order what we observe and uses imagination to fill in the
gaps. A scientist may find continuity between events that others would not, owing to
the imagination connecting separate past impressions. Smith said this ultimately leads
to a sense of admiration of the natural world. The pursuit of science, Smith argued,
brings pleasure, and therefore should be engaged in as in any other endeavor that brings
joy to our lives. Smith concluded that, since science is constructed from generalizations
(theories), we cannot consider these ideas to be the truth: our constructions are useful to
our minds to connect ideas, but other theories, other ways of connecting our observations,
could be equally valid.

The philosophies of Hume and Immanuel Kant (1724–1804) overlap in some respects
and diverge in others. In many ways, we can see the influence of Kant's Pietist background in his work. Kant attempted to reconcile the extreme viewpoints of empiricism
and rationalism that were prevalent during his time. As we have seen, Hume was an
empiricist who believed the only source of knowledge was from observable data. Kant
acknowledged the importance of empirical data, but also identified a role for reason.
Therefore, he also rejected the absolute notions of the rationalists who believe that
reason is the only path to knowledge.

Kant maintained the mind actively interprets data, organizes it, and provides understanding. The mind is not passive in this processing. General categories of interpretation
are innate within the mind, and Kant referred to this as *a priori* understanding. Some of
these categories include space, time, and causality. We don't directly observe these
categories, but we know they exist and we can formulate ideas within them. For
example, cause and effect for Kant was something innate within the mind, something
real. For Hume, cause and effect were based on past observations and experience. These
categories allow us to interpret data: they are not, as Hume would argue, revealed by
the interpretation of data. For Kant, science is a creative process in which imagination
plays a key role in the construction of theories that can lead to deduction of facts.

Kant had a Pietist upbringing in eighteenth-century Germany, which influenced his philosophy of morality and religion. He rejected the argument for God as primary cause, just as Hume did. Religion, he believed, is necessary for morals and ethics, and also to understand and solve practical problems. The purpose of religion is not to solve the theoretical problems that are investigated in the realm of science. Kant believed that ethics and morals should be universally applied, and that they should not be dependent on any particular religious doctrine. God is, in this sense, a postulate that is useful for guiding our laws and determining our morals and ethics. God's will requires us to accept a moral obligation (categorical imperative).

Therefore, according to Kant, the realms of science and religion are very different. Science does not have to invoke design in the explanation of phenomena, while religion does not examine and comment on the natural world, but rather explores and explains morality. Kant's influence reached far into the nineteenth century. We see, in his philosophy, the beginnings of our current attitudes toward science and religion: science is used to understand facts, whereas religion helps us to understand moral issues.

The Rift Emerges

Against the background of the Enlightenment, with its emphasis on rationality and empiricism in science, and of Romanticism, with its renewed emphasis on personal experience in religion, the stage was set for a separation of these disciplines in the nineteenth century. Although there was not a complete separation of science and religion in this period, a rift had developed which was to widen and deepen, and which has led to our present situation. Those who subscribed to natural theology deemphasized the notion of deism and again saw God working in the natural world. Most scientists adopted this view and continued to support the points of contact between science and religion. Many contend that the final blow to the relationship came with Darwin and his ideas regarding evolution (see chapter 8). This also represents the end of Aristotelianism in science, when the last of Aristotle's prevailing notions, teleology, was finally expunged. And thus, today, we have a distinct separation between science and religion. However, as we shall see, there are ways of integrating the two fields, particularly at the boundaries of their limits.

Conclusions

We cannot apply our current world view, on any topic, to people in different times, different places, and different cultures. Our popular understandings of science and religion, notably the distinction we make between them, are very different from those of most of our ancestors. Interactions in the past are varied, and span the continuum from direct conflict to integrated consonance. The remainder of this book will highlight topics, ideas, and people that fall somewhere within this range. We need to understand the complexity of the issues, the diversity of opinions, and the history of the disciplines to gain a complete picture of where we've been and where we may be headed. For now, we need to be cognizant of the notion that science and religion have had a complex interaction in the past that defies a simple, all-encompassing description. And if we look closely, this also illustrates the situation as it exists today.

Primary Literature

Useful primary sources include Thomas Aquinas's "Five Ways of Knowing God" from *Summa Theologica* (Question 2, Article 3); and the opening chapters of three famous texts: *Metaphysics* by Aristotle, *A Treatise of Human Nature* by Hume, and *Critique of Pure Reason* by Kant.

Questions to Consider

1   What terms would you use to describe the relationship between science and religion historically? Provide an example of each. Do any of these terms apply to their relationship today? Support your answer.
2   In your opinion, why did Aristotle's ideas persist for so long as the basis for much of science? Why were his ideas so important for religion?
3   What was the impact of Augustine's handmaiden formula? Some modern philosophers have used this analogy to describe the application of science to politics, medicine, society, etc. as well as to religion. Can you identify any examples of the handmaiden formula, given this expanded definition, in modern times?
4   Given the relationship between the church and the practice of natural philosophy (science), what affect do you think placing a scientific work on the *Index of Prohibited Books* would have on science? Keep in mind that the first Roman *Index* appeared in the late 1550s.

2

How We Know What We Know

Overview

We rely on many different ways to come to know ourselves and our universe. Science and religion ask different questions, and employ different methodologies to answer these questions. The natural sciences use empirical evidence to investigate natural phenomena, which includes a system of extensive testing to support or refute hypotheses. Theology has its own methodology, which relies heavily on biblical texts and their interpretations. History, revelation, and reason are also important in formulating understandings of God. Each discipline has its limits, and there are many parallels between them. In addition, culture helps to shape investigations into and interpretations of science and theology. Our understanding of humanity cannot be complete without these two important fields.

Introduction

We have many different ways of trying to understand the world, as we saw in chapter 1, and the knowledge that we gain is dependent upon the way in which we undertake our enterprise. Epistemology is the branch of philosophy that studies the nature of knowledge. It analyzes methods of inquiry and comments on their validity. Some categories of epistemology include empiricism (knowledge is gained from sensory experience), realism (objects have properties that do not depend on human experience or knowledge of them), and rationalism (knowledge is gained from pure reason and logic). We also recognize other ways of knowing, including experience, instinct, and reliance on authority. Any of these epistemologies can be used to study any subject matter. So, in the pursuits of science and religion, just how do we know what we know? How do these categories help inform us about these disciplines?

Humans have a need to categorize, separate, organize, and compartmentalize. As we just saw, this applies to epistemology as well as to ideas, objects, events, ways of thinking, etc. You don't study "science," you study biology or chemistry or physics or geology. As time passes and technology advances, our need to classify and specialize grows. We have become a culture that desires, and perhaps needs, to analyze and to be precise. Consider medical doctors – we rarely refer to someone as just a doctor. Instead we have cardiologists, gastroenterologists, oncologists, neurologists, and dermatologists, to name just a few. And we rename our categories when deemed necessary – sometimes for political or economic reasons. We no longer sell "used cars." They are "preowned vehicles."

This trend of creating categories, precise language, and "politically correct" terms applies to both science and religion. In chapter 1, we saw that the lines between these disciplines have not always been distinct. However, today it is difficult to imagine how the two fields could be considered in the same breath. This chapter examines how science and religion are studied in our modern age, as separate fields, and how we come to know what we know. We will look at the methodologies and the types of questions belonging to the different disciplines. And we will examine how one specific aspect of our culture can affect our modes of thinking and investigation. An appreciation of these methodologies will greatly enhance our understanding of topics and issues that affect the disciplines.

Modern Science

We can define a natural science as a field that investigates observable phenomena in the natural world. But the methodology used in these investigations is critical to the definition. The questions we investigate and the methods we use are intimately intertwined. This process is commonly referred to as the scientific method (see fig. 2.1), and it is an approach that came out of the Enlightenment/Scientific Revolution. Recall that the use of reason and the gathering of empirical data (information that our five senses observe) are the hallmarks of this period. "Natural philosophy" is no longer a term that can be accurately applied to the study of the natural world. As technology advances, instrumentation can enhance our abilities, as with microscopes (to see the very small) and telescopes (to see things far away). We also have a process of testing in the methodology. And science is progressive: we build on previous ideas to advance our knowledge.

The process usually begins with an observation that leads to a question. Maybe I walk my dog at the same time every night and notice the stars appear to be moving a little bit each night. I may ask the question, "Why are the stars moving?" An earthquake shakes my house, and I ask, "How does the earth move?" I notice a nest of apparently helpless baby birds outside my window and wonder, "How do they get their food?" I then try to answer my questions.

A valid answer, according to the scientific method, invokes natural explanations for natural phenomena. We do not use the supernatural to explain what we observe. We do not, for example, say, "God made it so." This does not help in scientific pursuits – it does not lead to further testable questions, and therefore does not allow for progress. The Enlightenment had a major effect on this aspect of science. As Pierre Laplace and others contended, any gaps or unanswered questions regarding natural phenomena should not be ascribed to God, but should be investigated further to find a natural explanation. Isaac Newton's laws of motion could not explain certain aspects of planetary movement, and he invoked a designer (God) to fill in the gaps. By using only natural laws, Laplace was eventually able to explain some of what Newton could not. When Napoleon commented, "M. Laplace, they tell me you have written this large book on the system of the universe, and have never even mentioned its Creator," Laplace answered, "I have no need of that hypothesis."

The failure to invoke God as an explanation for natural phenomena does not mean that all scientists are atheists and deny the existence of God. For example, deism affirms the existence of God but denies any divine intervention in the workings of the natural world. In our current culture, surveys taken at different times in the twentieth century show a fairly consistent proportion of scientists (about 40 percent) who believe in a God who answers personal prayers. The scientific method does not prevent an individual from believing in God. As we shall see, the very question of God's existence is outside the realm of science.

Hypothesis Generation, Testing, and Communication

Once we have posed a question, the next step in the scientific method is to find an answer. As we have seen, the answer cannot rely on the supernatural. We use logic, reasoning, and natural explanations to come up with a possible answer, known as the "hypothesis." What is important is that we also use the work of others who have come before us. Science builds on itself, which prevents us from having to start back at square one all the time. It also allows for progress in the various fields of science. Consider the tremendous leaps we have made in recent decades in all areas of science and technology, most notably in computers and electronics. Newton's famous quote, "If I have seen further, it is by standing on the shoulders of giants," reflects this important aspect of scientific methodology.

The construction of the hypothesis can be done using two different types of reasoning: inductive and deductive. With inductive reasoning, we take individual, specific observations and try to draw a general conclusion (hypothesis) from them. This conclusion should be applicable to all future observations. It relies on both observation and experience. So, if I observe, in several avian species, adult birds regurgitating food into a baby bird's mouth, I might draw the conclusion that all birds feed their young in this manner.

Deductive reasoning uses a general statement, idea, rule, or principle and applies it to specific, individual situations. These general rules allow us to make predictions about a system, explain an observation, and determine probabilities for the specific situation. For example, let's say I know I live on a geological fault line, and I know a little (the general ideas) about plate tectonics. I may predict that some day I will experience an earthquake, and, if my house does start to shake, I may explain this event by concluding that I am indeed experiencing an earthquake. Inductive reasoning can lead to the theories and laws that deductive reasoning uses to make predictions and provide explanations.

Logic and reasoning are not enough to ensure the hypothesis is scientific and useful. Consider for a moment fields that appear to be science but really aren't, such as astrology and the ancient art of alchemy. Both rely on empirical data and use logic and reasoning to come up with explanations. However, the hypotheses used in these pseudosciences lack an important criterion: they cannot be falsified. The philosopher Karl Popper (1902–94) used this notion to separate true sciences from pseudosciences, and concluded that all hypotheses must be able to be proven false if they are to be considered viable for scientific use. When we talk about proving the hypothesis false, what we mean is not that we will prove it false, but that there is a way to prove it false. If we can conceive of an experimental design or a particular observation that would prove the hypothesis false, then we have a scientific explanation. We may never encounter a situation where the hypothesis will be proven false, but we can imagine such a scenario. With pseudosciences, data that do not fit the hypothesis (that might prove it wrong) would be somehow explained away, typically through *ad hoc* explanations. No hypothesis will be falsified in a pseudoscience. Consider your horoscope, which, on any particular day might give you the following advice: "Finances can really hang you up – now is the time to tackle any and all cash-flow issues head on." In addition to its telling us nothing about the natural world and providing no insight into a natural phenomenon, there is no way to falsify this statement. Finances *can* cause problems, but will they? The statement is ambiguous, therefore it cannot be falsified.

The notion of falsifiability brings us to the next step in the scientific method: hypothesis testing. Testing involves the gathering of data to support or disprove the hypothesis. Testing can be done in two basic ways. In the process of naturalistic science, more observation is done, which may include the recording of historical data. In experimental science, the phenomenon is subjected to manipulation by the researcher. Both processes are valid to investigate scientific questions, and the choice of which to use depends on the system being studied. For example, we may want to determine whether or not a certain chemical is toxic. We could easily test this using experimental science; we could expose cells or organisms to different doses of the chemical for different lengths of time in the lab and observe any affects on these living systems. On the other hand, if we are interested in determining the exact movements of the stars and planets, we could not manipulate the system. In this instance we would use naturalistic science to study our questions and test our hypotheses. Another aspect of the hypothesis that determines its validity is its ability to help us make predictions. We should be able to make "If…then…" statements that can be tested via experimental or naturalistic science, or both.

Although testing may occur in different ways, there are key features of testing that must be addressed. This is easily illustrated with experimental science. First of all, when manipulating a situation, we are testing variables, various factors that may, or may not, be important in the system (temperature, light, time of day, size of the lab, the clothes you are wearing, etc.). We can change only one variable of the system at a time. If we change more than one variable and we see a different outcome, we have no idea which variable caused the change. Second, we always include a control. This is a situation where nothing is altered, so we can compare the outcomes between the system that was altered and the system that was not.

As stated above, our testing may falsify our hypothesis. If this happens, and we are confident that we have done our testing correctly, we consider the hypothesis to be proven false. We then attempt to come up with another explanation and we proceed to test the new hypothesis. If, however, our testing continually supports the hypothesis, we come to a point where we are confident our explanation is accurate. We then call our explanation a theory. The term "theory" does not have the same connotation as its colloquial sense of "it's just an idea." When we apply the term "theory" to a scientific idea, we are saying that large amounts of data support this notion, and we conclude that we are on the right track. It is the best explanation for a phenomenon, better than any that has come before.

You may have noticed that we do not use the term "prove" when referring to the hypothesis or theory. We cannot make a statement saying we have proven anything in science, because it is very unlikely we could ever test our hypothesis in every conceivable way – we could not test every variable, since there are potentially an unlimited number of them. Therefore, the possibility exists that some day we may show the hypothesis to be invalid.

Given this lack of proof, many question why we should accept what science is telling us now, knowing that at some point in the future it may be shown to be inaccurate or totally wrong. We accept the answers of today because the scientific method is progressive. What we know now is more accurate and closer to the "truth" than anything that we have proposed before. Although some may consider science a way to find truth, it actually is a way to approximate what really exists in the natural world. We strive constantly to advance our understandings to the point where we come closer to the "truth."

Last, and perhaps most importantly, the results of experiments and observations must be communicated with the rest of the scientific community. This usually takes the form of papers or manuscripts published in peer-reviewed journals, or through presentations at meetings and conferences of scientific societies. Communication is critical as it allows for official documentation of data, results, and ideas. This provides others in the scientific community with the opportunity to consider the work and to build on it, as well as for further testing of the ideas by researchers working with other systems. It allows for progress in the field.

The Way Things Really Work

Although the scientific method is well defined and accepted, it does have variations in different fields. For example, in some branches, it is customary to ask a question first, then design an experiment to answer the question. This may appear to bypass the generation of the hypothesis, but in reality it does not. The hypothesis will be formulated once the results of the experiment are interpreted (see the dashed arrows in fig. 2.1). For example, if I isolate a piece of DNA containing a gene in my lab, I may want to determine the function of the gene. I could formulate the hypothesis, "The gene produces an enzyme that will turn sugar into gold." I could test this hypothesis with an experiment, and I would probably determine that my hypothesis was wrong. I would then need to come up with another hypothesis. How many possible hypotheses could I come up with to test in this fashion? Too many. A better approach in this situation would be to not formulate the hypothesis initially, but instead to design an experiment that will provide a possible function for the gene. For example, I could place the gene in a bacterial cell and, using unaltered bacteria as a control, I can look for biochemical or growth differences between bacteria with the gene and those without. I can then take those preliminary experiments, come up with an explanation (hypothesis) as to the function of the gene, and further test my idea. Whatever the exact approach, the scientific method is at the heart of all investigations in the natural sciences.

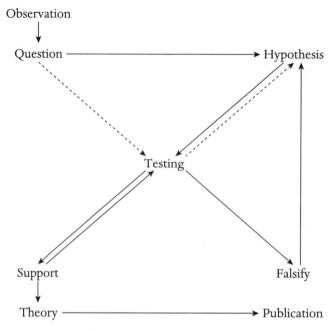

Fig. 2.1 Synopsis of the scientific method

Models are also important in science. They provide ways to organize and understand data, ways of thinking about phenomena, and ways to extend theories and knowledge. They are very useful when considering abstract and theoretical concepts. A model may be discarded when we have a better understanding of the phenomenon or if we falsify the hypotheses and theories on which the model is based. A relevant example of this is the notion of light. Newton originally modeled light as a particle until evidence contradicted his model, whereupon he changed his understanding of light and deduced it behaved more like a wave. Albert Einstein (1879–1955) concluded that light does indeed behave as if it were a particle. Today, we use the model that light behaves sometimes like a wave and sometimes like a particle. (It is interesting to note that religion also makes use of models: for example, we often use the model of God the father. As with science, these models are never completely accurate, but they provide a conceptual framework to interpret our personal experiences.)

Many people have an image of how science is done. They consider researchers to be objective and open-minded, and their ideas to be rigorous and well tested. However, science is done by human beings, who are flawed and imperfect. The scientific method represents a guideline for how science should be done, but the ideal levels of objectivity and open-mindedness are not always present. Thomas Kuhn (1922–96), a physicist and philosopher of science, considered this issue in his influential book, *The Structure of Scientific Revolutions* (1962), which introduced the term "paradigm" to our common vocabulary. Kuhn discussed how data is interpreted through a world view (paradigm). If we work within a certain set of assumptions, using specific equipment and technology, then we will fit the results of our observations and experiments into that paradigm. What happens when we accumulate data that do not fit into the paradigm? Kuhn called these "anomalies." Some anomalies cannot be explained at the present time, but are left for the future, when other resea[...] and advances in technology may be able to solve them. However, sometimes anomal[...] accumulate to the point where the theory no longer appears to be supported. In this case, we may change our paradigm. Kuhn called this a "paradigm shift." This may lead to a fundamentally different view of the natural world, known as a scientific revolution. Researchers working under a paradigm for many years will resist the shift. Therefore, it is usually the young, up and coming scientists that cause revolutions. According to Kuhn, paradigm shifts and revolutions are how progress is made in science.

Other dynamics we have not touched on also contribute to the advancement of science. We should not forget, or minimize, the role of creativity, inspiration, and imagination in scientific endeavors. These qualities certainly cannot be considered objective, yet they are instrumental to scientific investigation and progress. Without these factors, we could not generate hypotheses, design models, or determine ways to test our ideas, and thus science would not be possible.

Limits of Science

The scientific method has served us well for the past 400 years, but it has its limits. It is designed to study natural phenomena, to answer questions of how things happen in the natural world. Therefore, if a question cannot be tested through the use of the scientific method, it is not a scientific question. What are some questions that science cannot investigate? Certainly questions of ethics are out of the realm of science. We cannot, for example, resolve the debates in American society over the issues of abortion, euthanasia, and embryonic stem cell research. In each of these cases, definitions of life are important. Although science can provide information that may be useful in deliberations, it is ultimately society that must determine ethical standards. We will discuss this in further detail in Part IV.

Science cannot be used to investigate most issues involving religion. We cannot, using the scientific method, prove or disprove the existence of God. We cannot set up a controlled situation to test this, and we would, by necessity, invoke supernatural explanations. Again, as with ethical questions, science may be able to help inform certain issues, but would not be able to resolve them. An example would be the authenticity of religiously significant artifacts, such as the Shroud of Turin. Carbon dating, fiber and pigment analysis, and other tests could help establish the age of the artifact, for example, but this would not resolve the issue of what the cloth actually represents.

Ontological questions, regarding the purpose and meaning of existence, are also outside the limits of science. We cannot answer the philosophical and theological questions of why we are here. Science can provide understandings of biological processes, but these are not appropriate or satisfying responses to questions about purpose. Other questions, such as why suffering and evil exist (theodicy), also cannot be addressed by the natural sciences.

Since there are limits to what science can investigate, it can never be used to understand our existence in totality. It is one way of coming to know our world, our universe, and our existence. The scientific method does not determine truth; it only provides data

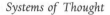

efute ideas about the natural world. Given its limitations, however,
erty of the method: if we are incorrect in an assumption, conclusion,
entually figure it out. According to the ideas of Kuhn and Popper,
ulate to a point where the current paradigm is useless, or we will
eory. With science, we don't construct a theory and then forget it
ing else. As new data, new techniques, new technologies, and new
those data and ideas are constantly reassessed and reevaluated.
Although this is truly a wonderful aspect of the methodology, it is not without its
problems. As discussed above, this means that the science we accept today may be totally
different in the near future. But again, what we know today is the best information we
have with the current technologies and methods. The scientific method works, and
therefore what comes out of the method can be trusted, with the overarching provision
that as more data accumulate, ideas may be modified.

Theological Inquiry

The close association, indeed the entwinement, of science and religion explored in
chapter 1 is in stark contrast to what we experience today. As with science, a major force
of change in theological methods occurred during and after the Enlightenment. Today,
we have many ways of thinking about God, and different religions have different
traditions, rituals, and doctrines to help their followers come to an understanding of
God. An in-depth discussion of the plurality of theology and religion is beyond the scope
of this book. However, there are some basic methods used in theology, and these will
be explored below. As stated before, we will focus almost exclusively on Christian
theology in this book.

Theology addresses many issues, but at its core, it is the discipline that studies how
we come to an understanding of God. Most theologians will admit that the attempt to
understand God is inherently flawed: how can a finite human mind understand the
infinitude of God? We acknowledge that this is not possible, but, in our attempts to
improve our relationship with God, we strive to achieve these understandings. Indeed,
we cannot do God's will without some understanding of God. Just as with science, we
may never know the "truth," but our investigations will supply us with progressively
more (and better) understandings and insights.

Some Basics of Theology

In contrast to the image of science as being objective, open-minded, progressive, and
critical, religion is often viewed as subjective, close-minded, resistant to change, and
uncritical. This is not an accurate view. We must look at the methodologies involved in the
study of religion (theology) to understand how we know what we know (see fig. 2.2).

First, let's take a brief look at what theology is and at some of the different branches
of theology. We defined theology a moment ago as the study of how we come to our

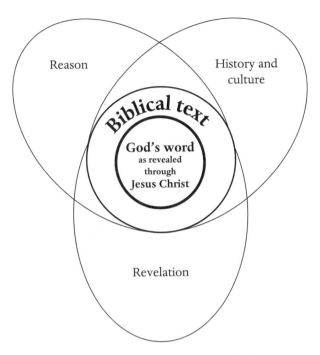

Fig. 2.2 Intersections of the ways of knowing in Christian theology

understanding of God, but this is a simplistic and incomplete definition. Within a faith context, theology helps to describe the faith, which entails communicating that faith with a community. Theology also considers important issues of the day on both an intellectual level and a practical level through the practice or works of faith (praxis). Contrary to the description above, theological studies are not uncritical or resistant to change, but instead rely on continuing inquiry. Theology does not rest simply on belief. Asking questions, however, does not mean that the answers will be forthcoming. And the conclusions we do arrive at today may not be useful to us in the future. Thus a new set of answers will often be sought when the culture changes and new events unfold. And we will never have all the answers, as God will always remain a mystery.

Theological language is not empirical; it is constructed and therefore is subjective. However, theology is not blind reliance on and adherence to dogma; it is the examination of faith. It is reflection on the teachings of the church and of the practices of the members of the faith community on many levels. Central to Christian theology is the word of God as revealed through Jesus Christ, as recorded in the Bible. It is through Christ that we can form a relationship with the living God. The different levels of theological inquiry rely on different approaches to understanding God, the church and the community. Four types of theological approaches that are important for our discussion are biblical theology, historical theology, natural theology, and systematic theology.

Biblical theology is the study of biblical texts and the history within them. Debates regarding science and religion today often employ biblical texts to support or refute scientific conclusions, and to provide guidance for ethics in the application of science.

Therefore biblical theology can play an important role in these conversations. For Christians, the Bible is the main source of information about God. It documents revelation, and the stories in the Bible explain the human experience and shape religious doctrine. The Bible attests to the living God, the creator and redeemer. It is a witness, a conduit of God's word. One of the tasks of theology is to make the text relevant to people in a particular culture. Prior to the Enlightenment, many passages in the Bible were not taken literally, but were understood to be metaphorical. After this period, critical reading and rationalism prevailed. The importance placed on reason resulted in a radical change in how the Bible was interpreted, as the events depicted in it, including miracles and the resurrection, could not be proven empirically. The Bible was still seen as authoritative, but it was read in a very different way.

"Hermeneutics" is the term used to describe the diverse ways in which the texts can be interpreted. Today, most scholars use the historical-critical method of interpretation. This approach takes into consideration the culture in which the writing was done – the period when the text was written, the author of the text, the intended audience, etc. It involves trying to uncover the true message of the text, and the reasons behind the specific representation of a subject matter. When texts are used in the dialogue between science and religion, the historical-critical method is particularly helpful. Is the account in Genesis an accurate description of the beginnings of the cosmos? Early readers would not have interpreted the Bible in this way, and modern science concludes this is not how the universe and our Earth were formed. However, we do look at this text to provide meaning and purpose. Are there texts that can help us determine the ethics of embryonic stem cell research? No mention of this specific technology exists in the Bible, but we may find passages regarding human life and dignity, and our obligations to those who suffer, that could prove useful in our discussions. When we identify a text of this nature, interpretation will be critical.

Historical theology examines Christian doctrine in the past: what it was, how it was applied, etc. This type of reflection will help us understand the reaction of the church to science and scientific discoveries at various times in history. We saw some examples of this in chapter 1, for example with Thomas Aquinas and his efforts to bring Aristotelian ideas into the framework of Christianity. By using the approaches of historical theology, we can examine the attitudes and events of the time, and consider how they impacted the decisions made. Perhaps the most famous conflict in the realm of science and religion that benefits from this type of examination is the case of Galileo. As we shall see in chapter 4, observations of the natural world and technological innovations provided the impetus for Galileo to make his discoveries. This was not the most stable time in church history, however, and his conclusions conflicted with some teachings of the church. And, perhaps most importantly, he did not present his case very tactfully and offended the clergy. It was this unique mixture of time and personalities that ultimately led to Galileo's trial and conviction. If we don't understand the history surrounding these events, it is difficult to understand how the church could have rejected Galileo's science.

Natural theology is a branch of theology that deals directly with science. This approach uses natural reason, what can be seen in the natural world, to prove the existence of, and to understand, God. This is in contrast to special revelation (see below). Throughout history, the notions of reason and revelation have changed, and so the approaches and conclusions of natural theology have also changed. Over time, natural theology increasingly emphasized that the order seen in nature, indeed its design, must be due to a supernatural force, and therefore nature was used to provide proof of and insight into the divine. In the seventeenth century, Robert Boyle, like many of his contemporaries, marveled at what he saw under the microscope. He thought the examples of complexity in nature, such as the eye, showed that an intelligence must have designed living things. Boyle argued that we cannot know God's intentions, but that scientific investigations could support revelation. Newton's views on the structure of the universe also helped to increase the popularity of natural theology in the seventeenth and eighteenth centuries. He argued that only an intelligent being could have calculated the correct paths of the planets. But natural theology had its problems and its critics, including David Hume (see chapters 1 and 6). Notably, there was a tendency to anthropomorphize God. Some conclusions that could be drawn from natural theology were polytheism, pantheism (the notion that God and nature are one and the same) and deism (whereby, as we have seen, God created the world but is not actively involved in it now: Newton countered deism by contending that God was active in correcting the orbits to keep the solar system stable). The arguments from design were very resilient and could be adapted to fit the major scientific discoveries of the day (see chapter 11). Darwinian evolution in the nineteenth century was a distinct challenge to natural theology, and twentieth-century events also diminished its impact on theological discourse. However, natural theology can still be found in some areas, such as the process theology of Alfred North Whitehead (1861–1947), in ecofeminist theology, and some fields of scientific inquiry where the roles of contingency and necessity are questioned.

Many of our investigation into the relationship between science and religion rely on systematic theology, the branch of theology that is informed by all the other branches. This method of inquiry tries to arrive at a complete and comprehensive understanding of the Christian faith. In relation to science, we can look at Darwinism for an example of how this approach can be used. As we shall see in later chapters, the development of and response to evolution was based on the interpretation of certain biblical texts, the attitudes of the church toward science, and the prevailing view of design in nature. These must all be analyzed to provide a full and complete picture of the controversy.

Revelation and Reason

As we saw in chapter 1, theological inquiry has a history of placing different emphases on revelation and reason in different eras. These two ways of knowing have been important in our understanding of God.

Revelation reveals hidden meanings and helps us to understand the will of God: however, God always remains a mystery. But revelation is more than just an acquisition of knowledge: it is often life altering. It forces us to reinterpret the events, people, and factors in our lives. Many biblical texts are considered to be records of revelation.

Subjective or special revelation is a personal experience that cannot be observed by someone else. Therefore, it can't be empirically validated. This type of knowledge was excluded from theology in the eighteenth century, as a result of the stress on empiricism during the Enlightenment. However, in the nineteenth and twentieth centuries revelation was again accepted as a valid way of knowing. Another type of revelation, general revelation, allows everyone to gain access to knowledge of God. General revelation is universal, such as when people look up at the stars and marvel at the nature of the cosmos.

Faith is personal commitment, trust, and involvement. It is based on revelation, but it is not blind. Revelation must be interpreted by the individual. This involves reflection and reason. In addition, theology is based on inquiry, and so the use of reason is necessary to achieve understanding. Therefore faith alone is not enough. Reason, referring to how one thinks and constructs knowledge, is an important tool in theology.

The 1998 encyclical by Pope John Paul II (1920–2005), *Fides et Ratio*, explores the relationship between faith and reason. John Paul argued that reason needs faith, as there arc limitations to reason, and that we cannot reach God only through reason because of sin. In this sense, human reason is weak and needs faith. But people, events, and history are observable, and we therefore need to employ reason. The Bible time and again values reason. And we can use reason to help us understand the gospel and to experience revelation. John Paul's conclusion is clear: faith and reason can support and enhance each other.

John Paul's commitment to reason and to science can be seen in many of his writings. In his address to the Pontifical Academy of Sciences in October 1996, he acknowledged the validity of the scientific theory of evolution. He also commented on the interplay of science and religion in a letter to the Reverend George Coyne, Director of the Vatican Observatory, in June 1988:

> Science develops best when its concepts and conclusions are integrated into the broader human culture and its concerns for ultimate meaning and value. Scientists cannot, therefore, hold themselves entirely aloof from the sorts of issues dealt with by philosophers and theologians. By devoting to these issues something of the energy and care they give to their research in science, they can help others realize more fully the human potentialities of their discoveries. They can also come to appreciate for themselves that these discoveries cannot be a genuine substitute for knowledge of the truly ultimate. Science can purify religion from error and superstition. Religion can purify science from idolatry and false absolutes.

Limits

As with science, religion has limits. It is able to respond to questions of ethics and morals, purpose and ontology, and theodicy. These are the "why" questions. Religion cannot provide information to answer the "how" questions. As we saw with the scientific method, invoking supernatural explanations to answer questions about the natural world does not help the progress of science. Therefore, to claim that a particular text offers a scientific account of a natural phenomenon, particularly if it appears in the context of the writing as a miracle, is not a viable scientific explanation. It provides no hypothesis that can be tested. And most theologians will agree that interpreting a text in this manner is a failure to place the writing in its cultural context, and a failure to understand the message the author was trying to convey.

Barth and Tillich

Two modern Protestant theologians are recognized as having a significant impact on the methodologies of theology today: Karl Barth (1886–1968) and Paul Tillich (1886–1965). The theologies of these men are almost diametrically opposed to each other. We will look briefly at their theologies and examine how each regards and approaches science.

Barth espoused a Christocentric theology, that is, the church must examine itself, its teachings, and its practices against its own norm, the revelation of God through Jesus Christ in the biblical text. The focus should be on the word of God. For Barth, culture should not influence theology, nor should theology be compromised by culture. He was steadfast and uncompromising on this point. Christocentric theology looks beyond culture to try to find the true meaning which, for Barth, is in the biblical texts. He saw the achievements of the Reformation, namely the return to biblical authority, as being undermined in his lifetime. Barth influenced theology to a huge extent because of his fervor over the exclusive use of the Bible as the way to understand redemption through Jesus Christ. Barth did not, however, accept the inerrancy of the Bible. The use of words to communicate the word of God is horribly flawed, as all language relies on and reflects the culture in which it is spoken and written. Even the Bible cannot avoid this. For Barth, the task of theology is to try to understand the true meaning of the words, even though the words cannot reveal the truth; they cannot penetrate the impenetrable. Barth set theology above all other disciplines, including science. The word of human enterprises cannot compare with, and should not be placed on the same level as, the word of God. Barth's most famous work is his multivolume *Church Dogmatics* (1936–62).

Tillich had a vastly different approach, which incorporated philosophical (existential) questions. His approach is often called the "correlation method," and his most famous work is his three-volume series *Systematic Theology* (1951–63). Although Tillich placed Jesus Christ at the center of his theology, he contended that human endeavors (including art, science, philosophy, and literature) are part of, and necessary for, understanding God. Culture and history provide sources for revealing the word of God in Jesus Christ. In Tillich's theology, there is a conversation, a dialogue, between culture and revelation. According to Tillich, the Bible is symbolic, and can be paraphrased and analyzed within a given situation.

Other theologians also emphasize the role of culture. It is difficult to understand fully a religion or a theology without understanding the people, time, and place in which the notions about God were constructed. Conversely, we cannot fully understand a culture without understanding its religion. The culture determines what is ultimately acceptable regarding its belief system. Some people will try to change the belief system (for example, prophets) while others will try to hold on to tradition (typically the clergy). Theology also asks how religious tradition is influencing culture today, and what role culture may play in the future of theology.

On a critical level, it can be said that Tillich's correlation method is too broad and generalized and can include anything to help us understand God's word. On the other hand, Barth's Christocentric approach is very narrow and excludes the culture of the people who live the Christian life. This runs the risk of making theology irrelevant to the individual.

Remarks on Science

Barth and Tillich each commented on scientific endeavors. Barth's emphasis on understanding the word of God, above all other human endeavors, is reflected in his attitudes regarding science. He was opposed to natural theology, and claimed this approach was in direct conflict with the teachings of the Reformation. Faith must be based wholly on God's revelation in Jesus Christ, and faith alone provides knowledge of God. We can know nothing about God, nature, or humans except through Jesus Christ. Science as an endeavor should be undertaken, but the goals of humans should not be placed above the understanding of God. Science is limited, because it cannot inform us about ontology; it simply describes natural phenomena.

Tillich examined the history of science and religion. He recognized the separation of science from religion (beginning with the Greeks) by the process he called "demythologization," the removal of any divine actions from natural phenomena. But as natural philosophy replaced mythology, conflicts arose, which often caused the church to reject the new science as it was seen to be dehumanizing and amoral. Tillich was aware of, and opposed to, the dehumanizing implications of technology. However, he did not consider societies in a state of pretechnology as being any better. Instead, he sought to understand both. Tillich specifically denied any advantage in choosing one scientific theory over another on theological grounds. He saw the use of theology in science as causing the split between science and religion. He regarded religion as a source of inspiration for science, allowing for the courage to create, which is necessary for progress in science. He contended that science and religion complement each other: we understand the universe through science, but its meaning and purpose come from religion. Tillich envisioned a reconciliation and reunification of science and religion, which he called "New Creation."

Common Ground

Although there are differences in the methodologies of science and religion, there is also common ground which can provide for understanding and dialogue between the disciplines.

- Both science and religion use models and paradigms in their explorations.
- As culture changes so must the disciplines (see below).
- In science, fundamental alterations of understanding are usually caused by a crisis and result in a paradigm shift. This is analogous to revelation in religion.
- Just as we look at and interpret science through a paradigm, we use hermeneutics to interpret biblical texts.
- Science and religion are investigated by fallible human beings: revelation and data must be recorded, and texts and experiments must be interpreted, by imperfect entities.
- We ask questions that we may not answer. And the questions we do ask, even when they are answered, inspire additional questions, which allows for the continuation of the never-ending cycle of inquiry.

- Both disciplines recognize that the knowledge obtained yesterday is not as good as what we have today, and that tomorrow will bring even better understanding and more answers.

Although the questions we ask and the ways in which we derive answers may be different in science and religion, the underlying reasons for asking the questions and searching for answers are the same. We are trying to describe the human experience. We are searching for truth, a truth that we will never find. We can never know God, who will always be a mystery. We can never prove a theory, as we can never test all variables. But on a fundamental level, the human mind and spirit value the quest and consider it of central importance for existence. The core of humanness is to contemplate our existence, our worth, our purpose. Science and religion, in their own venues, attempt to provide understanding of humanity and of the universe. We have in our midst two dynamic fields, each investigating the crux of human existence, each fascinating in its own right, and each absolutely necessary for an understanding of ourselves.

The Effect of Culture

We have mentioned several times in this chapter the notion that culture can affect both religion and science. Culture can influence the types of questions we ask, how we go about our investigations, and how we interpret the answers. The results of our inquiries reflect back on culture. In some cases, these results will support and affirm the culture; in other cases, the results may change culture. The individuals engaged in these investigations are themselves the products of their culture: the assumptions they bring to the work, how they think, the very language they use are all determined by cultural context. Sometimes these effects are subtle, but at other times they are overt, at least to the trained eye. We will now look at one specific example of the influence of culture: we will consider some issues that have been revealed when we look at science and religion critically through the lens of gender.

The historical context of gender in our culture has seen the exclusion of women from many facets of life. Women have been denied any real power for most of Western history. And they have been excluded from participation in science and religion for millennia. Today, we look at our society and see women obtaining degrees and participating in these disciplines, and also filling some prestigious leadership positions. However, a closer look reveals that women have a long way to go to achieve equality with men. For example, statistics from the United Methodist Church show that women are grossly underrepresented: women make up only 13 percent of all ordained elders, 15 percent of district superintendents, 8 percent of all bishops (active and retired), and 2 percent of clergy serving as lead pastors of churches of 1,000 members or more. On the basis of scripture and tradition, the Catholic Church still denies ordination to women, and believes the exclusion of women from the priesthood is part of God's plan for the church. Women are also lagging in equality in the sciences. A report to the National Academy of Sciences in 2007, *Beyond Bias and Barriers: Fulfilling the Potential of Women in Academic Science and Engineering*, highlighted the loss of women at every level of educational transition (the pipeline loss) and the discrimination in the appointment, retention, and advancement of women in every field of science and engineering. It found that most people, both men and women, are biased against women in science and engineering, and that evaluation criteria for advancement and promotion are not objective and are disadvantageous to women. Incredibly, the report also had to dispel many commonly held beliefs, including erroneous ideologies that women are not as good in mathematics as men and that women are not as competitive as men and don't want jobs in academe. Women make up a large percentage of the lower ranks in academia, as instructors, lecturers, and adjunct faculty, with fewer women in tenure track positions, and few full professors. In the US, approximately 18 percent of professors (all science and engineering fields considered) are females.

How have the historical exclusion of women and the continued inequalities affected science and theology? Biology (sex) has been seen as determining the behavior and abilities of individuals and their roles in society (gender). The disciplines of science and religion were developed and practiced in societies that were sexist (where men are seen as superior to women), patriarchal (where men are at the top of the social hierarchy and hold the power), and androcentric (where male behavior is the norm for the society). Almost all aspects of these societies, from the educational system to language, underpin gender differences and affect how we study the natural world and how we come to an understanding of God.

The pioneering work of Evelyn Fox Keller, professor of the history and philosophy of science at the Massachusetts Institute of Technology, points out that there are multiple issues that need to be considered when we examine the exclusion of women from science: the practice of science becomes distorted and we begin to question scientific methodology when we uncover male biases. The participation of more men than women in science is problematic, because it limits the contribution of female perspectives and insights. Prejudice occurs in the choice of problems and questions that are investigated, as seen, for example, in the almost exclusive focus on women in the investigations of and resulting methods designed for contraception. Bias in the design of experiments and the interpretation of data is also apparent, as when the males of a species are used exclusively in a research study, but the results are interpreted as being representative of females as well. Metaphors and analogies for scientific models often use age-old sexist dualisms, such as action for the masculine (think of the valiant free-swimming sperm and its perilous journey in the female reproductive tract) and passivity for the feminine (the waiting, immotile egg which cannot bring forth life until it is penetrated by the sperm).

Sexism has restricted the inclusion of women in scientific fields, for fear that they were not intelligent enough for these pursuits, or that they were not strong enough to handle the stress of "masculine" work. Patriarchal concepts are applied to science, as when we describe DNA at the top of the hierarchy, controlling everything about the cell (and consequently the organism), and when we model reproduction in primate species as a competition between the strongest males for passive females. Androcentrism has dictated that there is one right way to approach science that will allow us to discover the truths about the natural world. But Keller argues that what is needed is critical self-reflection, a constant assessment of how the science is being done (which, paradoxically, is a hallmark of the methodology) to purge science of this cultural bias. Women are clearly capable of scientific research, and many throughout history have made major and important contributions even when excluded from the educational systems and the laboratories. Hierarchical systems have been shown to be simplistic in some cases and downright incorrect in others: it is the relationship between the cell and the DNA that determines the cell's fate, and when women became involved in primatology, and actually examined the roles of males and females in primate society, it was found that only one out of 175 known primate species conforms to the competing males/passive females model. Keller's in-depth look at two women who won Nobel Prizes, Barbara McClintock and Christiane Nüsslein-Volhard, has revealed that both of these talented scientists did not follow the androcentric model of how science is done, but instead used their instincts to help them proceed in their ground-breaking research.

Preconceived notions can taint our interpretations and lead us to erroneous conclusions, hinder our complete understanding of a system, and prevent us from making progress in science. Those involved in all scholarly pursuits need to be aware that we are products of our culture, and to understand that our "knowledge" is also a product of a biased system. For the sciences, we need to utilize the scientific method in its ideal state: we need to question our results and interpretations constantly, to reexamine our theories, and to test our understandings continually. Some regard science as truth, but the objectivity of science is based on relative values. There is not only one truth, whether within or outside of science. Therefore, the more voices that contribute to the enterprise, the better will be our understanding of our world.

We also find that Christianity is inherently patriarchal and sexist. Just as it took female scientists to help reveal the biases in "masculine" science, it has taken female theologians, and feminist theology, to uncover the prejudices in the church. Women have been marginalized by the church, seen as incapable, and left with no power. Through self-fulfilling prophecy, women have come to view themselves as inadequate. If the result of a system is to denigrate human beings, through sexism, racism, etc., then it cannot be a reflection of the divine. It is not redemptive. Theologically, it must be changed; the system must be transformed.

Women such as Rosemary Radford Ruether, Carpenter Professor of Feminist Theology at the Pacific School of Religion and Graduate Theological Union, have been instrumental in calling for the inclusion of female voices in theology. Ruether's holistic, personal approach has challenged many aspects of Christian theology with regard to sexism, racism, and classism. Ruether and other feminist theologians see these issues as interconnected, and, along with liberation theologians, seek to transform the system and find justice for those who are oppressed. They are not proposing a reversal of sexism, where women dominate men, or the inclusion of women in the existing system. Rather, feminists seek to transform the system, to include all perspectives. The goal of most feminist theologians is to critique the oppressiveness of theology by examining theological language, symbols, and attitudes, to seek alternative understandings, to recover lost history, and to imagine and suggest new ways of thinking and acting that are inclusive, hopeful, and constructive, especially in light of the global concerns we face today. We have been denied feminine insights into and understandings about God throughout history owing to the subordination of women. Specifically, feminists point to the notion that patriarchy has led to classical theism, a conception of God as having absolute power in a hierarchy where God is above men (and men are above women). God is external to the world, does not depend on the world, and is eternal, infinite, and unchanging.

God is all-powerful and all-knowing. This authoritarian view of God, feminists argue, has been designed by men to "create" God in the image of man, a reflection of the patriarchal system.

Feminists explore alternative ways of thinking about God. How can this be done? We will examine one aspect of this: the notion of language in theological texts and religious doctrine. Elizabeth A. Johnson, distinguished professor of systematic theology at Fordham University, is an important voice in this aspect of feminist theology. She examines critically the roles of language and symbols in Christianity, and argues that the use of masculine language for the divine is oppressive and idolatrous. It is oppressive because it relegates women to the margins and undermines the equality of men and women, both of whom were created in the image of God. It is idolatrous because it is seen as the only, or best, way of speaking and thinking about God, which limits our understandings of the divine mystery. Is it wrong to speak of God in masculine terms? Johnson argues that this is not problematic per se. But when these terms are used exclusively and literally, promoting the image of God *only* as a ruling man in a patriarchy, we need to change the system. The language we use to symbolize God is powerful. It ultimately justifies and supports patriarchal, androcentric, and sexist societies, and upholds these concepts as being holy.

Many feminists have discussed similar problems with the male images of God. Thinking of God as male is in no way superior to thinking of God as female. Indeed, many throughout history have argued that the divine is neither male nor female; God has no gender, no sex. Jesus spoke of God as father (*Abba*, in Mark 14:36), but he also spoke of God in a multitude of other terms, including feminine images (a woman searching for a lost coin in Luke 15:8–9; a woman leavening dough in Matthew 13:33; bringing people to new life through birth in John 3:5–8). Historically theologians have stressed the mystery and incomprehensibility of God, impressing upon us that words and images are incomplete and that we can never approach a true understanding of the divine. Words are powerful, but ultimately they are insufficient and imprecise. There is no "correct" way to think and talk about God. We also need to keep in mind, when looking at sacred texts, that these words have been translated, again adding to their ambiguity. We must be careful in our interpretations also to consider the individuals who wrote the words, to take into account the cultural context and the target audience (the historical-critical hermeneutical method).

Feminists argue for a critical examination of the words and encourage inclusive language whenever possible. What does inclusive language look like, particularly when we are trying to be faithful to the meaning of the original text? Masculine terms, such as "men," "son," "father," "brother," "brethren," "fraternity," "brotherhood," etc. must be critically examined to determine if the text is addressing only men or if it is meant to include women as well. Most agree that certain passages in the Bible, particularly those referring to the Messiah, must use the masculine gender. However, translators can make changes to texts that were meant to include women as well as men. For example consider the Revised Standard Version translation of Psalm 8:

> what is man that thou art mindful of him, and the son of man that thou dost care for him? Yet thou hast made him little less than God, and dost crown him with glory and honor. Thou hast given him dominion over the works of thy hands; thou hast put all things under his feet... (Psalm 8:4–6)

Compare this with the gender-neutral language of the New Revised Standard Version:

> what are human beings that you are mindful of them, mortals that you care for them? Yet you have made them a little lower than God, and crowned them with glory and honor. You have given them dominion over the works of your hands; you have put all things under their feet... (Psalm 8:4–6)

The meaning does not change, but the gender neutral language is more inclusive.

Since our culture is patriarchal and is based on sexism and androcentrism, the suppositions that result from these ideas have been read into the natural sciences and theology throughout history. The barriers placed in women's paths in the way of opportunities for education and participation in these disciplines, and the androcentric underpinnings that cause these disciplines to focus on and to use male imagery, models, and analogies almost exclusively, need to be eliminated. We have made progress in this direction, but much still needs to be done. The goal of feminists in theology and in the philosophy of science is transformation of the systems, where women and other minorities will be included, and where knowledge will be broader and more extensive. Theology and science can only benefit from the different perspectives that women bring.

Where Science and Religion Meet

If we respect the validity of both science and religion as ways of knowing, we must recognize that, even though they are separate, there are concrete points where they meet. These areas are usually at the limits of each discipline, and we may make errors in the progress of our knowledge and understanding if we extend the application of one or other discipline beyond its limits. It is natural, at these points, to try somehow to reconcile these views, and often this involves grappling with the question, "Where is God in science?" We are now asking questions about causality: exactly how is God involved in the universe?

If we accept that science is correct, given its limitations and the notion of progress, then we are looking to fit God into our prevailing theories. This is not a "God of the gaps" scenario, where we invoke God to explain what we can't at this point in time (recall that, according to the scientific method, this cannot be done). Instead we are acknowledging that we are at the limits of science, approaching questions that science cannot answer. We have a scientific theory to explain the origin of the universe, but we cannot explain what came before. It's beyond our limits. Primary causation is the notion that God set up the natural laws (for example, by engineering the big bang), but then these laws proceeded without divine intervention to form the cosmos and ultimately us. God exists, but does not get involved (this is the deism that rose out of the Enlightenment).

On the other hand, we are told in the Bible that God is a living God who hears our prayers and is directly involved in our lives. Given these theological points, deism is problematic. If we accept what science and the Bible tell us, we have to reconsider how and where God acts in the natural world. Secondary causation is the notion that God actively works through natural laws. This is more compatible with a personal God than primary causation. God not only established the natural laws, but also directed the formation of the stars and the planets, and pushes evolution toward complexity. God continually acts in the world through nature. It is generally accepted, in this scenario, that God does not violate the natural laws, but does work within them. Many interesting ideas arise from secondary causation, particularly in the realm of quantum mechanics, as we will see in chapter 6.

Conclusions

Although science and religion are considered two separate and distinct fields in today's culture, and, as we have seen, the methods used to study each are different, we must still recognize that each is devoted to understanding the human condition and the universe. As with a jigsaw puzzle, we cannot solve these mysteries with only one or two pieces. The topics we have separated and categorized into different disciplines are like those puzzle pieces. We need the natural sciences, religion, philosophy, art, poetry, medicine, music, the law, politics, social sciences, as well as scores of other fields, to come together to help us gain a comprehensive picture of who we are. For all our carefully crafted classifications, resulting in different disciplines that provide precision and expertise, we do not have a complete picture until we bring them back together. And we must also include the ideas and creative talents of all of God's people in this endeavor.

Primary Literature

Useful primary sources include an essay by Paul Tillich, "Man, the Earth and the Universe," *Christianity and Crisis* 22 (1962), 108–12; a paper by Thomas Kuhn, "Historical Structure of Scientific Discovery," *Science* 136 (1962), 760–4; and a piece by Rosemary Radford Ruether, "Why do Men Need the Goddess? Male Creation of Female Religious Symbols," *Dialog: A Journal of Theology* 44 (3) (2005), 234–6.

Questions to Consider

1   Consider the three major branches of epistemology identified in this chapter (empiricism, rationalism, and realism). What do you see as some advantages and limits of each? Which is used most in science? In religion? In society today? Support your answer. Which one is most appealing to you personally? Why?
2   Would you consider a discipline such as psychology to be a natural science? Support your answer. Be sure to include a discussion of the scientific method.
3   Can you name some scientific ideas that have been falsified?
4   What similarities between the methodologies of science and of theology do you think are important? What differences are most critical? Justify your answer.
5   How do you respond to the methods of Barth and Tillich? Are they incompatible? Are they complete?

6 How important do you think reason is for Barth?
7 In this chapter we discussed the interplay between gender issues and science and theology. What other evidence do you see of culture influencing, or being influenced by, science and religion?
8 How would Barth and Tillich respond to issues of gender in the studies of science and theology?

3

Common Threads and
Ultimate Truths

Overview

The science and religion dialogue forces us to examine closely some of our core beliefs and understandings of ourselves, our society, and our universe. Each discussion can bring into play a number of recurring themes that, if addressed in a thoughtful manner, can help to facilitate conversations and understandings, and possibly bring about consensus and direction for further inquiry and action. Common issues such as contingency and necessity, interpretation of biblical texts and scientific data, dynamic relationships, causality, and theodicy are essential to our understanding when we engage in this interdisciplinary perspective. Throughout these discussions, we must always keep in mind the inherent limits in both disciplines. The quest for truth is the vital component of the human condition that inextricably links science and religion together.

Introduction

We will examine some complex issues in this book. However, many of these topics often boil down to a few underlying concepts. As we encounter these recurring themes, we will scrutinize them from various vantage points, not only from different lenses in science and religion, but also from philosophical and historical perspectives. In this chapter we will visit some of these important themes. You'll be introduced to some overarching concepts that can be used to bridge science and religion, to bring diverse topics together, and to provide a different framework for conceptualizing some of the vital issues in the science and religion dialogue. You should revisit this chapter from time to time as you continue your explorations.

Underlying Notions of the Relationship

In our post-Enlightenment world, we tend to ask how science can inform religion, but we don't ask the reciprocal question enough. Surely science, in its explorations, can contribute much to theological understandings. Science has peered into the beginnings of the universe, and has some idea of how it will all end. We can now plausibly contemplate how life began and see how and why it has changed. The mysteries of development, space time, subatomic particles, and human diseases have unraveled before our eyes. And we can manipulate our world in our attempts to improve the human condition. These understandings can inform theologians as they ponder creation and eschatology, bioethics and stewardship. But in our empirical paradigm, can theology help to inform science? Indeed it can. Science is a fast-moving discipline: conclusions from five years ago are already outdated. Technologies resulting from science, such as artificial reproduction, stem cell research, recombinant DNA, and medical advances, change at a blistering rate. Society ultimately decides the correct uses for these technologies, and the religious voices are some of the most important in these deliberations. Religious traditions have standards and ethics that have withstood the test of time, and the practice and use of science benefit from these seasoned contemplations. Theology can and should be the leader in many areas involving science and religion. Perhaps it can play a key role by reminding science that it is not the only way of obtaining knowledge, and that there are other ways to know reality. If science is going to help humanity flourish, then it cannot be disconnected from ethics and philosophy.

Innate curiosity drives our desire to understand. It is not for power or glory or money that we investigate our world, but for understanding. For some, one way of knowing is enough. Consider the scientist who bases all her understandings on scientific laws, who breaks everything down to physical principles, who places every aspect of her life in the realm of the empirical and concludes nothing is out of the reach of scientific understanding. Or think of the pious religious cleric, who interprets the Bible in a literal fashion, content in the conviction that God speaks only through these sacred texts, and that truth can be found only in its pages. The scientist cannot understand the value of a good philosophical debate and denies God exists because, for her, a materialistic and reductionist approach can explain the world. The cleric sees only the bad, and not the good, that secular society has to offer, with a narrow paradigm that minimizes the glorious works of God by preventing a full appreciation of the universe as understood through science and other disciplines. Most of us, however, welcome different approaches and viewpoints, and use these to find deeper meaning in our lives. Different epistemologies allow us to examine the universe and to come to know it in different ways. We stretch our minds and challenge our intellect. We take on some daunting tasks to understand our lives better. And we find that one way of looking at the world is limited and confining.

Curiosity drives us. Our quest to understand ultimately unites us, even when it looks as though we are at odds. One notion we will examine in this book is dualism, such as that between mind and body, between soul and body, and between nature and nurture. Science and religion can be seen as one of the ultimate dualisms. How can we have a holistic view of our universe when these concepts and disciplines are so far apart and so opposed to each other? But we will see, time and again, that classical dualistic thinking is not necessarily accurate, and science and religion do not have to be at odds. Thus, this notion of dualism can drop away. We may never again enjoy the pre-Enlightenment era of unification, but we do not have to tolerate a battle between science and religion.

We still need to be cautious in trying to bring science and religion together. Natural theology is one such attempt that is inherently flawed. Using design in nature to understand God was dealt a death blow by Darwin and his theory of natural selection. Organisms evolve, and they do so in response to the environment. There is no design and no goal (*teleos*) in Darwin's theory. However, natural theology has enjoyed a recent resurgence with the argument for fine-tuning: how could the universe have everything just right for the evolution of life? Many see this as the evidence for God. We need to be wary of this approach and others like it, including scientific creationism and intelligent design. With these approaches, one discipline often exploits the other (in a similar way to the handmaiden formula popular in the Middle Ages) and disavows its intrinsic value and its autonomy. Another way to bring science and religion together is the untenable "God of the gaps" approach. In our quest for understanding, we rely on the constancy of God. When we cannot explain something, we often invoke God. Recall that Newton believed that God helped to keep the planets in their orbits when he could not explain this with his science. However, this technique is problematic from both a scientific and a theological perspective. The scientific method does not allow for supernatural explanations, even when we cannot explain our observations with natural laws. If we do, however, use God as an explanation, then when science progresses and we can explain the phenomenon, we must inevitably push God out of the process, as Laplace did. God's role is diminished each time we fill in the gap. But God is always there. Where God is at any time cannot be determined by our perspective and knowledge of the world. We cannot include God and then exclude God. Theologically, the God of the gaps notion is not a reasonable foundation for a relationship between science and religion.

So how do we avoid the errors of natural theology and the God of the gaps explanation? How do we provide for a respectful view of both disciplines, to cultivate and value the significance of each, as we try to bridge the persistent apparent divide? We need to foster a relationship where each discipline is appreciated for its own merits, and where each is explored to help inform the other. Where there can be no "proof," no ultimate "truth," there can still be support, insight, knowledge, and wisdom.

These notions of knowledge and wisdom are important and can be seen as a conduit between science and religion. Knowledge and wisdom are often seen as two different things, with wisdom being the province of religion and knowledge the product of science. However, wisdom affirms the natural world while emphasizing our responsibility to it (ethics). And one cannot have wisdom without knowledge. Therefore wisdom can and should affect science in its methodology and approach, and knowledge will contribute to wisdom. Thus, the relationship between science and religion is a necessary one.

What is Truth?

The curiosity and the search we have just spoken of often leads us to the question of truth. Can we know the truth about anything? Our epistemology, on a cultural level, is based in empiricism: if science says it's true, then it must be. But science never says anything is true. The methodology does not allow for "proof." We acknowledge that the way we investigate the natural world will give us answers, but further investigations and better technology will allow us to discover more, and so our understandings today will be different from tomorrow. Thus science is dynamic. Theology is also dynamic: it reacts to society, and needs to reevaluate its doctrines from time to time. Since each discipline is dynamic, the relationship between them is dynamic as well. Science and theology also have limits. As we have just seen, science cannot prove anything, and science cannot investigate the supernatural. Theology is limited in two similar respects: it cannot tell us how the natural world works, and it cannot bring us to a complete understanding of an infinite God. Therefore theology and science will advance us, get us closer to the truth, but we will never ultimately "find" it.

These limits do not need to be viewed as shortcomings of either discipline. Instead, we could call on the concept of complementarity: science and religion are different ways of looking at the world and each can show us things the other cannot. Therefore, our quest to understand the universe should include both. But there are more issues to consider and to keep in mind when examining questions and the answers generated by different epistemologies.

Interpretation is a critical component in this discussion. Biblical hermeneutics can provide different interpretations for the same passages. Different paradigms allow for different conclusions to be drawn from the same data. As long as we are willing to examine and consider other modes of interpretation, we have a good chance of progressing towards the truth. But holding steadfastly to biblical inerrancy, or protecting a theory in spite of the accumulation of anomalous data, will hold us back. We must also be aware of how science and theology are influenced by society. The view of the world our culture provides us with cannot be separated from our actions and conclusions. Our culture has provided us with insights into life, the universe, and ethics. We are products of our cultures, and we cannot dispel all that is engrained in our minds, hearts, and souls. And we must remember that this is true for those who came before us. We must acknowledge that our understandings are based on our culture, and therefore are constructed. Our conclusions may be far indeed from the truth.

Another aspect that science and religion share, with regard to the attainment of truth, is the use of models. Both disciplines are trying to explain the unknown (and unknowable) in ways that humans can understand. Models are very useful in this respect. They are, however, imperfect and limiting. If we see nature as a constant struggle for survival, with competition as the main driving force, then how can we explain altruism and other examples of cooperation? If we refer to and view God as an omnipotent lord or king, then how can we understand the powers, such as free will, that have been given to us? As long as we accept these models as imperfect explanations, then we will be open and willing to look further, at other possibilities, and acknowledge that doing so will help us come closer to knowing the truth.

Is It Science or Is It Theology?

Some see science and religion as incompatible, others view them as being different and independent of each other. Still others point to issues and topics that are addressed by both which tie the two together. Below are some notions we will encounter that span the disciplines. In some cases, they are merely observations that can be discussed from the two different perspectives. In other cases, religion and science have, in a sense, merged to form explanations that are not possible from only one vantage point.

- *Rationality*. The world can be understood. We may never have a complete under-standing of it (we may never know the "truth"), but we know there are natural laws that allow us to investigate and predict events in the natural world. And we know that God is rational, steadfast, and constant.
- *Indeterminacy*. After the Enlightenment, the natural world was viewed as a mechanistic, predictable place. A reductionist approach allowed us to envision a world in which we could predict with certainty everything that could happen, as long as we understood all the laws and forces acting in the universe. However, quantum mechanics has shown us that indeterminacy exists. From a theological perspective, God has given us free will, allowing us to choose our paths. No natural laws, no coercions, are in place to force us to do anything. The choice is ours.
- *Contingency and necessity*. Do things have to happen? And do they have to happen the way they do? Is there another way they could happen? God created: most people see this as a choice. God did not have to make anything, but did so out of love. There was no necessity to creation. Scientifically, we cannot find a natural law that says there has to be anything. Necessity does not explain why things exist, although it can help explain how things are once they do exist, once the natural laws have been established.
- *Causality*. Tied in with contingency and necessity is the notion of causality. If the universe is contingent, then God created. God is the primary cause. God created the natural laws that we can study in the pursuit we call science. But is God acting further in the world? If God is only primary cause, then the natural laws act as secondary causation and determine the events we observe. The notion of a personal God who cares for us and about us must be abandoned, and we are left with deism. Does God take more of an active role, influencing events in our personal lives? Although some would describe daily events as miracles, most of us understand that natural laws control these events. If God does act through events, then God is acting through natural laws (secondary causation). We can study secondary causation with the scientific method. As these events are amenable to empiricism, then God does not violate these natural laws. Some contend, using the notions of indeterminacy and quantum mechanics, that God could act at a quantum level without violating any natural laws.
- *Our place in the world*. We are part of the world. We were created just like all other life forms, all other matter, by God. We are chemically made up of the same elements as all matter, and our molecular and cellular processes are the same as those of other living things. Therefore, we are entrenched in and part of the world. However, God created us with special intent and special attributes, giving us a unique place in the world. We alone have the capacity to enter into an intimate relationship with God. We

have the capacity to think on a level no other creature can. We can think about the moral consequences of our actions, about our death, about thinking. We have responsibility. We are like all living things and, at the same time, we are special and unique.

- *Our role in the world.* We were created in the image of God (*imago Dei*). We have dominion over and responsibility for part of God's creation. We are co-creators, having the ability to alter our world on many levels. What exactly is our responsibility? How are we to act ethically? The Bible tells us to care for one another, and also for the environment. Science can provide opportunities for both, but the responsible use of technology cannot be determined by science. Religion is needed in these decision-making processes.
- *Theodicy.* How can a loving and just God allow the suffering we see in the world? Theologically, this can be explained by several concepts, one being free will. We have the ability to choose our paths, and therefore the suffering that we see around us. Another explanation centers on eschatology and the notion that something better is coming: suffering and pain are a necessary part of this progression. The world to come will be one in which pain and suffering will not exist. We need to trust in God and God's plan. From a scientific perspective, the issue of waste and death is not a matter for moral discussion. Natural processes cause the formation and destruction of stars and galaxies. All life requires energy and nutrients to survive, resulting in predator–prey relationships and much apparent waste. And in all the death and suffering, there is the promise of new life. Theologically, there is the new kingdom and the resurrection. Scientifically, stars explode and make the elements necessary for life, and individuals die and species become extinct, allowing for other organisms to flourish.
- *Relationships.* A deterministic, mechanical view of the world leads to a reductionist mode of thinking. All things are knowable if we break them down into their component parts. However, science is learning that this way of thinking is not tenable. The whole is not the sum of its parts, and relationships determine what events will occur. DNA does not tell the cell what to do until the cell tells the DNA how it's doing. Similarly we can look at our understanding of God from the same viewpoint. The soul can be seen as our relationship with God, and sin as a turning away from God, which leads to a deterioration of this relationship. Our concept of humanity cannot focus on individuals: we are social creatures living in societies and depending on others. God's covenants were with whole populations, not just individuals. Biologically, we live in a complex society, some would say, because we evolved to do so: it was the best mechanism for our continued survival. We are part of the web of life, where changes to any part of the web can affect the other parts. Therefore, relationships are important and defining characteristics of ourselves: our relationships with the other living things on this planet, our relationships with other humans, and our relationship with God.

Conclusions

Are science and religion fighting for the ultimate truth? Is there one truth that someone will find one day? Will we crown science or theology the winner, with the defeat of the other seen as a falsification, and ultimately an annihilation, of all that the loser stood for? These are questions many in our culture are asking. The conflict model between science and religion is often taken as "truth." But the best we can say regarding this notion is that it is an exaggerated conflict. Human nature, including curiosity, creativity, and imagination, will help us understand more about the human condition and about our world. This will be done via many paths. Our approach to the truth is a journey, and, as with most journeys, it is not the destination that is important, but the journey itself. The more people who contribute, the more we'll see and understand. The important thing is to keep both sides talking, to keep the discussion going. It will not always be a smooth ride, and we're in it for the long haul. But it's sure to be an interesting and enlightening trip.

Primary Literature

A useful primary source includes an article written by the head of the Committee on Science and Human Values of the National Conference of Catholic Bishops, David M. Byers: "Religion and Science: The Emerging Dialogue," *America* 174 (13) (1996), 8.

Questions to Consider

1   Which of the common threads mentioned in this chapter do you think are critical to the science–religion dialogue? Why? What other notions should be included in the list?
2   What ideas, discoveries, policies, issues, or historical realities can you identify that could be used to support the idea that science and religion are separate and incompatible? Which could be used to support the notion that science and religion are not at odds? Using the list you created for the previous question, cite at least two specific examples from different periods or diverse topics. How do these compare and contrast?
3   John William Draper and Andrew Dickson White postulated what is known as the warfare thesis in the late nineteenth century, emphasizing the conflict between science and religion. They contended that science and religion have always been at odds, that religion has always been opposed to science. They cited many incidents in history that supported this notion. The epistemologies of science and religion make them incompatible, and therefore they compete and are often hostile toward each other. Do you agree with their assessment?

Part II
Cosmology

4

Scientific Explanations of the Cosmos

Overview

The ancient Greeks, including Plato and Aristotle, had a geocentric and geostatic view of the universe. However, other points of view existed, particularly that of Aristarchus, who advocated a heliocentric system. In the second century, Ptolemy expanded the geocentric system in his *Almagest*, which was for hundreds of years the authoritative text on the structure of the cosmos. In the sixteenth century, Copernicus placed the Sun at the center of the solar system. Galileo's observations, using the new technology of the telescope, brought down Aristotelian notions about the universe, and falsified the Ptolemaic system. However, he did not provide evidence that uniquely supported the Copernican system. The discord between Galileo and the Catholic Church over this has often been cited as a prime example of the conflict between science and religion. Tycho, Kepler, and Newton continued investigations of the cosmos, developed detailed records, and formulated laws of planetary motion and gravity. Both Kepler and Newton included God in their cosmologies.

Introduction

An understanding of the universe has always been of great importance to humans. The awe inspired by the night sky excites and delights us today, much as it must have done with our ancestors. Observations of the heavens allowed ancient cultures to create calendars that marked time and predicted the changing of the seasons. The place we occupy in this vastness was basic to understanding nature and ourselves. This naturalistic interpretation of the universe has great implications in the realm of philosophy and religion: we need to understand why we exist, what our purpose for being is. Thus, science (to explain the natural world) and theology (to understand our purpose) come together to help us contemplate the universe that exists just beyond our doorstep.

"Cosmos" is a term that is synonymous with "universe," implying an ordered and integrated whole. Cosmology is the study of the universe as a whole, and astronomy is the study of the matter in outer space, with an emphasis on the positions, motion, and composition of celestial bodies. Cosmology and astronomy are linked, in that we can use each to understand the other. Therefore it is difficult to separate the two totally. In chapter 5, we will focus on cosmogony, the study of origins of the universe, and look at myths surrounding the creation of the cosmos. In chapter 6, we will study the scientific explanations of the beginning of the universe. In this chapter, we will look at early ideas about the structure of the cosmos. Beginning with the Greeks, we will see how understandings developed, and we will examine the influence and impact of science on religion and vice versa. We will consider the Galileo affair, and examine the contributions of Tycho, Kepler, and Newton to our concepts of the movement of the planets.

Here Come Those Greeks Again

Although we may think of ancient cultures as primitive and "unscientific," we find amazing examples of their knowledge of the cosmos, stemming from meticulous, long-term observations. Some surviving written records of the Mayan culture show a complex calendar system based on the movement of celestial bodies. Structures, such as Stonehenge and the great pyramids of Egypt, have been shown to highlight celestial events. Most, if not all, of these observations of the heavens were correlated with the culture's belief system. The Greek philosophers also had myths, but their reliance on deities was minimal compared to the cultures that came before them. The Greeks explained the Earth and the universe in more naturalistic terms, some of which we have briefly discussed. We will consider some additional details here.

As we saw, Plato believed in a deity that had created the world but was distanced from it. His view of the universe was geocentric and geostatic: the Earth was in the center of the universe and did not move. Aristotle and other Greeks also adhered to this view. Within this notion, planets, stars, and the Sun moved around the Earth in concentric, perfect circles. This had common sense and aesthetic appeal: based on our daily observations, it is the Sun that moves across the sky. We do not feel the ground moving, and objects don't fly off the ground as they should if the Earth were in motion. Therefore, the Earth is at rest and the Sun moves. The heavens (the celestial realm), according to Aristotle, is perfect, whereas the terrestrial realm is corruptible and imperfect. According to Aristotle, major differences exist between the celestial and terrestrial realms, notably in how objects move. Aristotle argued that the stars were fixed on orbs that moved around the Earth. This established the basis for understanding the universe that was to dominate for centuries.

The Greeks had observed retrograde motion of the planets, where the movement of the planets over time appears to slow down, stop, and change direction, in essence moving backwards (see fig. 4.2(a); we'll discuss this in more detail in a moment). Plato challenged philosophers to find a natural explanation for this movement: Eudoxus of

Cnidus (c.400–c.347 BCE), an excellent mathematician, concluded that attached concentric circles could explain the paths of the planets. His system used a total of 27 spheres
to account for all the movements of the planets, the Sun, and the Moon.

Among the Greeks, there was no consensus about the position or motion of the
Earth, and it appears that Plato and Aristotle were aware of, and possibly sympathetic
to, other viewpoints. These different ideas coexisted for a long period of time, without
a tremendous amount of discord. A heliocentric (Sun-centered) solar system was first
introduced by Aristarchus (310–c.230 BCE). He was not interested in the movement
of the stars and planets, but rather in the size of the universe and the distance between
heavenly bodies. Most Pythagoreans held the view that the Earth moved; some of
them believed the Sun and Earth moved about a central "fire." And Heraclides of
Pontus (c.388–c.310 BCE) proposed that the Earth rotates on an axis. It was during
this period that a new age of mathematics was dawning, when geometrical problems
could be solved quantitatively. And so the logic used, and the answers produced, by
these new methods were more important than the ontological issue (whether the Earth
or the Sun was at the center). However, over time, the geocentric model became more
appealing: it was better able to explain the movements of the stars and planets using
circular motion.

The geocentric system was delineated in great detail in *Almagest*, written by Claudius
Ptolemaeus (c.90–c.168). Ptolemy's multivolume work was, like most ancient Greek
texts, preserved in Arabic and translated into Latin in the twelfth century. The Ptolemaic
model places the Earth at the center of the universe (see fig. 4.1(*a*)). The celestial
bodies (the Sun, the Moon, the stars, and the five observable planets) rotate around the
Earth. Each planet moves on a circular path called a deferent. However, these paths
could not account for all of the movements of the planets, particularly retrograde
motion. Therefore, other circular paths were added, called epicycles, to explain these
motions (see fig. 4.1(*b*)). The epicycles had their centers along the deferent. Not only
did the epicycles describe retrograde motion (see fig. 4.2(*b*)), they also accounted for
why planets appeared to be at different distances from Earth at different times. One
problem with this system was apparent to Ptolemy: it did not work if the Earth was
exactly in the middle of the planets' orbits. Aristotelian logic dictated that heavenly
motion was uniform. Observation showed that it wasn't. From Earth, the planets are
observed to move at varying speeds which does not mesh with a model of the Earth at
the center of a perfect circle. Ptolemy positioned the Earth off center, creating an
eccentric (unconventional) circle, which explained the varying speed problem. As observed
from Earth, when a planet was relatively near, it would appear to be moving faster than
when it was farther away. The position in the circle, opposite the Earth but equidistant
from the center, was called the equant. If an observer were to stand at the equant, then
the speed of the planets would not vary, but would appear uniform. Thus, Ptolemy
"solved" the uniform motion problem (for the sake of simplicity, the figures in this
chapter do not show eccentric circles or the equant).

The geocentric model was a geostatic model, wherein the Earth did not have any
motion. The system was appealing from the perspectives of both science and theology.
On the scientific side, it was in concert with observations of the time, and allowed for
fairly accurate predictions of the movements of the stars and planets. Theologically, it
supported the notion that human beings are special: we are at the center of the universe,

(a)

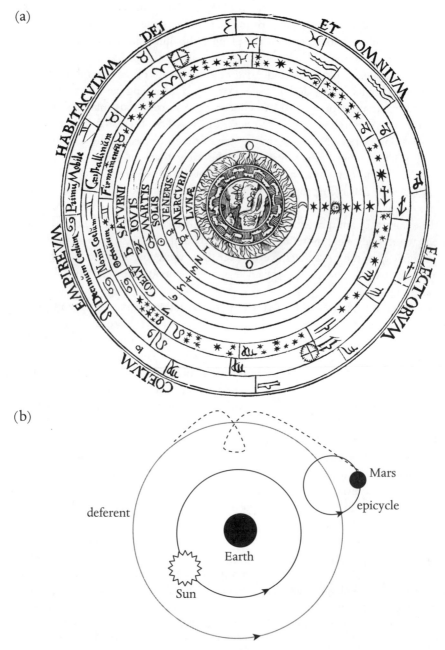

(b)

Fig. 4.1 (*a*) Medieval drawing of a geocentric universe. The Earth is at the center, with the major celestial bodies orbiting in perfect circles: first the Moon, then Mercury, Venus, the Sun, Mars, Jupiter and Saturn. Beyond was the firmament of fixed stars. (© The Print Collector/ Heritage-Images) (*b*) Movement in the Ptolemaic system. The Earth is unmoving, at the center. The Sun and other celestial objects move in perfect circles, called deferents, around the Earth. Planets also move in epicycles, smaller circles, around the deferent. This movement (represented by the dotted line) accounts for the observed movement of the planets. The Sun does not travel on an epicycle. (*c*) This diagram of a heliocentric universe was published

(c)

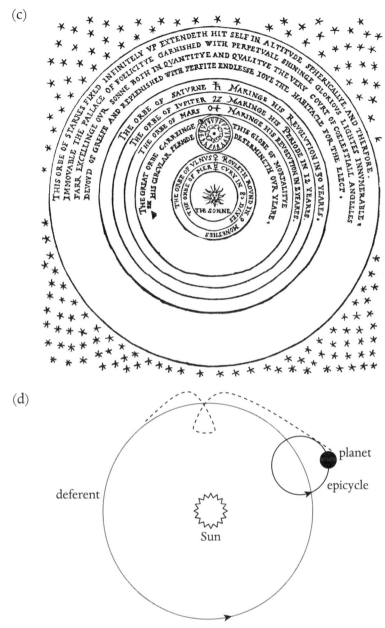

(d)

by the English astronomer Thomas Digges (1546–95) in *A Prognostication Everlastinge* (1576 edn.). The heliocentric theory of Copernicus had been published in 1543, and Digges was one of the first people to publish it in English. He added this diagram in an appendix to the original book by his father, which had featured the older Ptolemaic theory of a geocentric universe. In this diagram, the Sun is at center, with the six known planets in successive spheres, followed by an outer sphere of stars. (© Royal Astronomical Society/Science Photo Library) (d) Movement in the Copernican system. Copernicus still used perfect circles and epicycles, but he placed the Sun at the center of the universe, and the Earth was just another planet orbiting the Sun. The dotted line represents the movement of the planet.

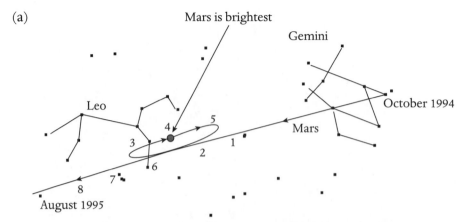

Fig. 4.2   (*a*) An observation of the retrograde motion of Mars. Note the positions of Mars at different times, labeled 1–8. The planet appears to travel from east to west, but at position 4 appears to reverse and travel from west to east. The planet continues its westerly motion at position 6. (*b*) Ptolemaic explanation for retrograde motion. Positions 1–8 correspond to the observed positions in (*a*). The east to west movement is along the deferent. The reversal of movement is attributed to the movement of Mars along its epicycle. (*c*) Heliocentric explanation for retrograde motion. Positions 1–8 correspond to the observed positions in (*a*). The model shows the movement of both the Earth and Mars and determines how we perceive the path of the planet from Earth. Earth's orbit around the Sun takes 365 days; Mars' orbit takes about 687 Earth days.

and the celestial bodies are for our enjoyment. There is a location for heaven in the perfect celestial realm, and a place for hell in the corruptible terrestrial realm. The geocentric/geostatic model also correlated with some biblical texts. For example, as we saw in chapter 1, the Sun stood still for Joshua:

> On the day the Lord gave the Israelites victory over the Amorites, Joshua prayed to the Lord in front of all the people of Israel. He said, "Let the sun stand still over Gibeon, and the moon over the valley of Aijalon." So the sun and moon stood still until the Israelites had defeated their enemies. Is this event not recorded in The Book of Jashar? The sun stopped in the middle of the sky, and it did not set as on a normal day. (Joshua 10:12–13)

Other references can be found in Psalms:

> In them he has set a tent for the sun, which comes forth like a bridegroom leaving his chamber, and like a strong man runs its course with joy. Its rising is from the end of the heavens, and its circuit to the end of them; and there is nothing hid from its heat. (Psalm 19:4–6)

> Yea, the world is established; it shall never be moved. (Psalm 93:1)

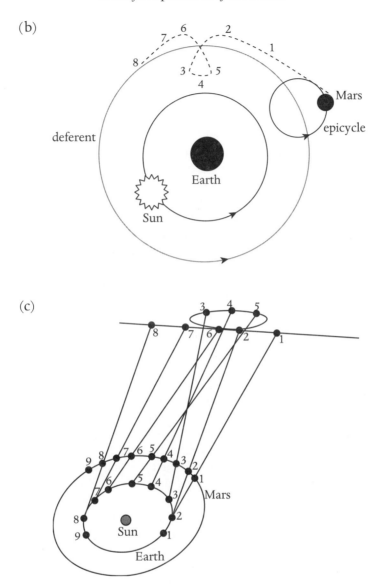

Fig. 4.2 *(Cont'd)*

But adjustments to the system had to be made, to account for accumulating observations of celestial movement that did not fit the model. These adjustments were mainly in the form of adding more and more epicycles, surrounding other epicycles. The system became ever more complicated. In Kuhn's philosophy, the anomalies were mounting. By the sixteenth century, a paradigm shift was on the horizon.

A Challenge to Geocentrism

We credit the first modern heliocentric system to Nicolaus Copernicus. Copernicus was born in Poland and raised by his uncle. He became a canon (priest) in the cathedral chapter of Frombork when his uncle became the bishop of Varmia. He attended several universities, including Krakow, Bologna, and Padua, and officially studied canon law and medicine. However, Copernicus had a passion for astronomy and was well versed in the subject. He remained at Varmia for most of his life, where he built an observatory, watched the skies, and formulated a new astronomical system. He wrote an anonymous sketch of his system some time around 1510 called *Commentariolus* (Brief Commentary), but he expanded on it in *De revolutionibus orbium coelestium* (Revolutions of the Celestial Spheres), published in 1543. In *De revolutionibus* he proposed that the Sun was the center of the universe, and the center of the orbits of all the planets was the center of the Earth's orbit (see fig. 4.1(*c*)). His justification for this was based largely on aesthetics (the Sun at the center was more pleasing and logical, as a lamp that lights up the celestial temple) and simplicity (it is less complicated than the Ptolemaic system). However, observations did help establish and support his system. Some of the data supporting the new system included information on conjunctions (when planets align with the Sun) and oppositions (when planets are "opposite" from the Sun), the positions of the Sun (including equinoxes) and the Moon, and lunar and solar eclipses. Copernicus set the correct order of the planets based on the extent of their retrograde motion (see fig. 4.2(*c*)). The heliocentric system explained why the outer planets (Mars, Jupiter, and Saturn) were brightest in opposition (they are on the opposite side of the Sun from the Earth and reflect the Sun's light), and delineated the twofold movement of the Earth (revolution on its axis and rotation around the Sun). Importantly, he made observations on the heavens, used mathematics in his reasoning, and came up with his own explanations, as opposed to the prevailing scientific method of commenting on the already existing Ptolemaic system. However, he kept several assumptions of the Ptolemaic system. He advocated circular orbits for the planets and uniform motion, and he made use of epicycles (see fig. 4.1(*d*)). On a positive note, he avoided the use of the equant. His system did not provide any better predictive value, but, as discussed above, it was simpler than the geocentric model, and it was aesthetically more appealing.

The problem with the Copernican system was that it was contrary to the understanding upheld by three powerful bodies: the church, the universities (still entrenched in Aristotelianism), and the astronomers. All were using Ptolemy's system. Copernicus may have feared the wrath of all three. With regard to the science of his system, he had no definitive evidence to support his system. The academics would reject it because it went against the teachings of Aristotle, and the church would have seen it as contradicting biblical text. A heliocentric view takes humans out of the center of the universe: we are no longer special. In 1541, Copernicus received a letter from Andreas Osiander (1498–1552), a Lutheran theologian, regarding church tradition. In it, Osiander told Copernicus that his system was an astronomical hypothesis, meaning it could be used for mathematical computations and as a device to model observed phenomena. It did not need to be considered "true," and therefore did not have to contradict the teachings of the church. Osiander encouraged Copernicus to emphasize this in his book, as it would appease the Aristotelians and the theologians. Osiander helped oversee the completion of *De revolutionibus*, and added, anonymously, a preface delineating the system as a useful hypothesis, but not necessarily the truth. Copernicus received the first printed copy of the work on his deathbed, but probably never knew about the preface written by Osiander.

Copernicus dedicated his book to Pope Paul III. It was not his intent to undermine a belief the church subscribed to, but rather to help in creating an accurate calendar. As Osiander had advocated, the work could have been considered a treatise on astronomy alone, with any theological implications left out. This certainly seems to be what occurred in the years directly following its publication: few took much notice of the book. Although it was placed on the *Index of Prohibited Books*, this did not occur until 1616. Why did the controversy take place so long after the initial publication of *De revolutionibus*? The hoopla was due to the response by both scientists and theologians to another scientist who advocated the system.

Galileo and His "Evidence" for Heliocentrism

As we have see, the Copernican system did not have better explanatory or predictive power than the Ptolemaic system, and it was not rejected or outlawed by the church. Copernicus and his writings did not cause much of a stir, and many clerics read his work and were intrigued by it. It was Galileo Galilei (see fig. 4.3) who ultimately raised the heliocentric system to the status it now has.

Recall that the science of the day was still firmly entrenched in Aristotelianism. Galileo came along and broke this mold. During his years teaching at the University of Padua (1592–1610), he observed natural phenomena through experimentation. His investigations focused on mechanics and motion. Two important concepts resulted from these endeavors: Galileo realized that the weight of a body was not a factor in its rate of fall, as Aristotle had claimed, and that the period of oscillation (the swinging motion) of a pendulum is constant no matter how wide or narrow the swing, an understanding that led to the manufacture of more accurate clocks. Although these contributions to science were ultimately more important than anything else Galileo did, it was his use of a new technology that resulted in our popular conceptions of him. In 1610, Galileo built his own telescope. With it, he was able to observe the heavens in a manner no one else had ever done before. Let's take a brief look at each observation and its significance:

- Galileo observed craters and mountains on the Moon. This was directly in contrast to Aristotle's claim that the Moon was perfectly smooth.
- Galileo was the first to detect four moons orbiting Jupiter. This showed there could be two types of motion: the moons rotating around Jupiter, and Jupiter (and its moons) rotating around the Earth or Sun (depending on which system was subscribed to). In a geocentric system, all celestial bodies orbit the Earth. Galileo's observations showed that not all objects directly orbit the Earth.

Fig. 4.3 Galileo Galilei, by (school of) Justus Sustermans. Oil on canvas. (Galleria Palatina, Palazzo Pitti, Florence, Italy/The Bridgeman Art Library)

- Galileo saw sunspots, dark spots on the Sun that moved from left to right. To Galileo, this meant that the Sun was moving, rotating on its axis. Aristotelian thinkers held that the Sun and other celestial bodies were perfect and pure, and that any movement would be in perfect circles.
- Many stars could be seen through the telescope, many more than with just the naked eye. And these stars could be very far away, given how faint they appear. If the stars were made by God for our observation, why would there be stars we could not see? And if some were very far away, the universe might be infinite, which presented a theological difficulty.
- But perhaps the most important observations Galileo made were of Venus. Through his telescope, Galileo could see that Venus has phases, just as our Moon does. Theoretically, these should occur in both the geocentric and heliocentric systems. However, the phases are predicted to be different in the two models (see fig. 4.4). Galileo's observations were consistent with the heliocentric view. Indeed, this evidence, in the philosophy of Popper, falsifies the Ptolemaic system.

We can summarize Galileo's findings in this way: Galileo discredited many assumptions of Aristotelianism and disproved the original Ptolemaic system. He did not, however, provide any evidence to support heliocentrism directly. Certainly his observations

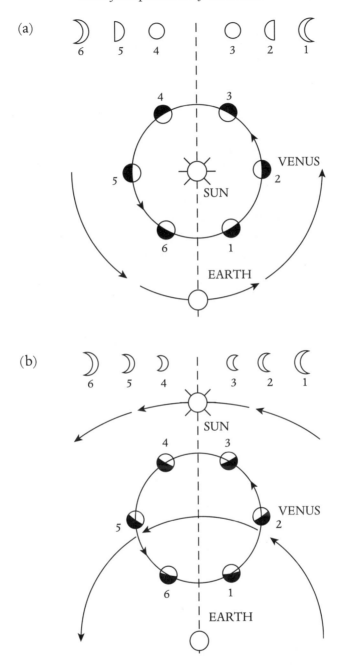

Fig. 4.4 (*a*) Phases of Venus according to the Copernican system. As Venus orbits the Sun, its appearance from the vantage point of Earth changes. The different shapes observed include spheres and crescents. (*b*) Phases of Venus according to the Ptolemaic system. Venus, on its epicycle, is also moving along its deferent, just as the Sun moves along its deferent. The phases predicted by the Ptolemaic model are different from those predicted by the Copernican model, and include only crescents. Galileo observed the phases associated with the Copernican model, thus disproving the Ptolemaic model.

were consistent with the notion, but they could have been explained by other systems. We need to keep this in mind to help us understand the later controversy.

Galileo recorded his initial telescopic observations in 1610 in *Starry Messenger*. This work brought him much fame and notoriety, but it also angered many of his academic peers, who still held to the Aristotelian ways. He left the University of Padua and became the mathematician and philosopher in the court of the grand duke of Tuscany. Galileo enjoyed much popularity during this time, and often spoke about heliocentrism. Had his telescopic observations, and his support of the Copernican system, been his only concerns, the story would be done at this point. But there is much more.

As we discussed before, several biblical texts support a geocentric universe. Therefore, with talk of heliocentrism, the implications for religion were sure to surface. And they did. Galileo wrote two important letters, one in 1613 to the Benedictine priest, Benedetto Castelli, and another in 1615 to the Grand Duchess Christina. In these letters, he explained his ideas about how to interpret the Bible in light of scientific evidence that may appear to contradict it. In summary, Galileo said that God was the author of both the Bible and the natural world, and therefore truths found in each could not contradict each other. As the Bible uses metaphors and figurative language to allow everyone to understand its messages, we must be careful not to interpret the Bible literally. The Bible is a source for religious and moral teaching and should not be consulted for a scientific description of the world. Galileo echoed the sentiment of Cardinal Cesare Baronius (1538–1607), who said the Bible tells us how to go to heaven, and not how the heavens go.

Reaction of the Church

As we saw earlier, the church was at the beginning of a particularly painful episode in its history, starting in 1517 with the Protestant Reformation. Some of the major issues surrounding Luther's separation from the church concerned the authority of the church and the interpretation of scripture. One of the church's reactions to this was the Council of Trent (1545–63), where church officials called for a reaffirmation of the authority of the church and an emphasis on a literal interpretation of the Bible. The Council declared that interpretation could be done only by bishops and church councils. Galileo's notions of interpretation were similar to Augustine's, who advocated that we need to understand the difference between literal and figurative use of language in the Bible. Many theologians of Galileo's day accepted this idea. However, Galileo took it upon himself to claim that the biblical passages discussing the position and movement of the Earth and the Sun should be taken figuratively.

Cardinal Robert Bellarmine (1542–1621) was the main theologian who commented on Galileo's ideas. Although he concurred with Galileo regarding the truth of nature and the Bible, he believed every statement in the Bible to be true, if understood properly, and that Christians must accept this truth by faith. If science could prove something false in the Bible, then a literal interpretation of the text would have to be reassessed. If science could not yet prove it to be false, but may do so in the future, Bellarmine argued, the traditional reading should still be accepted, because the interpretation of the

Bible by church authorities is a higher truth than the word of scientists. He proposed that the Copernican system be acceptable as a hypothetical idea, and be used for astronomical calculations, but that it not be accepted as true, because there was no substantial evidence to support it.

In 1616, Pope Paul V (1552–1621) commissioned several theologians to examine the matter of heliocentrism. They came back with the opinion that placing the Sun at the center of the universe was heresy, and saying the Earth moved should also be censured, although they did not go so far as to consider it heretical. Thus, the teaching of the Copernican system was prohibited, and any works that defended the system were placed on the *Index* (including *De revolutionibus*). A meeting was set up between Bellarmine and Galileo, where Bellarmine was to tell Galileo exactly what the decree said and to persuade him to agree not to teach or hold the Copernican position. This is where the controversy exists: it is not known exactly what Bellarmine told Galileo. There is no record of the meeting. However, there are two documents related to this topic:

- a letter from Bellarmine to Galileo dated three months after the meeting, saying the Copernican view should not be defended or held;
- a paper in the files of the Holy Office stating that Galileo had been told the heliocentric system could not be defended, held, or taught in any way.

The basic discrepancy lies in whether or not the teaching of heliocentrism was forbidden to Galileo. Regardless of what he was told, Galileo kept quiet regarding the Copernican system, for a time.

In 1623, Maffeo Barberini (1568–1644), a good friend of Galileo, was elected Pope Urban VIII. Galileo was granted meetings with the Pope, six in all, in which the heliocentric system was discussed. Apparently, the Pope told Galileo he could once again write about the system, as long as he made it clear it was hypothetical. In 1632, Galileo's *Dialogue Concerning the Two Chief World Systems* was published. It was in the form of a Platonic dialogue, perhaps to appease the Pope that the ideas proposed were "hypothetical." There are three characters in the book: Salviati, who presents the heliocentric system; Simplicio, who defends the geocentric model; and Sagredo, who is the open-minded inquirer learning about the two systems. Although, in the end, Salviati concedes to Simplicio, it is clear that Salviati has the better explanation and has won the argument. In the dialogue, Simplicio espouses a position often adopted by Urban. This was interpreted to mean that the Simplicio character was the Pope. Needless to say, Urban felt angered and betrayed by his "friend," and called for an investigation of the book. This led to the trial of 1633. The decree of 1616 and the two accounts of the Bellarmine–Galileo meeting were considered, and the judgment came down against Galileo, who was "vehemently suspected of heresy." He was sentenced to house arrest for the remainder of his life. The *Dialogue* was placed on the *Index*, and was not officially removed until 1822.

Although he was banned from discussing the heliocentric system, Galileo continued his scientific inquiries. It was during this time that he wrote *Discourse on Two New Sciences*, published in 1638, where he documented his work on falling bodies and pendulums. This book contained major contributions to the field of mechanics (physics). He eventually became blind and died in 1642.

The Success and Downfall of Galileo

There is no doubt that Galileo was a brilliant man, and that his methodology of experimentation and observation helped create modern science. His overall success, and his downfall, can be attributed mainly to his personality and to the times in which his ideas were proposed.

First of all, Galileo was a good Catholic. He never left the church, and never questioned the authority of the Bible (just the interpretation of it). He felt he was doing the church a favor by purging incorrect scientific information from its teachings, and never intended any embarrassment or disrespect. His celebrity status was probably due to his persuasive abilities as an orator and writer. He wrote in Italian, not in Latin, so his work could be read by a wider audience. However, he was pushy and arrogant in his attempts to convert academics and church officials to the heliocentric system. He thought his relationship with Urban VIII would protect him, but the *Dialogue* only angered the pontiff. Galileo was in the wrong place at the wrong time, and his actions could not be tolerated. The church was still trying to recover from the Reformation, and it was in the midst of the Thirty Years War, another struggle with the Protestants over the religious fate of northern European countries. It had little time or patience to deal with Galileo.

The response to the science by different factions of the church was varied. While the Dominicans thought the Copernican system could not be true because it was based only on mathematics, the Jesuits thought the mathematics was valid. However, they did not consider Galileo's proofs to be complete. Others in the church thought the science was good, and that the Bible should be reinterpreted. Although the phases of Venus were a strong argument against the Ptolemaic system, none of Galileo's observations strictly supported only the heliocentric system. One of the major problems with heliocentrism was the lack of observation of parallax, or parallactic shift of the stars (see fig. 4.5). This phenomenon would occur only if the heliocentric system were correct. As the Earth orbits the Sun, our view of stars close to the Earth would shift position in relation to stars farther away. So, when the Earth is on one side of the Sun (for example, in December), a nearby star would be in a different position in relation to other stars than we would observe when the Earth is on the other side of the Sun (in June). No parallax was seen in Galileo's time, but it does exist. The shift is so slight that a more powerful telescope was needed to observe it. The first parallax was detected in 1838 by Friedrich Bessel (1784–1846).

Regardless of the science, Galileo was seen as overstepping his bounds when he interpreted the Bible. The Council of Trent had been clear on the matter of interpretation. Galileo may have been able to escape the country after his trial, but he chose to stay in Italy. He never renounced his faith. In 1741, the Holy Office gave permission for the *Dialogue* to be included in a collection of Galileo's works. Some mark this as the official date where the Catholic Church accepted the heliocentric view.

Tycho's Observations and Kepler's Laws

While Galileo was silenced on matters of the universe, others were actively pursuing a better understanding of the heavens. In the latter part of the sixteenth century, a

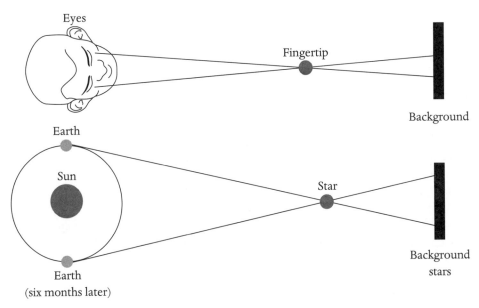

Fig. 4.5 Parallactic shift. If the heliocentric model is correct, then the appearance of a star close to the Earth (lower figure) will change relative to the background stars, which are further away, when the Earth is at different positions in its orbit. A simple demonstration (top figure) is to extend your finger at arm's length, and then look at its position relative to background objects while alternating one eye open and one eye closed. This is analogous to the Earth (your eyes) at different positions in its orbit. The parallax was not seen until 1838.

Danish astronomer, Tycho Brahe (1546–1601) made observations that would contribute enormously to the future of astronomy. Born into the nobility, Tycho's family enjoyed a high position in society and politics. He attended the Lutheran University at Copenhagen. His observation of a solar eclipse in 1560, at the age of 13, and his disappointment at the failure of both the Ptolemaic and Copernican systems to predict a conjunction of Jupiter and Saturn accurately led him to his profession. On November 11, 1572, he observed a new star (actually a supernova) in the constellation Cassiopeia. Tycho concluded what he observed was indeed an object in the celestial realm, and not simply an atmospheric event. If the object was in the terrestrial realm, it would display parallax, which it didn't. This had great significance in natural philosophy, as Aristotle and Ptolemy had concluded the heavens were immutable and unchanging. The star faded with time and ultimately disappeared the following March. His observation of this event thrust Tycho into the position of leading astronomer of his day. In 1576, the king of Denmark, Frederick II (1534–88), gave him an island, Hven, for his work, and supported him financially (it is estimated more than 1 percent of the Danish national budget went toward these endeavors). Tycho had the best instruments for astronomical observations. Two observatories were built on the island: Uraniborg ("Castle of the Heavens") and later Stjerneborg ("Castle of the Stars") which had more secure foundations to stabilize Tycho's instruments. The island also had a variety of other buildings, including a papermill and a windmill, as well as its own printing facilities. There were farms, indoor plumbing, a library, domestic staff, and room for eight assistants. Hven became the center of astronomy for all of Europe.

Tycho was a meticulous observer. He verified his readings through repetition, and was obsessive about checking and rechecking his equipment. This allowed him to determine the positions of the stars and planets with unprecedented accuracy. In his lifetime, Tycho studied the planets, the Sun, and almost 800 stars – all before the invention of the telescope! He also is well known for his lunar theory, in which he was able to predict the movements of the Moon more accurately. Unfortunately, he did not have a good relationship with Frederick's successor, Christian IV (1577–1648), and left Hven in 1597. Initially he went to Hamburg, but ended up in Prague in 1599. It was here that he hired Johannes Kepler as his assistant. Tycho died in 1601, leaving his astronomical data in the hands of Kepler.

Tycho was fully aware of the Copernican system, and as early as 1574 was lecturing on the absurdity of both the Ptolemaic and Copernican models. He objected to Ptolemy's equants, and thought a moving Earth, as in the Copernican system, could not be possible. Two of his observations discredited the Aristotelian notion of an unchanging celestial realm: the new star in Cassiopeia in 1527 (see above), and the appearance of a comet in 1577. Aristotle said that comets were in the realm of the terrestrial: they were beneath the Moon, and therefore did not violate the notion of the unchanging heavens. Tycho concluded the comet he observed was beyond the Moon, a changing event in the unchanging realm. Another problem Tycho noted with the existing systems was the movement of Mars: if the planets and stars were fixed on moving orbs, as Aristotle, Ptolemy, and Copernicus had assumed, then the orbs of Mars and the Sun would intersect. This was not physically possible. The paths of comets would take them through the orbs, which also challenged the notion of physical orbs. In addition, the paths of comets were clearly around the Sun – not around the Earth. And so Tycho proposed his own system. Based on his observations, he concluded the five planets moved around the Sun, and the Sun moved about the Earth. He contended that the heavens contained a fluid wherein the planets moved freely, and the orbs were not actual physical objects but rather the boundaries of this fluid. Some scientists and theologians of the time adopted the Tychonic system, almost as a compromise between the Ptolemaic and Copernican models.

There is no doubt that Tycho was a great astronomer, who made careful observations of the heavens and kept detailed records. However, he was not a good mathematician, and therefore could not deduce the correct orbits of the planets. This had to wait for Kepler.

Kepler's work represents an important advancement in astronomy: he used physics to understand astronomical observations. He was not the first to do so, but he was working at a time when Aristotelian explanations were being criticized and rejected. Kepler studied at the University of Tübingen, where he learned of the Copernican system. The Lutherans were willing to adopt some of Copernicus's ideas that did not directly go against their theological understanding of the universe. In 1594 Kepler began teaching mathematics at the Lutheran school in Graz. It was during this time that he came up with an interesting idea: he applied geometry to the study of astronomy. He was able to construct a scheme whereby the distance between the orbits of the planets could be explained by geometric figures. If the orbits were expanded into three dimensions (spheres), then these spheres could enclose other geometrical shapes (specifically a cube, a tetrahedron, a dodecahedron, an icosahedron, and an octahedron). His model fit in almost perfectly with the Copernican system. This scheme had great significance in Kepler's thinking.

Like many in his day, Kepler was interested in astrology. He used his astronomical observations to aid his understanding and application of this "science." He did not just accept the traditional notions of astrology, but earnestly tried to integrate mathematics into the field. The geometric scheme he advocated helped to support his astrology. Kepler argued that the human soul reacts to this geometric organization. In a sense, we have an innate understanding of the shapes in the universe, which may be the basis for all of astrology. (Money was often tight for Kepler, and so he often kept himself afloat by preparing horoscopes.)

The geometric scheme was important not only to astrology, it was even more crucial to theology and science. Kepler used the mathematics he developed as an argument from design. The geometric scheme demonstrated divine providence: the universe had to have been planned by the creator. He showed how this creation was based on mathematical principles, supporting the notion that mathematics was a valid and important tool that could help us understand nature, and hence understand God. The scientific importance of Kepler's claim rested on what caused the orbits: he was not just observing the movements of the planets (astronomy), but also determining why the orbits were the exact length they were (cosmology). That Kepler could explain the cause lent more credence to his science over other ideas about the universe.

Kepler searched for the cause of the central position of the Sun in the solar system. He thought that understanding it would be the key to understanding planetary movement. He was aware that a planetary period (the time it took for a planet to rotate once around the Sun, or a "year") depended on the distance the planet was from the Sun: the farther away, the longer the period. He tried to develop a mathematical law to describe this. His initial ideas were published in *Mysterium cosmographicum* (*The Sacred Mystery of the Cosmos*) in 1596, but his thinking was flawed. Eventually he was able to determine the correct mathematical relationship between the period (T) and the radius of the orbit (R): $T^2 = R^3$. Thus, if you knew the period of a planet (which is easily observed), you could determine its distance from the Sun (see fig. 4.6 (c)). He published this ratio in *Harmonice mundi* (Harmony of the Worlds) in 1619. It is commonly known as Kepler's third law of planetary motion. (We'll encounter the other two in a moment.)

In 1598 Kepler was forced to leave Graz by the Catholic authorities. He found his way to Prague in 1600 and was employed by Tycho. The data that Tycho had amassed allowed Kepler to determine an accurate orbit for Mars. However, Tycho was very secretive and possessive of his data, and it was only after his death that Kepler had access to all his observations. In addition, Kepler no longer had to adhere to the astronomical system of his employer. Using Tycho's data, Kepler determined the correct distances of Mars from Earth.

The actual force that caused planetary movement was the next object of Kepler's investigations. He thought a magnetic-like force from the Sun was the cause of these motions. He explained planetary movements using the notion that this force diminished the farther away a planet was from the Sun. This is his second law: the speed of a planet decreases as its distance from the sun increases. If you draw an imaginary line from the Sun to the planet, follow the path of the planet for a time, and draw another line back to the Sun, the figure will encompass an area in space that is shaped like a slice of pizza. The area of this slice will be the same for a given interval of time, no matter where in

(a)

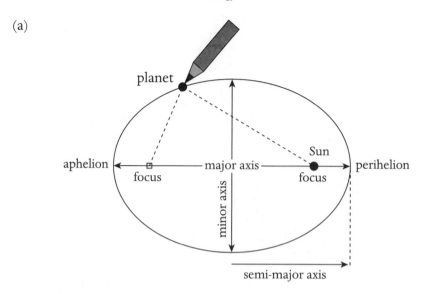

Fig. 4.6 (*a*) Kepler's first law of planetary motion: planets orbit the Sun on ellipses. The Sun is at one focus of the ellipse, the other is empty. In reality, the foci of the planetary orbits are close to the center point, making the ellipse very nearly circular. To draw an ellipse, loop a string around thumb tacks at each focus and stretch the string tight with a pencil while moving the pencil around the tacks. (*b*) Kepler's second law of planetary motion: a planet moves faster when it is close to the Sun, and slower when farther away. However, the areas (indicated in gray), derived from the distance traveled by the planet in a given length of time, is the same, no matter where it is in its orbit. (*c*) Kepler's third law of planetary motion relates the average radius of a planet's orbit (*R*, measured in astronomical units (au), the distance of the radius of the Earth's orbit) to the period, or time it takes a planet to make one full orbit around the Sun (*T*, measured in Earth years). $T^2 = R^3$, and so the ratio between the two will equal 1. Therefore, if you know the period of a planet, you can calculate its average distance from the Sun. This equation can also be used to determine periods and radii of other celestial bodies (for example, moons orbiting a planet).

the orbit the planet is (see fig. 4.6(*b*)). He published this idea in 1609, in *Astronomia nova* (New Astronomy).

Kepler was still encountering problems with the obit of Mars: a circular orbit could not explain the observations made by Tycho. However, an elliptical orbit could. Thus Kepler concluded that planets travel in elliptical orbits with the Sun situated at one focus of the ellipse (see fig. 4.6(*a*)). This is known as Kepler's first law of planetary motion. He published it in 1609, in *Astronomia nova*.

Kepler published *Epitome astromoniae Copernicanae* (Epitome of Copernican Astronomy) in 1618–21. This was a defense of the Copernican system. Kepler used many of his own ideas in this work, including an analogy between the arrangement of the universe and the Holy Trinity. This, and his support of a moving Earth, caused *Epitome* to be placed on the *Index*.

(b)

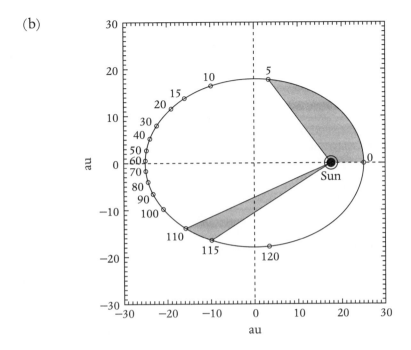

(c)

Planet	R (in au)	T (in years)	T^2/R^3
Mercury	0.387	0.24	0.994
Venus	0.723	0.615	1.001
Earth	1.000	1.000	1.000
Mars	1.523	1.881	1.002
Jupiter	5.203	11.86	0.999
Saturn	9.54	29.46	1.000
Uranus	19.18	84.10	1.002

Fig. 4.6 *(Cont'd)*

Ultimately, Kepler changed astronomy. His extensive use of mathematics led to a new age, and a new direction, for the science. His laws regarding planetary movement, and his understanding of the force necessary for movement, formed much of the basis for Newton's ideas. And his clarification of the orbits (as ellipses, not circles) finally provided more accurate predictions for the movement of the planets. Interestingly, he invoked divine providence as support for the science of astronomy.

Newton's Science

Isaac Newton was born on Christmas day in the year Galileo died (fig. 4.7). Newton's father had died a few months before his birth, and he was raised primarily by his grandmother after his mother remarried. Newton entered Trinity College, Cambridge, in 1661, where he became interested in mathematics and science. He was forced to return home for about 18 months owing to an outbreak of plague. In 1669, he became a professor of mathematics at Cambridge. Among his great achievements were the invention of the calculus, investigations of light and color, and studies in mechanics and gravity that led to an understanding of orbital dynamics. He was warden and master of the Royal Mint, and, in 1703, he became the president of the Royal Society of London, a position he held until his death. He was very interested in alchemy and astrology, and the volume of his writings in theology exceeds those in science.

By 1661, Newton was aware of Kepler's third law of planetary motion, and by 1664 he had developed ideas regarding centrifugal force. Together, these led Newton toward

Fig. 4.7   Sir Isaac Newton, by James McArdell. Mezzotint, 1760, after painting, c.1726, by Enoch Seemann. Paris, Bibliotheque Nationale. (akg-images)

an understanding of gravity. However, he had little data to support his ideas, and he discontinued this work for 20 years. By the early 1680s, he was corresponding with Robert Hooke (1635–1703), the curator of experiments at the Royal Society. Hooke had been conducting research on gravity for years. As early as 1674, he is known to have thought that all celestial bodies have an attractive force, or gravitational power, that can act on other celestial bodies. This force decreases the farther away the bodies lie: specifically, the force decreases as an inverse of the square of the distance (if planet B is twice the distance from the Sun as planet A, then planet B will experience only one-quarter of the force that planet A will; if planet C is three times the distance from the Sun as planet A, it will experience only one-ninth the force). Hooke and Edmund Halley (1656–1743) were working with these ideas, but they were unable to explain why the planets traveled in ellipses, as Kepler had observed. During a visit with Newton in 1684, Halley asked him, given the inverse-square law, what path a planet would take. Through the use of the calculus, Newton determined it would be an ellipse. Newton published his proof of this in 1687, in *Philosophiae naturalis principia mathematica* (Mathematical Principles of Natural Philosophy), one of the most important works in the history of science. *Principia* laid out Newton's famous laws of motion and gravity. We will discuss them briefly here.

Newton's three laws of motion can be described as follows:

1   *An object that is not being pulled or pushed (in other words, has no force acting on it) will either remain at rest or continue to move in a straight line.* Often this is restated as: an object in motion will stay in motion until it is acted on by another force. If you throw a ball, it does not continue forever in the direction you threw it: friction with the air will slow it down and gravity will act on it to change its direction (in other words, it falls). However, if you were to throw the ball in space, it would continue in the same direction, with the same velocity, forever, unless it came in contact with a gravitational field.

2   *If a force is applied to an object, it will move (accelerate) in the direction of the force. The magnitude of the acceleration depends on the mass of the object.* The equation $F = ma$ summarizes this, where F is force, m mass, and a acceleration. A common example of this is a shopping cart: when it is empty, you need apply only a small force (a light push) to make it go. Once full, the force you apply to move it must be much greater (you increased the mass with your groceries). Now compare the force you use in the supermarket to push your cart: it is less when the cart is empty, more when it is full, but you move the cart at the same speed (acceleration) through the aisles. If you use the same force to push an empty cart as you do with a full one, the empty cart would move (accelerate) much faster.

3   *If an object is pushed or pulled, the object will push or pull back with equal force.* This is often known as the law of equal and opposite reactions. You stand on the floor, and your mass pushes down on it. The floor is pushing up with equal force. If it wasn't, you would either fall through the floor (the floor pushes with less force) or you would be propelled up into the air (the floor pushes with more force).

Newton also described his ideas regarding gravity.

• *The force of gravity decreases with distance* (as discussed above).

- *The attraction exerted by one object on another object will depend on the mass of both objects.* Two massive objects, such as the Sun and a planet, will affect each other, although the body with the larger mass (Sun) will have a greater effect on the smaller body (planet). The primary effect will be on the orbit of the planet, but the planet can also affect the movement of the Sun. Also, a body with relatively little mass, say an apple, will not have much effect on a body with a relatively large mass, say the Earth. So the force in this example will pull the apple to the Earth, whereas the apple will have little or no effect on the Earth.

This aspect of Newton's work is critical, as he used the same force, gravity, to describe motion on the Earth as well as in the heavens. Objects, both terrestrial and celestial, obey the same laws. Recall that Aristotle said the terrestrial and celestial realms were different, including how things moved in them. With Newton we have a universal law of gravity that can account for the motions of the planets, satellites, and comets, and the motion of objects on Earth.

These laws of motion and gravity provided a theoretical explanation of Kepler's laws, which were based entirely on observation. Using these ideas, Newton was able to make predictions:

- *Orbits should deviate slightly from those predicted by Kepler's laws, as the planets have different masses.*
- *A planet should be spherical, because of gravity, if there is no other force acting on it.* A spinning motion (as in rotation around an axis) would cause a bulge at the equator of a planet. Newton was able to calculate the amount the Earth should deviate from being a perfect sphere, using size, mass, and spin rate. His calculations were within 1 percent of the currently accepted value.
- *The path of comets could be predicted.* Halley used Newton's ideas to propose that the comets seen in 1531, 1607, and 1682 (observed by Halley himself) were the same comet, whose orbit took it around the Sun every 76 years. Indeed, the comet returned in 1758, just as Halley predicted. He had, of course, died by then, but the comet now bears his name.

Newton's other *tour de force* was *Opticks*, published in 1704. This is a study of the nature of light, color, and diffraction, which, by itself, without the calculus and the *Principia*, would have made Newton one of the greatest scientists of all time. Newton used experimentation in *Opticks*, as opposed to the mathematical proofs he had employed in *Principia*. This helped set the stage for how experimental science should be done. It is amazing to think of the contributions of this one man to our understanding of the natural world. It is even more amazing to examine this alongside his theology.

Newton's Theology

Newton was both a mechanical philosopher and a natural philosopher. He concluded that nature could be explained by natural laws and mechanisms as well as by divine will.

Both are apparent in his scientific work. For example, Newton could calculate the effects of gravity, but he did not know exactly how it acted. He attempted to explain it in different ways, including divine intervention, throughout his life. Different conclusions could be drawn from his writings, and both theistic and deistic notions could be supported by his work.

Newton envisioned God as a divine intelligence, skilled in mechanics and geometry. The evidence, he claimed, could be seen in the exact orbits of the planets. It is a very easy jump from this notion of design to deism, the belief that God acted at the creation of the universe but no longer exerts providence over this creation. Newton never subscribed to deism. He saw divine providence everywhere in nature. For example, his understandings of gravity would mean that the "fixed" stars should fall into each other. They don't, therefore God must be actively involved in preventing this. He also saw the solar system as needing some help now and again. He thought space consisted of an ether, and that, as the planets moved through this ether, they would encounter friction, which would throw them off their orbits. A comet could also create a force on the planets that would affect them similarly. And the Sun's pull on the planets could cause them to crash into the massive body. Newton's solution to these difficulties was divine intervention. Interestingly, as his laws demystified comets by making them predictable events, he reintroduced them into the religious realm. He proposed that comets acted as agents of divine will: they supplied material to the solar system to keep the masses of celestial bodies constant, which would preserve their orbits. Newton also saw God as existing everywhere in space. There was no space without the presence of God in it. He used this as one way to justify gravity as a universal law.

Newton's theology did not just involve science. He studied the biblical texts and the ideas of early theologians intently. He utilized the same type of questioning in his theological studies as in his scientific studies. He rejected many authorities, but he most vehemently opposed the Trinitarians, referring to them as blasphemers and criminals. Newton believed that Jesus was a created being and not co-eternal with God. He argued, from biblical texts, that Jesus is always subordinate to God, and that God had to elevate him to sit at the right hand. He researched passages supporting Trinitarian notions, and saw evidence of tampering, as the versions printed before the introduction of the Trinity were different from the present-day texts.

Newton was also interested in prophecy, and studied the Book of Revelation carefully. He collected some 20 different versions of Revelation to try to determine the true text. He also studied Jewish literature to gain more insight into prophecy. His manuscript *Theologiae gentilis origines philosophicae* (The Philosophical Origins of Gentile Theology) was never completed, but it presented his most radical and important theological ideas, some of which are reflected in his scientific writings. Newton thought there was one true religion that could be deduced from the study of nature. Human history follows a cyclical pattern, wherein this religion is continually distorted. People stray from the true religion by engaging in false worship. God sends prophets to persuade people to come back to the true religion. Newton saw Christianity as just another episode in this history. He believed Christ was one of God's prophets, and the worship of him as God was idolatry.

Newton kept his theological ideas private, and the full extent of his views was not well known until the twentieth century, when his manuscripts were made public.

However, on his deathbed, after a lifetime of secrecy, he refused the sacrament of the Anglican Church. He was buried in Westminster Abbey.

Conclusions

We have covered many topics in this chapter. Table 4.1 provides a comparison of the geocentric and heliocentric systems, and a brief summary of key concepts.

The importance of astronomy and cosmology to our lives, and those of our ancestors, cannot be understated. We are part of a big universe, and we strive continually to understand the role we play in it, our part and our purpose. We seek knowledge and

Table 4.1 Comparison of heliocentric and geocentric systems

	Geocentric	*Heliocentric*
Basic tenets	Earth is the center of the solar system: the Sun, planets, and stars rotate around the Earth	The Sun is the center of the solar system: the Earth and the other planets rotate around the Sun
Important ideas	*Plato* Planets move in perfect circles around the Earth *Aristotle* Sharp distinction between terrestrial and celestial realms, including movement *Ptolemy* Developed a grand geocentric system; wrote 13-volume compendium; system lasted 13 centuries	*Aristarchus* Sun at the center; Earth rotates on an axis and revolves around the Sun *Copernicus* Devised heliocentric system; used mathematical elements of the Ptolemaic system *Kepler* Devised laws regarding orbits; realized orbits were ellipses, not circles; did not use epicycles *Newton* Laws of motion explained terrestrial and celestial movement; concluded gravity was the force for planetary movement in orbits
Evidence	Epicycles and deferents allowed for direct and retrograde motion; predicted movement fairly accurately; predicted no parallax; coincided with Greek philosophical and physical doctrine; consistent with medieval physics; had common sense appeal	Predictive accuracy of the system is no greater, but also no worse, than the Ptolemaic system; simpler than the Ptolemaic system; Galileo's observations contradicted Greek philosophy
Problems	Multiple epicycles were required to explain movement; observations of Tycho (new stars, path of comets) and Galileo (phases of Venus)	Common sense appeal of Aristotelian motion; no observation was explainable by the heliocentric system alone; no parallax observed

understanding on many levels, and this is reflected in the long and rich history of humanity. The stories of these investigations are complex, interweaving science, religion, philosophy, society, and politics. Those involved include clergy, nobility, and academics; Catholics and Protestants; popes and kings. The history has been interpreted and reinterpreted from many different viewpoints. The issues we have investigated represent only the tip of the iceberg, and numerous intriguing stories lie just beneath the surface. The most well known, of course, is the Galileo affair.

The analyses of what happened between Galileo and the church range from vehement conflict to unfortunate misunderstanding. The issues involve the nature of science, interpretations of the Bible, and the strong personalities of the authorities. It is a very complex issue, and there are many interpretations but no easy answers. In order to understand it, we have to ask what Galileo did. What did his science show? Was he wrong to take it upon himself to interpret the Bible? How much of a role did his ego play in this situation? How did he really intend the *Dialogue* to be read and interpreted? What did the church want from his trial?

In 1979, Pope John Paul II commissioned the Pontifical Academy of Sciences to investigate the Galileo affair, in order to gain a better understanding of the views of the scientists and the theologians involved, which could shed new light on the relationship between science and religion in the past and present. In 1992, the commission, made up of scientists, theologians, and historians, presented their report. The commission relied heavily on the views of Bellarmine, and concluded that, as Galileo had not "proven" the heliocentric system, there was no need for the Catholic Church to reinterpret scripture. However, the judges in the 1633 trial were in error in their condemnation of Galileo. In the opinion of the commission, the judges did not dissociate their faith from the "science," and they wrongly believed that the heliocentric view would weaken the authority of the Catholic Church and that they had a duty to prevent the heliocentric system from being taught. John Paul acknowledged that Galileo suffered under the church's authority.

History will always be reinterpreted when new facts come to light and new approaches are taken. Is there a "truth" that can be deduced? Like science and religion, history may seek the truth, but it is doubtful it will be found.

Regardless of whether it is "right" or "wrong," science and faith have been yoked together in the study of the cosmos. It is difficult to investigate this vast universe without asking questions about our significance and our purpose. As we shall see in chapter 6, our modern scientific theories of the nature of the universe raise these same issues. For all of our "advancements," we are still trying to answer the questions our ancestors asked thousands of years ago.

Primary Literature

Useful primary sources include a selection of Aristotle's *Metaphysics* (Book XII, Part 8), describing the number of orbs in the celestial realm; the letter Galileo wrote to Castelli in 1613; an excerpt from *Dialogue concerning the Two Chief World Systems* ("The Third Day"); and four letters Newton wrote to Richard Bentley in 1692–3 discussing God's role in the universe.

Questions to Consider

1 Imagine yourself as a geocentrist, and a contemporary of Galileo and Kepler. What evidence, if any, would be sufficient to convert you to the heliocentric system? Explain your reasoning.

2 The period of time we covered in this chapter is often called the Scientific Revolution, reflecting the fact that this era changed how science is done. However, many deny it was a true revolution, in that it took place over the course of almost 145 years, from the publication of *De revolutionibus* in 1543 to the publication of *Principia* in 1687. Consider Kuhn's notion of scientific revolutions. Would you consider the shift from the geocentric to the heliocentric system a revolution, or is it a logical progression of ideas that relied on the gradual accumulation of theories and data? Justify your answer.

5

Creation Myths

Overview

All cultures have stories of creation, depicting the origin of the cosmos and of human beings. All myths provide etiology and purpose, and most serve other functions, such as providing understandings of the culture from historical, ethical, societal, and scientific perspectives. A limited number of themes are found in these myths which explain the origins of the gods, of the universe, and of humans. Genesis shares many of these themes, but it also has some unique features. In addition, it is important to realize that the meaning of Genesis cannot be determined from just the opening chapters of the Bible. This creation myth must be placed in a wider context: it needs to be understood in the context of the entire Bible and within Christian tradition.

Introduction

Every culture has its myths and legends, stories of how the universe and humans came to be, and of the trials and tribulations that followed. These stories, richly poetic and symbolic, delight our imagination and spark our curiosity. They provide an insight into how these cultures view the world and their own existence. They awaken in us a desire to understand our reality further. In discussing these stories, we must first define a few key terms, and examine the function of myth. In this chapter, we will consider a few creation myths, compare and contrast the underlying elements in each account, and dive a bit deeper into the creation story in Genesis, including some important reflections on the interpretation of the biblical text.

We defined cosmology in chapter 4 as the study of the universe as a whole. The study of the origin of the universe is call "cosmogony." However, today the two terms have been conflated, and we use cosmology to mean the study of both the origin and the structure of the universe. The creation myths we will examine are cosmogonies, and they are also theogonies, which describe the origins of the gods. As we have seen, an understanding of the cosmos is of great importance to humans, and creation myths reveal this to be a common quest across cultures and throughout history.

It is important for us to understand just what a myth is. The term "myth," as used colloquially today, denotes a fictitious story, a fairy tale that is so fantastic it cannot possibly be construed as real. However, the term has other meanings that are central to our discussion here. On the surface, our definition of myth focuses on the stories a culture tells to explain the origin of the cosmos and of humans. But at a deeper level, myths transmit morals and lessons from one generation to the next, and provide meaning, social structure, and other important cultural identities. Thus, it is not appropriate to dismiss a myth as an imaginative story that is pure fiction. There are deeper meanings and critical information behind these traditional legends. Most myths have been passed on orally through time, and several variations of the same myth may exist, reflecting modifications that were made to adapt the myth for a particular time and a particular people.

The Function of Myth

It is difficult to discover exactly what function a myth serves if we are not familiar with the culture. Thus, if we know little about a society, we may only guess the importance of its creation story. One could argue that myths are simply the result of the imaginations of the people relating the story. Everyone loves a good story, and so myths could represent a tall tale that was passed down through the generations. Like good craftsmen, individuals constructed and wove these stories to fashion the narratives that exist in the culture today. However, these stories would not have survived, and would not have the importance they do, unless they conveyed some vital meaning to the culture. Thus, there must be a function for the myth: it is more than "just a good story." The following are some of the roles myths play.

- *Etiology*. What we see as the obvious message in many myths is the etiology, or origin, of the universe. How did everything begin? Although this appears to be the primary function of many myths, closer examination will reveal other meanings conveyed in these stories. The function usually goes well beyond etiology.
- *Purpose and meaning*. Humans have a deep-seated need to understand the purpose of things, and to find meaning in the events in our lives. Myths provide reasons for our existence. They explain and justify the nature of the heavens and the Earth, and the nature of humans.
- *Teaching*. Myths can be used to teach morals, ethics, philosophy, and social structures that are important to a society. These stories are a way of indoctrinating individuals into a culture.
- *Primitive science*. We can view myths as "science," attempts to explain the natural world through the action of gods. In many cultures, pleasing the gods became important for life, agriculture, fertility, etc. This was often done through magic, which eventually evolved into ritual. When the rituals remained, but the meanings behind

them were long forgotten, new myths, indeed new theologies, were created to explain, or to reinterpret, the customs.

- *Specific explanations.* Some cultures focus on just one or a few aspects of the physical world, such as the Sun, the Moon, or weather patterns, not the cosmos in its entirety. They use myths to explain these elements.
- *Historical accounts.* Some myths are probably based on fact, on events that actually occurred. These myths are interpretations of great floods, fires, or celestial occurrences (such as supernovae) whose significance resonated through the society for thousands of years.

In many cultures, the creation story is told and reenacted during yearly celebrations. This is a vital component in the lives of the people, to remind them of important aspects of their culture and their beliefs. Creation myths usually convey eternal truths and provide lessons to help the culture in the present day. Their retelling is believed to revitalize nature and provide for the prosperity of the population.

Recurring Themes

All myths are meant to impart meaning and purpose to a culture. Human experience is similar no matter the history or location of a population. All humans have difficult lives and must deal with evil, suffering, disease, natural disasters, and death; all humans look at the world with awe and wonder; and all humans observe and live within the physical and biological world. Therefore, we find several common themes and recurring elements within creation myths. The vast majority of myths use one of the following to explain the creation of the world:

- *Watery chaos.* The world is often depicted as rising out of the water. Land appears from the water, or it is made within the water. Water may be a god, or the birthplace of the gods. As water is a powerful force in nature and a sustaining element for human existence, it is no wonder that many myths use it to symbolize chaos and to emphasize its life-giving properties. In addition, many myths include a deluge, whereby a flood is important in the creation of the world and/or of humans.
- *Egg myths.* Some myths describe the world as coming from a cosmic egg. The egg is usually split open, and different parts are used to create the heavens and the Earth. This is a logical way for humans to view the "birth" of the world, employing a process they have witnessed time and again in nature.
- *Procreation of the gods.* Sky and Earth are often depicted as gods in myths, and their mating produces other gods, the universe, or life on Earth. After the union of father sky and mother Earth, the children are often responsible for a violent separation between the gods. Humans may have deified the sky for its warmth and light, and seen the Earth as a womb.
- *Creation edict.* In these myths, the universe, and sometimes the creating deity, appears solely by a spoken word. We may be seeing, in these myths, the importance humans place on words and language.

- *Dismemberment*. In many myths, the cosmos is created from the cutting up of a god or monster. Often these stories detail exactly which body part became which element in the cosmos. It is interesting to think about why humans would view their world as originating in this gruesome manner. The underlying notion may be that death is necessary for the beginning of life. This may reflect the cyclical nature of the universe, where seasons occur in a regular, repeated series, and death and (re)birth are continuing themes in nature, in agriculture, and also in the human condition.

Humans are self-conscious beings. We are able to reflect on our existence and to ask how we came to be. Therefore, myths usually tell of the specific creation of humans along with the creation of the cosmos. Again, several common themes emerge:

- *Catastrophe*. In some myths, humans exist but are wiped out by a flood, fire, or other disaster. Often only one person, or a small group, remains to repopulate the Earth. The birth of the next generation may require some extraordinary circumstances. In some cases, when males are the only ones to survive, mating with a wooden fetish, or with other men, miraculously produces offspring. Where the only survivors are women, some of them may become pregnant through immaculate conception or mating with an animal. Or humans come directly from animals mating. We also see animals becoming helpers to humanity in these worlds where there are few people.
- *Clay or dirt*. Many myths describe how humans were fashioned from clay or dirt by a god. However, the clay or dirt figures have no life until a god performs a special act, usually by breathing life into them. A correlate to this is the idea that humans existed inside the Earth, and the true birth of humanity occurred when they rose from the interior to populate the land.
- *Stones and plants*. Some creation myths tell of humans created from stones or from various parts of plants (seeds, wood, sticks, etc.). Often the gods use trial and error in this creation, to see what form is best. This accounts for different races, or for deformities seen in humans.
- *Descendant of gods*. Humans may originate from a god. For example, the god may divide himself in two, to create male and female, or humans may be formed from the tears of a god. Some myths explain the different castes in a society by their origin from a different body part of a god. Still others tell of urination and masturbation as necessary for the origins of humans.

Most myths have a clear and elaborate theogony, recounting the origin of the divinities. The efforts of the gods in creation are detailed. Myths explain the relationship of the gods to humankind and sometimes provide a justification for why the cosmos was created. Some common themes related to the divinities are:

- *Polytheism*. The vast majority of myths have multiple gods contributing different aspects to creation.

- *Origin*. Some myths assume the deities are already in existence. Others assume the existence of the godhead and detail the origin of lesser deities. Still others tell of the creation of the main deity as well as of the other gods.
- *Power struggles*. In the polytheistic stories, one god is usually dominant over the others. Power struggles are common, and often result in battles and deaths of the gods. Many myths attribute the existence of good and evil to different gods.
- *Relationship of gods to nature*. Many creation stories have a pantheistic model, where the gods are in nature, and the world is a mode of existence for the gods. In others the gods are separate from their creation (a theistic model).
- *Relationship of gods to humans*. In most myths, the creation of humans is not a directed, good process. Humans are sometimes created as servants or slaves. Some stories have humans created as companions for the gods, or almost as a hobby for the gods. Some myths allow for the continuing involvement of the deities in human life, others do not. In some myths, humans are responsible for the separation of the created world from the gods, which results in suffering and explains the existence of evil.
- *Material for creation*. In the act of creation, the divinity may use preexisting materials or, rarely, create from nothing (*ex nihilo*).
- *Male and female*. Some myths have gods only of one sex, who create other gods and humans male and female. Other stories have both male and female deities as the original gods.

We will now look at several different creation myths and examine Genesis in detail. Keep in mind the functions these myths serve, and see if you can identify some of the recurring themes noted above in the following stories.

Greek Myths

The Greeks, like every culture, had their own creation myths. We will not examine the myths involving the popular gods of Mount Olympus here, but rather the cosmologies of the rational thinkers of ancient Greece. We will focus on two examples: Anaximander and Plato.

Anaximander's cosmology provides a comprehensive natural philosophy of the beginning of the world. He relied heavily on notions of change, which probably came from Near Eastern traditions, but he rejected any divine cause. Anaximander avoided some difficulties with the Greek notion of the primary material, the stuff from which all things were made. He did not propose that one of the four elements (earth, air, fire, and water) was the primary material: he identified *aperion* as this substance. When acted on by heat and cold, aperion transformed into the four elements.

For Anaximander, the universe began as chaos. A primary force caused a vortex that formed our world. The elements were separated into different strata based on their densities: earth (being the heaviest) was at the center, water covered the earth, which was also enveloped by mist, and fire (being the lightest) escaped and formed the heavenly bodies. The motion of the vortex also disrupted the separation of the elements.

This caused combinations of fire enclosed by air, which formed the Sun and the Moon. The vortex also caused the formation of the Earth and living creatures. The mud of the Earth was exposed to fire which created dry land and mist, and the Sun warmed the mud which brought forth the animals. Fish were first, when there was still mostly water. The fish came on land (when it appeared), and continued to change into other animals as the environment changed. Man eventually developed from fishlike creatures.

Unlike Anaximander's cosmology, Plato's is religious and teleological. Described in *Timaeus*, it was influential in the Middle Ages. Plato's myth is, naturally, grounded in his philosophy, which is based on purposeful design. The "idea" (what is understood by the intelligence of the mind) is constant and unchanging, but what humans can sense (that is, empirical evidence) is not constant and is not real. Whatever can be sensed cannot be eternal. Therefore, Plato concluded the world (universe) cannot be eternal, because we can sense it, and so it must have had a beginning. If it had a beginning, it had a cause, and the cause must be the best possible, because we have a beautiful world. For Plato, this cause was God. The world was a copy of a pattern in the divine mind of a perfect, intelligent animal. The universe is a living creature which God fashioned from preexisting material. God used fire to make the world visible, earth to make it tangible, and water and air to allow the union of the elements. The shape of the universe is a globe, as the world is one living animal: as such, it is a whole. The soul was made prior to the world's existence and it resides outside of the "body." After the corporeal universe was made, the soul and the body were joined. God then made the Sun to light the heavens so that man could learn arithmetic by observing the stars. Lesser gods were also created, who bore other generations of gods, including Zeus and Hera. The gods were responsible for fashioning human bodies.

Plato goes into detail regarding the shape of the human body and the function of many organs. For example, the head is spherical, analogous to the spherical universe, and the heart is the guard of reason and sends the fire of passion to all other parts of the body. Man's immortal soul, which God created by diluting the universal soul, is contained in the head and is responsible for acquiring knowledge. The lesser gods also placed a mortal soul within man. The mortal soul lies outside of the head and is responsible for the passions of man. When man dies, the immortal soul is released and is brought back into the next generation. The soul may degenerate, and appear in different life forms in the second generation, depending on how a man lived his first life. If he was cowardly and criminal, the soul would form into a woman. If he was "harmless but light-witted," he would turn into a bird. If he had no use for philosophy, he would turn into a four-legged beast. And if he was foolish and stupid, he would turn into a fish. These "outcomes" were probably used to mock some of Plato's predecessors and their ideas, especially those who did not value abstract thought as he did.

Although these two accounts differ, we see the hallmarks of ancient Greek thoughts in both myths. Anaximander uses an entirely naturalistic account for his cosmology. There are no gods involved in the creation of the universe or of man. Plato's account consists of a well-constructed and rational plan by God. Our observation of the cosmos allows us to make some reasonable assumptions regarding why the world is the way it is. The universe is good and it can be understood by us.

Enuma Elish

Enuma Elish is an ancient Near Eastern creation story. Its name is taken from the first words of the story, "When on high..." Cuneiform writings have been found dating back to at least 1700 BCE, but the Babylonian myth itself is probably much older. This epic poem was recited to celebrate the new year. It was written on seven tablets, most of which have survived largely intact. Thus, *Enuma Elish* is one of the oldest and most complete creation stories we have. The story was first discovered in ruins in what is now Mosul, Iraq. Ancient Israel was part of the same ancient Near East, and many parallels have been noted between *Enuma Elish* and the Genesis account of creation, thus adding to the importance of this story. We will compare these two stories a bit later, but first let's look at a summary of *Enuma Elish*.

All that existed in the beginning were the sweet-water god, Apsu, and the salt-water god, Tiamat, and their son Mummu, which was the mist rising from the waters. Apsu and Tiamat gave rise to other gods, including Nudimmud (also called Enki or Ea), the most powerful of the gods. The children gods were loud and upset Apsu, Tiamat, and Mummu. Apsu planned to destroy them. When the other gods heard of this plan, they were frightened. Ea slew Apsu and imprisoned Mummu. Tiamat, whose army was led by her new husband, Kingu, waged war on the gods who had been involved in the death of Apsu. The gods were frightened and called on Marduk, the son of Ea, to fight for them. Marduk agreed, as long as the gods would make him supreme over them. The other gods approved of this. Marduk killed Tiamat and cut her body in half. One half Marduk used to create the sky, the other he used to create the Earth. He then organized the calendar by creating the stars (months) and the Sun (days). The Moon he fashioned for the night. The enemy gods were made the slaves of the other gods, and provided food for them. However, this was such tiring work that Marduk created humanity to do this job. He spilled the blood of Kingu, which formed people, who would now toil for the gods. The poem ends with the gods building a temple for Marduk and assigning him 50 names that the people are encouraged to study.

A Hindu Myth

The Hindu myths of India are numerous and varied. One figure that is venerated and respected by all traditions is Brahma (who goes by other names as well). He is the god who created the universe. However, Brahma is not an object of worship. The following myth is from the *Bhagavata Purana*.

At one time, the beings and objects in this world were without form or name. Matter was dissolved in *prakriti* consisting of three fundamental materials that could not be separated: matter (*prakriti*), selves or souls (*atmas*) and god (Bhagavan). When the time was right, Bhagavan decided to become many, to become present in the world and to give form and names to everything. By shaking his body, Bhagavan generated the three *gunas* of matter: *sattva* (being, existence, goodness), *rajas* (activity, passion), and *tamas* (darkness, idleness). The matter he produced became the five elements: ether, air, fire, water, and earth. The fundamental materials and beings were unable to do anything by themselves. The divine beings praised Bhagavan. Bhagavan entered into the substances and mixed them. The substances then appeared in the form of a lotus bud in Bhagavan's navel. Brahma was formed in the lotus bud, and remained there for 1,000 years with the *atmas*. Brahma searched for the cause of the lotus bud, but could not find it. He next considered how he should make the world, and meditated for a long period of time. Then Bhagavan showed his world to Brahma. Brahma was pleased and asked Bhagavan to provide him with the knowledge to create such a world. Brahma found the Earth, the higher worlds, and the highest worlds to be submerged in water. He first drank the water. Bhagavan told him to meditate, so that he would see clearly how to create the three worlds. He would also see Bhagavan in all the worlds. Brahma was instructed to create beings in accordance with their past *karma*. Bhagavan was pleased with Brahma, as Brahma had shown his eagerness to know and praise Bhagavan, and gave Brahma his blessing. Brahma first created all kinds of plants and the lords of the forest. Next he created the beasts of the land, air, and sea, who are full of *tamas*. Then he created humans, who are full of *rajas* and *karma*. Lastly Brahma created the eight classes of supernatural beings, the *devas*. The creation and form of different beings was entirely dependent on Brahma's actions or moods. These other beings were the creative agents who filled the world.

African Creation Myths

Some creation myths focus on the creation of humans rather than on cosmogony. The Nigerian creation stories of the Yoruba and the Igbo are examples of this. In the understanding of the human saga, the social order is highlighted and explained for these peoples.

In the Yoruba story, the supreme deity is Olodumare. He lived in heaven as the king of other deities, which included a prime minister, deputy divinity in charge of knowledge, and a guardian of rituals. Olodumare also had a chief deputy (and arch-divinity) named Orisa-nla. Olodumare decided to begin creating when he saw a watery marsh below heaven. He sent Orisa-nla to make solid earth. To do this, Olodumare gave Orisa-nla some clay, a white hen, and a pigeon. Orisa-nla spilled the clay, and the bird scratched the clay into the marsh, which became dry land. Olodumare sent the chameleon to inspect the work. The chameleon declared all was well and recommended that the work continue.

In another version, Orisa-nla suggested to Olodumare that the Earth be filled with life. Olodumare agreed, and Orisa-nla descended into the watery marshes on a golden chain. He brought with him some sand, a white hen, and a palm nut. The hen scratched the sand to make earth, and Orisa-nla planted the palm nut.

After the creation of the Earth, humans were formed. The Yoruba story has several variations of this event.

- Olodumare told Orisa-nla to make birds and trees, for food and drink, to prepare for the beings who would inhabit the Earth. These beings later put humans on the Earth. A water shortage occurred, and Orisa-nla asked Olodumare for help. It was then that Olodumare sent the first rain.

- Olodumare told Orisa-nla how to make humans, which he did, and Olodumare then breathed life into them.
- Orisa-nla's only companion on the Earth was a black cat, and he was lonely. So he took some clay from the ground and formed humans. While the clay was drying in the sun, he drank some palm wine and became intoxicated. He continued his work, but he had an unsteady hand, and made some of the clay figures with deformities. He called on Olodumare to breathe life into the humans. When Orisa-nla sobered up, he saw his mistakes, vowed never to drink again, and became a guardian to all people with handicaps and special needs.

The Yoruba myth accounts for different races and social classes of humans. In one version of the story, some of the created humans went to cold climates, where the cold and sea breezes caused them to become white. In another version, the people complained how they were all the same. Olodumare was saddened by their comments, and gave the people what they wished for: he decreed that they have different skin colors, different languages, and be given different social statuses (landowners, servants, and slaves). This created disharmony among the people. There was also disharmony between humans and Olodumare. Initially, the rapport between man and the deity was good, but bad manners on the part of humans caused a souring of the relationship.

In the Igbo myth, the supreme deity is called Chukwu or Chineke. The root of the word "Chukwu" is *chi*, meaning spirit. The Igbo believe that every person has a *chi* that is given by Chukwu and the *chi* will return to Chukwu when the person dies. Thus, *chi* is very much like the Christian concept of the soul. As with the Yoruba, there are several versions of this myth.

- Chukwu made the first man, a superhuman, called Eri. Eri was sent to Earth, but he found it too wet. He asked Chukwu for a blacksmith, who would use his bellows to dry off the earth. Soon dry land appeared, and Eri married. His children populated the earth.
- Other beings existed with Chukwu, prior to the creation of humans. However, they were not equal in status with Chukwu. One of Chukwu's favorites was a female divinity called Edo. Chukwu gave her part of his scepter, made from white chalk, and a small clay pot filled with water. Edo went to Earth with her gifts, but she became lost and disoriented. She took some of the chalk and spread it out, and it became land. She broke some of the chalk into four pieces and put them in the water pot. When Chukwu found Edo, he used the four pieces of chalk to make people. He named each piece (First Son, Second Son, Third Son, and Last Son) and breathed life into them. When they became adults, they married four beautiful sisters.

The Genesis Story

The Genesis account of creation takes place in two parts. Genesis 1:1–2:3 is mainly a cosmogony, recounting the creation of the heavens and the earth. Genesis 2:4–3:24

focuses on humans: their creation and the story of the fall, the cause of all evil and suffering. We will first look at a summary of the story, and then examine its meaning more closely.

In the first account, the six days of creation are described. Although water exists, God created all from nothing (creation *ex nihilo*) simply by calling things into being. On the first day, God created light and separated it from darkness. On the second day, God separated the waters with a firmament, and called the water above the firmament Heaven. On the third day, God created the dry land, Earth, in the water below the heavens, and called forth vegetation from the land. On the fourth day, God created the Sun, the Moon, and the stars. On the fifth day, God created birds and animals in the sea. And on the sixth day, God created animals on the land and humans, both male and female. Humans are created in God's image and given dominion over the Earth. On the seventh day, God rested. In the text, on several occasions, the separate acts of creation are judged to be good. On the seventh day, all of creation was declared to be very good.

In the second account, the order of creation is different. God formed man, Adam, from dust and breathed life into him, and then made a garden, Eden, for Adam to till and to keep. God made trees for food, and also made the tree of life and the tree of knowledge of good and evil. God commanded that the man not eat of the tree of knowledge. God did not want Adam to be alone, and so made animals as helpers. Adam gave names to all the animals, but none was a suitable companion. God caused the man to fall asleep and made woman, Eve, from one of his ribs. The serpent of the garden convinced Eve to eat of the tree of knowledge by telling her she would be like God if she did. She shared the fruit with Adam, and both realized they were naked and were ashamed. God found them and learned of their disobedience. God cursed the snake and punished the man and the woman with suffering and eventual death. God then made clothes for Adam and Eve, and expelled them from the garden.

Genesis as a Myth

When we consider Genesis as a myth, we can see some of the themes present in all creation myths. In this section we will look more closely at Genesis as myth, and compare it with the other myths in this chapter. In some cases, we will see that Genesis has similarities to all creation myths, but it also has some distinct and unique features.

We would classify the Genesis story as a creation edict: the cosmos and humans are called into existence. God does not fashion anything from preexisting material. Although water is present at the beginning of Genesis, and indeed we do see chaos ("without form and void"), water is not used to make anything. God creates through word alone. Although *ex nihilo* creation can be found in other myths, it is not common. In most myths, matter already exists and the deities fashion the Earth and humans from this material, as with the Igbo myth, where the first men are made from chalk. Importantly, God is not part of creation in the Genesis account. God is separate from the created. With other myths, such as *Enuma Elish*, the cosmos is made up of the body parts of the gods. In the Hindu myth, matter already exists, and Bhagavan refines it. Procreation is not a theme in Genesis: God creates man and woman, and therefore creates procreation. Contrast this with *Enuma Elish*, where the gods come from a mixing of the waters (Apsu and Tiamat).

An interesting exception to the *ex nihilo* doctrine of creation can be found in the second Genesis account:

> then the Lord God formed man of dust from the ground, and breathed into his nostrils the breath of life; and man became a living being. (Genesis 2:7)

Recall that, in creation myths, dirt and clay are common materials from which humans are formed. Humans are the only exception to *ex nihilo* creation in Genesis. Humans are created, not by an act of will, but by divine effort, and require the breath of life from God. This reinforces the uniqueness and importance of humans.

Water does play a role in the biblical creation story. Creation is not limited to the first verses of Genesis: it is found throughout the Bible (we will look at this in more detail in a moment). The story of Noah is reminiscent of many catastrophic creation myths, where a great flood destroys most of humanity, leaving only a handful of people to repopulate the earth.

Genesis is monotheistic and lacks any theogony. There is only one God, and we are not provided with a "biography" of God. God's nature is revealed to us through God's action in creation. Each of the other stories we have examined provides a polytheistic view of the world. In some cases, as in Plato's *Timaeus* and with Olodumare in the Yoruba story, one deity is clearly the authority, and has powers the others do not. In other cases, as with *Enuma Elish*, there are battles between the gods to determine supremacy.

The reason for the creation of the cosmos is not always clear in myths. In the Genesis account, we are told repeatedly that the creation is good. Humans are special creations. This tells us much about the character of God (as we will discuss below). Other myths provide a simple, yet not always flattering, reason for the existence of humans. As we saw in *Enuma Elish*, humans were created as slaves to do the work for the gods. In other myths, as in one of the variations of the Yoruba myth, the gods may have wanted companionship. However, humans were created when the gods were intoxicated: not a very prestigious beginning! The goodness of creation is also echoed in Plato's creation myth. However, he uses this notion to argue for a creator, and hence for our ability to understand the universe (the intelligible world).

The relationship between God and humans is explained in Genesis. The separation that exists is a direct result of the disobedience of humans. Although some stories, particularly when humans are created as servants or slaves of the gods, do not require an explanation of this relationship, others are similar to the Genesis account. For example, in the Yoruba account, humans, with their demands and bad manners, caused the separation with the gods. In Genesis, the disobedient humans are punished with suffering, which accounts for the hard life that humans must endure. However, God does not abandon humans and still cares for them (as when God makes clothes for Adam and Eve). Even in separation, God is involved in, indeed is central to, human life. Orisa-nla, in the Yoruba myth, also remains involved with humans: he acts as the guardian for the lame and deformed.

One of the functions of myths is to elucidate social structure and norms within a culture. Genesis provides a good example of this regarding the marital relationship.

> Then the man said, "This at last is bone of my bones and flesh of my flesh; she shall be called Woman, because she was taken out of Man." Therefore a man leaves his father and his mother and cleaves to his wife, and they become one flesh. (Genesis 2:23–4)

The *Enuma Elish* accounts for the status of humans as slaves in Mesopotamia, while the formation of Babylonian leadership is seen in the story of Marduk, while the hierarchy of the state is clearly reflected in the Yoruba myth.

Many other comparisons can be made between Genesis and other creation myths. But for now we will switch gears and discuss the meaning of the story.

The Meaning and Function of Genesis

With many myths, different versions of the story exist, which may have provided meaning to more than one culture at various periods in time. Within the Bible, as noted above, two creation stories are chronicled in Genesis. They were written at different times and serve different functions, but they complement each other. The first account, Genesis 1:1–2:3, was written in the fifth century BCE in the Priestly tradition, which focused on rituals and origins, and portrayed God as transcendent. The second account, Genesis 2:4–3:24, was written in the tenth century BCE in the Yahwist tradition, characterized by an epic style, where God was often represented in human form. The first account provides an organized, detailed cosmogony. The "environment" is created in the first three days, and the objects and living things that inhabit the environment are created on days four, five, and six. The seventh day is a day of rest, providing justification for the Sabbath. Genesis 2:4–3:24 has a different function. It is a narrative that does not contain a detailed cosmogony, but instead highlights the human experience. It conveys what it means to be human, including the roles of males and females and the responsibility of free will. Humans are created in the divine image and have dominion over nature. Free will allows for the disobedience of Adam and Eve, and results in a separation from God. Although punished by God and expelled from the garden, God takes care of the humans. God is still in our lives, still loves us and cares for us, even though we do not always do God's will.

We have already examined Genesis as a myth. As such, we see similarities between Genesis and other accounts. Given the common experiences all humans share in this world, no matter the time, culture, or place in which they live, it is not surprising that Genesis contains the common themes outlined above. We must look more closely at what Genesis says about our culture and our beliefs. We look to the unique aspects of this story to find deeper meanings for our lives today. In addition, we must realize that the creation story in Genesis does not stand alone. We cannot look at the early chapters in Genesis to tell us everything about creation. Other references to creation are found in the Bible, particularly in Isaiah chapters 40 to 66, the book of Job, and some of the Psalms. However, we need to examine creation in the larger context of the Bible and the history of the Jewish and Christian traditions. The primary theme in the Bible is not creation. Rather, the focus of the Bible is God's acts in history, particularly in the Exodus and in redemption and salvation through Jesus Christ. Genesis provides a framework for all creation, declaring the absolute sovereignty of God over the universe. Creation is just the opening event in a long, continual historical process.

So what are the messages we can find in this creation story? Genesis affirms themes that resonate throughout the Bible, most notably the nature of God, the nature of creation, and the nature of man.

The creation story tells us emphatically that God is omnipotent and the source of all that exists. God's presence and power is wholly and unequivocally evident. The creation is orderly, and there is a divine plan for everything. God is the creator, not part of the creation, and the creation is not yet finished: it is ongoing. Not only does God create but God also sustains. God is transcendent and generous, giving life and community. This demonstrates not only God's omnipotence but also the self-limitation of God. We see that the act of creation was a free act, a contingent act, done out of love.

The nature of creation is, in a word, "good." The goodness of creation is expressed repeatedly in Genesis, but is also conveyed in many other biblical texts. This is important when we consider the problem of evil in the world. Suffering is not inherently evil and, if we keep in mind the entirety of creation that will be revealed in the fullness of time, we are assured that suffering has a role in God's plan (this topic, termed theodicy, will be discussed in later chapters). There is a place for every created thing in God's plan. Therefore all of nature deserves our respect and admiration. God's continuing activity in creation expresses the value of the world.

Why exactly did God create the world? The answer to this question has come from different interpretations of Genesis. We are told that the creation is good. For Augustine, it was a moral necessity for God to create: it would have been cruel for God not to. For Thomas Aquinas, creation was God sharing the divine goodness. Love is the motivation for the free, unconstrained creation. We also look at creation in relation to Christ. The purpose of creation is found in the life, death, and resurrection of Jesus. In redemption, the created world will realize peace and joy in a community of God and all of creation. Although creation is independent of God, it is wholly dependent on God. All of creation is finite and contingent: everything exists because of God's will, and the continued existence of creation is dependent on God as well. And all of creation is interdependent: God did not create life to exist independently, but in an environmental web of mutual dependence.

The nature of humans is also revealed in Genesis. Humans are special, created in God's image and given dominion over the Earth. The message regarding human existence is positive and life-affirming. We have been given free will: God is not a tyrannical ruler, but a leader who calls us to follow. We alone decide what we will do. We can choose to be disobedient, as in the story of the fall, and in our choice lies the cause of suffering. We must take responsibility for our actions. Our dominion over the Earth does not give us free rein to take and destroy. Instead, we are the caretakers, the tenders, of the garden. We are unique from all other creatures in our degree of separation from the rest of nature, yet we are ultimately dependent upon it. God has also given us the role of co-creators. We are called to help fulfill the will of God, and we have been given the power to do so.

Part of the function of the Genesis creation narrative was to counter the beliefs of other religions, and to show the distinctiveness of the Hebrew God.

- Genesis is clearly monotheistic, in opposition to polytheism, which was prevalent in most cultures.
- There is no theogony in this story. God exists and always has. The account begins with creation; it is not a story of the origin of a deity.
- The monotheistic God is all-powerful, unlike the weak, dependent, petty, warring gods of other myths.
- The ambiguous ethics present in polytheistic models are not found in the Genesis account. God has moral standards that are knowable, absolute, and unchanging.
- God is separate from the creation. Thus, the magic rituals of the polytheistic religions do not apply: there are no deities in nature to cajole or petition.
- The way God creates is also unique in the Near Eastern tradition. God speaks to create. God is not a craftsman who fashions the created order from a preexisting substance.
- The creation of humans also displays a break from the polytheistic religions. Humans are dependent on, but uniquely separate from, nature. Humans are given dominion over the world. We have purpose, freedom, and power.

Interpretation of the Biblical Text

Myths provide an explanation of our existence prior to the development of modern science. We need to use caution if we approach any creation myth from a scientific perspective. The epistemology of Western culture is based in rationalism and empiricism. We are a product of the Enlightenment. This is not a conscious notion for most of us. We live in a highly technical world, and we believe that science can provide us with truth and is therefore the only, or at least the most important, source of knowledge. When we examine the beliefs of other cultures, we need to be aware of our own perspectives. Science, as we know it, was unthinkable to people living thousands of years ago. They could not have conceived of our notions of reality, and they did not need empirical data and scientific "proof." Instead, their thinking was imaginative, and the expression of their ideas emotional and poetic. To apply our notions of modern science to the biblical text is naive. The text cannot be reconciled with our modern theories. A literal interpretation of the creation narrative would be a gross misreading, robbing the text of its meaning and distorting its message. When we apply our perspective and world view to the Bible, we may fail to see the significance of what the authors were trying to convey. Genesis tells us of the goodness of creation and of the plan and purpose of God. It is life-affirming. The Bible in its entirety tells of redemption and love. It is not a scientific document. It provides meaning, and answers the *why* questions. It communicates statements of faith. Our modern science answers the *how* questions.

A literal interpretation of the Bible is a relatively recent phenomenon, resulting from the Enlightenment, when reason and empiricism were exalted to a status previously unthinkable. There is a long tradition among theologians, prior to and after the Enlightenment, of arguing against a literal interpretation. For example, Origen (c.185–c.254), one of the most important early Christian theologians, focused on describing Christianity on an intellectual level. In *On First Principles*, he rejected strict adherence to the Genesis text as an accurate historical account, calling the statements, in their literal meaning, "absurd and impossible." Augustine accepted a figurative interpretation of Genesis, on the principle that God teaches us about salvation, and that the intent of scripture is not to instruct us on other matters. In *The Literal Meaning of Genesis* (c.415), Augustine advised Christians not to display their ignorance to pagans by claiming that the biblical text describes the natural world. How can we convince non-Christians of resurrection, eternal life, and heaven if we hold to nonsense regarding the physical world, whose truth is clearly knowable to all? Friedrich Schleiermacher (1768–1834), sometimes referred to as the father of modern theology, greatly influenced the reformulation of theological positions. In *The Christian Faith* (1821–2), he argues that science needs to be separated from the Bible. As we shall see later in this book, the literal interpretation exemplified in the creation science movement of the twentieth century and today arose as a reaction to advances in science, specifically evolution. We must understand that this exegesis of the Genesis creation narrative is not a common one throughout most of history.

In the past, humans were not unaware of nature, nor did they refrain from thinking about it and trying to explain what they saw. However, their explanations were not based on the methodologies we use today. They did not observe the world in the same way as we do, and there was no concept of experimentation. The "science" of the Hebrews, at the time Genesis was written, was consistent with the beliefs of other Near Eastern cultures. To them the universe was tiered and the Earth flat (see fig. 5.1). Water existed above and below, separated by the firmament ("firmament" does not mean land: it is usually understood as a thin sheet of metal). Heaven is above the water in the sky. Some pillars, such as mountains, support the sky, while others support the Earth. Water comes up from under the Earth (think of floods) and falls from storehouses above the firmament through holes in the sky. The cosmology in Genesis had to be consistent with this view of the world. There are no hidden meanings and no great truths to be ferreted out of the Genesis text that could in any way be interpreted to represent our scientific understanding today.

If the biblical text is not empirical, if it is not "factually based," according to our definition, then how are we to interpret it? Why should we believe it? What meaning are we to gain from it? We need to shake off our empirical epistemology and see the text as containing different kinds of "truths." We need to look at the other functions of myths to understand the true meaning of Genesis. The text tells us of God's nature and relationship to humanity, of the importance and uniqueness of humans, and of the goodness of creation. These messages are the truths of Genesis. If we focus on these messages, we preserve the integrity of the text.

A Common Creation Myth for All Humanity?

As we have seen, humans need to answer some basic questions that are common to us as a species. We want to know about the physical world around us, its origin and nature, and we need to understand the existence and experience of being human. Thus, our creation stories are essential to understanding ourselves, to providing purpose and

1 Waters above the firmament
2 Storehouses of snows
3 Storehouses for hail
4 Chambers of winds
5 Firmament
6 Sluice / windows of heaven
7 Pillars of the sky
8 Pillars of the earth
9 Fountain of the deep
10 Navel of the earth
11 Waters under the earth
12 Rivers of the nether world
Sheol is the underworld, the bottom of the Earth,
the land of the dead.

Fig. 5.1   Three-tiered universe of the ancient Near Eastern tradition

meaning to our lives. As we shall see in the next chapter, science has come a long way in understanding the beginnings and the nature of the universe. Many believe that science is a transcultural field, that is, all humans have access to this way of thinking. This leads to a question: should we, and can we, use the scientific description of the universe as a creation story that is relevant to all peoples and cultures?

This idea could give humans a wonderful sense of community, in a coming together of all humanity. It could give us a basis for uniting in an unprecedented, common creation story. The story itself has been formulated by scientists from different religions, nationalities, and cultures. It presents all of humanity as being equal, and excludes no one. All people would then be seen to have had a common beginning. We would stand on the same ground and share the same answers to our most fundamental questions. A common creation story could be a powerfully uniting force in our small, but important, corner of the universe.

The main problem with such a common myth is the same as its major appeal: it has been formulated by the neutral, empirical field of science. Like science, this "myth" provides us with answers to how the universe came to be. But it does not, and cannot, provide meaning for our existence. If a story cannot provide purpose, then it cannot succeed as a cosmology.

A different use of science has been proposed, not to replace existing creation myths but as a way to open up dialogues between various faith traditions. If we focus on the ecology of the Earth itself, and what human existence has done and continues to do to this life-sustaining resource, then we may find a common starting point. If we commit ourselves to act for the Earth, then we may be able to formulate some common ethics. These ethics would provide a shared starting point from which each religious tradition could work. A common point of interest would help bring different religions together, to understand each other and to work for common goals.

Conclusions

The presence of creation myths in every culture attests to the importance humans place on self-understanding. We are special in nature, a part of nature but also different from all other creatures. Regardless of our understandings of how we came to be, all humans have a unique ability to reflect back on ourselves, our surroundings, our beginnings, and our fates. The meaning we each find in life lies within our particular cultural context. As such, there is no ultimate truth, no right answer. Should we be searching for a common creation story, to bring together different religions and cultures and to unite all people through a common origin? Or should we rejoice in the diversity of our species, and respect the ideas of our ancestors and neighbors who understood/understand the world differently? The struggle to understand meaning and purpose will always be part of the human condition, to be continually reexamined in every epoch of the history of humanity.

Primary Literature

Useful primary sources include a portion of *Enuma Elish* (the fourth and fifth tablets, the fifth being the most incomplete of the poem), telling the story of the battle between Tiamat and Marduk; Genesis 1:1–3:24, containing the two creation stories; and short excerpts from Origen (*On First Principles*, Book IV, 16, 18); chapter 19 of Augustine, *The Literal Meaning of Genesis*; and Schleiermacher, *The Christian Faith* (1821–2), on interpretation of the biblical creation story.

Questions to Consider

1   Research a creation story that is not highlighted in this chapter. What similarities does your story have with other creation myths? Which of the recurring themes discussed above are present? Is it a cosmogony or does it focus more on human existence? Can you find any parallels between your story and the Genesis account? Is there something unique about your myth? If so, what does it convey about the cosmos and/or humanity?

2   Do the ancient Greek creation stories count as myths? Does Anaximander's account provide purpose and meaning? What if a story is not believed by a culture, such as Plato's *Timaeus*? Does a story have to be believed by a culture to be considered a myth? If *Timaeus* is not a myth, what is it?

3   We stressed that Genesis cannot be fully understood or appreciated unless it is considered in a larger context, that is, in relation to the rest of the Bible and Christian tradition. How might this line of thought influence our perception and interpretation of other creation myths?

4   Most creation myths have long oral histories (including Genesis). Some were eventually written down. Do you think a myth that was recorded in literature would have less variations than one that is transmitted via an oral tradition? Give reasons for your answer.

5   Myths in general provide a lesson, or explain something about our world. There are many myths in American culture, such as George Washington and the cherry tree, and the stories of Paul Bunyan, Johnny Appleseed, Pecos Bill, and John Henry. Research one of these legends or another similar one. What ideas or message does the story convey? In what period is the story set? What do you need to know about the psyche and structure of the society and culture to better understand their importance?

6

Current Understandings
of the Universe

Overview

Einstein's "year of wonders," 1905, saw the birth of two critical theories that are vital to our understanding of the universe today. Relativity theory helps to explain spacetime, and quantum mechanics provides a framework for understanding sub-atomic particles. The outcomes of these theories, in particular the scientific theory of the beginning of the universe and notions of indeterminacy resulting from wave functions, have impacted theology. Science has provided possibilities in which we could conceive of God acting in our universe without violating natural laws. Other issues, such as contingency and theodicy, are points of contact between the two disciplines.

Introduction

Scientific progress in the twentieth century was staggering. Tremendous strides were made in all disciplines, and our understanding of the universe was no exception. Astronomers explored space to reveal to us a dizzying, incomprehensible number of galaxies and stars, at times making us feel even smaller and less important than when Copernicus removed us from our central position in cosmology. What's more, *everything*, including time and space, began as a singularity, the size of an atom with incredible density, 13.7 billion years ago. It all sounds very mythical but mostly, it is science.

We thought we understood mechanics long ago – how the universe was constructed, how materials behaved, etc. Newton explained terrestrial and celestial motion with his laws, providing a framework in which the mysteries of the cosmos could be unraveled. And his laws work well, for the most part. However, when we study objects that are very small or moving very fast, Newton's laws do not hold up. Hence, we needed new models, new theories, new paradigms. This chapter will examine the events in the

twentieth century, beginning with Albert Einstein, that have led to our current understandings of matter, energy, and the origin of the universe. Of course, advancements
were made in the field between the times of Newton and Einstein. However, the major
events that have led to our current understandings can be traced directly to Einstein and
his contemporaries. One of the most astounding aspects of Einstein's work is that he
contributed to both the very large and the very small: relativity led to explanations of
time and space, and the photoelectric effect demonstrated the nature of energy, which
led to quantum mechanics. And, if that weren't enough, Einstein had a lot to say about
God as well.

In this chapter we will examine the science behind our current understandings of the
universe. We will explore the big bang theory and quantum mechanics, and, of course,
consider the theological implications and responses to these ideas. Most scientists agree
that, at some point, the universe will come to an end. The scientific notions of how and
when this will happen will be addressed in the next chapter, along with the theological
concepts of eschatology.

The Year of Wonders

Newton's work on gravity had a significant impact on cosmology and helped us to
understand the movement of the planets. Given that gravity was a force exerting a pull
between two objects, Newton thought there must be some material in space itself
through which the force was transmitted. He also noted a problem with measuring
movement: if the Earth is spinning on its axis, and moving around the Sun, then our
measurements of an event on Earth are not true, absolute measurements, as we do not
normally take into account the movement of the Earth when measuring the terrestrial
event. This means that all motion is relative, and is based on the position of the observer.
Newton thought there was a place from which the observer could see absolute motion,
a place that was not moving. This place, he concluded, was in space, in a material known
as the ether. The idea of this material had a long history, dating back to the ancient
Greek philosophers. Newton reasoned that, if the ether did not move, and if we could
position ourselves in the ether, we would detect absolute motion. According to this logic,
then, if we could measure motion from the ether, we could detect the ether based on
the motion we see in space. But what movement could be used?

One of the leading scientists in nineteenth-century physics was Michael Faraday
(1791–1867), who studied electricity and magnetism. He showed that these two forces
could be converted into each other, and today we call this phenomenon electromagnetism.
James Clerk Maxwell (1831–79) showed that visible light was part of this electromagnetic
spectrum (see fig. 6.1). Electromagnetism is made up of waves with varying frequencies.
Therefore, to contend that light was part of this spectrum contradicted the notion that
light was a particle. Visible light occupies a range of frequencies in the spectrum, as do
radio waves, microwaves, gamma rays, and infrared rays. Light waves move through
space (we see light traveling to us from distant stars), and it was thought that this movement could be used to detect the ether. Despite many attempts, no one could detect the
space-filling substance.

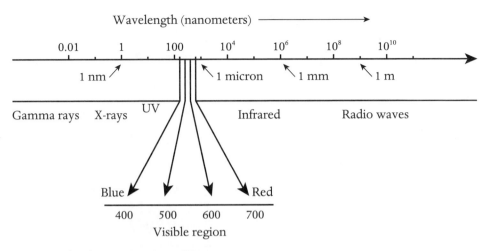

Fig. 6.1   The electromagnetic spectrum.

Into this world of undetectable ether and strange light that no one could fix as a wave or a particle emerged a budding physicist named Albert Einstein (fig. 6.2), who, by the age of 16, was already interested in the connection between electromagnetic waves and the ether. Einstein was highly critical of his formal education in Germany, but nevertheless, after his family moved to Italy, the necessity of earning a living led to his attending the Swiss Federal Polytechnic School in Zurich, where he was to follow in his father's footsteps and become an electrical engineer. He was, however, more interested in physics. After graduating in 1900, he held a few temporary teaching positions, became a Swiss citizen in 1901, and gained permanent employment at the Swiss Patent Office in Berne in 1902. This position provided him with a stable income, and time to work on his physics. In 1905, he published four seminal papers in *Annalen der Physik* that were to change the face of physics forever. These papers described the photoelectric effect, Brownian motion, and special relativity.

The Photoelectric Effect

Einstein's paper "On a Heuristic Viewpoint concerning the Production and Transformation of Light" described the photoelectric effect. Up until then, there had been no theoretical explanations for how a hot body radiates energy into space. When high frequency light (for example, blue light, with small, high energy wavelengths) strikes a metal plate, electrons of high energy are given off by the plate. If low frequency light (such as red light, with long, low energy wavelengths) strikes a metal plate, electrons with low energy are emitted. Increasing the intensity of the light (its brightness) causes more electrons to be released from the metal plate, but it does not affect the energy of these emitted electrons, as had been predicted. In 1900, Max Planck (1858–1947) proposed an idea that fitted the experimental observations. He suggested that radiation is emitted

Fig. 6.2   Albert Einstein. Photograph, 1951. (akg-images)

in bursts of energy, and not as a continuous flow. Einstein expanded on this idea. He proposed that light should be thought of not as a wave, but rather as a collection of particles. These particles are produced by discrete changes within an atom, what he called quanta. Today these particles are known as photons. When photons hit the metal plate, the energy causes the release of electrons from the atoms in the metal plate. If the photon has high energy, as with blue light, then the electrons emitted will also have high energy. Low energy photons (red light) cause the released electrons to have less momentum. When the light intensity changes, more photons hit the metal plate, releasing more electrons, but the energy of the photons doesn't change. Thus the energy of the electrons remains the same; there are just more of them because more photons are hitting the plate.

Einstein was awarded the Nobel Prize in Physics in 1921. Although he is better known for relativity, only his work on the photoelectric effect was specifically mentioned by the Nobel committee. The photoelectric effect is no less important than relativity, but it was probably less controversial at the time the prize was awarded.

Brownian Motion

Einstein's second paper was titled "On the Motion – Required by the Molecular Kinetic Theory of Heat – of Small Particles Suspended in a Stationary Liquid." It described a unique type of motion called Brownian motion, first described by the botanist Robert

Brown (1773–1858) in observing pollen grains under the microscope. When he mounted the pollen grains on slides containing water, Brown noted the grains moved slightly, in a random fashion. Einstein determined that the water molecules were constantly moving, due to the energy from the heat of the microscope. The water molecules collided with the pollen grains, and, as a result, moved the grains. This was strong evidence for the existence of molecules and atoms, something badly needed by the scientific community at that time.

The Theory of Special Relativity

In "On the Electrodynamics of Moving Bodies," Einstein described the theory of special relativity. Recall that Newton thought there was absolute motion, which could be observed from the ether. However, no one had been successful in detecting the ether. Einstein denied its existence, and thus denied the existence of absolute motion. He believed that electromagnetic waves (including light) move at the maximum speed that was possible in the universe (about 300,000 km per second), and that no ordinary body could move at that speed. But he also claimed that light moves at the same constant speed regardless of how an observer is moving (see fig. 6.3). The implications of these ideas are quite remarkable.

- Speed is defined as a distance traveled per unit time ($v = d/t$, where v is velocity (or speed), d distance, and t time). If speed is relative, so is distance. Length, or distance, will decrease in the direction of the motion.
- If speed is relative, so is time. The time it takes for something to happen depends on the relative motion of the observer. Say there are two observers, A and B, who have two identical watches in proper working order, which they synchronize. Observer B gets in a rocket ship and travels very fast, approaching the speed of light. When B gets back to Earth, and the two compare the passage of time on each watch, less time will have passed on observer B's watch than on observer A's watch.
- The dimensions of an object (height, width, length, mass) depend on the relative motion of the observer. Two observers may see an object very differently, depending on their relative motion. Measurements of distance, as stated above, will decrease in the direction of the motion. Mass will increase as velocity approaches the speed of light.

The "special theory of relativity" is so named because Einstein applied his ideas only to bodies that are moving at a constant speed ("special"), and emphasized that all motion is measured relative to an observer ("relativity"). In yet a fourth paper written the same year, "Does the Inertia of a Body Depend upon Its Energy Content?" Einstein expanded his ideas on relativity to show that mass and energy are interchangeable. This led to the famous equation $E = mc^2$, where E is energy, m the mass of the object, and c the speed of light. As c is so large (about 300,000 km, or 186,000 miles, per second), the amount of energy contained in a very small amount of matter is huge.

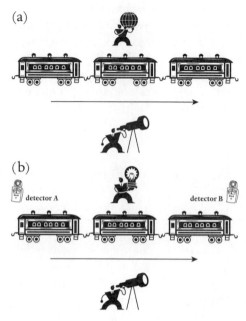

Fig. 6.3   Special theory of relativity. (*a*) Relativity of measurement. Imagine two observers, one on a fast moving train, the other on the ground. If the observer on the train were to throw a ball up in the air and catch it again, he would only observe the up and down motion of the ball. However, the observer on the ground would also notice the movement of the ball with the same direction and speed as the train. Thus, the two observers see different motion depending on where they make their observations. (*b*) Speed of light. The speed of light is constant and does not depend on the motion of the observer. Imagine a similar situation as in part A, with the train moving very quickly. Two light detectors are positioned equidistant from the observer on the train, one toward the front of the train and one toward the rear of the train. The observer turns on a light, and sees both detector A and B receiving light at exactly the same time. However, the observer on the ground sees something different. In the example in (*a*), the observer on the ground sees the ball as moving from left to right: it has momentum because it is moving with the train. But the speed of light is constant, and would not gain any momentum from the movement of the train. Therefore, the observer on the ground would see detector A register the light before detector B. Why? After the light is turned on, the train moves, so detector A will be "closer" to the light source, and detector B "farther away." The two detectors are no longer equidistant from the source. (What would happen if, instead of a light source, the observer on the train shot two guns, at the exact same moment, toward two targets replacing the detectors – when would each observer see each bullet hitting its respective target?)

The Aftermath

Einstein's contributions to physics were not appreciated initially. He was working in virtual isolation, and did not have much evidence to support his theory of relativity. He finally procured teaching positions at the University of Berne, the University of Zurich, and the German University in Prague. He eventually moved to Berlin in 1914 and resumed his German nationality. However, he did not like the regimented society of Germany and, with the outbreak of World War I, found himself at odds with most German scientists in light of his pacifist stance. His work at this time focused on applying acceleration (when bodies change speed) to special relativity. By including acceleration in his theory, Einstein could also include gravity. He proposed general relativity in 1915, which provided a very different view of gravity. Einstein suggested that gravity could be seen as a distortion, or bending, of the space around an object (see fig. 6.4), not as a pull exerted by the object, as Newton had claimed. A massive object, such as the Sun, curves space. If another object, such as a planet or light, moves towards the Sun, its path will be disrupted by the distortion of space (gravity) from the Sun. In the case of a "slow moving" planet, this bend may cause the planet to move in an orbit around the Sun, or, in the case of "fast moving" light, the curvature may cause a slight deviation from its original path. And gravity doesn't just curve space, it curves time as well. Space and time are no longer seen as separate entities: we now refer to them as "spacetime."

Although Einstein's and Newton's ideas of gravity were very different, each predicted almost the same events, except where things moved very quickly or where objects were very massive. The only evidence Einstein had to support his theory was from the orbit of Mercury. There was a slight shift in Mercury's orbit, which Newton was aware of but could not explain using his theory. However, it could be explained by Einstein's theory of general relativity. This alone was not enough for the scientific community to abandon Newtonian physics. Arthur Eddington (1882–1944), a British astronomer, devised a test of Einstein's theory. Both Newton and Einstein predicted that light from stars "behind" the Sun should be deflected by the Sun's gravity, but Einstein's theory predicted a greater shift than Newton's. During a solar eclipse, light from stars "behind" the Sun could be seen and this bending could be detected and measured. Eddington planned to take this measurement during an eclipse on May 29, 1919. Two observation teams were set up, one in West Africa and the other in Brazil. A shift in light was observed, and the shift was exactly what had been predicted by Einstein's theory of general relativity. Einstein became world renowned after this event.

Einstein was in the United States when Hitler came to power in 1933. He remained in the US, took up a position at the Institute for Advanced Study at Princeton, New Jersey, and became a US citizen in 1940. In the last decades of his life, Einstein tried to unify gravity and quantum mechanics, in what is often called the "grand unified theory." Although he was not able to do this, others have continued on the journey, and theoretical physics is still trying to realize his dream. The impact of Einstein on modern cosmology and quantum mechanics cannot be understated. His ideas, most of them developed in the "year of wonders," led to progress in understanding our universe that is unparalleled in the history of science. Let's examine these understandings further.

The Beginnings of the Universe

Newton's law of gravity predicted that a finite and static universe would collapse on itself owing to the pull of gravity, by the inner bodies, on the bodies on the outer edge

(a) (b)

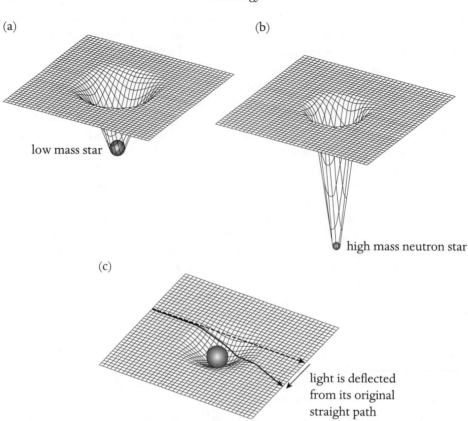

low mass star

high mass neutron star

(c)

light is deflected
from its original
straight path

Fig. 6.4 Einstein's theory of general relativity. (*a*) and (*b*) Einstein described gravity as a warping of spacetime around a massive object: the stronger the gravity, the more spacetime is warped. (*c*) Light travels along the curved space, taking the shortest path between two points. Therefore, light is deflected toward a massive object. The stronger the local gravity is, the greater the light path is bent.

of the universe. Most physicists in the early twentieth century held to the idea of an infinite, static universe. When Einstein applied general relativity to the universe, spacetime became "curved," "closed," and "unbounded"; if we picture the universe as the surface of a sphere, a line could be drawn without any ending point. Mathematics also predicted a nonstatic universe, implying that it was unstable, either contracting or expanding. Einstein, however, could not accept this, and so included the "cosmological constant" in his equations which retained the static model. To use Kuhn's terminology, he was having trouble accepting a new paradigm. (Einstein himself later admitted the cosmological constant was the "biggest blunder of my life.")

There were other problems with the infinite, static model. For example, Heinrich Olbers (1758–1840) drew attention to the paradox that now bears his name. He reasoned that, if the universe is homogeneous and infinite, the stars must be uniformly distributed throughout the universe. Why, then, does the sky appear dark at night? Shouldn't all those stars light up the night sky? Two solutions were proposed to Olbers's paradox. One posited that the dust in the space between the stars and the Earth might block out the light, and therefore the light would not reach us. However, if this were the case, the dust would absorb the energy and reradiate it. The radiation would be observed as light, and again the sky would not be dark at night. The second explanation was that the universe is young, and the light from all the stars has not yet reached us. Therefore, the universe cannot be infinite.

In 1917, Willem de Sitter (1872–1934) used general relativity to formulate his own equations in which the universe was expanding. Further developments of this idea caused others to predict that all the matter in the universe was moving away from itself. In the 1920s, Georges Lemaître (1894–1966), a priest and physicist, proposed that, if objects are indeed moving away from one another, the light we see from distant galaxies would be shifted into the red frequencies of the electromagnetic spectrum. To better understand this, think for a moment about sound and the Doppler effect. Imagine a car moving toward you with the radio playing very loudly. As the car approaches, the sound waves become compressed, and you hear the music at a higher pitch. As the car moves away from you, the sound waves are expanded and you hear the music at a lower pitch. This is similar to what happens with light. White light is made up of many wavelengths (see fig. 6.1), with blue light having a relatively short wavelength and red a relatively long wavelength. If an illuminated object, such as a star, were moving toward you, the wavelengths of light would be compressed, much like the sound waves from the radio in the car. This would shift the light into the blue spectrum. If the star were moving away from you, the shift would be toward the longer wavelengths in the red spectrum. Edwin Hubble (1889–1935), in his studies of nebulae, confirmed the red shift, and formulated Hubble's law in 1927: the speed at which a nebula is moving away from us is proportional to its distance from us. The red shift provided evidence to support the idea that the universe is expanding. By 1930, most physicists accepted the data and adopted the paradigm of an expanding universe. Einstein was among them.

Lemaître took the expanding universe a step further. He reasoned that, if galaxies are moving apart from each other, then at some point in the distant past they were close together. And at some point all matter in the universe was contained in a small space that was very dense. Lemaître called this the "primeval atom." His ideas were published in an obscure Belgian journal, but Eddington brought Lemaître's work to a larger audience.

Other predictions were made based on Lemaître's primeval atom. George Gamow (1904–68) and his colleagues calculated the heat required for nuclear reactions to occur in this scenario, leading to a detailed account of the temperature and size of the universe at different times following the decay of the primeval atom. They were able to explain some of the elements that could be formed from the decay of the primeval atom, such as hydrogen and helium, but could not explain the heavier ones, such as carbon and oxygen. In addition, Hubble's estimate of the age of the universe was younger than the estimated age of the Earth and some stars! These estimates were eventually found to be incorrect, due to inaccuracies in measuring the distances of galaxies.

A second theory was proposed, known as the steady state theory. Thomas Gold (1920–2004) and Hermann Bondi (1919–2005) used a philosophical argument to conclude that the universe is eternal. If one accepts that the universe is expanding, and it is eternal, then there is a problem with the density of matter. If the density must be maintained, where does the new matter come from? Gold and Bondi posited that all that is needed to maintain the density is one atom to come into existence every 100,000 years in the area the size of a school auditorium. This would be so rare that physicists would never be able to detect it. Fred Hoyle (1915–2001) developed equations to describe the steady state theory, and tried to debunk the "big bang" theory of Lemaître. Although Hoyle stood by the steady state theory, evidence supporting big bang essentially falsified steady state.

Description and support of big bang

The mathematics and physical laws we work with today can help us understand how the universe evolved (see table 6.1), but they are meaningful only after the first one-ten-million-trillion-trillion-trillionth of a second (10^{-43}) after the big bang. The time before this is known as Planck time. This is when the laws of physics break down, general relativity does not apply, and we need a new theory to explain the singularity. We predict, in Planck time, that the four forces of the universe were united into one. These forces are gravity, electromagnetism, weak nuclear forces (responsible for radioactive decay), and strong nuclear forces (which hold atomic nuclei together). The understanding of Planck time involves quantum theory (see below). Already, three of the forces (electro-magnetism, and strong and weak nuclear forces) have been explained by one theory. A theory that allows for the inclusion of gravity would unite all four forces, and, as we saw with Einstein, represents a holy grail for physicists.

Gamow and his colleagues predicted the two lightest elements, hydrogen and helium, would make up the bulk of matter in the universe, with approximately 75 percent hydrogen and almost 25 percent helium. These estimates turn out to be very accurate. Heavier elements, we know today, were not formed initially from the big bang, but are created within stars. When hydrogen burns in stars, helium is formed. When enough hydrogen is burned, the star contracts, which increases the core temperature. The helium then ignites, which ultimately converts it into carbon and oxygen, the necessary stuff of life. Helium has an atomic mass (the number of protons and neutrons in the nucleus) of 4. Carbon has an atomic mass of 12, and oxygen 16. Beryllium's atomic mass is 8. So, in a star, two helium atoms combine to form beryllium ($4 + 4 = 8$), and the beryllium combines with another helium atom to create carbon ($8 + 4 = 12$). The carbon can then react with helium to form oxygen ($12 + 4 = 16$).

Besides the hydrogen–helium ratio and the red shift, two other key pieces of evidence support the big bang theory. Both center on the radiation (energy detected as electro-magnetic waves and heat) resulting from the first instances after the big bang. This radiation should still be observable today. Given the expansion of the universe, there should be long wavelength radiation left over from the big bang, in the microwave range of the electromagnetic spectrum. In the 1960s, Robert Dicke (1916–97) and James Peebles (b. 1935) were working at the Holmdel Laboratories of Princeton University in New Jersey to find a way to detect the predicted radiation. Just a few miles away at Bell Laboratories, Arno Penzias (b. 1933) and Robert Wilson (b. 1936) were developing

Table 6.1 Timeline for the big bang

Time	Temperature (°C)	Events
0 second	?	The universe is a singularity – very small and very dense All four forces are unified General relativity does not apply here Quantum physics may explain this time
10^{-43} seconds (a unit of time known as Planck time)	10^{32}	The universe is the size of an atom The density of the universe is 10^{96} times that of water All forces except gravity are unified
10^{-35} seconds	10^{27}	Rapid expansion occurring The universe is the size of a tennis ball Strong forces separate from others
10^{-33} seconds	10^{25}	Formation of quarks
10^{-12} seconds	10^{15}	The universe is 10^{13} meters in diameter All four forces separated
10^{-5} seconds	10^{13}	Protons and neutrons form from quarks
1 minute	10^{10}	Formation of hydrogen nucleus
3 minutes	10^{9}	Protons and neutrons begin to form nuclei Universe consists of about 75% hydrogen, 25% helium and trace amounts of deuterium, lithium, beryllium, and boron
100,000–1 million years	$\approx 3,000$	Hydrogen nuclei capture electrons to form stable atoms Radiation can no longer interact with background gas; it propagates freely to this day Radiation is losing energy because the wavelength is stretched by the expansion of the universe (radio/microwave frequency today)
600 million–1 billion years		Galaxies and stars forming Heavier elements are created in stars
9 billion years		Formation of Sun and Earth
10 billion years		Life first appears on Earth
Today	−270	

satellite communications systems that would transmit information at microwave frequencies. Penzias and Wilson were working with a receiver that could detect signals bounced off balloons in the Earth's atmosphere. They also used the receiver to study radio waves in the cosmos. When observing the radio waves, Penzias and Wilson ran into an annoying, recurring problem: background radiation, which interfered with their studies, and, no matter what they did, they could not get rid of it. Penzias and Wilson contacted Dicke and Peebles for advice. Finally, the group realized these background signals were the leftover radiation from the big bang. Gamow, Dicke, and Peebles had estimated the temperature due to these microwaves to be −268 °C. The temperature of the observed waves was −269.5 °C. Thus, a serendipitous observation led to the most convincing evidence for the big bang. Penzias and Wilson won the Nobel Prize in Physics in 1978 for their discovery.

Not only should we be able to observe the leftover background radiation, but we should see variation in this radiation, depending on where we take our measurements. Our observations of the universe tell us there is heterogeneity: galaxies are scattered across the universe, and some of these galaxies form clusters. This implies that there must have been fluctuations in the early universe, to disrupt the homogeneity. If this were true, we should be able to detect temperature variations in the cosmic background microwave radiation. In 1992, the NASA COBE (Cosmic Background Explorer) satellite detected these variations, again supporting the big bang theory.

Atoms and Quantum Mechanics

We now turn our attention from the very large to the very small, and examine what we know about atoms and the world of quantum mechanics. Early in the twentieth century, not all physicists recognized atoms as real entities. Many thought of "the atom" as a convenient model, but not necessarily true. Moreover, the prevailing view predicted that atoms would collapse after a very short period of time. Neils Bohr (1885–1962) created a model of the atom based on Einstein's photoelectric effect (see fig. 6.5). He envisioned a positively charged nucleus surrounded by negatively charged electrons, similar to a

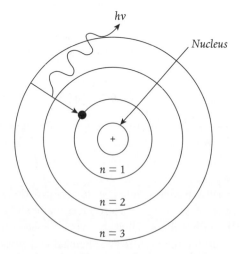

Fig. 6.5 Bohr's model of the hydrogen atom. The Bohr model has a nucleus, with protons and neutrons in the center, and electrons circling the nucleus in fixed energy levels, or orbits. Movement to an orbit closer to the nucleus causes the release of radiation.

solar system. Electrons move around the nucleus, and each has a specific angular momentum, or spin, which confines it to fixed areas (orbits) around the nucleus. Electrons can jump to different orbits: if the jump is toward the nucleus, radiation (energy) will be given off. If the jump is away from the nucleus, radiation will be absorbed. Either way, the radiation always occurs in bursts (quanta); it is not continuous. Ernest Rutherford (1871–1937) expanded this concept and determined the nucleus of the atom contained more than one type of particle that can be made unstable. In 1944, Otto Hahn (1879–1968) was awarded the Nobel Prize in Chemistry for discovering nuclear fission, the process whereby the nucleus breaks down into two fragments. When fission occurs, a loss of mass is observed. It was hypothesized that the mass lost during fission would provide the source for energy in Einstein's famous equation, $E = mc^2$. This led to the development of the atomic bomb, an endeavor that Einstein supported to begin with. Later he regretted his part in setting up the Manhattan Project, but he was also glad that the Germans had not developed the bomb first.

Another puzzling aspect of the very small was the observation that light (and other electromagnetic waves and subatomic particles) had a wave–particle duality: we cannot explain all the properties of light using just one model. In 1923, Louis de Broglie (1892–1987) proposed that particles could act like waves. If particles can exist in any place within a particular region, then, given a large number of particles, there will be a distinct probability where each particle will be at any given time. The sum of these probabilities for many particles appears to us as a wave. These waves, therefore, occur only in distinct frequencies (quanta). This led Erwin Schrödinger (1887–1961) to create a mathematical formula to describe the wave. Werner Heisenberg (1901–76) introduced his uncertainty principle in 1927, which states that if you determine the position of a particle, you cannot know its exact motion, and if you measure its momentum, you cannot know its position. He emphasized the role of the observer in these measurements: the observer is not an objective entity, but one who influences the system. A particle is everywhere in the wave (an idea known as superpositions) until a measurement is taken. At the moment of the measurement, the wave is said to collapse and we see only one outcome. Therefore, the observer interferes with the system being observed.

A familiar example of superpositions is radioactive decay. Some atoms are unstable and will emit subatomic particles (detected as radiation or energy). When a radioactive material emits energy, it is said to decay. It is impossible to predict when an atom will decay. When we talk about decay, we use the term "half life." This is the amount of time it takes for half of the material to decay. So, if the half life of a radioactive substance is one year, then half of the substance will decay in one year. In two years, three-quarters of the substance will have decayed, in three years seven-eighths will have decayed, and so on. Each atom, however, could decay at any time. So, if we examine a single atom, it could decay within the first minute of our observation, or within the first year. Or it may not decay for 10 years. We have no way of knowing when it will happen. Any given atom is both intact and decayed at the same time.

Schrödinger's cat is a thought experiment that provides a macroscopic example of superpositions. Imagine that a live cat is placed in a box with a radioactive atom and a vial of poison out of the cat's influence. If the atom decays, the vial will break and the cat will die. If the atom does not decay, the cat lives. So, once we place the cat in the box, the question becomes, "Is the cat alive or is it dead?" The answer is, "Yes." Since we can't know the exact state of the atom because of superpositions, the cat is alive and dead at the same time.

If we can see this type of strange behavior with subatomic particles, on the microscopic scale, why can't we detect it on the macroscopic scale (aside from the hypothetical killing of cats)? Three primary ideas have been used to explain this:

- *The Copenhagen interpretation*: all possibilities can occur, and all are equally probable. However, by observing a system, we collapse the wave function so there is only one outcome. One state is randomly realized based on the probabilities determined by the wave function. The problem with this idea is the lack of a mathematical equation to describe the collapse.
- *The many worlds interpretation*: this idea was proposed in the 1950s by Hugh Everett (1930–82). It states that all possibilities actually do occur. Each superposition is realized. This creates parallel worlds, each corresponding to a different superposition. The problem with this is that all outcomes are equally real, and all worlds equally real. We just happen to be in one of them. And we do not, at this time, have any way of detecting the other worlds.
- *Decoherence*: something in the environment causes one outcome to be realized. This could be anything from a photon of light to a gust of wind. The observer in this case does not cause a collapse of the wave function, as in the Copenhagen interpretation. Therefore, there are no violations of Schrödinger's equations.

Bohr argued that measurements can also influence how we interpret the outcome of an experiment. Consider, for example, the wave–particle duality of light. Depending on how we set up an experiment and how we take our measurements, we will see light behaving as a wave or as a particle. He called this "complementarity," meaning that the results of two experiments set up in two different ways will complement each other. Our understanding of a phenomenon cannot be understood by a single observation system. And, moreover, the two methods of observation are mutually exclusive (wave vs. particle). Bohr ultimately argued that the ideas of causality and reality, as defined by classical physics, had to be radically altered, and that the physical world does not exist in any classical way except when it's being measured.

So what does all this wave stuff mean? Well, based on probabilities, we can predict where a particle (an electron, a photon, etc.) will be, but we cannot know exactly where it will be at any given time. If we try to measure the location or momentum of the particle, our very act of measurement will disrupt the system (for example, if we use light to detect electrons, the photons can interact with the electrons, changing their position or altering their momentum). The wave theory indicates that there is fundamental randomness with these very small particles. We do not know precisely where an electron is, only the probable place where it might be – somewhere within the wave. In addition, according to Schrödinger's wave function, a particle can exist in two places at one time. Thus, the mathematics gives us some pretty amazing predictions and counterintuitive conclusions. However, on a practical level, quantum theory is extremely useful. Many technologies today rely on it, such as nuclear power, semiconductors, lasers, and magnetic resonance imaging (MRI).

Relativity and Quantum Mechanics Meet

Physicists are searching for a basic theory that will describe the four fundamental forces of the universe (gravity, electromagnetism, and the strong and weak nuclear forces). To date, quantum mechanics can unify electromagnetism and the nuclear forces, but gravity has been problematic. The notion of not being able to explain all four forces under a unified theory seems "untidy" to physicists. In addition, the pictures we get from relativity and from quantum mechanics are contradictory which, again, is problematic for physicists. Most of the time, relativity and quantum mechanics are separate, and are used in very different situations. Practically, there is no problem with the independence of the theories. However, when the curvature of spacetime is very large, relativity and quantum mechanics meet. There are two realms where this happens: at the big bang and in the center of black holes. Thus, we need a new theory, a new paradigm, of gravity that conforms to the quantum behavior of everything else in the universe. One area of inquiry is string theory. Strings are very small (approximately 10^{-33} centimeters) one-dimensional vibrating objects. They exist in a multidimensional (10 or 11) universe and make up all matter and forces. Other ideas have also been proposed, such as holographic theories, where the characteristics of materials or forces, such as gravity, in three dimensions can be explained by studying the properties of the phenomenon in two dimensions.

Cosmological Questions

Twentieth-century physics fundamentally affected three key areas that were important to prevailing notions of mechanics: realism, reductionism, and determinism. As a result, all these concepts came into question for the modern human. We have relativity and quantum mechanics to thank for this upheaval in our epistemologies. And the situation afforded ample opportunities for dialogue between science and religion.

The big question surrounding cosmology is, "Why are we here?" Scientifically, this question is not an ontological one; it refers not to purpose, but to the process of how the universe originated. We need to rephrase the question: "How did we get here?" The big bang theory gives us some of the answers. It tells us what the universe was like beginning at 10^{-43} seconds after the big bang. It does not tell us about anything before that time. According to the theory, there was rapid expansion and cooling, atoms formed, and, over the course of millions and billions of years, stars, planets, and galaxies formed. And, on at least one of those planets, life emerged. Not only life, but intelligent life. In order for life to emerge, physicists tell us, the conditions had to be just right: there had to be certain constants established at the big bang that determined not only matter but time. If these constants had been only slightly different, the universe would not have the properties it has today, and would not support life:

- *The rate of expansion*: If the expansion rate following the big bang had been too slow, the universe would have collapsed back on itself. If it was too rapid, no stars or planets would have formed.

- *The strength of the strong nuclear force*: The strong nuclear force is required to keep protons and neutrons together in the nucleus of the atom, and has to overcome the repulsion between the positively charged protons. A decrease in the strong nuclear force would have had several consequences, depending on the exact reduction. Basically, it would have thrown off balance the possible elements that could have been created, which would have resulted in a range of possibilities, from altering the rate of production of carbon and oxygen (preventing the possibility of life) to eliminating all elements except hydrogen. If the strong nuclear force had been greater, some have argued, all hydrogen would have been converted into helium and no heavier elements would have formed. And others have argued that, again, carbon and oxygen would not have formed at the correct rates to allow for the formation of life.

- *The proton–neutron mass difference.* Neutrons have a slightly greater mass than protons. If the mass of a neutron had been just slightly larger, then the conversion of hydrogen to helium could not have occurred, and stars could not have existed. Less massive neutrons would have resulted in an all-helium universe. The stars in this universe would have been much less stable than hydrogen–helium stars, which would have resulted in stars with shorter life spans and dramatically reduced the time available for the evolution of life.

- *The particle–antiparticle ratio.* Quantum theory states that even in a vacuum there is a wave function. Particles can appear and annihilate each other in this wave. For every one billion antiprotons that appeared in the early universe, there were one billion and one protons. If this ratio were slightly larger or smaller, it would have been impossible to form our universe.

It would appear that, in order for life to emerge in the universe, precise conditions had to be formed at the very beginning, within the first second after the big bang. These and other considerations have led many to talk about the fine-tuning of the universe, the notion that everything had to be just right for life to evolve. When we include the idea that life not only exists but evolved into intelligent life, indeed to human life, we are talking about the anthropic principle. Could other universes have formed with different properties, different forces, different natural laws? This is possible. Could these different universes support life? Most are skeptical that they would be able to. So it is very possible that only a universe with just our properties could have allowed for the evolution of intelligent life, such as us. The fine-tuning argument can be seen as circular reasoning: we are here, and thus the conditions required for us to get here are what we would necessarily observe. But there is no scientific principle that specifies things have to be this way. And we should be careful about focusing on the anthropic principle, as we may be placing too much emphasis on intelligent life, rather than life itself. We need to consider three options to help us understand the probability of the formation of a universe that could evolve intelligent life: necessity, chance, and design.

Necessity refers to the formation of our universe based only on natural laws and the relationships between forces and matter. The outcome of these laws, our universe, would be predicted to occur, given the nature of forces and matter. What is required for us to consider or adopt this viewpoint fully is a more fundamental theory that can show us why the constants have the precise values they do. We have no such theory yet. Einstein and others talk about the grand unified theory, or the theory of everything, which will describe how the four forces can be united. If such a theory is ever formulated, maybe we will see that the universe is necessary, and not contingent.

If the universe is not necessary, then could it have arisen by *chance*? There are several models that address this. All are based on probability: given enough time and multiple opportunities, the right conditions would have come about at some point. Three of these theories are discussed below.

- *Oscillating universe*. The universe may have been created through expansion (big bang) and destroyed through contraction (big crunch) multiple times. Eventually one of these universes would have the properties necessary for life to emerge.
- *Multiple isolated domains*. One big bang could have created multiple domains, all existing at the same time. However, these universes would be completely non-overlapping. These other universes would lie beyond our "horizon" in space, the farthest point we could possibly see, given the limitation of the speed of light and the expansion of the universe. Communication would be impossible between them. Given a large number of domains, many universes, potentially with different laws, would be feasible. Our universe is just one of the multitude of possibilities, the one where the conditions were right for life.
- *Many worlds quantum theory*. This is the idea proposed by Everett, whereby universes branch off for each possible outcome of the wave function. Therefore many worlds could exist, ours, again, being one that can support intelligent life.

These multiple universe ideas are difficult to support. It is generally acknowledged that we cannot communicate with other universes, if they do exist. And communication with universes that came before ours (as in the oscillating universe notion) would also be impossible. However, just because we currently cannot detect other universes doesn't mean they don't exist. How can we envision these other universes? Computer simulation could help us understand the alternate realities; black holes may create new spacetime arenas, different from our own; and parallel universes, as in Everett's theory, are a solution to quantum mechanics, and so their existence may be supported by mathematics. But the detection of these universes cannot be confirmed or refuted with our current technologies and theories. And the possibility of such multiple universes certainly calls into question our notions of realism.

If the universe was not created out of necessity or as a result of chance, then it must have been designed. The anthropic principle argues for this. The probability of a universe appearing with just the right conditions to support life by chance is inconceivable to many. Thus, a designer, such as God, must have created the universe. We will discuss this in more detail below.

Quantum Conundrums

The plethora of questions posed by the big bang is mirrored in our discussions of quantum mechanics. Quantum theory invokes the wave function to help us understand the behavior of particles at the subatomic level. As we discussed earlier, we cannot know both the location and the momentum of the particle. And, as Heisenberg showed, a particle can be in two places at one time. The wave equation tells us that fundamental randomness is built into the laws of nature. In other words, there is indeterminacy. This directly contradicts the determinism central to Newtonian physics, which held that, if we knew the natural laws, fundamental forces, and properties of matter, we could predict everything that would happen to an object. Quantum theory changed that, forcing us to face the notion that we cannot predict the behavior of matter because there is indeterminacy in nature.

Related to this is the understanding of parts and wholes. Classical physics looks at a system as being the sum of its parts (reductionism), but in quantum mechanics, the systems display properties that cannot be predicted based on the integration and inter-action of its parts. The following are some examples.

- *Quarks.* These subatomic particles make up protons and neutrons, but they cannot exist on their own: they must be part of a larger whole.
- *Electrons.* In an atom, no two electrons can have identical properties (such as energy, momentum, and spin). Therefore, when an electron is added to an atom, its properties are dictated by what is already present in the "system."
- *Bell's theorem* (also known as the EPR effect). This thought experiment proposed by Einstein has been verified experimentally. Two particles, such as a pair of electrons, are said to be entangled and can communicate with each other faster than the speed of light. If we separate the two electrons by an incredible distance and force a change in one of the electrons (for example, its spin), the other electron will also change. This is a violation of locality, the notion that a force can affect a change only in a nearby system and cannot have an effect over a huge distance. The system must be regarded as a whole to understand these changes, not as a conglomeration of parts that are affected only by locality. This also has implications regarding causality: if forces can act over distances faster than the speed of light, we may not be able to determine causation. Einstein called this "spooky action at a distance."
- *Measurement.* As we have seen, the act of measuring can affect the system. Therefore, we even need to include our experimental design, our method of observation, as part of the whole system.

It is difficult for us to comprehend many aspects of quantum mechanics, and we still do not fully understand what the equations are telling us. However, testing of the theory and development of technologies based on it tell us that it is correct, at least on several levels. As we have seen, many scientists are searching for another theory to incorporate everything that may supersede quantum mechanics and, once again, change our percep-tions of the universe and of what is real.

Theological Inquires: Natural Theology

As we have seen, physics in the twentieth century challenged our notions of realism, determinism, and reductionism. What is reality, when, as quantum theory states, we can't describe the world apart from the observer? And how can we have reality when space and time are no longer absolute, and physical properties such as length, velocity, and mass are no longer independent of an observer? How can we think of systems as deterministic when there is indeterminacy at the quantum level? And what happens to reductionism when the components of a system form a whole that cannot be described as the sum of its parts? Nature transformed itself from a law-abiding machine to a subjective hodgepodge with strange, almost incomprehensible, properties. How does this paradigm shift impact on theology? John Polkinghorne (b. 1930), a mathematical physicist and Anglican priest, and winner of the 2002 Templeton Prize for progress toward research or discoveries about spiritual realities, sees this as a positive advancement. He contends that a mechanistic view of the universe, indeed of anything in science, leads us to think that we can know everything. We are humbled when our ideas are shown to be wrong, and this can allow for opportunities of exchange between science and religion. In the remainder of this chapter we will examine some of the issues that may be covered in such an exchange.

Let's begin with the concept of natural theology. Recall that one argument for the existence of God, and a way to gain knowledge of God, is through evidence from nature. Design is cited as the key to this argument: the natural world shows complexity and order that points to a designer. Although Darwin essentially discredited this notion with the theory of natural selection in the nineteenth century (see chapter 8), new ideas about cosmology have brought it back. The anthropic principle emphasizes that all conditions had to be just right for intelligent life to form in this universe. This fine-tuning can be explained by necessity, chance, or design. Currently, we have no scientific theories that can be tested to support necessity or chance. Of course, this situation may change in the future. But proponents of natural theology argue that fine-tuning is what we would expect from design, from God.

The natural theology argument has been criticized by many. Karl Barth was staunchly opposed to this viewpoint, as we saw in chapter 2. He stressed that God cannot be known through nature, only through faith. Science is limited: it describes only natural phenomena. Another important voice in the opposition to natural theology was David Hume. Hume began writing *Dialogues concerning Natural Religion* in 1751 but was dissuaded from publishing it during his lifetime because of its controversial nature (it was published posthumously in 1779). In it, Hume showed the limitation of natural theology and its inadequacies in providing support for the existence of God. He asserted that human reason cannot comprehend divine truths, and that our attempts to use empirical evidence to help us understand God are flawed. Natural theology rests on analogy: because we see an organized, orderly world, we infer design and compare this design to human design. For Hume, this was the flaw: the analogy is not a good one. The universe is unlike anything that a human can make. What's more, we cannot possibly comprehend how it was fashioned. The only way we know of design, how things are made, is through observation. No human was present to observe the creation of the universe, so we can't judge how valid the analogy to human design is. Hume stated that first cause cannot be an argument for the existence of God; it is inconclusive, and other causes could account for what we see in nature. Hume cited some examples, including growth (as a tree grows from a seed) and attraction between matter (natural forces may allow for the formation of matter and the universe). He also cautioned that the analogy between a divine designer and a human one presents several problems. If we compare the human and divine minds, we must conclude that the divine mind is confused, changeable, and subject to influences. God would be prone to error and imperfection. These notions are incompatible with our view of God. And if we were to use only our senses and empirical data to comprehend God's attributes, we are limiting our opportunities for understanding. Interestingly, Hume stated that more scientific information would only increase our perception of design. The difficulty lies in the source or cause of the design. Ultimately, Hume concluded, natural theology does not help us understand the moral character of the designer.

Creation and Design

Natural theology and the argument from design stem from the observation of an apparently purposeful and orderly universe. It is a teleological argument based on what we can empirically detect at the present time. However, when we consider the "other end" of the timeline, the creation or origin of the universe, design can have a different connotation.

Many theological inquiries focus on the creation of the universe. The big bang theory, as opposed to steady state, is more consistent with the biblical account of creation. The big bang was formally endorsed by Pope Pius XII (1876–1958) in a speech to the Pontifical Academy of Science in 1951. Although most scientists accept a finite universe, some, such as Stephen Hawking at the University of Cambridge, have developed theories concluding that there may not have been a specific beginning. And Hoyle never gave up the notion of steady state, the theory that contends that the universe is infinite and that new matter needs to be formed continually to maintain density. This theory, even though it holds that the universe is infinite, contrary to theological notions of creation, has been preferred by some religious writers. The big bang can be viewed as deistic: God established the natural laws and allowed the universe to evolve according to them, without any divine intervention. Steady state theory requires the continuous creation of new particles to keep the density of the expanding universe constant. Therefore, this could be seen as the role played by an active God.

However, the big bang is supported by convincing evidence and has been adopted by the vast majority of scientists. If we accept the big bang, we accept that there was a beginning to the universe, and we have to ask whether or not this creation required a transcendental cause. Could the universe have arisen spontaneously? Quantum theory does predict the existence of a singularity from "nothing." Therefore, even in a finite universe, a creator is not absolutely necessary. However, neither is the existence of that universe. If the universe is contingent, then why does it exist? And why is it the way it is? As we have seen, exact parameters are required for life, indeed intelligent life, to have emerged. We can't scientifically support the argument that these conditions arose from chance or necessity. So what about design?

If design is the answer, it raises more questions. Why was the universe designed? What is its purpose? Some contend that the universe was designed for us. Again, this would be supported by theological notions, reflecting the biblical account of creation in Genesis: the world is good, creation is good, humans are good. But there are problems with this design argument. The indeterminacy specified by quantum mechanics provides for randomness in the universe. How could intelligent life be guaranteed from such laws? Maybe God acted at the quantum level at critical moments to ensure the evolution of humans; maybe he still acts at this level today. Given the uncertainty of the quantum world, God could influence or direct events freely. All possibilities exist, as predicted by quantum theory, but God may "collapse the wave function" in certain directions; there may be "divine guidance" along the path. We would not detect any violations of the laws of physics, as there would not be any. To accept this point of view we would need to know if quantum influences could truly affect the world on a macroscopic level, where God's activities could be realized. Experimental evidence and computer simulations have shown that small changes on the microscopic level in a system do indeed have profound effects at the macroscopic level. Therefore, via one event or a series of events, God could direct actions from the quantum level.

In considering necessity, chance, and design, we must also take into account a combination of these factors. God could have designed a universe with the laws we know. Observance of those laws would account for necessity. Quantum theories would allow for chance. Are necessity, design, and chance mutually exclusive? In a word, no.

Design also inevitably leads to the question of theodicy: what is the source of the evil and suffering we experience? Christians believe in a benevolent and loving God, which often seems to contradict the pain and agony we observe. If God designed the universe, why not design it so there is no suffering? One answer focuses on the notion of continuing creation. The universe is not finished yet. We are not done evolving. Evil and suffering are part of the creative process: evil and suffering are a result of the laws that govern the universe. They are the cost of a world that is in the process of creation. It is analogous to the whole versus the sum of the parts: part of the creative process requires evil and suffering, and we cannot imagine what the outcome will be when this process is complete. The idea of theodicy and continuing creation applies to biological evolution as well, and we will explore this notion further in chapter 11.

Indeterminacy

Indeterminacy in nature has been supported by quantum mechanics, but it also has been doubted by many. There are three interpretations of the indeterminacy issue.

- *Indeterminacy could be due to human ignorance.* We may not have the technology or the theories to understand all the variables and interactions that make quantum systems not appear to be deterministic (this was Einstein's point of view). These laws will eventually be discovered (the grand unified theory, or the theory of everything) and we will regain determinism and reality.
- *Indeterminacy could be due to limitations in our experimental designs, or in our ability to understand nature.* This means there are some things that we will never be able to know. We may have come to a limit of science, where the true nature of the atom is inaccessible to us. From this point, observation, and not theory, will be our only mechanism of understanding.

- *Indeterminacy could be real, and the universe is not deterministic.* There is a range of possibilities in nature, and the future is not yet determined. As observers, as participants in the system, we may cause one or another value to be realized.

As with design and creation, suffering also comes into the discussion of indeterminacy. Indeterminacy can be seen as a cause of suffering. The same types of mutations that result in biological evolution can also cause cancer. If indeterminacy exists, then the course of any event cannot be predicted, not even by God. This notion provides new meaning for human freedom and divine activity. It implies free will, consistent with Christian theology. Indeterminacy may appear to contradict God's omnipotence and omniscience. However, God's self-limitations on these powers, as exemplified in reccurring themes of free will and suffering, are expressed in numerous biblical texts and have been argued by theologians. Quantum mechanics provides room for omniscience: the field theories essential to quantum mechanics, as seen in Bell's theorem, can provide an analogy for God's presence, activity, and knowledge of all things in the universe.

Contingency

Scientifically, we cannot say that the universe was *necessary*, that there is some law that would eventually lead to the universe we have, or to any universe for that matter. So we are left with the notion of contingency: everything is an unforeseen event emerging from some cause not based on natural laws or necessity. Ian Barbour, the Templeton Prize winner in 1999, divides this notion into four categories:

- *Boundary conditions.* Regardless of whether the universe is finite or infinite, there are limits to what science can investigate. As we have seen with the big bang and a finite universe, our physical laws do not apply until 10^{-43} seconds after the big bang, and cannot be applied before that time. And if the universe is infinite, there are still some unexplained situations, the givens, that have to be assumed before we can begin a scientific investigation.
- *Laws.* Why are the physical laws the way they are? Why is the speed of light just what it is? Why are there four forces, and why are they the exact strengths they are? We do not yet have a unified theory that would reveal these laws to be necessary. Some day we may. But even if these laws are no longer found to be contingent, then we just push the question back a step, to the contingency of the unified theory. And a unified theory, describing forces and constants, would do little to inform us about the complex life we see today on Earth.
- *Events.* As quantum mechanics reminds us, the whole is not the sum of its parts, and there is indeterminacy. Even when the laws are in place, and result in necessary outcomes, we still cannot always predict exactly what the end products will be.
- *Existence.* Contingency, particularly from a theological viewpoint, often centers on the question, "Why is there anything at all?" Even if science will some day explain that this universe is the only one possible, it still has not told us that it is

necessary. The biblical tradition tells us that God created the universe by choice. This reveals the purposefulness, transcendence, and power of, as well as our dependence on, God.

Einstein's Theology

Not only did Einstein contribute to physics, but he was also politically active (particularly with regard to war and the state of Israel) and had some much popularized views on religion. In some of his writings, he espoused a deist attitude, surmising that God created the universe but is not personally involved with humans. Some of his views have also been described as pantheistic: he saw wonder and amazement and glory in the universe, and identified God with its orderly structure. Even though Einstein's scientific ideas were critical to the development of quantum theory, he held to the views of classical physics, namely that the universe was real and independent of observers, and that it was causal and deterministic. Einstein reasoned that, because God is rational, humans should be able to have a complete understanding of the natural world, and that, if we know the natural laws governing a system, we will be able to understand the causes of events and to disregard the observer as influencing the system. He saw contingency as a threat to rationality.

Quantum mechanics fails to describe the state of systems between measurements and observations. Einstein concluded that it must therefore be incomplete and that a more general theory would one day be discovered that would reveal the forces and causes of what we see at the quantum level. The result will be a deterministic universe. One of his most famous quotes reveals his disagreement with the randomness predicted by quantum mechanics. Einstein did not believe that God plays dice with the universe.

Conclusions

A search for intelligibility in the universe has its roots in the ancient Greeks and in the Bible. We continue this tradition in our scientific and theological investigations today. Bohr's idea of complementarity, where a phenomenon cannot be described in just one way, can be seen as an analogy to the dialogue between science and religion. We cannot describe the universe, our existence, and the things that happen to us using just one viewpoint. Both science and religion are needed for a fuller appreciation of the human experience. However, as Bohr recognized, the problem with this is that, with scientific measurements, the results from the two methods of observation are mutually exclusive. Although some would apply the notion of complementarity to the science and religion interface today, many are examining ways in which the two disciplines can interact without excluding each other.

The scientific understandings of cosmology have not generated as much discussion in the religious realm as have other topics, such as evolution. There are several possible reasons why this may be so.

- Few examples of astronomical evidence have been found to support the cosmological claims. Even though this limited evidence is very strong, there is a view held by some that the big bang should still be considered speculative.
- The mathematics involved in describing the big bang is very complex and incomprehensible to most. Therefore, it is difficult for not only nonscientists, but even scientists outside of physics, to understand and evaluate the conclusions.
- The subject of the beginnings of the cosmos and the properties of particles we cannot see are very far removed from daily life – much more so than the origin and evolution of life.

Modern physics has led us to abandon many absolutes, such as space, time, and mass, which were previously thought to be objective. However, we have replaced them with other certainties, such as the constancy of the speed of light. Realism, reductionism, and determinacy may be in question, but we realize that design, contingency, and free will are not inconsistent with each other. The implications of modern physics are exciting for both science and theology, and leave open many avenues of discussion. Principles basic to Christian theology, including free will, theodicy, and the uniqueness of our world and ourselves, are issues that are central to physics as well. It is an exciting time to be involved in the science–religion dialogue.

Primary Literature

Useful primary sources include a speech entitled "On Science and Religion," given by Albert Einstein in 1941, an excerpt of which can be found in *Science & Spirit* 16 (6) (2005), 34–5; and John Polkinghorne, "The Universe is a Mystery," *Science & Spirit* 12 (6) (2001).

Questions to Consider

1 Consider the equation $E = mc^2$. If we specify mass in kilograms (kg) and the speed of light in meters per second (ms^{-1}), then our unit of energy will be kg m^2 s^{-2}, which is defined as a joule (J). A joule can also be defined as a watt second (Ws; think of a light bulb to grasp the idea of a watt). If we could harness all the energy from a 1 kg mass (2.2 lb.), how long could we keep a 100-watt light bulb burning (use 3×10^8 ms^{-1} for the value of c)?

2 We cannot verify any claim about the uniqueness of our universe and, scientifically, the existence of other universes is possible. How do you think this idea impacts on theology? Is it contrary to or easily integrated into Christian belief? Explain your answer.

3 One key issue discussed in this chapter is origins, a topic fundamental to both science and religion. How should theologians view scientific concepts regarding the origin of the universe? Should theological concepts change when new scientific data are revealed? Does theology have any bearing on science with regard to this issue? Consider in your answer the notions of limits – what questions can and cannot be answered by the two disciplines.

4   How do the notions of indeterminacy and contingency impact on science (specifically physics) and theology? What difficulties do these notions present to each discipline? What aspects of science and theology are enhanced by these ideas?

5   Bohr's notion of complementarity can explain scientific conundrums, for example the wave–particle duality of light. Can you think of any theological notions that could fall under this category? Do you think complementarity is an adequate way to view the fields of science and religion? Support your answer.

6   What is the basis and significance of Einstein's notion that God does not play dice with the universe?

7   We can trace the idea of intelligibility back to the ancient Greeks, who believed that we can come to know and understand the natural world. Did quantum physics destroy this notion? Give reasons in support of your answer.

7

Eschatology

Overview

Eschatology is the study of the end, or culmination, of time. It is based on the promise of God for a new world without sin, suffering, or death, for an eternal life in God. This promise can be viewed as an extension or fulfillment of creation, and is intimately intertwined with redemption. Different theological notions have focused on individual death, as well as the end of communities and of the cosmos. The timing of the eschaton has been debated: it has been seen variously as a future event, as an event that has already happened, and as an occurrence that has already begun but has not yet been completed. Scientifically, we have little doubt that human life as we know it will come to an end, along with the Earth and the universe. These scientific notions highlight the importance of focusing on the meaning of the eschaton, rather than on the actual events that will bring it about or the exact structure of the new creation. By integrating eschatological ideas into our present life, as opposed to thinking of the consummation as a distant event, we can gain perspective for our existence, hope for our future, and insight into God's character.

Introduction

In our discussion of creation, we noted that humans are considered special; indeed we are the culmination of creation in the Genesis account. Whether through divine grace or evolution (or a combination of both), we have consciousness and, more importantly, self-consciousness. We have the ability to contemplate our own mortality. We know that some day we will die. In the Judeo-Christian tradition, we look for life after death, and find hope in God that something lies beyond death. This hope is not only for us but also for our communities and for the cosmos. Eschatology, from the Greek word meaning "last," is the term used for our study of the final events of this world, the destiny of humankind, and the end (or culmination) of time. Many biblical texts point us toward a violent end to this world, with a promise of a new age and a new world that is the kingdom of God, free from death, sin, and suffering. In addition to the biblical and theological concepts of the eschaton, we also need to consider what science has to say on this subject: cosmological theories predict the end of the human species, the Earth, and the universe. Against the scientific backdrop of annihilation and theological doomsday prophecy stands the Christian concept of hope.

In this chapter we will examine the theological, biblical, and scientific understandings of eschatology. We will consider such topics as hope, time, and eternity, life after death, and the kingdom of God. The concepts we will cover are speculative, as the future hasn't happened yet, at least not in our conception of time. We will see that, if nothing else, the subject of eschatology contains much fodder for discussion in the dialogue between science and religion.

Some Historical Eschatology

Anthropological investigations of the human race from prehistory to the written records of ancient cultures show us the importance we have always placed on death, and the beliefs we have had in an afterlife. Burial rituals from simple Neanderthal graves to the elaborate tombs of the Egyptian pharaohs have included objects for the dead to take with them into the afterlife. Mythologies in many cultures tell in detail of the worlds encountered after death, such as Tartarus and the Elysian fields. The realization of mortality, and perhaps a denial of the finality of death, fueled ancient peoples to imagine a life beyond death that gave hope and purpose to human existence. The Christian views of eschatology do no less than this.

As with many theological notions, eschatology has been interpreted in different fashions, and the eschaton has been envisioned in many forms. In the Jewish tradition, early eschatological ideas centered on the emergence of an ideal ruler of Israel, a descendent of David. The kingdom of God would be a supreme state of affairs within this world and within history. Peace and prosperity would reign. This state would be achieved only through the spirit of God. Later ideas placed the kingdom of God outside of history and outside of this world. Discontinuity, brought about by a sudden apocalyptic divide, would separate this world from the new one. The Son of Man would usher in this new age. This viewpoint was dominant during the lives of the New Testament authors, and was reinforced in many of the teachings of Jesus. It was believed that the second coming of Christ was imminent, possibly within their lifetimes. For example, Jesus tells the disciples that the kingdom of God would soon be realized:

And he said to them, "Truly, I say to you, there are some standing here who will not taste death before they see that the kingdom of God has come with power." (Mark 9:1)

When they persecute you in one town, flee to the next; for truly, I say to you, you will not have gone through all the towns of Israel, before the Son of man comes. (Matthew 10:23)

And Paul also implies an imminent second coming:

> Besides this you know what hour it is, how it is full time now for you to wake from sleep. For salvation is nearer to us now than when we first believed; the night is far gone, the day is at hand. (Romans 13:11–12)

> May the God of peace himself sanctify you wholly; and may your spirit and soul and body be kept sound and blameless at the coming of our Lord Jesus Christ. (1 Thessalonians 5:23)

Although this notion is clearly seen in many New Testament references, other texts point to an undetermined time:

> "But of that day or that hour no one knows, not even the angels in heaven, nor the Son, but only the Father. Take heed, watch; for you do not know when the time will come. (Mark 13:32–3)

> But as to the times and the seasons, brethren, you have no need to have anything written to you. For you yourselves know well that the day of the Lord will come like a thief in the night. When people say, "There is peace and security," then sudden destruction will come upon them as travail comes upon a woman with child, and there will be no escape. (1 Thessalonians 5:1–3)

The early Christians soon abandoned the idea that the end was imminent. They looked for the second coming of Christ in the future, and also believed in the bodily resurrection of the dead and an apocalyptic end to this world. The belief in premillennialism was predominant – it was based on a 1,000-year (millennial) reign of Christ as foretold in Revelation:

> Then I saw an angel coming down from heaven, holding in his hand the key of the bottomless pit and a great chain. And he seized the dragon, that ancient serpent, who is the Devil and Satan, and bound him for a thousand years, and threw him into the pit, and shut it and sealed it over him, that he should deceive the nations no more, till the thousand years were ended. After that he must be loosed for a little while. Then I saw thrones, and seated on them were those to whom judgment was committed. Also I saw the souls of those who had been beheaded for their testimony to Jesus and for the word of God, and who had not worshiped the beast or its image and had not received its mark on their foreheads or their hands. They came to life, and reigned with Christ a thousand years. The rest of the dead did not come to life until the thousand years were ended. This is the first resurrection. Blessed and holy is he who shares in the first resurrection! Over such the second death has no power, but they shall be priests of God and of Christ, and they shall reign with him a thousand years. (Revelation 20:1–6)

For the premillennialist, this 1,000-year reign was considered to be in the future. Tertullian, often considered the father of the Latin church, introduced the term "Trinity" to the Christian vocabulary and was an influential proponent of premillennialism. Origen, however, rejected this viewpoint. As we have already seen, Origen denied a literal interpretation of the Bible. To him, the kingdom of God was not an earthly realm. He focused more on the eschatology of the individual soul, thus emphasizing a spiritual rather than a material transformation at the eschaton. But the real challenge to premillennialism came from Augustine, in his book, *City of God* (426). According to Augustine's amillennialist approach, the kingdom of God is already here, taking place through the church. This view was favored by the church, and led to a decline in popular apocalyptic views. Augustinian amillennialism was popular through the medieval era, and was accepted by the leaders of the Protestant Reformation, including Luther and Calvin. However, the sixteenth century in Europe saw another rise in apocalyptic eschatology. With the Enlightenment, another paradigm emerged, chiefly the liberal Christian notion that the kingdom of God is not a futuristic event, but rather the age brought on by humans in establishing social equity and justice: human activity, guided by morality, would result in the transformation of this world. This led to the postmillennialism of the eighteenth century, which was also popular in America in the late nineteenth and early twentieth centuries. In this view, the millennium begins in our present age, the time between Christ's two appearances on Earth. An age of righteousness will be realized before Christ's return.

Regardless of the timing, the message within the biblical text is what is important. In our discussion of modern notions of eschatology, we will focus on the meaning of the message and consider some issues of time.

Individual Death

Christian theology has viewed death in two different ways: as a result of original sin, and as the end of a biological life. In the Augustininian tradition, death was seen as punishment for original sin, the turning away from God. This ending was not only an end in time, it was also an eternal exclusion from a relationship with God, known as eternal death. Church doctrine distinguished three different types of death: death of the body, death of the soul, and eternal death. Once the body died, the soul was judged by God, and the result was either eternal life or eternal death. Since death was the inherited consequence of sin, the final judgment brought anxiety to most people. The fear of death was actually a fear of hell. Grace would bring relief to the dying who feared this eternal damnation.

Once death of the body was acknowledged to be a natural end of earthly life, a distinction was made between physical death and sin in Protestant theology. Friedrich Schleiermacher, the German philosopher and theologian, argued that physical death should not be viewed as evil: it is only in our awareness and consciousness of death as divine punishment that we experience guilt. Our redemption through God's grace is not redemption from death, but from the fear of death. Eternal death, or the loss of a relationship with God as the result of sin, is still possible, but it has nothing to do with the death of the physical body. Barth agreed with Schleiermacher that death is the natural physical end. He believed that grace can free individuals from fear. Our temporal life is kept in God's memory: Barth saw this as the meaning of redemption, not a resurrection of the physical body, but our life made eternal in the mind of God.

The natural physical death of the body leaves behind the soul. In Plato's philosophy, the soul is immortal: it cannot die because it was never born. It has nothing in common with the physical realm, and cannot experience suffering and happiness. In this way, it is "lifeless." Death divides the soul from the physical body. Modern ideas of the soul view it not as a substance, but rather as the relationship between the whole mortal individual and the immortal God. This "spirit" is the relationship with God into which we enter, which only God can terminate. Remaining in a relationship with God is immortality.

Eschatology, Creation, and Redemption

The eschaton, or consummation, raised questions that needed to be addressed not from a futuristic perspective, but from a reality that is present and ongoing. Early in the twentieth century, theologians reconsidered eschatology in ways that could provide meaning and practical significance in our time. We can view eschatology as an ongoing process, just like creation and redemption. Therefore, we must consider eschatology alongside, and interwoven with, the doctrines of creation and reconciliation. These three themes recur in the Bible and are emphasized by Christ. Just as the doctrine of creation does not necessarily mean there was a beginning to our world, eschatology does not mean there has to be an end. Creation refers to our dependence on God, reconciliation in our relationship with God, and consummation in fulfillment of God's plan. The three cannot be separated, but instead represent different aspects of God's activity.

But how are we to view the consummation as something that is ongoing? One way is to consider the effect it has on the present time. Eschatology says something about our existence and about our ontological status: we can gain perspective on our lives by contemplating what awaits us. We also focus on the future we have been promised: this provides us with hope. And we can look to the promised events to provide us with insights into the character of God.

On an individual level, as we face the notion of death, we can gain a new attitude, a new perspective on our lives, and come to a fuller understanding of our existence and of ourselves. Just as our own mortality can help us appreciate our lives from an existential and ontological perspective, the end of a community or the end of the world may also provide for reflection on the meaning and purpose of being. As we bring the doctrines of creation and reconciliation into the picture, we come to realize that our finite existence is within God's promise and plan for us. God's faithfulness and commitment to us will be realized: the world is called to the creator for a new creation, one without suffering, sin, or death.

This promise provides hope. Although we cannot know the future, we have faith in God's promises and therefore we have hope. Can we know anything about the future? Whatever lies ahead will have to be consistent with what we already know about the world and human existence, and what we already know about God.

God created, and continues to create, with a purpose. The life, death, and resurrection of Jesus were part of this purpose. And any eschatological conjectures must be consistent with creation and reconciliation. The consummation will be a fulfillment of the potentialities of all things, a gathering into God. It may never be a precise point in time, a true "ending" that will some day be reached. If we imagine the "end" as a state of perfection, then we envision a static existence, where the kingdom of God would be "frozen." Creation is anything but static, so we should think of the consummation as a dynamic process as well. For individuals, we will be closer to God, and become more like God in our selflessness and love. However, we must retain our individuality. Looking again to creation, God made the world, and humans, with an amazing amount of diversity. If, at the culmination of time, we become the same in a union or unity with God, then the pain, suffering, and death of creation will have been pointless. The consummation can be viewed as continuing creation, an ever expanding quest toward perfection, where new stages will open new horizons for us.

The Timing of the Eschaton

Two ways to interpret the biblical text with regard to the timing of the eschaton include a futurist viewpoint, where the events are pushed to a remote future, and a realized eschatology, in which the promised events have already taken place. Recall that within all of these notions we need to examine eschatology from an individual, community, and cosmic stance.

Futuristic views include the millennial ideas we discussed above. In some cases, we can see the New Testament authors shifting from an imminent to a futuristic second coming: the final days would arrive when Israel had been saved (a community focus). For the individual, there would be a judgment of the soul at death, and, on the cosmological side of things, the new age would be otherworldly. The problem with this interpretation is that it puts the consummation in a distant, remote future, relying on mythological understandings and divine intervention. This removes eschatology from the here and now: what significance can it have for us in the present time? Is it just a flight from reality? And what of science, which tells us that the end of the world will not necessarily occur via supernatural forces (see below)?

Realized eschatology may be lacking as well. According to this view, the promised events have already taken place (this is also referred to as a preterist view). Believers already have eternal life, and the judgment of the world is happening now: we live in the face of death, and our decisions and actions are judged each day. The problem with this view is that the realized eschatology is at the level of the individual, and does not include the community or the cosmos. This creates a paradox: the kingdom of God is present but has not yet come.

Can we find an interpretation that incorporates all eschatological levels, remains true to biblical teachings, and provides meaning for us in the present time? If we consider consummation to be intimately connected with creation and reconciliation, a new view of eschatology emerges, in which eschatology is a continuing event. The kingdom of God is now, but has not yet been fulfilled. This will occur with the parousia (the second coming of and judgment by Christ). Viewed in this manner, eschatology can provide perspective for the individual, foster hope, and help us understand God's character.

Notions of Time

In Western culture, which is based on biblical notions of time, we think of time as linear. Historical events occur as a sequential progression. Not all cultures see time in this fashion. For example, the Buddhist tradition is based on cycles rather than linear time. However, time was not a concern for many Christian theologians, including Augustine. For Augustine, the past was non-existent and the future was not yet: the present will soon become the past, but if the present could remain and not transform into the past, then it would be eternal and not temporal. Thus, Augustine's view of eternity was one in which everything remains in the present and nothing passes away. The reason humans can remember the past, anticipate the future, and understand the present is because of our souls, which can extend into the past and the future. The soul is an enduring presence, able to span time ("time-bridging"). Augustine referred to this as the distention of the soul, and our participation in eternity can be achieved only through our souls. For God, the past and the future are present. Think of performing a piece of music: the present is the exact note we are performing at the moment, but the piece is not whole if we do not remember the "past" and anticipate the "future" of it. Thus, eternity is analogous to the performance: past, present, and future are all woven together to create the whole.

Eternity was timeless for Augustine. Time was created by God along with everything else and is separate from eternity. Wolfhart Pannenberg (b. 1928), professor emeritus of systematic theology at the University of Munich, took Augustine's ideas further. He proposed that God looks at the whole of time, which directly relates to the concept of "everlasting": God's existence and identity are continuous through time. He also incorporated his ideas about time and eternity into the Trinity. Paul Tillich, on the other hand, focused on the future. He saw our awareness of time as opposite to our experience of it: we see our past and present with respect to the future. The future is the loss of the present, and, eventually, each individual's "now" will end at death. This can result in a denial of death or of a belief in an afterlife. Unfortunately for Tillich's view, we can see that time has an end, and that therefore eternal life will come to an end. Tillich, however, did not see eternity as a future state or a temporal event. For him, creation was not a temporal event, and neither was the eschaton. Instead, he saw eternity as the *telos* of creation, and eternal life as being always present. God is inclusive of all time, but humans are finite and are enslaved by time. Ted Peters (b. 1941), professor of systematic theology at Pacific Lutheran Theological Seminary and the Graduate Theological Union in Berkeley, California, critiqued Tillich's ideas. Although he agrees that eternal life does have a role in the present, especially with regard to a relationship with God, Peters saw Tillich's view as creating anxiety for the future, not the hope of resurrection and new life promised in the New Testament. Peters pointed out that Tillich's theology stresses an end, a finish, to time, as if it were mortal, just like humans. Peters uses Pannenberg's ideas of eternity as the whole of time, which is necessary in order to place the meaning of our lives within the history of the cosmos. He contends that the end of time should be thought of as the fulfillment of time, not as a temporal, finite event. God's creation of time allowed the universe to have a future, to become something new. Thus, our three underlying themes – creation, reconciliation, and eschatology – all have a common promise: a future.

As we have seen, science has also considered the topic of time, particularly when it comes to relativity. Einstein's special theory of relativity tells us that our observations depend on our frame of reference. There is no absolute measurement we can take, as everything is in motion. The only situation that violates this idea is the speed of light: it is constant, no matter how we are moving. Not only are mass and length relative, but so is time. Consider the example we saw in the last chapter: if we were to synchronize our watches, and I were to board a rocket ship and head into outer space for a while, traveling near the speed of light, and we compared our watches when I came back, we would find that more time had elapsed on your watch, here on Earth, than on my watch. A real world, practical example of this is seen with the clocks on global positioning systems (GPS) satellites: they appear to lose time each day, and thus their clocks must be synchronized with ground-based technology. Time and space are interrelated and interdependent (spacetime). So what does this mean? It means that our perception of time is faulty. Time is relative: in moving from the present to the future, "one second" may be the same to each observer in the exact reference frame of the observer, but it will be different to another observer in a different reference frame. There is no way to determine a universal "present." The concept of "present time" is defined by each independently moving observer. So how do we define "past" and "future" if we cannot universally define "present"?

These observations regarding time can be integrated into a theological framework, which raises many questions. What is God's frame of reference? Does this help us understand our notions of eternity, where God can look at all of time? Is there time in eternity? If time was created in a material universe, then will time still depend on matter and forces in the new age? The subject of time is one that provides lots of opportunities for dialogue between science and theology.

Scientific Predictions

The questions we ask regarding the kingdom of God, the afterlife, resurrection, immortality of the soul, etc., cannot be answered by science, and the answers provided by theology cannot be supported with empirical data. However, we can examine the end using scientific methodology, and make some predictions as to what may await us in the future. And, as we have already seen with the concept of time, scientific notions can have a bearing on theological views.

The recurring theme we see with science is the understanding that nature is orderly and can be known through reason and observation. Natural laws and our knowledge of the structure of the universe allow us to make predictions. Quantum physics provides for randomness and indeterminacy on a subatomic level, but all in all, we have a solid cosmological understanding of the universe. We can't say for sure what the future holds but, based on natural laws and our knowledge of the history of the universe, we can make predictions that are reasonable. One of the important lessons from the history of life, and the history of the cosmos, is that death allows for the emergence of new life.

The death of a star results in the formation of elements that can be used to form new celestial bodies, and even life itself. The extinction of species here on Earth allows for the evolution of new life forms. Even a forest fire, which destroys all the vegetation in a given area, clears away the underbrush, and allows for seed germination in some plant species, providing for the growth of new trees. Individual death does not mean the end of a community or of the cosmos. This is a common theme that science shares with theology.

So what comments can we make regarding the end? As with theological reflections, we can examine the end from a scientific perspective on different levels. We can look at individual death, the extinction of the human race, the destruction of the Earth, and the end of the cosmos.

Human End

The Christian hope is for the resurrection of the dead. Scientifically, we know that resurrection of the physical body is impossible. Resurrection cannot be a physical event, so it must be spiritual. Can science comment on this? Can we gain insights into life after death with an empirical epistemology? Thanatology is the study of death and dying, and includes research from the medical, psychological, and sociological communities. Although a purely empirical study is impossible, there have been attempts by the natural sciences to peer into what happens after death. Stories of near-death experiences abound, and most have some common features: sensations of bright light and fire, a calm feeling, and images of one's past life flashing before one's eyes. Some sensations can be explained by physiological responses in the brain, for example, from a lack of oxygen. But others are not experienced by individuals unless they are in actual danger of dying. So what can science say about death? It is inevitable, but we cannot use our methodology to study what comes afterward.

And what about the human species as a whole? Will we survive? A survey of the fossil record tells us that extinction is the fate of most, and probably all, species. How will it all end? We could envision a natural infectious disease that may wipe out our species. But, more likely, we will be the authors of our own death. The amazing advances that have improved our lives, such as medicine and agriculture, may ultimately be overshadowed by some of our other accomplishments: nuclear and biological warfare and environmental disasters. Historically, we have seen many civilizations vanish owing to the exploits of their citizens. We now have a global community: our actions not only affect our neighborhood but the world as a whole. Global warming, pollution of the air and seas, the increasing size of the ozone hole, acid rain – we are too familiar with these problems and their potential consequences.

If we reverse some of our activities, and take better care of the Earth, will we survive? Natural disasters, such as floods, droughts, hurricanes, earthquakes, and volcanoes will always be devastating to human populations, but these tragedies do not affect the entire human population at once. Mass death is limited to a local region – it is not on a planetary scale. However, an examination of this planet will quickly show that Earth has been pelted with space debris for much of its history, and this is potentially bad news for the whole of the human species.

Asteroids and comets have periodically impacted the planet, often with devastating results for many species. About 50,000 years ago a meteor 30 m in diameter created a crater 1.2 km wide in Winslow, Arizona. The extinction of the dinosaurs was caused by a meteor 10 km in diameter that impacted in the Yucatan in Mexico about 65 million years ago. The crater is about 180 km in diameter! Indeed, at least three mass extinctions of life on this planet have been attributed to asteroids and comets. These cosmic collisions can still be observed today. In 1994, the comet Shoemaker-Levy 9 impacted Jupiter. The "scars" and "blemishes" left by this impact could be seen for over one year. Some of them were larger than the size of the Earth. Our Moon is covered with craters from previous impacts. Our planet must have encountered at least as many of these collisions. However, owing to our atmosphere and other natural forces, such as erosion and biological processes, the Earth does not show many of these scars.

Asteroids are generated in a belt between Mars and Jupiter. Sometimes the orbits of these small rocks cross the orbits of other celestial bodies, and collisions occur to knock particles off track. The size of these projectiles varies greatly, from fine dust particles to objects larger than 10 km in diameter. Statistically, we could expect an impact of an object greater than 1 km in diameter every 300,000 years, and one collision with an asteroid 10 km wide or larger every 100 million years. Comets are generated from the Oort Cloud (which envelopes the Solar System) and the Kuiper Belt (just outside the orbit of Neptune). Sometimes one of these comets is knocked out of its orbit and forms a new one around the Sun. Comets range in size from 1 to 30 km wide and travel much faster than asteroids.

If the orbit of an asteroid or comet were to cross that of a planet, and it ultimately crash into the planet, the results would be spectacular. Let's imagine a 20-km-wide comet hits Earth at 20 km per second. The initial impact would cause rocks and steam to be ejected into the atmosphere. Massive earthquakes would result and 200-m-high tidal waves would wreak havoc even in communities not directly on the coasts. The rock ejected by the collision would be returned to Earth, all over the globe. These fireballs would cause conflagrations that would consume oxygen and generate massive amounts of carbon dioxide and dust. The dust would block out the sunlight for years, causing acid rain, and resulting in massive global warming owing to the greenhouse effect. This is what happened 65 million years ago, and it could happen again. NASA's Near Earth Object Program monitors large cosmic objects that have orbits "close" to Earth. NASA has listed over 4,000 near-Earth objects, identifying almost 800 asteroids as potentially hazardous (passing within 7.5 million km of Earth). We have had several near misses in the past few years. Two asteroids in the 1990s passed within about 105,000 km of Earth (less than the distance to the Moon). In 2002, an asteroid about 80 m in diameter came within 120,000 km of Earth, and in 2004 another asteroid, measuring 30 m in diameter, came within 43,000 km.

Although the ultimate fate of life would depend on the size and speed of the object hitting Earth, it would also depend on the life forms themselves. Some life would survive even a devastating impact that wiped out most species. So, even if humans died, life on the planet would probably continue. Where's the hope in all this? Well, if it weren't for such a massive extinction, we would not be here. The death of the dinosaurs allowed for the emergence and evolution of other animals, for example the mammals, which would not have had the same opportunities had the dinosaurs survived. Thus, the evolution of humans may not have come about without this disaster. If such an impact were to occur again, and the human species on Earth were exterminated, there is still the possibility for life to go on, and for new and wonderful species to evolve.

If an impact with an asteroid or a comet is not enough to destroy all life on this planet, how about the impact of our galaxy with another? From the red shift we observe from other galaxies, we know that the universe is expanding. However, the close proximity of the Milky Way and the Andromeda galaxy counteracts this expansion model: our galaxies are moving closer together at about 100 km per second owing to gravitational pull. We can expect a collision in as little as 3 billion years. The collision of stars within the two galaxies may not occur, but the gravitational pull from stars in the two systems would likely alter the orbits of planets, flinging them into interstellar space. Without the Sun, without our stable orbit, life on Earth would almost certainly not survive.

Thus, any sort of galactic impact would likely destroy much of life on Earth, and would probably count the extinction of the human species as one of its consequences. But let's say we get lucky: we don't destroy ourselves and we avoid catastrophic collisions with large celestial bodies/galaxies. Will life (and humans) survive? In a word, no. Other hazards are lurking. Massive stars, toward the end of their lives, explode in supernovae, which cause the formation of heavier elements that become dispersed throughout the galaxy. These elements are the stuff that life is made of. However, if a supernova occurred close to Earth, it could destroy all life. There are no stars within 30 light years of Earth, the critical distance, predicted to have this fate. But supernovae from distant regions could increase cosmic radiation, amplifying the mutation rate in species on this planet for thousands of years, and potentially causing massive extinctions. We can also look to black holes for another catastrophic scenario. Black holes are formed when two neutron (very small and extremely dense) stars come into close proximity. The collision of the stars causes the emission of gamma rays which would be lethal if they occurred within 3,000 light years of Earth. We expect three such occurrences in the Milky Way every 100 million years. We know of two systems within this critical distance from Earth: one system will see neutron stars merge in 410 million years, and the other in 2.73 billion years.

The Fate of the Earth

Even if humans do survive all these catastrophes, all of life on Earth, and indeed the planet itself, will not survive the fate of the Sun. The Sun was formed about 5 billion years ago, and has another 5 billion years left to its life. The Sun burns hydrogen in its core. Once this is gone, the hydrogen in the shell will burn, and the core will contract, causing the temperature to rise. The burning shell will extend outward, and the Sun will increase to about 2,000 times its present luminosity. The temperature will decrease, and the Sun will become a red giant. Its atmosphere will envelop the inner planets – definitely Mercury and Venus, and probably Earth as well. Even if Earth is not consumed, life will no longer be possible as all the oceans will boil away. After about 1 billion years, the remaining hydrogen in the Sun will be burned, and the core will shrink, increasing its temperature. This will ignite the helium, making the Sun a yellow star. After the helium is consumed, the Sun will go through a red giant phase again, expanding beyond Earth. The outer layers of the Sun, containing carbon and silicon dust, will be pushed away from the Sun. The result will be a planetary nebula. The core will eventually collapse, and the Sun will be left as a white dwarf, roughly the size of the Earth.

The End of the Universe

So, let's say we advance enough technologically to send humans off the planet to colonize other planets in other solar systems or other galaxies. We avoid the end of the human race as foreseen by cosmological events. Will we exist forever? Again, the answer is no, because the universe will not survive. One way to determine the ultimate fate of the universe is to consider how much mass it contains. If its mass is above a critical threshold, the force of gravity will stop the expansion and the universe will contract and collapse in a "big crunch" (imagine a reversal of the big bang). The contraction will cause an increase in temperature which will destroy everything. However, if the mass is below a critical level, then the universe will expand forever: matter will become dispersed, preventing the formation of new stars and planets. So what is this mass and why don't we know precisely how much of it there is? Some of the mass is ordinary matter, the stuff that makes up atoms and molecules and larger particles. But there is another type of matter that contributes mass to the universe: dark matter. Dark matter is something different. We do not yet know what it's made of, but we know it's out there (this will be discussed below). Current evidence suggests the expanding universe theory is more likely. How long do we have? Something in the order of trillions of years.

But there is also the possibility of a "big rip": a tearing apart of galaxies, planets, and even atoms. In 1998, astronomers stumbled on evidence that indicated the expansion rate of the universe was accelerating. General relativity predicted the expansion rate would decrease because of gravitation between celestial bodies. So a theory was introduced to explain these results: the presence of dark energy, a force that counteracts gravity and causes galaxies to be hurled away from each other. Exactly what dark energy is, no one can say. Even its existence was questioned. But in 2003, the Wilkinson Microwave Anisotropy Probe (WMAP) made new measurements of the cosmic microwave background radiation, the same electromagnetic waves that confirmed the big bang theory. The satellite was able to detect the regions in the cosmos caused by the compressions and expansions of gas in the early universe. This led to a strange picture of the universe: WMAP told us the universe is made up of 4 percent ordinary matter, 23 percent dark matter and 73 percent dark energy. It also provided a better estimate of the age of the universe (13.7 billion years), gave us the current rate of expansion (71 km per second per megaparsec) and told us the shape of the universe (flat). Another project, the Slogan Digital Sky Survey (SDSS), analyzed the distribution of galaxies and reached the same conclusion as the WMAP data: the universe is made up largely of dark energy. And, when the data produced by WMAP and SDSS were combined, the question of the existence of dark energy could no longer be disputed. Currently, scientists are considering the nature of dark energy: if its strength is above a critical value, then the universe will end suddenly and violently in a big rip in about 20 billion years.

Views of the Eschaton

The scientific outlook for our future is quite dismal. There is no doubt about the fate of the Earth, and the only questions about the end of the universe concern the exact mechanism, not the ultimate outcome. As for the end of the human species, again, it's inevitable, but we don't yet know the path it will take. So what does all this mean for theology and eschatology? Does the scientific evidence help us in our understandings? Does it inform us about the consummation? And what of the greater message that eschatology conveys concerning the meaning and purpose of our lives? Is there hope in this world without a future?

The questions surrounding eternal life, heaven and hell, the kingdom of God, and hope are important ones, critical to our understanding of ourselves and our existence. Not surprisingly, there have been many thoughts on these and other issues. We will consider some of these views briefly, focusing on how theologians have incorporated scientific notions into their ideas.

Eternal Life

In our understanding of eschatology, some of the most prominent questions surround the concept of eternal life. Notions of time and eternity are complex issues, as we have already seen. In examining the concept of life after death, many of us tend to equate eternity with immortality. The New Testament speaks of resurrection, not immortality, so the conflation of the two terms may not be an accurate picture of what's to come. In our lives, we continue to develop constantly, particularly with our understanding of time. Think of a young child, who cannot remember her past or think of her future. To her, there is only the present, only the here and now. But as we grow and expand our understandings, we gain perspective, and we can begin to unify our existence from our past, present, and future. This is what eternal life is about: the unity of past, present, and future. Many believe the "eternity" we are promised after death is available to us in this life. But there is much more to come. In eternal life we will fulfill the potential God has given us.

Intimately associated with eternal life is the notion of judgment. We believe in the final judgment from God for all evil:

> The Son of man will send his angels, and they will gather out of his kingdom all causes of sin and all evildoers, and throw them into the furnace of fire; there men will weep and gnash their teeth. Then the righteous will shine like the sun in the kingdom of their Father. He who has ears, let him hear. (Matthew 13:41–3)

Many theological notions contend that judgment is not what happens only at the final judgment day, but that it is an ongoing process. The providence of God involves both judgment and grace, and thus judgment must be continuous. Providence is God's activity and guidance for creation. In opposing evil, God advances the divine plan toward the eschaton. Therefore, judgment is not left for the end, but is occurring now.

Jürgen Moltmann (b. 1926) is a Protestant theologian and a professor emeritus at Tübingen University whose work is embedded in the concept of hope. He began his theological studies in Allied prison camps during and after World War II. For Moltmann, death is an intermediate state between the life just lived and the eternal life yet to come. In this state, God completes our lives. Moltmann believes that God's judgment consists in righting the injustices of the life, and allows for the development of lives not yet complete, those cut short by premature death. The dead are in a community of hope with the living. We are all awaiting God's future.

Heaven, Hell, and What's in Between

We have many mythological notions of the place to which we may go after death. Heaven and hell have been described in many ways, but Christian theology stresses that our experience of eternal life will be our relationship, and our closeness, with God. Heaven can be seen as being close to God, and being like God, in a state of selflessness and loving. It is the goal of human existence. Hell is the loss of this closeness. It is the lack of fulfillment of potential. However, this loss will never be complete: we are never beyond the reach of God, never beyond reconciliation. Therefore, heaven and hell can be seen as two extremes in our relationship with God.

Some view hell not as punishment, but as a state of the working out of sin. We cannot sever our connection to God, only God can do this. Therefore, we can always improve our relationship with God. This means there are intermediate states between heaven and hell, a concept known as purgatory in the Catholic Church. The notion of purgatory is not universal: Protestant theologians tend to reject it. However, several beliefs force us to consider that there must be some intermediate state: heaven and hell are "limits" that we approach in our closeness to God; God's reconciliation is available to both the living and the dead; and all of creation will be saved. Purgatory and hell can be considered as a continuum, with purgatory being a process of purification. This purification does not mean the suffering of external pain, but rather suffering with Christ, experiencing the death and resurrection of Jesus in order to become closer to God.

> For there is no distinction; since all have sinned and fall short of the glory of God, they are justified by his grace as a gift, through the redemption which is in Christ Jesus. (Romans 3:22–4)

What makes us alive? Is it the beating of our hearts, or our closeness to God? We can think of being dead in the spirit when we are away from God, even though we are biologically alive. We can be in hell while we are living. But redemption is ongoing. We can become closer to God while we are alive and after our biological death.

The New Testament stresses that individual death will not sever our relationship with God.

Kathryn Tanner of the University of Chicago Divinity School has formulated an eschatology within a foundation of hope. She contends that we have eternal life in God: beyond death we no longer just have a relationship *with* God, but *in* God. This relationship cannot be broken by sin or death. We are always alive in God, no matter our faults. The end will see our total dependence on God. Eternal life is ours now. It is not a futuristic notion, and it is not otherworldly. Therefore, the fate of the world is not what matters. Eternal life has not yet been fulfilled. More is to come once we are fully dependent on God. We are immortal, both before and after our deaths, because we are dependent on an eternal God.

The Kingdom of God

What will be the ultimate fate of all humans, the world, and the cosmos? It will be the full manifestation of God's plan, a united creation in God and in love. The kingdom is partly realized now, and humans can help to make the kingdom. But it ultimately requires the action and grace of God. It is beyond history, and will not be realized on Earth.

Science is telling us the end of the world does not have to come about through supernatural intervention – nature will take care of this. If the end is discontinuous, if we await a new creation, then science cannot comment on it. But if God will usher in a new age that is discontinuous, this begs the question, "Why didn't the creation begin without pain and suffering?" John Polkinghorne, Anglican priest and former professor of mathematical physics at the University of Cambridge, has written much in the field of science and religion. He contends that God is not starting over with a new age, but rather redeeming the old world. We will see it as discontinuous yet also continuous, just as we can view the resurrection of Jesus: the scars of the crucifixion were retained but Christ appeared in a transformed, glorious body. If this view is correct, Polkinghorne contends, then science may be able to contribute to the conversation on a metascientific level: we may be able to use some of the views and principles of science to understand the possible continuities of a new creation.

If discontinuity will prevent a rehash of the old, then where does continuity fit into the picture? Continuity stems from the notion that each person will be resurrected after death, and we will hold on to our identity. How can we understand this apparent contrast between the aspects that will be different (everything) and those that will remain the same (our identities)? Polkinghorne looks at models of energy and patterns to help in this venture. Energy, matter, and natural laws have to be different in the new creation, because death and suffering will no longer exist. This is impossible in our current world: the old creation has been able to construct itself through evolution, where death is the cost of life. The continuity to the new creation will be the soul, which can be understood as a pattern, or form, of our individual bodies. Polkinghorne argues that what will be important in this identity is relationships: much of who we are is based on our interaction with other people and with God. We will all be incorporated into the one body of Christ. The complex pattern that makes up an individual will be held in the divine mind at death, waiting reembodiment in the new creation. Polkinghorne ties this idea into the scientific understanding of relativity, which he says is a general characteristic of created order: space, time, and matter are all together, and thus resurrected beings will be located in space, time, and matter as well. The continuity will be the everlasting destiny, not a temporal eternity. The time in the old creation versus the new creation does not have to be sequential, thus these worlds could exist along side each other. Continuity could also represent the resurrection of souls from one "space" to the other, at the same "time." There would be no "gap" or "holding pattern" from one world to the next.

Hope

Before we begin our discussion of hope, we need to understand that hope is different from optimism. Fraser Watts, the Starbridge lecturer in theology and natural sciences at the University of Cambridge, identifies four characteristics that separate these two concepts:

- *Optimism is a measurement of the probability of an occurrence*: the more likely the event, the more optimistic we will be. Hope occurs in uncertainty, indeed in some of the most trying of times and in the face of overwhelming adversity.
- *Hope is circumscribed by moral values*; optimism is not. We can be optimistic about any event, but we are hopeful only about good things.
- *We hope for what is important to us*. We do not hope for things of little value. We can be optimistic about trivial things, such as the weather, but we are hopeful about the recovery of a critically ill child.
- *We take action for hope*. We will do what we can to make things happen when we are hopeful. We do not act on optimism.

As we have seen, eschatological ideas are not just about the end of the world or the end of life. They help to shape our attitudes about our past, present, and future, about ourselves and our efforts in this life. Christian eschatology centers on the resurrection of Christ, his triumph over death. And an important part of eschatology is hope. Hope can be viewed as realized eschatology: it is eschatology that has entered the present. Hope is the faith we have in God that we carry into the future. We have seen the power and creativity of God, and we can wait for the future that God has in store for us. We have been promised resurrection after death, so hope can be valid for life only if it is valid for death. We will have a new relationship with God that will not be limited by our earthly life, or tainted by sin. God has promised a good future. This is a promise, not a prediction.

We have hope in God, in the kingdom where there will be no more suffering. Some have argued that science has deflated hope. The mechanical models of science prevalent in the seventeenth century can certainly be seen in this light. Our confidence in technology, progress, and control over our lives and over nature have led us down some blind alleys and created problems we did not foresee and cannot seem to solve. We have even been so bold as to think we were "playing God," or seeing like God. Our epistemology separated the "natural" and "spiritual" worlds, that is, the real world of facts from the inner knowledge of our values. By admitting that we are part of nature, that we are created beings, we can again enter into a better relationship with God. By understanding that we cannot see or do as God does, we open ourselves to the promise and wisdom of God. We have seen what is possible with God. Hope maintains a link between the foreseeable future and the ideal future, and calls us to work toward the ideal. Hope calls for action, for commitment to a better future. Our commitment to God's future will help us discover what it means to be human.

But we are still left with the scientific understanding of the fate of life and of the universe. Can we reinterpret theology to provide hope for a world that science says must end? Tanner takes a page from past reflections: theology was able to cope with the possibility that the universe is eternal by stressing that the world is a creation of God, whether or not it had a beginning and regardless of the exact process. She argues that we can take a similar approach with eschatology. The actual end of the world has just as little importance as its actual beginning. Creation teaches us that we are dependent on God. Eschatology is a focus not necessarily on the future, but rather on the world as a whole. Our relationship with the redeemer God is an important facet, and not the ultimate end, of life. Our hope today is not in nature, that it will prevail, but in God's promise. Recall that Tanner contends that we already have eternal life, which itself leads to many questions. If we already have eternal life, what does this mean for hope and for action? Is there any hope? What is there left to hope for? And why should we act? If we already have eternal life, is there any point in trying to relieve the suffering of the here and now? Tanner believes that life in God calls us to action. We are obligated to fight against poverty, injustice, and the myriad other evils of this world. Action takes on new meaning in this view: it is unconditional. We are more like God, giving of ourselves and helping to continue the divine creation. By these actions we express our gratitude and love.

Conclusions

Comparing theological notions of eschatology and scientific notions of the end of life highlights some interesting parallels. God promises us new life, a new world, and a new age, which depend on the death and destruction of the old. Science also illustrates the importance of death before new life emerges: supernovae are the death of stars, but the resulting material can be used for the formation of new celestial objects and life. After the mass extinction of species, we see an increasing diversity of new species that flourish and evolve in the absence of the old. Thus, the end can be a new beginning, in both science and theology.

However, we must ask if the end in theology is the same as the end in science. Theologically, the end is a continued life in God. Scientifically, our understanding of the end, similar to our understanding of the beginning, is not yet complete. Our universe may fade away in a never-ending expansion, till all that's left is space dust. But our fate may be one of unending cycles, of successive big bangs and big crunches, or oscillating universes. And we can still consider the possibility that ours is not the only universe. If other universes exist, the matter, energy, and laws of physics may be very different from what we have in our universe. The end of our universe would not necessarily mean that others would also terminate. Here we have another parallel between science and theology: we cannot know our ultimate fate until we get there.

Lastly, the ideas in theology and science are interrelated. The events that occur in the cosmos directly affect life on Earth, as we have seen in several instances. And life on this planet is also closely interrelated in a complex and fascinating web, which we will continue to explore in later chapters. In Christian theology, the concepts of creation, reconciliation, and eschatology are bound together, and our conception of ourselves cannot be complete without considering all three. A common thread between science and religion is the study of the unseen, and a common thread for all humanity is hope for a unknowable future:

> For the creation waits with eager longing for the revealing of the sons of God; for the creation was subjected to futility, not of its own will but by the will of him who subjected it in hope; because the creation itself will be set free from its bondage to decay and obtain the glorious liberty of the children of God. We know that the whole creation has been groaning in travail together until now; and not only the creation, but we ourselves, who have the first fruits of the Spirit, groan inwardly as we wait for adoption as sons, the redemption of our bodies. For in this hope we were saved. Now hope that is seen is not hope. For who hopes for what he sees? But if we hope for what we do not see, we wait for it with patience. (Romans 8:19–25)

Primary Literature

Useful primary sources include two biblical texts: Mark 13:1–37 and 2 Peter 3:1–18; an excerpt from Origen's *De principiis* (Book I, Chapter VI); and an excerpt from the Catechism of the Catholic Church regarding the Profession of Faith (Part I, Section 2, Chapter 2, Article 7). It would be interesting to revisit, at this time, the article by Paul Tillich, "Man, the Earth and the Universe."

Questions to Consider

1   Consider the shift from apocalyptic eschatology to postmillennialism that began in the Enlightenment. How is this shift consistent with the change in thinking that occurred during this time period?
2   How are creation, redemption and eschatology related?
3   How important is the concept of the soul in eschatology? Discuss one understanding of soul (as an immortal entity, as a relationship with God, or as a "time-bridge") and the role it plays in one view of eschatology.
4   How important is the notion of time for the different concepts of eschatology? Do your views of time correspond to any of those discussed in the chapter (consider the views of Augustine, Pannenberg, Tillich, Peters and Einstein)?

5   How important is the timing of the eschaton in relation to its meaning in our present life?

6   Consider a current or recent tragedy that has affected a large number of people (a war, hurricane, earthquake, disease outbreak, etc.). Compare and contrast elements of hope and elements of optimism for that population. How will these elements change as time passes? Does this notion of change over time say something about eschatology? Explain your answer.

7   We focused in this chapter on humans. However, as we discussed earlier, all of creation is good and special to God. And, as discussed in this chapter, creation is interwoven with eschatology. What might this mean for species other than humans?

Part III
Evolution

8

Darwin Changes Everything

Overview

Ideas regarding evolution go back to the ancient Greeks, but a literal interpretation of the Bible denied the notion of change. Mounting anomalies from geology and paleontology forced a paradigm shift from that of special creation and the immutability of species to Darwin's idea of evolution via natural selection. Advances in other fields, including taxonomy, comparative anatomy, and economics, helped formulate and support Darwin's evolutionary theory. His conclusion that change was not driven by divine intervention was in direct conflict with natural theology. Some tried to fit evolution into this theological framework, but others totally rejected the scientific view. American society is still involved in this debate, particularly regarding what can and should be taught in the science classroom.

Introduction

We can look back at various periods in time and see when true scientific revolutions occurred – events that not only caused a paradigm shift, but that also changed the face of science forever. In some rare cases, these situations also impacted greatly on society, religion, and theology. The Galileo affair is one instance. Another is the development of the theory of natural selection, proposed in 1859 by Charles Darwin in his book *On the Origin of Species*. The controversy surrounding Darwin's ideas continues to rage, as we shall see in subsequent chapters. This is quite a legacy for a young man who dropped out of medical school!

As we shall see, evolution (change with time) was not a novel concept proposed by Darwin. It was an idea that had been considered for thousands of years. The importance of Darwin lay in his explanation of evolution, his proposal of how things change with time. Not only did his ideas alter our understandings of science but the impact of these ideas on religion and culture had long-lasting effects and widespread repercussions. In this chapter we will begin a journey to understand the theory and implications of evolution. We will examine ideas about evolution before Darwin, take a look at his background and events that helped him formulate his ideas, and consider some of the effects he had on science and religion. In later chapters we will discuss the evidence for evolution and other related topics.

Ideas before Darwin

We cannot understand how Darwin's ideas were formed, nor can we understand the responses to them, until we have some knowledge regarding the world in which he lived. Like all of us, Darwin was a product of his time and his culture.

As we discussed in chapter 1, the ancient Greeks did not use gods and magic to explain natural phenomena. The notion of change through time was no different. Anaximander, as we saw in chapter 5, invented a cosmology based on logic and reasoning. He proposed that fishlike creatures came onto the land and changed as the conditions on Earth changed, and that eventually, man developed from these creatures. Empedocles (c.492–c.432 BCE) proposed a cosmic cycle where organisms developed in different stages: only those that had special skills survived and reproduced. As we shall see, both of these ideas parallel Darwin's notions of natural selection and descent with modification. The fossil record was also examined. Xenophanes of Colophan (576–490 BCE) concluded that the Earth and sea had changed places. How else could fossilized shells be found far from the seas, even in mountains?

The Greeks addressed notions of design and purpose (teleology) in their philosophies. Aristotle and Plato concluded from their studies of nature that biological organisms were designed. They differed in that Aristotle's teleology did not invoke a deity to explain the acts of creation. Theopharates (c.373–c.285 BCE) rejected the notion of teleology, observing that nature does not appear to act with purpose, and that design is not always evident. He argued that invoking teleology provided for quick answers to questions, but the conclusions were not necessarily meaningful. As we shall see, Darwin also rejected teleology.

Galen (130–200), the famous physician, commented extensively on design. He saw design in all things. Through his dissection of animals, he concluded that nature acts with perfect wisdom. All organs and parts of the body were made specifically for their unique functions; there was no waste. Although he did not comment directly on notions of evolution, Galen's work provided for future investigations that were vital to the development of evolutionary theories. Galen was considered *the* medical authority, and his work was treated much like Aristotle's. His writings were preserved by the Arabs and later translated for a European audience. Unfortunately, Galen's appeal to relying on one's own work and not on authority, was largely overlooked and lost in translation. Although his ideas were disproved in the sixteenth and seventeenth centuries, Galen's influence continued into the nineteenth century.

The "Modern Science" that Shaped Darwin's Ideas

Science in the Middle Ages, as we have seen, was based mainly on consultation of the authorities. The period was not fertile ground for the advancement of evolutionary thought. However, the ideas of the Enlightenment helped to set the stage for the development of modern evolutionary ideas. Recall that one result of the Enlightenment was a literal interpretation of the Bible. With regard to the creation of living things as described in Genesis, the church, and the scientific community, set forth the notion that all living things had been created as they exist today.

> And God said, "Let the earth bring forth living creatures according to their kinds: cattle and creeping things and beasts of the earth according to their kinds." And it was so. And God made the beasts of the earth according to their kinds and the cattle according to their kinds, and everything that creeps upon the ground according to its kind. And God saw that it was good. (Genesis 1:24–5)

Species were unchanging, immutable. However, evidence began to accumulate that was to challenge these ideas. Scientific progress in multiple disciplines would ultimately provide the necessary pieces that Darwin assembled into a coherent theory of how evolution occurs.

The studies of Andreas Vesalius (1514–64) allowed for major advances in anatomy and provided some of the early evidence to support evolution. He was the first to perform extensive dissection of human corpses. He found much of Galen's writings to be inaccurate, because Galen had not been allowed to study humans in this manner. Vesalius compiled a masterpiece, *De humani corporis fabrica libri septum* (The Seven Books on the Structure of the Human Body), with magnificently detailed illustrations of human skeletons and musculature. Through his work, it became possible to compare and contrast living organisms accurately. It was now easy to observe, on this level, that humans were amazingly similar to other animals.

Another branch of science that was making progress was paleontology. Although fossils had been known since ancient times, exactly what they were remained a mystery. Nicolas Steno (1638–86) is credited with being the first to understand the nature of fossils. Steno's work also led him to propose a theory of how geological strata are formed. "Tongue stones," pieces of rock shaped like triangles, had been known for centuries, but their significance had not hitherto been understood. By studying the teeth of a modern-day shark, Steno concluded that tongue stones were actually shark teeth that had been turned to rock. He deduced that the material in the tooth was gradually replaced by minerals from the environment. Steno also accounted for the position of the tongue stones inside larger rocks with his law of superposition: the strata in the earth were laid out, over time, by the settling of rocks and minerals on top of each other (sedimentation). He proposed that fossils were once living beings that had been trapped in these geological layers. Therefore, these strata corresponded to the period in which the fossils had lived. William Smith (1769–1839) used these ideas to determine the relative ages of the different strata. He dated each layer based on the fossils found within that particular section of earth.

The field of paleontology advanced with the studies of Georges Cuvier (1769–1832). Cuvier used the anatomy of existing animals to deduce how fossilized animals functioned. As the fossil record grew, it became apparent that numerous animals had existed in the past that were no longer found in the present. Cuvier reasoned that these organisms had died out, or became extinct, and concluded that catastrophes had caused the extinctions.

Cuvier's ideas posed a distinct problem with regard to religious doctrine. Most people during this time believed that God had created the Earth and all life on it according to a divine plan. It was not logical to think that God would allow these special creations to die off. In addition, it was believed that all life constituted a great chain of being, a ladder-like hierarchy with the lower forms of life near the bottom, and man in the middle. Demons and angels were placed above man, and God was at the top. If organisms became extinct, this would interrupt the chain.

Beginning in the seventeenth century, extensive exploration and colonization exposed Europeans to new worlds and new wonders. More and more plant and animal species were being "discovered" and described. Cataloging the new finds proved difficult, and there was a need for a classification system to organize these diverse life forms. Carolus Linnaeus (1707–78) invented the system that is still in use today. He standardized the nomenclature of all organisms, using the categories of genus and species to identify an organism uniquely. But he also grouped genera into families, families into orders, orders into classes, and classes into kingdoms. The groupings were based on physical characteristics shared by the organisms. This led him to place humans, orang-utans, and chimpanzees in the same genus (*Homo*).

Linnaeus did not intend his ideas simply to allow for classification. He also saw his efforts as an extension of the work God gave to Adam:

> So out of the ground the Lord God formed every beast of the field and every bird of the air, and brought them to the man to see what he would call them; and whatever the man called every living creature, that was its name. The man gave names to all cattle, and to the birds of the air, and to every beast of the field; but for the man there was not found a helper fit for him. (Genesis 2:19–20)

Linnaeus believed that, by organizing life in this manner, he would approach an understanding of God's design in nature. Publicly, Linnaeus espoused the religious doctrine that all life was created in the forms present on Earth in his day. However, given his knowledge of animal and plant breeding, he was aware of variations that could arise, and he privately questioned the idea of organisms being fixed in their forms. It is interesting that Linnaeus considered humans to be God's special creation, and yet he treated them like every other living thing, by grouping them with similar organisms, in the same genus as the apes.

The last major scientific advancements we need to consider before our discussion of evolution were in the field of geology. Geology and paleontology are intimately connected, as we have seen in the work of Steno and Smith. The accumulating scientific evidence indicated that the Earth was very old. However, popular belief held that the Earth was less than 7,000 years old, an estimate that was based on the genealogical lineages in the Bible. Many geologists, including the Rev. Adam Sedgwick (1785–1873), saw evidence of the events in the Bible, particularly the great flood, in geological formations. Catastrophes caused changes in the Earth and supported the biblical accounts. Other geologists, such as James Hutton (1726–97) and Charles Lyell (1797–1875), argued that the Earth changed slowly, over long periods of time, a theory known as uniformitarianism. At the heart of uniformitarianism was the notion that the changes we see today are due to the same forces that existed, and acted, in the past. Changes occurred gradually, often imperceptibly, through processes such as erosion. Lyell's work was first published in 1830–3, in his three-volume *Principles of Geology*, which greatly influenced Darwin. Incidentally, Sedgwick recanted his views in 1831, and concluded that the Bible contained information to guide us in the moral sphere, not in the scientific one.

In a strange twist, Darwin's ideas were also greatly influenced by an area outside the natural sciences. The Rev. Thomas Robert Malthus (1766–1834) was an economist with a rather pessimistic message. In *An Essay on the Principle of Population as It Affects the Future Improvement of Society*, published in 1798, Malthus described the growth of the human population as geometric (exponential), but the growth of the food supply as arithmetic (linear). This meant the population would eventually outgrow the food supply, leading to famine, starvation, and death. Malthus stated that the only reason this had not yet occurred was due to natural checks on the population, such as diseases and plagues. He suggested some rather radical solutions to postpone the ultimate fate. For example, he argued that giving money to the poor would allow them to have more children, which would contribute to the problem, so, we could slow down the reproductive rate and delay the inevitable if we were to refrain from helping this segment of society. There were, however, some positive consequences from his work. Darwin extended Malthus's ideas to argue that, not only were reproduction and competition at work within the human population, but also within every other living thing. This was central to Darwin's theory.

Pre-Darwinian Notions of Evolution

As we have seen, many scientific discoveries were beginning to challenge religious notions about the creation of species. Whereas species were supposed to be fixed and unchanged, observations of fossils and the results of breeding indicated that organisms could change and even become extinct. Therefore, the idea that living things change with time, that evolution takes place, was becoming more evident and harder to ignore. Jean Baptiste Pierre Antoine de Monet, Chevalier de Lamarck (1744–1829) suggested exactly how and why living things change. Lamarck was a botanist by training, and later in life became an expert on invertebrates. He too noticed variations in organisms, and was struck by the ever growing fossil record. Lamarck concluded that life was not fixed, but changed with time. What caused the changes? Lamarck had two answers:

1   As environments change, so must the organisms that live in them, in order to survive. The changes would come about through the use or disuse of anatomical structures. If an organ was no longer used, it would eventually shrink and lose its function entirely. But if an organ was required, and if it was being used more and more, it had the capacity to change slightly (become larger, stronger, etc.). The changes made

within an individual creature during its lifetime would be passed on to its offspring. This inheritance of acquired characteristics provided a way to explain evolution. Eventually, given enough time, changes would accumulate and alter the organism. The classic example is the giraffe stretching its neck over many generations to reach the leaves on trees.

2   Lamarck didn't just try to explain how organisms evolve, he also tried to explain why they evolve. He concluded that life began through spontaneous generation (life from nonlife). Nature "called" these new life forms to become more complex with time, until they reached the ultimate life form, humans. Therefore, bacteria were spontaneously coming into existence all the time, and starting their long journey to become increasingly complex. If the environment changed, organisms produced modifications to survive. If the environment remained stable, organisms would continue on their journey toward complexity.

Although Lyell opposed Lamarck's ideas, it was largely his attacks on them that exposed the English-speaking world to Lamarck's notions of evolution. Many scientists rejected Lamarck's theory because of its theological implications, which we will discuss below. But some studied his ideas and adopted them. Others at the time formulated similar ideas. Erasmus Darwin (1731–1802), the grandfather of Charles, believed in the transmutation of species, that organisms had the ability to change, to gain new properties and behaviors, and to pass these on to their offspring. All living things were related through descent. He wrote three books, *Zoonomia*, *The Botanic Garden*, and *The Temple of Nature*, all of which were placed on the *Index of Prohibited Books* (the list of books considered by the Catholic Church to be immoral or to contain theological flaws that could corrupt the faithful).

Since the time of the ancient Greeks, nature had been used to demonstrate God's design, and the study of nature had helped to glorify God and understand this design. This idea became known as natural theology (see chapter 2). In 1691, John Ray (1627–1705) published *The Wisdom of God as Manifested in the Works of Creation*. Ray concluded there was order and purpose in nature, and that by studying nature one could see God's design. Like Linnaeus, Ray considered the classification of living things to be an extension of the work God had given to Adam. Most scientists in England worked under the paradigm of natural theology, accepting that the book of God (the Bible) and the observations of nature could not be in conflict. In Darwin's time, the writings of the Rev. William Paley (1743–1805) were well known. In his book, *Natural Theology; or, Evidences of the Existence and Attributes of the Deity, Collected from the Appearances of Nature* (1802), Paley used an analogy to explain the premise of natural theology. Imagine you are walking across a field and you come upon a pocket watch. As you examine it closely, you notice how complex it is, how perfectly all the pieces fit together, how well it works. You know it must have been designed. So the evidence from nature, its perfection and complexity, tells us there was a designer, God, who made all living things.

The conclusions of Lamarck and others meant that species were not designed by God, but were formed according to blind, random forces. Lamarck contended that change took place as a result of natural events, not through the intervention of God. This was in direct contrast to the notions of natural theology.

It was into this mix of natural theology and newly emerging ideas in the fields of science and economics that Darwin was born. He used these ideas to help explain his own observations and to formulate a theory of evolution that has withstood the test of time.

Along Comes Darwin...

Charles Robert Darwin (1809–82) was born to Robert Waring Darwin, a wealthy English physician, and Susannah Wedgwood Darwin, also from a well-to-do family (fig. 8.1). Charles was sent to Edinburgh to study medicine and to follow in his father's and grandfather's footsteps. Edinburgh exposed Darwin to a cosmopolitan atmosphere, where ideas were discussed freely, and where his horizons were broadened. He listened to radical views, including those regarding the feasibility of Lamarckian evolution. Although Edinburgh was intellectually stimulating, Darwin was not interested in medicine, and left after witnessing nineteenth-century surgical procedures. His father then sent him to Cambridge University to train for the Church of England. Darwin was not particularly enthusiastic about becoming ordained, but he was drawn to studies of natural history,

Fig. 8.1 Charles Darwin, by George Richmond. Watercolor on paper, 1840. (Down House, Kent, UK/The Bridgeman Art Library)

and came under the influence of two of his instructors, Adam Sedgwick, who taught geology, and John Stevens Henslow (1796–1861), who taught botany. It was Henslow who recommended Darwin for a position as a companion to the captain of the HMS *Beagle*. After much persuasion, Robert Darwin allowed his 22-year-old son to depart on the historic voyage.

The *Beagle* set sail in December 1831. Its task was to survey Patagonia and Tierra del Fuego, and it was to circumnavigate the globe (fig. 8.2). Life was not luxurious on the *Beagle*, to say the least. Darwin slept in a hammock and discovered that he was prone to horrible seasickness. He became the *de facto* naturalist on board when the ship's surgeon (and naturalist) left in April 1832. The *Beagle* spent much of its time surveying the coasts of South America, where Darwin observed and collected unusual creatures and interesting fossils. During September and October 1835, the ship traveled to the now famous Galapagos Islands, an archipelago located off the coast of Ecuador. Although it provided spectacular examples of evolution, the archipelago probably did not influence Darwin's ideas to the extent that is often thought. Darwin kept records and diaries of the voyage, and began to question the prevailing biblical view of the immutability of species, to which he had hitherto subscribed. When the *Beagle* returned to England in October 1836, Darwin had honed his observation and reasoning skills, and was a much better scientist. However, he had not yet tackled the problem of evolution, and he would not publish on it for over 20 years. In 1839 he married his cousin, Emma Wedgwood (1808–96). As the Darwins and the Wedgwoods were financially comfortable, he did not have to be employed in a profession. Darwin settled into country life in Downe, where he continued his studies of the natural world. He became well known in Britain for his expertise in geology. He joined the Geological Society and eventually became the secretary. Through his work, he met many influential scientists and intellectuals, including Lyell and the botanist Joseph Hooker (1817–1911), both of whom became trusted friends and advisers. Darwin's health steadily deteriorated after his journey on the *Beagle*, and he was chronically ill for the remainder of his life. Despite ill health, he lived to a fairly advanced age. He died in 1882, outliving three of his 10 children. Darwin was buried in Westminster Abbey, with scientists and church officials in attendance.

Let's take a moment to summarize the ideas that were prevalent during Darwin's time.

- Advancements in the fields of classification (taxonomy), anatomy, paleontology, and geology were changing ideas in both science and religion.
- Gradualism and the notion of an old Earth were discussed in the writings of Lyell.
- Concepts of evolution, as described by Lamarck and outlined in Erasmus's book, *Zoonomia*, were well known.
- Malthus described what would happen to human populations as a result of competition for limited food supplies.
- Natural theology, as described by Paley and others, was widely accepted by scientists of the day, including Darwin.

Within this framework, Darwin formulated his ideas: descent with modification and natural selection.

(a)

(b)

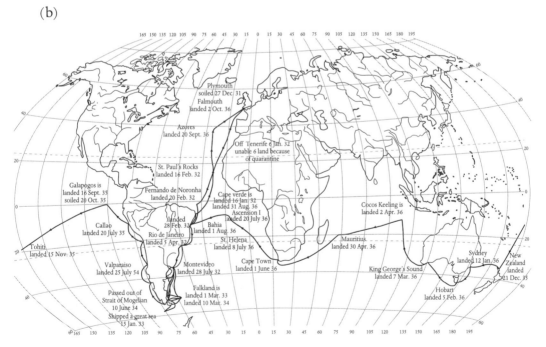

Fig. 8.2 (*a*) HMS *Beagle* carrying Charles Darwin's expedition in the Straits of Magellan, Mount Sarmiento in the distance, 1890. (© Bettmann/Corbis) (*b*) Map showing Darwin's voyages.

Darwin's Observations and Interpretations

What exactly did Darwin see and how did he interpret his observations? Time and again, on the voyage of the *Beagle*, as well as during his later investigations back in England, Darwin noted that all organisms produced more offspring than would survive to reproduce themselves (overproduction), and that each individual in a population has distinct and unique traits (variations). These variations would be inherited in the offspring. Darwin applied the principles of Malthus, namely the competition for food in human society, to all living things. If the individuals of any species have to compete for limited resources, then not all the organisms that are born will survive to reproduce. Therefore, there are checks that will limit the population size. Given that all individuals within a population have different traits and variations, some of those traits may give an individual an advantage in this competition, and these individuals are more likely to survive and reproduce. As variations are heritable, their offspring would also possess these advantageous traits. Given a long period of time, the population would gradually change on the basis of the selective pressures of the environment. Darwin called this idea natural selection. Such a selection is based on the environment: a change in the environment would make some traits more or less favorable to survival. The gradual changes caused by natural selection could accumulate, eventually forming a new species. By extending this idea over a long period of time, Darwin concluded that the species existing today came from one or a few common ancestors, an idea known as descent with modification.

Darwin wrote down his ideas in two papers in 1842 and in 1844 but did not publish them. His close friends, including Lyell and Hooker, knew of his work and encouraged him to publish. He began work on his book in 1856. However, before he could finish it, Darwin received a letter from Alfred Russel Wallace (1823–1913), a naturalist working in the Malay archipelago in 1858. The letter contained Wallace's paper entitled "On the Tendency of Varieties to Depart Indefinitely from the Original Type." Darwin and Wallace had corresponded before, and Darwin knew of another work by Wallace published in 1855 in the *Annals of Natural History*, which hinted at ideas on the divergence of species. However, in the 1858 paper, Wallace described what was essentially natural selection. Wallace asked Darwin to look over the paper and send it on to Lyell to read at a meeting of the Linnaean Society. Darwin was shocked at how similar Wallace's ideas were to his own. Lyell and Hooker arranged to have Darwin's 1844 essay, and a letter he had sent to the American botanist Asa Gray (1810–88) in 1857, read with Wallace's paper at a meeting of the Linnaean Society. Darwin finished his book and, finally, on November 22, 1859, *On the Origin of Species by Means of Natural Selection* was published. It went through six editions in Darwin's lifetime. Wallace and Darwin remained friends and collaborators, but Wallace has largely become a footnote in the history of evolution.

Although *Origin of Species* did not address human evolution, it was Darwin's conclusion that humans were no different from any other living species, and that the laws of nature apply to us as well, in other words, we have evolved to our present form. He addressed human evolution in *The Descent of Man, and Selection in Relation to Sex* in 1871. The ideas in this book show the predictive power of the theory of natural selection: although there was little fossil evidence, Darwin concluded that humans and apes had a common ancestor, and that humans originated in a warm climate, probably in Africa.

Questions

Two important questions are often asked about *Origin of Species* and Darwin, namely why he waited so long to publish, and what his religious views were. Neither has a straightforward answer.

Why did Darwin wait so long to publish his work? We can look at a variety of factors that probably contributed to the delay:

- Darwin realized his views would be considered unorthodox and offensive to many on religious grounds. He may have been reluctant to suffer the backlash, but he may also have wanted to spare his wife, Emma, who was a very religious woman (a Unitarian), this pain. One can only imagine the burdens she bore: caring for her children, tending to her frequently ill husband, and praying for his immortal soul.
- He wanted to accumulate as much scientific evidence as he could, to strengthen his argument. His omission of a discussion on the evolution of humans in *Origin of Species* was calculated. He knew that this would have detracted from the evidence he presented.
- His chronic illness, and the death of three of his children, may have influenced his decisions.
- Timing is important. The pieces were in place for developing the idea of natural selection; all that was needed was someone to come along and put them together. Lyell knew Darwin was not the only one who could do this. He encouraged his friend to publish before someone else did. Lyell was right, and it is an interesting turn of events that ultimately led to the reading of Darwin's paper at the Linnaean Society.

As for Darwin's religious views, he started out as a Christian, and accepted the views of natural theology. He did not want, or intend, to abandon Christianity. His faith faded through the years, and he eventually became an agnostic. Why did this happen? Again, we can look at several factors that may have contributed to his shift.

- The death of his father and his three children, especially his 10-year-old daughter Anne, took their toll on him. It is often in times of crisis that people lose their faith, and Darwin may have been no different.
- Natural selection, by its very definition, is a cruel process. Many organisms come into being only to die. Whole species are wiped out in extinctions. There is massive waste and suffering associated with natural selection. Darwin had difficulty with this theodicy, in reconciling the cruelty apparent in nature with a kind and loving God who had created it.
- He also rejected the idea of eternal damnation inherent in some religions on the grounds that it was immoral.

The Scientific Aftermath

Origin of Species is a work comprising extensive examples of natural selection. We will examine some of the evidence for evolution, both in Darwin's time and what we've learned since then, in chapter 10. The remainder of this chapter will focus on the responses to Darwin's ideas.

The evidence Darwin supplies is impressive indeed, and some would say overwhelming. However, there are specific issues he could not address, and problems he could not solve. He devoted an entire chapter in *Origin* to these problems. It is interesting to examine this situation through the lens of Thomas Kuhn. When a paradigm shift occurs, the new paradigm needs to answer the questions of the old one, and more. But it may not answer everything, yet.

Among the most intransigent of the problems that could not be addressed was the apparent inability of natural selection and gradualism to account for the formation of new species, and the lack of a mechanism to account for how traits are inherited. Darwin speculated that natural selection takes so long that we cannot see, in a lifetime, the accumulation of changes that would result in a new species. Although many of the geologists of the day subscribed to the notion of an old Earth, the estimates of its age were still too young to account for the production of new species via gradualism. William Thomson (1824–1907), better known as Lord Kelvin, was a physicist who estimated that the Sun could have existed for only 100–500 million years. Although this would allow for an Earth far older than the biblical estimates of 7,000 years, it would not provide enough time for natural selection to work. Thomas Henry Huxley (1825–95), an ardent supporter of Darwin, argued that geology and biology could also be used to estimate the age of the Earth, and so we have reason to believe it is much older. The physicists had to wait for Henri Bequerel (1852–1908) to discover radioactivity, which can be used to estimate the age of materials accurately. Today's science puts the age of the Earth at about 4.7 billion years, long enough for natural selection to form new species.

The lack of a mechanism for inheritance was perhaps the most difficult to counter of the objections to Darwin's theory. The commonly held idea of the day revolved around blending inheritance: the traits of the parents were blended to produce the offspring. If, as Darwin claimed, a variation occurred in an individual, then the offspring of the individual would not show the same trait, as it would be blended with the traits from the other parent. Therefore the trait would, in essence, disappear in subsequent generations. Interestingly, part of the answer to this question was not far off. Gregor Mendel (1822–84), a priest in an Augustinian monastery in Brno, now part of the Czech Republic, cultivated peas in the monastery garden to discover the true method of inheritance. Mendel realized that traits were not blended in the offspring, but were inherited in discrete units (today we call them alleles or genes). The combination of these units determined the appearance of the offspring and the traits it would have; blending did not occur. Mendel published his work in 1865, but it went largely unnoticed in his lifetime, and Darwin could never account for the inheritance problem. This had to wait until the turn of the century, when Mendel's work was rediscovered and expanded into the new field of genetics.

The Theological Reactions

In addition to scientific problems, Darwin's theory of evolution posed moral, philosophical, and theological problems.

- *The scientific method itself was in question.* Darwin provided much evidence for natural selection, but his critics did not think his speculations and probable explanations should be accepted over and above the truth of God's action in the world as revealed in the Bible.
- *God's agency in the world became a central problem.* Darwin assumed that only natural forces were at work. This meant there was no design by a creator. New species did not come about by miraculous divine intervention, but by forces that could be explained by natural laws. Natural selection may give the appearance of design, but it is a false impression. Here was an argument that directly challenged natural theology.
- *Teleology, or purpose, was a nonissue for Darwin.* There was no direction for evolution to follow, and no purpose for change, other than survival in a particular environment. Change was a matter of trial and error: some variations allowed for survival, but some were detrimental and caused suffering and death. Which variations were "good" and which "bad" was determined on a relative scale (the changing environment), not by any absolute standard. Where is God's plan in this randomness?
- *Humanity itself was also an issue.* If humans evolved just like every other biological organism, what sets us apart from the rest of nature? What makes us special?

Other ideas regarding evolution, such as those proposed by Lamarck, were easier to accept theologically. For example, although Lamarck emphasized the role of the environment in causing change, teleology was evident: there was purpose in evolution, there was an ultimate goal (see table 8.1).

Darwin's purposeless, random, and cruel view of evolution was in direct contrast to the prominent theology of the time. It was inconceivable for many that God was not the creator of species, and that nature did not have a purpose. These individuals branded Darwin and those who accepted his ideas as atheists. Others saw ways in which natural selection could be incorporated into natural theology. But even for those who accepted natural selection, many could not apply the theory to the ultimate special creation, humans. Charles Lyell is an interesting case study. Although he rejected claims by his contemporaries that geology supported the biblical accounts of creation and the flood, he could not apply the uniformitarian approach to biology. He believed species were created by a divine force and were fixed and unchanging. Even after Darwin persuaded him that natural selection was at work, Lyell remained unsure about human evolution. Ultimately, Lyell did not think Darwin's ideas were a threat to natural theology: he saw God initiating the chain of events that led to evolution.

Like Lyell, there were others who accepted natural selection and tried to fit it into natural theology. Teleology and theodicy were subjects discussed in much correspondence between Asa Gray and Darwin. Gray looked at evolution on a global, long-term scale, using a teleological argument, and surmised that natural selection could help solve the theodicy problem: if God acted through evolution, then suffering was part of the creative process. Frederick Temple (1821–1902), the bishop of Exeter and archbishop of Canterbury, also focused on theodicy. He concluded that death and extinction in the natural world are more of a problem if we hold on to the belief that God creates new organisms in special, separate acts than if we accept evolution. St. George Jackson Mivart (1827–1900), an English biologist, was an early opponent of Darwin who later tried to reconcile Catholic doctrine

Table 8.1 Comparison of the ideas of Darwin, Lamarck, and natural theology

Concept	Darwin	Lamarck	Natural theology
Creation of new species	Differential survival in distinct environments of individuals with the "best" traits eventually leads to dramatic changes (speciation)	The environment causes organisms to adapt and change; the "call" of nature encourages species to become more complex	God alone creates new species, through special acts of creation
Changes in species	Yes	Yes	No; variations exist, but species are fixed and unchanging
Source of change	Variations in individuals	Use and disuse of organs	—
Force for change	Natural selection	Inheritance of acquired characteristics	— (God)
Extinction	Species that could not survive changes in the environment died off	No extinctions occur; organisms that appear to be extinct actually changed into new species	Shows that God has been active since the creation; extinction is part of God's creative process; organisms died out owing to natural forces
Teleology	None	Ultimate goal is to become human	There is a divine plan which can be better understood through the study of nature

and evolution in his *Genesis of Species* (1871). He argued that natural laws, including evolution, were established by God; the human spirit could not be attributed to evolution, but instead is instilled by God. This is the basic view of the Catholic Church today: evolution is well supported by many branches of science and is accepted as the mechanism of change. However, the soul is believed to be of divine origin.

Evolution and Education in America

Although Asa Gray differed from Darwin in that he considered evolution to be driven by God, Gray was Darwin's major proponent in America. But even into the twentieth century we see difficulties in the acceptance of evolution, especially with regard to the mental and moral advances of the human species, because of Darwin's insistence that change lacks purpose and has no ultimate goal. The extrapolation of natural selection to society led to social Darwinism and the eugenics movement (which we will discuss in chapter 12). Furthermore, if behavior evolved just like every other human trait, then vices such as prostitution, gambling, and drinking could be seen as part of our natural biological makeup. It was these affronts to morality, coupled with other events of the time, such as World War I, that caused a backlash in the 1920s, especially in the South. Support for fundamentalism, creationism, and a literal interpretation of the Bible grew in strength. Those on both sides of the evolution controversy came to meet in one of the most famous court cases in American history, the Scopes trial.

In 1925, the state of Tennessee passed the Butler Act, which made it illegal to teach evolution in the public schools. As a test of the law, the American Civil Liberties Union, and some entrepreneurial members of the Dayton community, staged the arrest of a volunteer, John Scopes (1900–70), a substitute teacher. His trial unleashed a circus-like spectacle in Dayton, including a media frenzy and the recruitment of two famous lawyers who had volunteered their services. For the prosecution, William Jennings Bryan (1860–1925), a three-time candidate for president, upheld the Bible and its literal interpretation. For the defense, Clarence Darrow (1857–1938), a former campaigner for Bryan, tried to present the case for evolution. The issue in the trial was simple enough: did Scopes violate the Butler Act by teaching evolution? The answer was yes, and Scopes was convicted and ordered to pay a fine of $100. But the principals involved in the case were hoping to make the trial a confrontation between evolutionary and creationist views of the world. No experts on evolution were allowed to testify, as the judge ruled the information irrelevant, but Darrow was able to question Bryan on the witness stand. Bryan ultimately did not do much for his cause: Darrow was able to get him to admit that he did not subscribe completely to a literal interpretation of the Bible. Scopes's conviction was overturned in 1927 by the Tennessee Supreme Court because of a technicality. The court did not, however, find the Butler Act to be unconstitutional.

Afterwards, Scopes went back to obscurity, but the impact of the trial is still with us today. Many court cases since the Scopes trial have been heard at both local and state levels, and, in 1968, the Supreme Court ruled that banning the teaching of evolution was unconstitutional. Many other cases attempting to provide "equal time" or "balanced treatment" for creationism, creation science, and intelligent design in the science classroom have also been struck down. However, the battle continues, especially at the local level. We will revisit this issue in chapter 11.

Conclusions

When Darwin joined the ranks of the naturalists, the young science of biology was a historical one, based largely on observation, which lacked the theories that could lead to logical explanations and accurate predictions. There had been attempts to make biology a theory-based science, like physics and chemistry. For example, we can look to Linnaeus and his classification system, and Lamarck and Erasmus Darwin with their own ideas on evolution. What we see in these instances, particularly early notions of the transmutation of species, is a desire to formulate natural laws that apply to biology. But these early ideas were based only on speculation, not on evidence. Darwin and Wallace proposed natural selection, and provided the evidence to support it. We don't just notice similarities among species, as Linnaeus did, but we can now explain why these similarities exist – through common descent. Now there is a theoretical basis for biology, which allows for testing and prediction. These natural laws broke the fetters that had kept biology in the historical realm of documenting observations and provided some respectability for the science. However, the idea of natural selection transformed more than just the scientific world – it expanded into the culture and society, and influenced fields as diverse as theology and economics. Can one idea change the world? You need go no further than your local newspaper to find references to evolution. Modern medicine, especially with regard to communicable diseases, depends on theories of evolution. And it is a topic of discussion for many faith communities. Its implications have revolutionized science and society. Can one idea change the world? There is no doubt it can.

Primary Literature

Useful primary sources include a letter Darwin wrote to the *Gardeners' Chronicle and Agricultural Gazette* in 1855 entitled "Does Sea-Water Kill Seeds?"; Lyell and Hooker's introduction to the Linnaean Society for Darwin and Wallace's papers on natural selection; an abstract of the 1857 letter Darwin wrote to Gray describing natural selection, from Paul H. Barrett, ed. *The Collected Papers of Charles Darwin*, vols. 1 and 2 (Chicago: University of Chicago Press, 1977); and a letter by William Jennings Bryan published in the *New York Times* in 1922, three years before the Scopes trial, "God and Evolution," in Gail Kennedy, ed., *Evolution and Religion: The Conflict between Science and Theology in Modern America* (Boston: Heath, 1957), pp. 23–9.

Questions to Consider

1   How did theological notions influence the work of scientists prior to Darwin? What about after Darwin proposed the theory of natural selection?
2   What similarities and differences can you see between the story of Darwin and the story of Galileo?
3   Many of Darwin's supporters, including Lyell and Gray, did not fully accept all of Darwin's ideas (for example, that humans had evolved and that God plays no part in evolution). What effect do you think these views had on popular support for Darwin's theory?
4   From a theological standpoint, did natural selection disprove the argument of design as purported by natural theology? In your opinion, were attempts to reconcile natural selection and natural theology successful?
5   How would theodicy, teleology, extinction, and changes in species be explained by someone adhering to the ideas of Darwin? Lamarck? Natural theology?

9

Scientific Explanations of the Origin of Life

Overview

Investigations into the origin of life on Earth have shown that organic molecules can be produced through natural, nonliving processes from inorganic materials. These molecules could then have assembled into the first cells. Ideas regarding the exact manner in which life arose are numerous, as are the notions of how life evolved. Within this context, the evolution of eukaryotic cells and the Cambrian explosion have stimulated much interest over the years. Contingency undoubtedly was a force in the evolution of life, but the exact role contingency played (and continues to play) is debated. Theologically, if we change our metaphysics to focus on the future, then the evolution of life, and indeed of the whole cosmos, is entirely consistent with a Christian understanding of God.

Introduction

The number of life forms on this planet is staggering. We have catalogued fewer than 2 million distinct species, mostly mammals and birds. However, estimates of the actual number of species range from 10 million to more than 100 million. We classify approximately 15,000 new species each year. We have focused mostly on eukaryotic species – those whose cells have a nucleus containing DNA. Humans, plants, fungi, and some unicellular organisms are eukaryotes. Bacteria are prokaryotic species, single-celled organisms that do not house their DNA inside a nucleus. Of all the life forms we know, the prokaryotic species are woefully underrepresented. Some contend that most life on Earth is microbial and exists underground. The old paradigm of five kingdoms (one prokaryotic and four eukaryotic) as the first and most basic level in classifying organisms has been dethroned: we now use the three domain system, where only one domain comprises eukaryotes. Approximately 100 kingdoms are now recognized, only four of which are eukaryotic.

Even considering the dearth of our knowledge of the species that exist, the diversity of life is amazing. The 400 nm (4×10^{-7} m) *Nanoarchaeum equitans* found in submarine hot thermal vents stands in stark contrast to sea grass plants found in Spain (8 km in length), blue whales (up to 24 m in length and weighing 150 tons), and the honey mushroom (*Armillaria ostoyae*), which covers over 2,200 acres in Oregon. Microbes have been identified that can metabolize plastic, or neutralize acidic (pH of 1.0–0.1) runoff from mines. Genetic systems range from 9,750 individual units (base pairs) in the human immunodeficiency virus (HIV) to 500 million base pairs in *Nanoarchaeum equitans* to 670 billion base pairs in the amoeba species *Amoeba dubia*.

To contemplate the beginning of life, we need to define life somehow. This has been very problematic, as life is so variable. Instead of a definition, we use characteristics to identify life, including reproduction, growth and development, evolution, organization, energy conversion, and response to stimuli. A careful examination of anything we consider to be alive will display each of these characteristics. Thus, to define something as alive does not require a single attribute (such as a requirement for oxygen), but rather certain processes. We are still uncertain as to how to classify viruses: although they show many, if not all, of the above characteristics, they cannot engage in these attributes on their own. They require a living cell in order to perform these functions. However, as we identify more life forms, this interdependence, this symbiosis, does not seem so unusual.

In his theory of descent with modification, Darwin recognized that all life on Earth could have descended from a single common ancestor. We now think there was not a single trunk to the tree of life, but rather many stems and roots that make up a bush with many branches. The more we find, the more amazing we find life to be. This chapter will not address all of the diversity seen in nature, but rather focus on the origins of life, and some interesting aspects of its evolution. In chapter 6, we discussed some notions of origins, such as contingency and the fine-tuning of the universe. We will reexamine some of these concepts. Origin of life issues are, by their very nature, speculative, but as more research is done, and as more life is discovered, we uncover further possibilities, modify hypotheses, and refine our understanding of the basis of life.

Chemical Origins

How did life originate on Earth? Before there was life, the molecular components that make up cells must have existed. Otherwise, there would be no material with which to build living cells. Today, one of the basic tenets of biology is that all life comes from life. So how can we account for the first cells? To answer this, we must begin with the question of how organic molecules, those produced by living organisms, can form from "nonliving," inorganic materials. The issue was addressed by Aleksandr Ivanovich Oparin (1894–1980), a Soviet biochemist. Beginning in the 1920s, Oparin considered the origins of life and the possible events that led to the formation of the first cells. Based on the composition of other planets, he contended that the atmosphere of the early Earth was a reducing one: in other words, there was no molecular oxygen. He thought the early atmosphere contained methane (CH$_4$), ammonia (NH$_3$), hydrogen gas (H$_2$), and water vapor (H$_2$O). These inorganic substances were the fundamental molecules that would have given rise to organic molecules that would in turn have been assembled into living cells. Oparin thought cells would have formed first in the oceans. In addition to the chemical components, energy would also have been necessary to form the first organic compounds, and ultimately life. Ultraviolet (UV) light, electrical discharges (lightning), radioactive decay, volcanic energy, and cosmic rays were all possible sources of energy on the early Earth.

The proposition that prebiotic chemical reactions could produce molecules normally produced only in living organisms may sound like pseudoscience, but it is a falsifiable hypothesis. Laboratory experiments can indeed be designed to test such an idea. The first attempts to synthesize organic molecules from inorganic components in an oxidizing atmosphere failed. Then, in 1953, a graduate student at the University of Chicago, Stanley L. Miller (1930–2007) set up an experiment to test Oparin's ideas. In a closed glass apparatus, Miller placed methane, ammonia, and hydrogen gas (see fig. 9.1). Liquid water in the apparatus was boiled, allowing for all the gases to be mixed. It also forced the gases to circulate past an electrical discharge, the energy source. The gases were

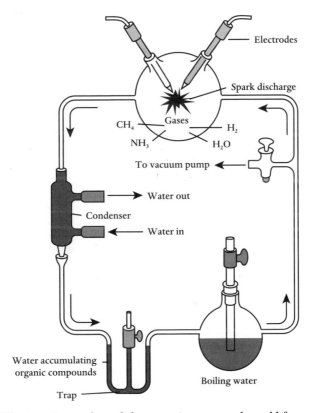

Fig. 9.1   The Miller experiment showed that organic compounds could form without there being life present beforehand, given the conditions on the early Earth.

cooled and condensed into a "trap." After one week, Miller analyzed the chemicals in the trap: he found many molecules, including amino acids, the building blocks of proteins. Miller's experiment was repeated by others, with alterations in the amounts and types of gases, as well as the energy source. As long as the system had a reducing atmosphere, amino acids and other organic compounds formed. Thus, it has been shown experimentally that organic molecules do not have to come from living organisms, and that these compounds could have been formed without life being present on the early Earth. Given enough time, many different types of organic molecules, from proteins to sugars to lipids, could have formed to allow for the evolution of life.

Many of our ideas regarding the chemical evolution of life have changed since Miller's experiment. Oparin's combination of atmospheric gases would cause a strongly reducing atmosphere. We now think the early atmosphere was still reducing, but that it contained carbon dioxide (CO_2), nitrogen (N_2), carbon monoxide (CO), water, methane, and hydrogen. Other ideas have challenged the notion that life began in the shallow waters of the oceans: new theories center on clay deposits on land, which could catalyze chemical reactions, and deep-sea hydrothermal vents, which could supply energy and inorganic nutrients to early cells. Other ideas center on extraterrestrial origins: it is possible for organic molecules to form in meteorites, which could then have landed on Earth (it may even be possible for cells to travel in this fashion, which could mean that life may not have originated on Earth at all!). Regardless of where these molecules originated, it is now accepted that, for molecules to form, it is not necessary for life to have been present first.

The Molecules of Life

So what are these organic molecules that are so essential to life? We classify organic molecules into four categories:

- *Proteins.* Twenty different amino acid subunits link together in different numbers and different combinations to form long chains (polymers), known as peptides or proteins. The potential diversity is enormous. Each protein folds into a unique three-dimensional shape which can then carry out its function. Proteins have a wide variety of functions, from enzymes that catalyze biochemical reactions, to proteins in the immune system that fight off foreign invaders, to transport proteins that carry nutrients from one place to another.
- *Lipids.* Although today we constantly watch our fat intake, some fats, or lipids, are good for our bodies and vital for our existence. Lipids make up cell membranes and other important biological molecules, including some hormones and energy storage compounds.
- *Carbohydrates.* In a word, carbohydrates are sugars. Simple sugars can combine to form complex carbohydrates, all of which can provide energy, and in some cases (as with cellulose in plants and chitin in insects) structural support.
- *Nucleotides.* The building blocks of our genetic material, deoxyribonucleic acid (DNA), and its cousin ribonucleic acid (RNA), are known as nucleotides. These molecules

also serve other roles in our cells. For example, the main currency of energy in living things, adenosine triphosphate (ATP), is a nucleotide.

To better understand life and its origins, we will focus on two organic compounds: proteins and nucleic acids. Let's first take a look at the structures and the relationship between these molecules, and then examine some thoughts regarding origins.

As we saw above, DNA is made up of subunits known as nucleotides, molecules comprised of a sugar group, a phosphate group, and a nitrogen-rich base. Figure 9.2 shows the four nucleotides found in DNA – all are identical except at their base. RNA differs from DNA in one of its bases and in a single oxygen atom in its sugar. We abbreviate each nucleotide with the first letter of its base: A for adenine, C for cytosine, G for guanine, T for thymine (only in DNA) and U for uracil (only in RNA). Nucleotides string together via their phosphate and sugar groups to form long polymers. RNA usually exists as a single-stranded chain, but DNA normally exists as a double-stranded molecule. The bases of one chain can form bonds, or pairs, with the bases on another chain. These pairs are specific: the A on one chain will pair with a T on the other, and a C on one chain will pair with a G on the other. In addition, the strands twist around each other. If we imagine the sugar and phosphate connections (often called the

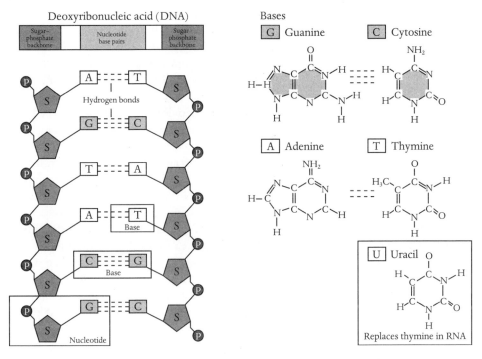

Fig. 9.2 The structure of DNA and RNA. DNA and RNA are made up of repeating units of nucleotides. The two main differences between the molecules are an extra oxygen atom in the sugar molecule of RNA (absent in DNA) and one of the bases (U in RNA substitutes for T in DNA). S, sugar; P, phosphate.

backbones) as the sides of a ladder, with the base pairs as the rungs between them, the structure of the double stranded DNA molecule is much like a spiral staircase. It is known as a double helix (see fig. 9.3(*a*)). This structure was first delineated by James Watson (b. 1928) and Francis Crick (1916–2004) in 1953. Their work was based on X-ray photographs taken by Rosalind Franklin (1920–58) and biochemical analyses done by Erwin Chargaff (1905–2002). Watson and Crick built a model based on these data, which led to their being awarded the Nobel Prize in 1962.

The pairing between bases can also occur with RNA. In this case, as there is no thymine in RNA, uracil pairs with adenine, making A–U base pairs. RNA can pair with DNA, but it can also pair with another molecule of RNA. And, interestingly, a single strand of RNA can fold and form base pairs within itself (see fig. 9.3(*b*)), creating elaborate three-dimensional structures similar to folded proteins.

DNA carries instructions that tell the cell how to carry out the biochemical reactions necessary for its existence. Soon after its structure was discovered, the function of DNA was also delineated. Crick was one of the key players in uncovering what is known as the central dogma. The instructions in DNA provide information for assembling proteins. The DNA is first copied into RNA inside the nucleus of the cell. The RNA is transported out of the nucleus, into the cytoplasm of the cell, and it is there that the information in the RNA is used to assemble proteins. The process of copying the information in DNA into RNA is known as transcription, and the relaying of the information in the RNA to make proteins is known as translation.

In transcription (see fig. 9.4), an enzyme known as RNA polymerase reads the DNA and builds a strand of RNA using the base-pairing rules: if there is a C in the DNA strand, the RNA will be built with a G in that position. If the next base in the DNA is A, then a U will be inserted into the RNA sequence, and so on. In this way, a "complementary" copy is made. The RNA is typically processed before leaving the nucleus, including the extraction of large stretches of sequences in the transcript. These sequences are known as introns, and the process of removing them is known as splicing. The RNA is called a messenger RNA (mRNA), as it carries the message from the region of the DNA known as a gene. Other regions of the DNA are transcribed into RNA but are never translated into proteins. Some of these sequences aid in the process of translation. Ribosomal RNA (rRNA) is a part of the ribosome, the large molecular complex that actually does the translation. Transfer RNA (tRNA) carries the amino acids to be assembled into the new protein.

Once the processed mRNA transcript has left the nucleus, it can be translated (see fig. 9.5). The ribosome, made up of rRNA and proteins, attaches to the mRNA and "reads" the mRNA in a pattern of three nucleotides (a codon). Codons are like words in our language: every three letters spell out a word, or in this case, an amino acid (see table 9.1). Thus, the codons tell the cell which amino acids need to be inserted into the protein and in what order. The ribosome builds the protein with the aid of the tRNA molecules. Each tRNA has a region, called an anticodon, that binds to a codon in the mRNA. The tRNA carries with it the correct amino acid for the corresponding codon. The ribosome connects the amino acids brought in by the tRNAs through a peptide bond. Thus, when the ribosome reads to the end of the mRNA, a protein has been built. This string of amino acids folds into a three-dimensional shape through molecular interactions and is sent to where it is needed inside, or outside, the cell.

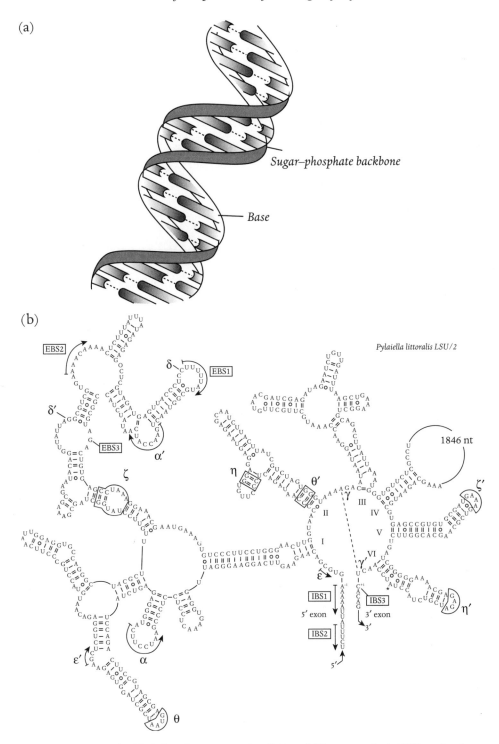

Fig. 9.3 (*a*) DNA double helix. (*b*) An example of RNA folding: a catalytic RNA molecule. The figure shows a single strand of RNA folded via base-pairing within the molecule.

- The bottom strand of the DNA molecule above is the template for RNA synthesis.
- RNA polymerase makes a copy of the DNA sequence but substitutes uridine (U) in place of thymine (T).

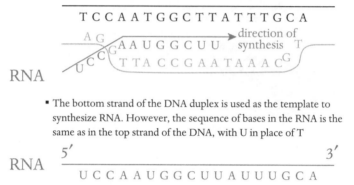

- The bottom strand of the DNA duplex is used as the template to synthesize RNA. However, the sequence of bases in the RNA is the same as in the top strand of the DNA, with U in place of T

RNA   5′ ——————————————————————————————— 3′
          U C C A A U G G C U U A U U U G C A

Fig. 9.4   Transcription of RNA from DNA.

Metabolism or Genetics: Which Came First?

Now that we understand a bit about proteins and DNA/RNA, let's get back to the origin issue. Once organic molecules of various types were abundant on Earth, how did they assemble into living cells? Two main hypotheses address this issue: the metabolism-first and the genetics-first (or replication-first) models. Metabolism is a termed used to describe the biochemical reactions that use energy to produce necessary components (molecules) for an organism. These reactions are often very slow, and so living systems depend on proteins that act as enzymes to speed up (catalyze) the reactions. Genetics refers to the material that is passed from parent to offspring (DNA), providing information that can be used to build proteins, such as enzymes needed for metabolism. When we examine life today, the "Which came first?" question is, in essence, a chicken and egg scenario: without metabolism (enzymes) the genetic material (DNA) cannot be formed or maintained, and without DNA enzymes cannot be produced.

The genetic system we have found in the vast majority of life on this planet is DNA. However, as we have seen, DNA and proteins cannot exist without each other. It is unlikely that this highly complex, interacting system could have come into existence without some intermediate or precursor steps. Some believe the precursor was none

mRNA

5′ end   A U G U U G A A G   3′ end

Initiation: The ribosome attaches to the RNA and recognizes the first AUG triplet codon near the 5′ end of the mRNA. A transfer RNA (tRNA) (shown as a gray rectangle) coupled to the amino acid methionine (MET) binds to the AUG codon in the RNA.

Elongation: The correct sequence of amino acids in a protein is assembled according to the sequence of bases in the RNA. The next codon (sequence of 3 bases) in the RNA is UUG and this encodes leucine (LEU). Another tRNA, this one coupled to LEU, recognizes and binds to the UUG sequence in the RNA.

A peptide bond joins MET to LEU:

A transfer RNA coupled to lysine (LYS) binds to the next triplet codon, AAG, in the mRNA:

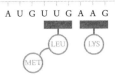

A peptide bond joins LEU to LYS, extending the peptide chain:

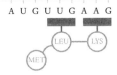

Termination: The ribosome completes the elongation of the chain of amino acids and releases the completed protein. The codon AAU encodes isoleucine (ILE). The next codon, UGA, is a stop codon. The ribosome stops adding amino acids to the chain, the protein is released from the ribosome, and the ribosome falls off the mRNA and is recycled.

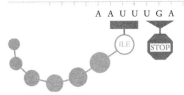

Fig. 9.5   Translation of mRNA into protein.

Table 9.1 The genetic code. The codons are represented by the three-letter nucleotides found in the mRNA. The amino acids are shown by their three-letter abbreviations (for example, "Ala" is the abbreviation for alanine). This chart can be used to determine the amino acid sequence from the mRNA sequence. For example, the codon AGU codes for the amino acid serine ("Ser" in the table). Three of the codons, UAG, UAA, and UGA do not code for any amino acids, but instead are used as punctuation marks by the cell: they are known as stop or termination codons, and tell the cell where the protein coding sequence ends.

Second letter

First letter (5′)	U	C	A	G	Third letter (3′)
U	UUU UUC } Phe UUA UUG } Leu	UUU UCC UCU UCG } Ser	UAU UAC } Tyr UAA UAG } Stop	UGU UGC } Cys UGA Stop UGG Trp	U C A G
C	CUU CUC CUS CUG } Leu	CCU CCC CCA CCG } Pro	CAU CAC } His CAA CAG } Gln	CGU CGC CGA CGG } Arg	U C A G
A	AUU AUC AUA } Ile AUG Met	ACU ACC ACA ACG } Thr	AAU AAC } Asn AAA AAG } Lys	AGU AGC } Ser AGA AGG } Arg	U C A G
G	GUU GUC GUA GUG } Val	GCU GCC GCA GCG } Ala	GAU GAC } Asp GAA GAG } Glu	GGU GGC GGA GGG } Gly	U C A G

other than RNA. Since RNA can carry genetic information, it could substitute for DNA. But what about the metabolism component? It turns out that, because of the ability of RNA to base-pair with itself and fold into three-dimensional shapes, it can perform catalytic functions and act as enzymes. The notion that RNA was the first genetic material and also acted to catalyze its own existence (and other functions in the cell) is known as the RNA world hypothesis. We have many examples in living organisms today of catalytic RNA, and we also know of many viruses that use RNA as their genetic material. So it is easy to envision how RNA could have been the molecule to carry out the basic necessary functions for the very first life forms. Thus the assembly of RNA, a genetic material, could have led to the formation of cells capable of metabolism, the genetics-first model.

One of the key problems with the genetics-first idea is the structure of the RNA molecule: it has been difficult to explain how such a complex molecule could have been the original source of material for life. Some argue that simpler molecules must have started it all, eventually resulting in the RNA world. This view, which is known as the metabolism-first model, focuses on enzymatic pathways. The original organic molecules that started life may have been amino acids, which are chemically much simpler than nucleic acids (recall that Miller was able to produce them easily in his experiment). The amino acids could have formed proteins capable of catalytic activity. Biochemical pathways could have been produced and the first cells could have formed without genetic information. This model does not necessarily reject RNA as the first type of genetic material, but it argues for a very different beginning to life.

The formation of the first cells would require not only genetic material and enzymes for metabolism, but also a way to separate the primitive cells from their environments. Today, lipid molecules form membranes that perform this function. In the past, "cells" (in reality, isolated environments) could have formed first on rock surfaces or in small ponds or aerosols, or membranes could have been made from other materials besides lipids. The acquisition of cell membranes, be it early or late in the evolution of the cell, is debated. Eventually, whatever these first life forms were and however they formed, they probably did use RNA as a genetic system, and then evolved to use DNA, a more chemically stable molecule.

Evolution of Early Life

The Earth was formed approximately 4.5 billion years ago (bya). Uncontested evidence for the first fossil finds of cells dates back to approximately 3.5 bya, but some claim that life is even older than that. Fossil evidence of cells living prior to the Archeoan eon (2.5 bya) usually cannot be distinguished from the rocks in which they are embedded. So, instead of looking for fossils, researchers look for other signs of life, known as biosignatures. This entails examining the rocks for carbon-based organic molecules, compounds that could be created only through life processes. These biosignatures indicate that life is older than 3.5 billion years – perhaps life was already present as early as 3.8 bya.

These first cells were probably very simple, in many ways similar to prokaryotic cells that exist today. There would not have been a nucleus to house the DNA, or any of the other special structures we find in eukaryotic cells, known as organelles. These structures provide the cell with different compartments in which to perform different biochemical reactions. For example, eukaryotic cells contain mitochondria, membrane-bound organelles that perform cellular respiration. This is the process whereby oxygen is used to break down organic molecules, mainly sugars, to produce ATP, the molecule that cells use as a source of energy. Photosynthetic organisms also have an organelle known as the chloroplast. This structure captures energy from the Sun and uses it, along with CO_2 in the atmosphere, to produce organic molecules. A waste product of the photosynthetic reaction is O_2, which is expelled into the atmosphere.

An important question in the evolution of life is "How did eukaryotic cells arise?" A theory about their origin was presented in 1966 by Lynn Margulis (b. 1938), now a distinguished university professor at the University of Massachusetts Amherst. Based on the structure of the organelles, particularly mitochondria and chloroplasts, Margulis proposed that these organelles were once free-living prokaryotic cells that evolved to perform special functions, such as respiration or photosynthesis. Other prokaryotic cells evolved the ability to engulf objects, a process known as phagocytosis, and to take these objects into the cell. The cell would then digest the material and use it as a source of nutrients. Phagocytosis is used by a multitude of cells today. Margulis thought that the early prokaryotic phagocytic cells may have engulfed some of the specialized prokaryotic cells, but failed to digest them. Instead, the specialized cells provided a benefit to the phago-cytic cell, such as energy or food production. Thus, the cells began to live in a symbiotic relationship. This is known as the endosymbiont theory (see fig. 9.6). Although Margulis's ideas received much criticism, the endosymbiont theory is now widely accepted, and has been supported through many lines of evidence:

- The process of endosymbiosis has been observed in living organisms today.
- These organelles are surrounded by membranes that resemble those of prokaryotic cells.
- Mitochondria and chloroplasts contain their own DNA, which has characteristics of prokaryotic, not eukaryotic, DNA.
- Ribosomes in organelles resemble those in prokaryotic cells more than those in eukaryotic cells.

Eukaryotic cells first appear in the fossil record about 2 bya, and the first multicellular organisms appeared about 1.2 bya. Table 9.2 shows the major events in the history of life.

The Cambrian Explosion

One of the most interesting time periods in the history of life occurred about 530 million years ago (mya) and is known as the Cambrian explosion. Prior to this, few fossils depicting different animal forms are found. Almost all the major animal groups are,

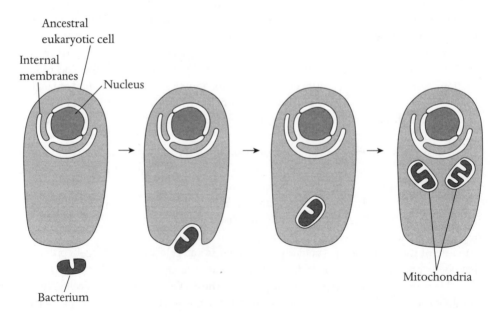

Fig. 9.6 The endosymbiont theory. An ancestral eukaryotic cell engulfed another, and the two entered into a symbiotic relationship. Eventually the engulfed cell evolved into an organelle.

Table 9.2   Major events in the history of life within geological time

Eon	Era	Period	Epoch	Major events in the history of life
Phanerozoic (543 mya– present)	Cenozoic (65 mya– present)	Quaternary (1.8 mya– present)	Holocene (10,000 years ago–present)	All of recorded history; domestication of animals and plants by humans; writing developed; metal working
			Pleistocene (1.8 mya–10,000 years ago)	Continents drifting; first appearance of *Homo species*; glaciation where ice sheet covered much of the northern USA
		Tertiary (65–1.8 mya)	Pliocene (5.3–1.8 mya)	Hominids; bipedalism
			Miocene (23.8–5.3 mya)	First apes
			Oligocene (33.7–23.8 mya)	Koalas evolve
			Eocene (54.8–33.7 mya)	Monkeys evolve
			Paleocene (65–54.8 mya)	First placental mammals; radiation of flowering plants; pollinating insects
	Mesozoic (248–65 mya)	Cretaceous (144–65 mya)		First flowering plants (angiosperms); extinction of the dinosaurs; marsupial mammals; continental drift

Table 9.2   (*Cont'd*)

Eon	Era	Period	Epoch	Major events in the history of life
		Jurassic (206–144 mya)		First birds; Pangea starts to separate into Gondwana and Laurasia; first mammals; gymnosperms and ferns disperse; age of dinosaurs
		Triassic (248–206 mya)		Gymnosperms dominate; first dinosaurs; continents separate; marine arthropods dominant; roaches and termites; mass extinction event
	Paleozoic (543–248 mya)	Permian (290–248 mya)		Mass extinction of plants and animals (including trilobites); decline of non-seed plants; land masses all together (Pangea); increase in reptiles and insects
		Carboniferous (354–290 mya)	Pennsylvanian (323–290 mya)	Rise of reptiles; winged insects
			Mississippian (354–323 mya)	Rise of amphibians; primitive insects; primitive ferns

Table 9.2 (*Cont'd*)

Eon	Era	Period	Epoch	Major events in the history of life
		Devonian (417–354 mya)		First seed plants (gymnosperms); origin and diversity of amphibians and bony fish; jawed fish; Appalachian mountains formed; primitive sharks; mass extinction event
		Silurian (443–417 mya)		First terrestrial invertebrates; first terrestrial (vascular) plants; golden age of fish; first jawed fish
		Ordovician (490–443 mya)		First vertebrates (fish); diversification of marine invertebrates (echinoderms); mass extinction event
		Cambrian (543–490 mya)		Cambrian explosion (first appearance of most phyla); algae dominate the plants; trilobites dominant; the large land mass Gondwana forms

Table 9.2 *(Cont'd)*

Eon	Era	Period	Epoch	Major events in the history of life
Precambrian (4,500–543 mya)	Proterozoic (2,500–543 mya)	Neoproterozoic (900–543 mya)		Decline of abundance and diversity of eukaryotes; planet-wide glaciation causing the first mass extinction; earliest evidence of metazoans (multicellular animals); continental drift
		Mesoproterozoic (1,600–900 mya)		Earliest evidence of sexual reproduction and complex multicellularity
		Paleoproterozoic (2,500–1,600 mya)		Oxygen atmosphere; first eukaryotes (about 2,000 mya)
	Archaean (3,800–2,500 mya)			Oldest rocks at 3,700 mya (Greenland); oldest uncontested fossilized life (cyanobacteria: photosynthetic prokaryotes) at about 3,500 mya
	Hadean (4,500–3,800 mya)			Earth formed; ozone layer forms; solidification of Earth's crust; condensation of atmospheric water into oceans

however, preserved in the fossil record in rapid succession over the course of a relatively brief (10–15-million-year) period of time. This "explosion" of life is puzzling to many who study evolution, and even Darwin noted it in *Origin*. A sudden appearance of such diversity seems contrary to the ideas of natural selection and gradual change. The main fossil finds just prior to this time are called "shelly fossils." As their name indicates, these organisms had hard shells that fossilized well. Many fossil finds from the early Cambrian, including the famous Burgess Shale, demonstrate an amazing radiation of the major animal groups. Many scientists argue that this supports the notion of a massive and sudden evolution of life. This has often been called a late-arrival model. However, an early-arrival model has been proposed in light of some recent evidence including:

- *Fossils of bilateral animals.* Recent finds of microscopic animals with bilateral (left and right) symmetry and multilayered bodies have been dated to 580–600 mya. It is speculated that animals must have evolved even earlier than this. This also demonstrates that complexity arose before a large body size. Microscopic fossils are difficult to find, and thus our understanding of evolution, based on macroscopic evidence from the early Cambrian, may be skewed.
- *Fossilized burrows.* As animals move and dig into the ground, they can leave behind "tracks" and burrows. These types of fossils have been found dating back prior to the Cambrian explosion, showing a greater diversity of animals existed earlier than previously thought.
- *The molecular clock.* In the past, fossils were the main evidence used to estimate how long ago different species had a common ancestor. If we can date the fossils, then we can date when species diverged. Today, we can compare DNA from two species, and look for differences between the nucleotide sequences of the same gene. These differences represent mutations that have accumulated through evolution: the more differences, the further back in time the two species diverged. This type of analysis is known as the molecular clock. Some studies using the molecular clock conclude that the major animal groups actually diverged hundreds of million of years before the Cambrian period.

In considering the late- and early-arrival models, we must examine some of the difficulties in explaining how the models can mesh with evolutionary theory. In the late-arrival model, the question of how such diversity could appear in such a short period of time needs to be addressed. In this case, several hypotheses have been proposed:

- *The evolution of specific sets of genes.* We know today that the major body plans of animals are controlled in development by specific sets of genes, known as the homeotic genes. These genes are found in many species, from fruit flies to humans, and determine exactly how the organism develops from an embryo to an adult. If these genes evolved during this time period, alterations of this precise regulation could have led to the diversity we see in the fossil record.
- *Macroscopic predation.* As animals became larger and more complex, and as they continued to prey upon other animals, an effective defense may have been hard body parts, such as shells and skeletons. This could result in the many different body forms we observe.

- *Environmental constraints.* If some factors existed in the environment that prevented the evolution of diversity, then a change in the environment may have lifted this constraint. Some believe the amount of atmospheric oxygen was such a factor. Once O_2 levels increased, it may have been possible for a massive evolution of different body plans to have taken place.

The major point that needs to be addressed with the early-arrival model is the time-line: if animals did diverge prior to the Cambrian period, why don't we find evidence for them in the fossil record? One distinct possibility is that these organisms were not very amenable to preservation. Animals found during and after the Cambrian explosion were hard-bodied and had skeletons that could become mineralized, a definite plus for preservation. If the development of hard body parts occurred during the early Cambrian, then we would expect to see more fossils at this time than in previous eras. And as we saw, the size of organisms would also affect our ability to detect fossil evidence. If animals were mainly microscopic prior to the Cambrian, it would be difficult to find them and document their diversity.

The debate as to whether the Cambrian fossil record depicts an actual explosion of life forms, or reflects the acquisition of an adaptation in organisms that diverged much further back in time, will continue for years to come. Evidence from the geological record, paleontology, developmental biology, and genetics will continue to add to our knowledge and ideas regarding this interesting period in the evolution of life.

Extinctions

As we have seen, extinctions of organisms in the fossil record are quite common. The loss of individual species was an important piece of evidence for Darwin and the theory of evolution. However, we find many periods of mass extinctions, times where a multitude of species became extinct, usually on a global scale. We are very familiar with the extinction that occurred about 65 mya, when the dinosaurs were wiped out. But this was not the only mass extinction nor was it even the largest one. At least five mass extinctions have been identified, and some scientists recognize many more. During the Permian extinction, 250 mya, approximately 95 percent of all marine species and 70 percent of all terrestrial vertebrates became extinct. Although many life forms die off at such times, another amazing event happens: those organisms that survive evolve to create greater diversity. For example, mammals were present during the reign of the dinosaurs, but they were not a dominant life form on the planet. After the extinction of the dinosaurs, mammals evolved into many different species, including the primates, which ultimately led to the evolution of humans (see chapter 12).

What causes mass extinctions? There are numerous possibilities, some of which we discussed in chapter 7:

- *Climate change.* The most notable type of climate change is glaciations or ice ages. The lowering of global temperatures alters the environment, including freezing large bodies of water. The oceans would not entirely freeze in this situation, as the heat from the Earth's core would prevent this. However, ice can, and in some cases did, accumulate to 1 km on the surface. Marine and terrestrial life that cannot adapt to the colder climate die out.

- *Tectonic plate activity*. The movement of land masses may alter the ecosystem and bring previously isolated populations together. Both of these events can lead to extinctions.
- *Impact events*. Collisions between the Earth and extraterrestrial objects can cause massive destruction. Asteroids and comets can create massive tidal waves, global forest fires, and dust in the atmosphere that would block out the Sun for years, creating a "nuclear winter." There is strong evidence that the extinction event at the end of the Cretaceous period (when the dinosaurs were wiped out) was due to an impact event.
- *Volcanic activity*. A massive sustained release of CO_2 gas during extended volcanic activity can alter the ecosystem by creating a greenhouse effect. Dust from volcanoes can also block out the Sun, leading to a scenario similar to that of an impact event.

One or a combination of these possibilities could trigger global changes in the environment that would cause a large-scale loss of life. Recent evidence suggests that the Permian extinction may have been caused by a meteorite. A crater under Antarctica, found in 2006, resulted from the impact of a 30-mile-wide meteorite about 250 mya. This event may have caused the breakup of the Gondwana supercontinent. Extinction events prior to the Cambrian period may have been due to four cycles of cold–hot climate changes that occurred between 750 and 580 mya. The "snowball Earth" model contends that glaciation events caused the global temperature to plummet to −50 °C. Due to the disruption of chemical cycles (which rely on liquid water) to consume atmospheric CO_2, accumulation of this gas from volcanic eruptions caused rapid warming, with average global temperatures of 50 °C. Organisms that could not adapt to the extreme cold and heat died off. As discussed earlier, extinctions led to the radiation of new species, and some think that the snowball Earth effect may have caused the Cambrian explosion.

Some scientists regard the present day as a period of mass extinction, and many claim the cause is human activity. We will discuss this prospect further in chapter 15.

The Necessities of Life

The only life we know of exists on this planet, and so our understanding of evolution is restricted to a particular set of circumstances. When we ask what is necessary for life, we have only one "event," the evolution of life on Earth, as our example. Statistically, this is not a significant sampling! So what we know about life, and our attempts to extrapolate how life forms and evolves, are myopic... or are they?

What exactly is necessary for life, for its origin and for its survival? Let's begin by briefly examining the chemistry of life. We can identify some key materials, including water and carbon, that appear to be necessary for life. All life requires water, and we cannot imagine life existing anywhere without it. Therefore, water appears to be an absolute requirement for life, and it is this substance that we search for in extraterrestrial environments to begin contemplating the possibility of life on other planets. What about carbon? Our organic molecules are made up of carbon backbones that bond with oxygen, hydrogen, nitrogen, phosphorous, and a host of other elements, including metals. Since carbon can form bonds with many other atoms, large diverse macromolecules can be formed which are necessary for carrying out biological functions and for transmitting genetic information. Carbon-based molecules can capture energy in their bonds which can be used to do work and to catalyze biochemical reactions, and they are also soluble in water. No other element has the versatility of carbon. Carbon forms in stars, and is thus a relatively abundant element in our universe. Therefore, for all intents and purposes, life must be carbon-based.

Complex molecules, such as proteins and DNA, are made up of repeating subunits. These subunits, such as amino acids, can be formed from inorganic substances, as Miller and others have shown. Amazing diversity can be obtained from relatively few types of subunits. Thus, no matter how life evolved, the use of subunits is probably a necessity.

Energy transformation is another key feature of life. Thermodynamically we can identify only two types of processes that allow for the biological production of organic compounds, and both processes exist on Earth today. The first is lithotrophy, the oxidation and reduction of geochemical compounds, which allows for the transfer of high-energy electrons to living cells. The second process is photosynthesis, where organic molecules use the energy from light (photons) to create high-energy electrons. The "excited" electrons, resulting from lithotrophy and photosynthesis, can be used to perform work.

Although much, if not most, of life on Earth relies on photosynthesis, and thus light from our nearby star is important, it is not required. However, it has been suggested by some scientists that light was necessary for the synthesis of organic molecules on the early Earth and for the generation of disequilibrium states necessary for chemical reactions in the first cells. This brings us to the question of the physical setting necessary for life. We often think in terms of a "habitable zone" where life could exist. This zone cannot be too close to the Sun (too hot for life) or too far from it (too cold for life and reduced light for photosynthesis). Today, given the multitude of species we have identified that are lithotrophic and can withstand extreme temperatures, this habitable zone has been greatly expanded. Life has been found existing at 131 °C in the ocean and growing in ice at −20 °C. We still consider some limits when it comes to temperature: based on the chemical properties of water, it is estimated that life could exist anywhere from −50 °C to 150 °C.

As we discussed, the ability of living organisms to reproduce and pass on genetic information is a characteristic of life. All life on Earth does this with DNA. In addition, the structure and function of DNA is identical in all life. This is what allows for the biotechnology that creates genetically modified organisms (see chapter 14). The function of DNA relies on the genetic code (see table 9.1). This code is (almost) identical in all organisms, hence it is usually referred to as the universal code. The nature of this code is very interesting and has raised questions. Since it must specify 20 different amino acids using four different nucleotides, the code must comprise at least three letters (which would allow for 64 possible combinations, more than enough to specify 20 amino acids). Did this genetic code evolve as a random combination in the first cell(s) that was passed on through Darwin's notion of common descent, or was it subject to natural selection? Crick adhered to the former hypothesis, and called the code a "frozen accident" of evolution. But some recent investigations suggest that the code evolved through natural selection. First of all, there are at least 16 variants of the code that occur across diverse lineages, including differences in the mitochondrial DNA code. Therefore, the code is not "frozen" but has evolved. Computer modeling programs have also indicated that the code we have is one of the best possible codes, again indicating that it may have been subjected to selection and did indeed evolve.

As the genetic code is almost identical in all living things, it means that it existed in the last common ancestor of all life. Carl Woese, professor of microbiology at the University of Illinois was the first scientist to use molecular data to help explore the tree of life and to understand evolution, in the 1960s. In the early version of the molecular clock, Woese chose to examine rRNA. As all cells need to produce proteins, all need ribosomes, and hence all need rRNA. Woese reasoned that rRNA would be common to all life and any changes in the sequence would help to establish the relatedness among living species. After painstakingly sequencing many rRNA molecules, Woese proposed a new view on life. In the 1970s, he introduced a three domain system (see fig. 9.7), where one domain included all eukaryotes, and the other two contained the prokaryotes. The eubacteria include prokaryotes that are fairly common to us (such as *E. coli* and *Salmonella*), and the archaea include organisms that live in "extreme environments" (hot thermal vents, high salt conditions, etc.). Woese concluded that the archaea are as different from the eubacteria as the eubacteria are from the eukaryotes. It is also thought that eukaryotes evolved from the archaea. In addition, the evolution of these three domains has not been linear: in other words, once they diverged, genetic information was still exchanged between the domains. We have already seen a major way in which the domains did this, with the evolution of organelles via endosymbiosis. But we also have seen the exchange of genes, known as horizontal or lateral gene transfer, between different organisms. The tree of life based on Woese's ideas looks more like a bush, containing multiple branches with connections between them. There was no single organism that was a common ancestor to all life. Instead, we look at this as a communal process.

The evolution of the DNA in complex organisms is another interesting topic. As we discussed earlier, not all of the DNA in humans codes for proteins: some sequences (introns) are removed after transcription. In 2003, the completion of the Human Genome Project (the effort to sequence the DNA in humans) left us with some surprises (see chapter 14). As it turns out, the 3 billion nucleotides of human DNA contain fewer than 30,000 genes, not much more than the common fruit fly, *Drosophila melanogaster*, or the lowly nematode, *Caenorhabditis elegans*. And less than 2 percent of our DNA codes for protein sequences. Another interesting observation, revealed with the sequencing of the genomes of other organisms, is that the complexity of an organism does not appear to depend on the absolute amount of DNA, but rather on the percentage of DNA that is noncoding: bacteria have very little noncoding DNA in their genomes, whereas lower eukaryotes have more, and vertebrates even more. In addition, we find that the noncoding sequences are still transcribed into RNA but not translated. And many noncoding sequences have been found unaltered over millions of years of evolution, in diverse vertebrate species, which indicates that these sequences are vital to the organism. How can we make sense of this information?

A new view of genomes and complexity has emerged recently. As we examine the noncoding RNA, we find that these molecules have a regulatory role: they help to

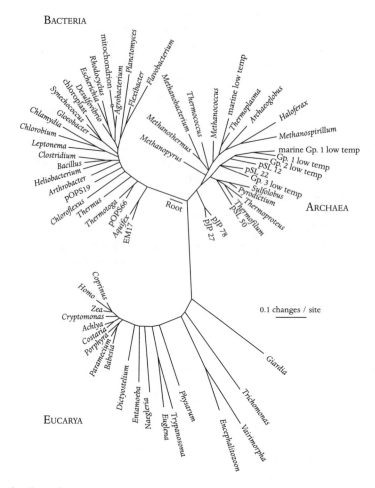

Fig. 9.7 The three domains. Woese's classification scheme, based on molecular data, drastically changed our paradigm of life.

control the expression of genes and the production of proteins. RNA controls the differentiation (specialization) of cells and the development of the organism. The more complex an organism, the more regulation is necessary to control development. Some have even proposed that the Cambrian explosion may be explained by the emergence of this system. And these mechanisms may also be the key to the neural systems necessary for human evolution.

The Necessity of Life

So was the evolution of life a contingency or was it inevitable? We looked at the fine-tuning notion, which argues that natural laws are just right for life and, if they had been any different, life would have been impossible (see chapter 6). What about the evolution of complex cells, of multicellular organisms, of beings with complex nervous systems, of humans? Was life, including complex life, destined to occur, or is it a chance, random "accident"?

Donald E. Ingber, of Harvard Medical School and the Children's Hospital Boston, defines evolution as the process that determines how matter self-organizes. He contends that the formation of organic compounds and the beginnings of cellular life may not have been a chance occurrence, but one that was inevitable. According to Ingber, the origin and evolution of life is actually a natural consequence of the makeup of the cosmos. Specifically, life is a matter of architecture. As organic and inorganic molecules are made from the same atoms, life boils down to how these building blocks are assembled. The parts of the system combine into something new and unpredictable: unique properties emerge from the architecture. Self-assembly is the process whereby the parts join together to form a stable structure that has new properties. This self-assembly in nature is based on an architectural form known as tensegrity: the system gains stability and support from its components based on the forces of tension and compression within the system. There are two types of tensegrity:

- *Rigid struts*, where each component (strut) of the system resists either tension or compression. The struts connect to make triangles, pentagons, or hexagons. Geodesic domes and buckyballs are examples of this type of tensegrity.
- *Prestress*, where the components of the system that resist tension are distinct from the components that resist compression. This system is established even before any external forces are applied (hence the term "prestress"). When an external force is applied, the components of the system rearrange to establish equilibrium within the structure. This is the basis for musculoskeletal systems.

Many biological forms in nature, including viruses, enzymes, organelles, cells, and even small organisms, have a geodesic architecture. Tissues, organs, and organ systems are examples of prestress systems. Ingber has used tensegrity to explain a wide variety of biological observations. For example, changes in cellular geometry have been shown to alter gene expression, forcing cells to divide, differentiate, or even die. But how does this help us to understand evolution and the origin of life?

Ingber reminds us that, although changes in DNA can cause diversity and contribute to evolution, genes themselves are the product of evolution. Thus, he argues, DNA cannot be considered to be the driving force for the evolution of life. The prebiotic formation of organic molecules was due to self-assembly. Ingber contends that tensegrity is the most economical and efficient way to build a structure. Clay exhibits loosely packed geodesic structures on the molecular level. The molecules can allow for catalysis, possibly resulting in the formation of the first organic molecules, the building blocks of life. With time, these molecules would begin to self-assemble into structures with specialized functions that could in turn assemble into the first cells. Cells would then self-assemble into multicellular organisms, which could further self-assemble into tissues and organs. DNA became the new mechanism for generating diversity: it accelerated evolution. But the rules for self-assembly, the hierarchy we see everywhere in nature, did not change. Natural selection first worked on architecture, which then led to life. Based on Ingber's ideas, the emergence of life can be viewed as a natural state resulting from the interaction and self-assembly of matter. Although emergent properties cannot be predicted based on the components of the system, Ingber tells us that we should not be surprised that life exists. It is a natural extension of the architecture of matter.

Stephen Jay Gould (1941–2002), a professor at Harvard University and an influential public figure, wrote prolifically on evolution, including a book entitled *Wonderful Life: The Burgess Shale and the Nature of History* (1989), examining the notion of contingency. Although the "quick" arrival of life, about 1 billion years after the formation of the planet, indicates inevitability, evolution was highly contingent. Gould stressed that natural selection is not the only force for evolution, and that other events, such as punctuated equilibrium (see chapter 10) and mass extinctions, are important factors. For example, if one specific group of organisms had not survived from the Cambrian explosion, then no vertebrates would have emerged on the planet. If an asteroid did not hit Earth 65 mya, then dinosaurs would still dominate the planet and mammals would be an insignificant class of animals. Some of life's evolution can be predicted by the physical constraints in nature: for example, the size of the largest organisms in the sea would logically be predicted to be larger than any terrestrial organism. Coevolution, whereby predator and prey evolve in response to each other, can also be predicted, as when crab claws become stronger with the development of harder shells in the crab's prey. However, there is no way to predict exactly what those large organisms in the sea or on the land would be, or why there are crabs and snails for them to prey on. Gould emphasized the contingency of life, even in the context of inevitability and the predictive ability of evolution. If we were to rewind history and play it out again, the evolution of life would most certainly be different. The life we know today would not exist, including humans. According to Gould, the contingency inherent in evolution would prevent the same events from happening a second time.

Gould denied the notion of increasing complexity in evolution. He contended that progress, whereby organisms become more sophisticated and complex with time, is a false idea. Bacteria, according to Gould, are the planet's greatest success story. They occupy every possible environment on the planet, and their numbers are staggering, greater than that of all other life forms combined. According to our standards, they are far from "complex." And most of life's history, 3 billion years of unicellularity capped by a few million years of intense diversity (the Cambrian explosion) and 500 million years of variation on these themes, does not, for Gould, represent a progression toward complexity.

Simon Conway-Morris, professor of evolutionary palaeobiology at Cambridge University and author of *Life's Solution: Inevitable Humans in a Lonely Universe* (2003), has a vastly different take on evolution. He contends that the conditions necessary for life are rare, but once these conditions are met, the evolution not only of life, but of intelligent life, is inevitable. If we replay the history of life tape again, we would see very similar events in evolution, and we would end up with strikingly similar organisms, including humans. Some of Conway-Morris's ideas echo Ingber's. He contends that the building blocks of life will combine in economical and elegant ways, that the templates for complex structures evolve long before the structure itself, and that life does evolve in a direction, where whatever is possible will evolve repeatedly. He cites specific examples of convergent evolution, whereby organisms that are not closely related evolve similar features. Eyes, legs, and wings evolved multiple times in diverse lineages. Mammals and marsupials evolved on different continents, and yet each class has rodent-like, mole-like, and cat-like organisms. And cooption, the use of existing structures in new and different ways, also plays heavily into Conway-Morris's ideas. For example, proteins known as crystallins in eyes were coopted from heat shock proteins, which evolved to fold proteins. It happened that these heat shock proteins were transparent, a good characteristic for the eye lens. Thus, according to Conway-Morris, while the exact environment necessary for life to emerge may be rare, once it does evolve, it will progress to increasing complexity. And the way in which this occurs will be similar every time.

And now for the big question: is life unique to Earth? We estimate that there are billions of galaxies, with billions of stars in each one. We have already found multiple examples of planets orbiting stars. How can we not suspect that there are other planets with similar conditions to our own? Investigations of our own galaxy have shown the presence of water outside of Earth: the Phoenix lander detected water on Mars in 2008, and Europa, a moon of Jupiter, contains liquid water. In 2005 the Cassini spacecraft detected eruptions of water from the polar region of Enceladu, a moon of Saturn. From discoveries on our own planet, we know that life can exist in a myriad of different conditions – in thermal vents deep under the ocean, in energy- and nutrient-starved caves, in the freezing temperatures and high UV radiation environment of Antarctica. Several claims have been made for fossilized life forms and biosignatures in meteorites (although most of these have been disproved). Do we think we are alone in the universe? It is highly unlikely that Earth is the only place where life exists. As Ingber has argued, self-assembly is a common principle for all matter and, if this is true, life could originate in many different places. If life does exist on other planets or moons, does it look like Earth life? Many contend that life, no matter where we find it, will require water, be carbon-based, and comprise macromolecular structures made up of simpler building blocks. Others go further and argue that we would recognize many specific biomolecules that would be remarkably similar to what exists on Earth, for example DNA as the genetic material and chlorophyll, necessary to capture light and drive the process of photosynthesis. And some, such as Conway-Morris, would argue that, if a planet had similar properties to Earth, we would also find intelligent life, including human-like creatures.

A Theology of Evolution

From the evidence and ideas presented in this chapter, it is clear that we now have scientifically plausible explanations for how life originated on this planet without the necessity of any supernatural forces. In chapter 6 we discussed extensively the notions of contingency and fine-tuning in the universe, and the roles of necessity, chance, and design. And in chapter 7, we looked at important ideas regarding eschatology. To conclude this chapter on the origins of life, we will not reexamine these issues, but instead use some of these notions to consider how evolution can fit in with a Christian understanding of God.

John Haught, professor of theology at Georgetown University and author of *God After Darwin: A Theology of Evolution* (2000) contends that evolution is wholly compatible with a Christian understanding of God. He is critical of the metaphysics that underlies both science and theology. The metaphysics of science is rooted in the past: the materialistic, reductionistic, and mechanical approach of science emphasizes history, explaining what we observe today as having been caused by past events. The metaphysics of theology is often rooted in the "eternal present," where the influences of ancient Greek philosophy are still apparent in the metaphysics of being. The natural world is viewed as an imperfect reflection of a perfect, unchanging, eternal realm. In neither of these metaphysics does true novelty play any role and Haught contends that this prevents evolution from being incorporated into theology at any substantial level.

The scientific focus on the chemical substances and the mechanical process of evolution doesn't address what life is. Pure design, as might be attributed to a creator, also doesn't take into account novelty, the bringing about of new beings. Haught argues that we need to understand God as the creator and wellspring of novelty. If we do, then Darwinian evolution is compatible with God and is even anticipated by God's nature.

A theology of evolution needs to take into account two images of God. The first is of God's unreserved self-emptying (kenotic) and suffering love. Critics of kenotic theology claim this understanding of God implies powerlessness. Haught counters this by emphasizing that God's power is the capacity to influence the world. The second image is of the God who makes promises, who invites us into an unpredictable future with a new creation. Haught contends that this image of God, which is firmly established in the Bible, provides us with a different metaphysics, a metaphysics of the future. This is the "power of the future," and God is the "Absolute Future." God's call to us, as humans rooted in the physical realm, as part of the universe, is also to all of creation. Instead of focusing on the details of the process of evolution, Haught urges us to examine the science with these understandings of God. Cosmic and biological evolution are part of this calling. What is this call? Haught believes that the principles of self-organization and assembly, and the emergence of complexity, are manifestations of this call from the future.

What kind of universe would result from God? Haught stresses that the infinite love of God allows for creation to be independent. Love is not coercive, and thus God does not overwhelm creation and does not direct the evolution of life. The randomness and contingency of Darwinian evolution, which causes theological difficulties for so many, actually allow for independence and for the opportunity for creation to become unique and distinct from God. An overpowering God, directing every aspect of creation, would not truly allow for the evolution of independence. Thus, the randomness and unpredictability of Darwinian evolution is compatible and consistent with the self-giving love and the "letting be" of God.

The infinite divine love that created the world allows it to be independent of God. The world has certain autonomous operating principles, the natural laws, which are as necessary as contingency. If there were no order, then there could be no novelty. God respects creation, and allows it to develop independently of divine action. This allows for tremendous freedom. This notion, however, can provoke a sense of anxiety and may be the reason why some people hold tight to the idea of a designer God. Freedom, independence, and randomness provide powerful forces for creation, but also have pitfalls, namely the suffering and waste that is so prevalent in evolution. If we stress the concept of divine love, Haught argues, and have faith in the promise of God, then the anxiety will subside, and we will gain a better understanding of God's plan.

Conclusions

The multitude of ideas regarding the origin of life, from exactly where life first formed (prebiotic soup, terrestrial clay, deep-sea hydrothermal vents) to the accumulation of organic material (inorganic reactions, extraterrestrial sources) to the possible energy sources (electromagnetic, thermal, chemical, cosmic rays) will undoubtedly be debated for years to come. However, the combination of all of these factors may be important in the origins of life on Earth: to adhere to a single possibility is myopic on our part. Life on this planet can be found in many different forms and in many different environments. If so many different conditions could produce life, and if it can be sustained in such a wide variety of environments, then life is truly adaptable. Is it so difficult to envision life on another planet or moon, in another galaxy, in multiple locations throughout the universe? Certainly not. Is extraterrestrial life inconsistent with what we know of God? God's creation includes natural laws and contingency. If God is calling the cosmos to some future, which we cannot know, then there is no reason to discount life on other planets. Exactly what this life is, we do not know. If we ever find it, the amazing new avenues and prospects that will open, both for science and for theology, will occupy our thoughts and endeavors for generations to come.

Primary Literature

A useful primary source is an article by John Haught, "Evolution and God's Humility," *Commonweal* 127 (2) (2000), 12–17, which further describes his ideas regarding a theology of evolution.

Questions to Consider

1 Using table 9.2 (and other sources, such as the internet) as a guide, construct a scale model depicting major events in evolution. Some possibilities include a timeline, a year-long calendar, and a 24-hour clock. What strikes you as most interesting about the history of life on Earth? Where are humans in the big picture? What conclusions can you draw regarding evolution?

2 Experiments like that for which Miller is famous have been criticized for not producing actual life. In addition, it is argued that Miller did not use the "right" components to mimic conditions on the early Earth. Are these criticisms valid? How can they be addressed?

3 Does the endosymbiont theory contradict Darwin's ideas about evolution? If we find evidence that does contradict his ideas, does it mean we need to shift paradigms?

4 Mass extinctions are one of the contingencies that occur throughout the evolution of life: some accidental chance event determines who will live and who will die. How does this contrast with natural selection?

5 How does a mutation (a change in a nucleotide) in the DNA cause a change in the protein sequence? Use the genetic code chart in table 9.1 to show how this could occur. Will all mutations cause a change in the protein sequence?

6 If we eventually find life on another planet, what impact will this have on science, and on theology?

7 Is Haught's theology of evolution consistent or compatible with the ideas of Gould, Ingber, and/or Conway-Morris? Explain your answer.

10

Evidence for Evolution

Overview

Discoveries after Darwin, including the development of genetics, have supported evolutionary theory. The inheritance of traits, the molecular mechanism behind this inheritance, the study of populations, and investigations into development have all confirmed and extended the notion of natural selection and its role in evolution. Other forces, such as genetic drift and reproductive isolation, are now known to contribute to the evolution of species. Changes at the species level (microevolution) can result in changes above the species level (macroevolution, or speciation). The definition of "species" is problematic, but most accept one that includes reproductive barriers. Today, we still use much of the same types of evidence as Darwin did (for example, paleontology, artificial selection, and homology), but, with the emergence of other branches of biology, we also have molecular data and population genetics. The neo-Darwinian synthesis, or modern synthesis, pools together all these data to provide us with overwhelming evidence for evolution. Evolution can be successfully integrated into theology, for example through the notion of continuing creation.

Introduction

"Nothing in Biology Makes Sense except in the Light of Evolution" is the title of a 1973 essay by Theodosius Dobzhansky (1900–75), one of the most important geneticists and evolutionary biologists of the early twentieth century. This oft-quoted phrase conveys a sentiment that is an underlying paradigm in biology today. In such diverse fields as immunology, virology, microbiology, genetics, anatomy, physiology, neurology, biochemistry, development, ecology, behavior, endocrinology, parasitology, biomechanics, histology, pharmacology, molecular biology, cell biology, and yes, even medicine, every discovery can and is interpreted in the light of evolution. All these branches of biology contribute evidence for evolution (along with other scientific disciplines such as geology and physics). And this evidence is overwhelming.

Evolution becomes important not only in basic research, where we try to understand the underlying causes and natural laws behind what we observe, but also in applied research, where we attempt to extend our understanding so as to be of direct benefit to humankind. As an example, stem cell research is basic research, whereas the development of a drug as a therapeutic treatment for cancer is applied research. Notions of evolution may help us understand the biology and differentiation of stem cells, but how does evolution help us with the testing of a new drug? Typically, drugs are not initially tested in humans. Animal models are used instead, to uncover any side effects. Why animals? Why not plants? And why do we usually choose a mouse rather than a fruit fly for these tests? Because animals are biologically more like humans than plants are, and mice are more like humans than flies are. The explanation for this is evolution: we share a more recent common ancestor with mice than with flies, and a more recent common ancestor with all other animals than with plants. Thus, human biology, and potentially our reaction to this new drug, will mimic more closely the response in the mouse than in the other two species.

Evolution is a theory, and we know what a theory is, in the scientific use of the term: it is a well-supported hypothesis. As a theory, there is always the potential for falsification. However, for 150 years, there has been no substantial challenge to evolution: there is no theory with better explanatory and predictive value, that is as progressive, and that can be falsified. Our accumulation of knowledge since Darwin's time has only helped to strengthen the theory. Evolution is also a fact. What is meant by this is that evolution happens: there is too much evidence to deny that life changes. The theory explains how these changes occur. This is similar to gravity: we know there is a force out there, the fact of gravity, but how do we explain that fact? We can use Newton's theory or Einstein's. Regardless of how we explain it, we know it's there, we know gravity exists. Evolution is a fact: the theory explains how it happens.

In this chapter we will discuss some major types of evidence for evolution and some specific examples. This is only the tip of the iceberg, but enough to give you a sense of what's out there. Over a century of evidence has extended our understanding of the forces behind evolution, but Darwin's basic tenets of natural selection and descent with modification are still the cornerstones of the theory. We will look first at the development of new branches in biology that have supported Darwinism and then discuss the types of evidence we have for evolution.

Neo-Darwinian Synthesis (Modern Synthesis)

Science is progressive, and evolutionary theory is no exception. Several key discoveries in the nineteenth and twentieth centuries and the establishment of new branches of biological science led to modern evolutionary thought. Taken together, the Darwinian notions of natural selection and descent with modification and these new additions make up what is sometimes called neo-Darwinian or modern synthesis.

We have already touched on the most significant post-Darwinian discovery which came just a few short years after the publication of *Origin*. In 1866, an Augustinian priest, Gregor Mendel published his work on plant breeding, in which he proposed how pea plants passed traits from one generation to the next. This breakthrough, whose significance was not acknowledged until the turn of the century, provided the fundamental understanding for what we now call genetics. Why was this so crucial? Darwin stressed the importance of variations that could be inherited from parent to offspring; however, he had no understanding of the mechanism behind this. Through his careful breeding experiments, Mendel was able to explain the basics of this mechanism. His work indicated that each parent contributes one "factor" to each offspring for each trait, and that the combinations of these factors determine what traits the progeny will have. Today, we use the term "allele" instead of "factor." An allele can be defined as a variation of a gene. For example, one of the traits Mendel examined was the shape of peas: they could be either wrinkled or smooth. Therefore, in modern terminology, we would say that there is a gene for pea shape, and two alleles: one that makes the pea wrinkled and one that makes it smooth.

The beginning of the twentieth century was an exciting time for biology. The Dutch botanist Hugo de Vries (1848–1935) and others rediscovered Mendel's work, and further plant breeding confirmed Mendel's results. Microscopic analysis of cells revealed that chromosomes, the threadlike structures inside the nucleus of the cell, behaved just like Mendel's factors, and thus it was understood that chromosomes store genetic information. From there, the floodgates opened, and the field of genetics was born. Thomas Hunt Morgan (1866–1945), at Columbia University, began working with fruit flies (*Drosophila*), confirming Mendel's rules in animals and uncovering additional pieces of the puzzle. In Morgan's lab, natural as well as induced variations (mutations) were studied.

But how could Darwin's natural selection work in a Mendelian world? Three scientists, Ronald Fisher (1890–1962), J. B. S. Haldane (1892–1964), and Sewall Wright (1889–1988) used mathematical models to understand how mutations could spread through a population, leading to change. This branch of genetics, known as population genetics, has had a major impact on our understanding of evolution, showing how natural selection could influence populations and, indeed, produce evolutionary changes.

Theodosius Dobzhansky, a Soviet-born geneticist who emigrated to the United States in 1927 and worked with Morgan, was another important figure during this period. Dobzhansky began to unravel the notion of what a species is, and determined that reproduction is important in this understanding: organisms mate with members of their own species, not with those of other species. In *Genetics and the Origin of Species* (1937) he presented an argument for how new species arise, contending that new mutations would produce variations. If a subset of a population began breeding within itself, and different mutations accumulated in the original population and the subset, then, given enough time, the two could become distinct, and would no longer be able to mate. Thus, the two would be considered different species.

On the biochemical side of the equation, chromosomes were found to be comprised of two types of molecules: DNA and proteins. Which molecule actually contained the hereditary information was unclear, and several experiments, most notably those done in the early 1940s by Oswald Avery (1877–1955) and his colleagues at the Rockefeller

Institute, indicated that it was DNA, not proteins. The structure of DNA was discovered by Watson and Crick in 1953 and soon the basic function of DNA was also deduced (see chapter 9). The latter half of the twentieth century saw astounding and amazing discoveries about life at the molecular level. Along with this knowledge came the ability to manipulate the genetic material of living organisms. In evolutionary studies, similarities and differences at the molecular level were examined to determine the degree of relatedness between species. Side-by-side comparisons of protein or DNA sequences indicate how closely two species are related. Moreover, the number of differences seen between the sequences can be used as a molecular clock to estimate the time of divergence from the most recent common ancestor (see chapter 9). Molecular genetics, the examination and manipulation of the genetic makeup at the molecular level, further confirmed evolutionary theory and expanded it. (We'll discuss some specifics of this later in the chapter.)

The importance of the ability to analyze DNA cannot be overstated. The passage of DNA from parent to offspring is the mechanism by which traits are inherited, and DNA determines, along with the environment, how traits are expressed. We now have a clearer understanding of how variations arise, and further insights into how natural selection can affect populations. Molecular genetics has also greatly affected the field of development. Researchers can now determine which genes are involved in various stages of development and how they are regulated. This has led to the branch of biology known as evolutionary development (often shortened to "evo-devo") and has contributed greatly to our understanding of how major variations can arise with only minor differences in genetic makeup.

And so breakthroughs in Mendelian genetics, population genetics, and molecular genetics have confirmed evolutionary theory and advanced our understanding of it. These advances have shed light on other mechanisms besides natural selection that can act on populations to cause change.

Other Mechanisms for Evolution

Evolution works at the population level. Individuals do not evolve: populations do. Individuals have variations/mutations that may impact or cause evolutionary change, but we must look at the population, over time, to see this change. The temporal aspect of this change makes the theory difficult for some people to accept. Gradual changes mean that evolution generally takes a long time to become apparent, much more than a human lifetime. But as we shall soon see, there is ample evidence on many levels that change does indeed occur.

As mentioned above, Fisher, Haldane and Wright pioneered the field of population genetics. Their insights and use of statistics helped to integrate the ideas of Darwin and Mendel. We can define evolution as a change in a population's genetic makeup, the most fundamental change being simply a change in the frequencies of alleles. So, if there are two alleles for a gene in a particular population, we can say the population is evolving if we see a change in the frequencies of these alleles from one generation to the next. This is the basis for a mathematical model derived independently in 1908 by Godfrey

Harold Hardy (1877–1947) and Wilhelm Weinberg (1862–1937). The Hardy–Weinberg equilibrium states that the allelic frequencies will change if a population violates any of the following five assumptions:

- *Large population size*. At the heart of population genetics is statistics. Allelic frequencies will fluctuate randomly, but, just as with any statistical analysis, the larger the sample (or population) size, the less these random fluctuations will affect the sample (population). So, when random fluctuations occur, large populations will "absorb" them better, and changes in allelic frequencies will not be significant. In small populations, these random changes can have a major effect on the overall frequencies.
- *Random mating*. All individuals in a population must have an equal likelihood of mating and producing offspring. This ensures all alleles will be passed from one generation to the next, and that the allelic frequencies will not change. If a subset of individuals is more likely to reproduce, then the allelic frequencies will change in the next generation.
- *No selection*. If certain traits are selected for, then the incidence of these traits in the next generation will increase, and allelic frequencies will change. The two main types of selection are natural selection and sexual selection, both of which were recognized by Darwin. With natural selection, if a particular trait (allele) is beneficial for the survival and reproduction of an individual, then that trait is more likely to be passed on to the next generation, and hence allelic frequencies will change. Sexual selection is the competition between members of the same sex for mates. If a particular trait attracts more members of the opposite sex and increases an individual's chances for reproduction, that trait will be passed on to the next generation and will increase in frequency.
- *No mutation*. Mutation is the source of variation in a population. If mutations (basically, new alleles) arise, then the frequencies of all the alleles for that gene will change.
- *No migration*. If organisms leave a population or enter it, then allelic frequencies may change, depending on the genetic makeup of the migrating organisms. This type of change is often called gene flow, the transfer of alleles from one population to another.

Most populations do not meet all five of the assumptions of the Hardy–Weinberg equilibrium, and thus most populations are evolving. This type of evolution, where allelic frequencies change and the characteristics of a population are altered slightly, is known as microevolution. Evolution involving lots of changes, where we no longer recognize the population as the same species, is known as macroevolution, or speciation. Darwin proposed that these small changes, over time, would accumulate and cause speciation. However, we need to ask how we can determine when a speciation event takes place. And that requires us to define the term "species."

The concept of a species is an artificial one. Humans created it in order to classify, organize, and make sense of what we observe in the natural world. There are various definitions of a species, but there is not one that is satisfactory for all life as we know it. The most widely accepted definition, known as the biological species concept, distinguishes a species based on the ability of individuals to mate and produce fertile offspring.

If two individuals cannot mate, or can mate but do not produce offspring capable of reproducing themselves, then the individuals are considered to be of two different species. For example, we would not expect a fruit fly to mate with a horse: they cannot, and are therefore considered to be two different species. However, we know that horses and donkeys can mate. They even produce offspring: mules. However, mules are sterile. Thus, horses and donkeys are considered two different species. There are many different species of *Drosophila*, some of which have almost identical morphologies. Most of us would not be able to tell them apart, until we attempted to mate them. Three major problems exist with the biological species concept:

- *How can asexual organisms be classified?* If the criterion for differentiating species relies on mating, then this definition cannot be used for organisms that reproduce only by cell division, such as bacteria.
- *How can we classify organisms that are extinct?* We classify fossils into different species, but we have no knowledge of their mating capabilities.
- *How do we distinguish between the ability to mate and the actual reality of mating?* Many organisms will not mate in their natural habitats, but will mate in an artificial environment. For example, lions and tigers do not mate in the wild, but can mate and reproduce in zoos and wildlife sanctuaries (in this instance, however, the species definition may still work: the offspring are sterile).

As we mentioned, the whole notion of a species is an artificial construct, and thus a single definition cannot be accurately applied to every situation. However, the biological species concept supplies us with a good foundation for classifying organisms, and a criterion for determining when speciation events have occurred. When we encounter different cases, such as organisms that reproduce asexually or fossil evidence, we use other criteria. For example, morphology and biochemistry can help us determine whether or not two individuals are likely to belong to the same species.

How does a speciation event take place? Darwin's notions stressed the gradual accumulation of variations, such that, over long periods of time, a species changes via natural selection to such an extent that it cannot be considered the same as the original population. Today, we would add some further caveats to this:

- *Reproductive isolation.* This is the idea discussed in relation to the work of Dobzhansky. If two species are to evolve from a single starting population, then there must be reproductive isolation. If two subsets of the population begin to diverge, but continue to mate randomly, there will be no differences in the genetics within the larger population. Speciation will occur only if the two subsets stop mating with each other. Each subset will evolve based on natural selection and other factors, and the changes that occur in one subset will not necessarily occur in the other. Given enough time, the two subsets may diverge to such an extent that they can no longer mate and produce fertile offspring with each other.
- *Punctuated equilibrium.* Darwin stressed gradual change. However, for some species in the fossil record, we find examples of relatively rapid change intermingled with long periods of stasis (note that "rapid" is a relative term and, geologically speaking, tens of thousands of years is rapid, compared to millions and billions of years). Is

this an actual phenomenon or an artifact of the fossil record? In 1972, Niles Eldredge (b. 1943) and Stephen Jay Gould proposed that this was not an artifact, and contended that evolution could occur at different rates: gradually as well as in stops and starts. They called the latter punctuated equilibrium. This idea does not violate evolutionary theory. It reveals another way in which life can change. Thus, speciation can occur in a relatively short period of time.

- *Genetic drift.* Another powerful force in evolution is genetic drift, whereby random changes in populations have a great effect. Recall that one of the assumptions of the Hardy–Weinberg equilibrium was large population size. In small populations, random changes can dramatically change allelic frequencies. These changes have no "direction" to them, as with natural selection (which increases the frequency of beneficial traits). But their accumulation can cause massive changes in the genetics of the population.
- *Bottleneck effect.* Another type of a random change in a population, similar to genetic drift, is due to the bottleneck effect. In this situation, a drastic event causes a large proportion of the population to die. Those who survive, however, do not live because of an advantageous trait, as would have happened by natural selection. Instead, those who survive do so by chance, and the only traits available to the next generations are those that randomly survived the catastrophe. For example, imagine an island that is devastated by a hurricane. By chance, 90 percent of the individuals in a particular population of birds are killed. The 10 percent that survive do so not because of any particular trait, but by sheer luck. Thus, a population could change dramatically because of a bottleneck.

Evidence for Evolution

In the following sections we will examine some of the evidence for evolution, both from Darwin's time and after. Note that this is not an exhaustive list, but a sampling of examples that increases every year.

Paleontology

Many of the fossils Darwin collected in South America appeared very similar to living (extant) organisms on the continent. Darwin concluded that the fossils were the remains of the ancestral species of those presently alive. In this way, the fossil record provides much support for descent with modification. It also illustrates gradualism, the long time it takes for a species to evolve, and can help us understand the biology and ecology of the past. In addition, we find extinct species which have no counterparts today. We have already discussed some of this fossil evidence, including the Burgess Shale (see chapter 9).

If evolution is indeed gradual, then we would expect to see transitional forms, intermediate stages in the evolution of major lineages and individual species, in the fossil record. However, with an estimated fossilization rate of less than 0.001 percent, transitional forms are not likely to exist. In spite of this, many key specimens have been found. One extraordinary example is seen in the evolution of marine mammals. As children learn from a very early age, whales are mammals: they give birth to live young, feed them with milk, have fur or hair, and are endothermic (warm-blooded). Mammals evolved on land, from tetrapod ancestors. Therefore whales must have evolved from these terrestrial, four-legged creatures. Indeed, we have a well-established fossil record for whales, showing the progression of their evolution from tetrapods to the form we know today (see fig. 10.1). In the case of horses, at least 10 intermediate genera have been identified, spanning over 58 million years of evolution. Multiple examples of intermediate forms also exist within each genera. We see general trends during the evolution of the horse, including an increase in size and a change from a multitoed foot to the now familiar hoof. The primate fossil record also greatly supports the evolution of humans, which we will discuss in detail in chapter 12.

Examples of transitional forms between major taxa have also been identified. *Archaeopteryx lithographica* (150 mya) and *Sinosauropteryx prima* (125 mya) had feathers and are examples of intermediates in the dinosaur-to-bird transition. Many Cynodonts, mammal-like reptiles, have also been discovered. And the *Acanthostega* genus represents the transition from fish to terrestrial animals. *Acanthostega*, which lived approximately 360 mya, had lungs and recognizable limbs.

Comparative anatomy: homology

When we compare the anatomy of extant species, we can see that, even though some structures are used for different purposes, their composition is remarkably similar, or homologous. A classic example of this is the forelimbs of mammals (see fig. 10.2). In primates, the forelimb is used for grasping and carrying, in seals it is used for swimming, and in bats it is used for flying. Regardless of function, all show a common arrangement of bones, from the long bones in the "arms" to the digits in the "fingers." Homology can easily be explained by descent with modification. Over long periods of time, the forelimb of the most recent common ancestor of these species evolved differently in the various lineages due to different environmental conditions and selective pressures. The different anatomies allowed for different functions. The taxonomic schemes of Linnaeus and others can be explained via the process of evolution: organisms placed in the same taxonomic grouping due to similar anatomical structures are descendents of a common ancestor.

Comparative anatomy: analogy (homoplasy)

Distantly related organisms may show similarities in their anatomical structures. Although these similarities may indicate a recent common ancestor, overwhelming differences indicate the opposite. So how do these similarities arise? Species may evolve similar adaptations in response to a similar environment. This is known as convergent evolution, and the adaptations are known as analogous, or homoplastic, structures. For example, two distantly related plants in very different regions may be subjected to the same

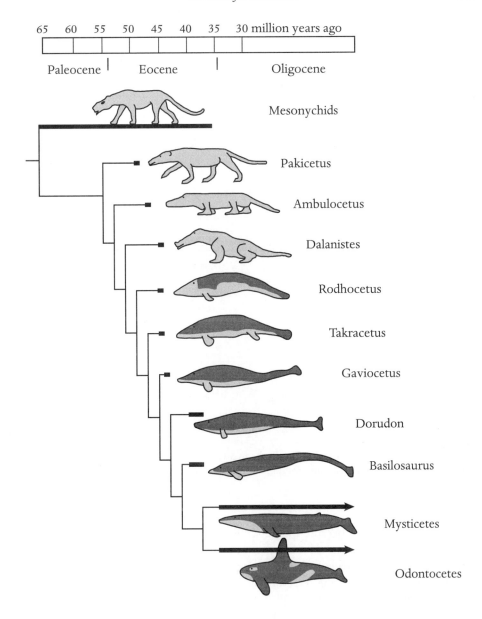

65   60   55   50   45   40   35   30 million years ago

Paleocene | Eocene | Oligocene

Mesonychids

Pakicetus

Ambulocetus

Dalanistes

Rodhocetus

Takracetus

Gaviocetus

Dorudon

Basilosaurus

Mysticetes

Odontocetes

Fig. 10.1 Transitional forms in the evolution of whales. Fossil evidence has allowed us to see the gradual transition from a four-legged terrestrial creature to the modern-day whale.

environmental change, say a gradual reduction in the amount of annual rainfall. Over time, the two environments become deserts. The two plant species will evolve in response to the change, or they will become extinct. In arid climates, many structures have evolved that help plants conserve water, for example leaves in a cactus evolving into needles. So, the two distantly related plants, placed under similar environmental conditions, may

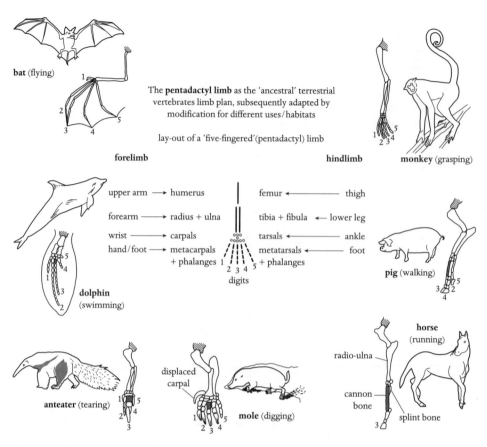

Fig. 10.2 Homology in forelimbs. Forelimbs in various species show amazing similarities in anatomy, even with diverse functioning, supporting the idea that all these species had a common ancestor.

evolve similar structures because of the same selective pressures. Thus, when we look at plants from different desert regions, we see this homoplasy (see fig. 10.3). Another example of analogous structures is the wing. Birds and insects have wings that allow these organisms to fly, but the structure of the wings is very different. With analogous structures, the function is the same but the structure may be different. With homologous structures, the function is different but the structure is the same.

Molecular biology

As we saw in chapter 9, all life uses DNA as its genetic material. The comparison of DNA and protein sequences has become a powerful tool in biology. Carl Woese redrew the tree of life based on sequence comparisons of ribosomal RNA. We now classify organisms according to his three domain system. Mitochondrial and chloroplast DNA show tremendous similarities with the DNA of existing prokaryotic organisms. These

Fig. 10.3 Analogy (homoplasy). Desert adaptations in plants. Similarities evolve from different structures in different organisms when natural selection exerts the same selective pressure. Modification of anatomy in desert plants is an example.

data have been used to support the endosymbiont theory of Lynn Margulis, which explains the formation of eukaryotic cells. The molecular clock can be used to indicate the time of divergence of two species from their most recent common ancestor. Molecular data can provide independent corroboration of conclusions from other lines of evidence. We saw an example of this with the Cambrian explosion. The following is a brief list of some of the uses and interpretations of molecular data.

- Sequencing of the genomes (the entire set of DNA) in multiple organisms, including humans, has allowed for better understanding of the evolution of individual species as well as for extensive comparisons between diverse species.
- Many regions of the DNA that do not code for proteins (more than 95 percent of human DNA) are conserved in other species, indicating these regions have been selected for over the course of evolution and play an important role in the cell. As we have seen, most of these regions are indeed transcribed into RNA, and may function as regulatory molecules in the expression of other genes (various types are called microRNAs and small interfering RNAs). In general, the more noncoding DNA, the more complex the organism.
- More than 19,000 pseudogenes, nonfunctional remnants of genes, have been identified in humans. These can help us uncover our evolutionary past. For example, humans

and other primates carry a pseudogene, $\Psi Gulo$ whose functional counterpart in other mammals, *Gulo*, allows for the organism to produce vitamin C. This supports the notion that primates diverged from the rest of the mammalian lineage more than 40 mya, and explains why primates rely on food sources to obtain this important nutrient. Many pseudogenes have been found to have activity within the cell: these pseudogenes have functional counterparts, and the nonfunctional genes may contribute to the regulation of the functional ones.

- Humans and chimpanzees share over 98 percent of their DNA, independently corroborating other data (from paleontology to comparative anatomy) that indicate the close relationship and recent common ancestry of these two species.

- The environment can affect the rate of mutation of cellular DNA. A change in the environment may cause biochemical changes in the cell that promote random mutations in the DNA, which may, in turn, allow the cell to survive in the new environment.

- Both small nucleotide alterations, as well as reorganization of large regions of the genome, can affect evolution. Many large rearrangements can be traced to ancient viruses that invaded the cellular DNA. These viruses allowed for DNA to be moved within the genome. The remnants of these viruses, transposons, are found scattered throughout many eukaryotic genomes (including humans) and provide another evolutionary mechanism that can alter the DNA.

- Examination of mitochondrial DNA (mtDNA) has been effective in determining the relatedness and evolution of various populations, including humans. The most famous example is the case of what is known as "mitochondrial Eve," where the origin of *Homo sapiens* has been traced, via mtDNA, to a population in Africa, approximately 200,000 years ago.

Embryology

Even the early embryologists noted that embryonic development was very similar in widely diverse species. Darwin made sense of these observations through the notion of common descent: the development of embryos would be similar if the species had a common ancestor. As the species changed over vast periods of time, development would also change, but similarities should still be apparent. For example, many animals go through a developmental stage where a set of blood vessels forms in the neck. In fish, these vessels remain in the neck and are used to obtain oxygen from the gills. However, in other animals, including humans, these vessels reorganize and are distributed to the lungs. Some of Darwin's examples in *Origin* included the larval stages of barnacles which appear as a shrimp-like arthropod, and in *Descent of Man*, he used the example of the tunicate, once classified as a mollusk, which shows a similar embryonic development to chordates. By studying an organism's development, we can predict some of the historical events that shaped the organism; we can better understand its evolution. For example, the jaw in reptiles and the inner ear bones in mammals develop from the same bones in the early embryos. This, along with evidence found in the fossil record, supports the notion of a common ancestor for reptiles and mammals. Marine mammals, such as whales and dolphins, have hindlimb buds during embryonic development. These buds, in other mammals, develop into the hind legs. However, in marine mammals, these buds degenerate before birth.

Vestigial structures

Vestigial structures, or rudimentary organs, are anatomical features that have degenerated through evolution. They help us understand the evolution of a species, and also indicate from what type of ancestor the organism evolved. The function of the vestigial structure, if there is any at all, was different in the ancestor. This is not a case of homology, however: vestigial structures do not function in a manner consistent with their complexity. The appendix is a vestige of the caecum, an organ used in extant animals to digest plant materials. Although it may play a role in the immune system, appendectomy survivors attest to the fact that humans no longer rely on their appendices for a specific function. Wings in the ostrich and other flightless birds may help the birds balance and may be used in courtship displays. They are considered vestiges because they do not allow the birds to fly, which is the primary function of a wing. Pelvic bones in whales and snakes no longer function at all. They are simply leftovers from tetrapod ancestors (see fig. 10.4).

Perhaps one of the most amazing examples of vestigial structures is the case of eyes in cave-dwelling organisms. These animals live in darkness, and, although the structure of an eye is present, it does not function in vision. Many modifications have occurred in subterranean organisms with regard to the structure of the eye. For example, in the mole rat *Spalax ehrenbergi*, the majority of the eye is malformed, including a degenerated lens, and the development of the eye occurs underneath the skin. However, the retina

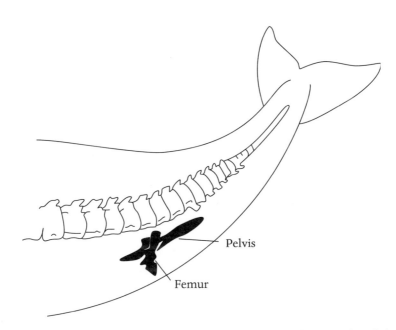

Fig. 10.4 Vestigial structures. Remnants of the pelvis and femur bones in the whale indicate it had an ancestor that once walked on four legs.

has undergone major restructuring and appears to retain a function: it may aid *S. ehrenbergi* in photoperiodism, the light-dependent regulation of circadian rhythms. Changes have also evolved in the brains of subterranean animals, with a regression of the regions involved in sight.

Vestigial structures had been a puzzle to naturalists long before Darwin. Aristotle commented on the reduced size of the eye in moles, and Lamarck noted in *Zoological Philosophy* (1809) the reduction of eyes and their location beneath the skin in *Spalax* and *Proteus*, a salamander that lives underground.

Biogeography

The investigation of the global distribution of living and extinct organisms is known as biogeography, and it can provide much information about evolution. For example, Darwin noticed that the species on the Galapagos Islands more closely resembled species on the South American mainland than species from another island with a similar climate, such as Cape Verde, off the coast of Africa. For Darwin this meant that the ancestors of the Galapagos species came from the mainland. According to Lamarck, the species on islands half a world away should be similar, as they have to adapt to the same environment. In addition, Darwin also noted that each island had different species. He attributed this to natural selection acting differently on each island.

Darwin also speculated on the distributions of species on continents, and attributed the patterns to glacial advances and retreats. Plate tectonics, unknown in his time, help to explain biogeography (see fig. 10.5(*a*)). For example, most marsupial animals are found in Australia, with a few species in South America. Marsupial fossils have been found in Antarctica, where no marsupials exist today. Australia, South America, and Antarctica were once connected in the land mass known as Gondwanaland, and thus the distribution of marsupials can be explained. Fossils of extinct species from the Permian and Triassic periods, such as *Cynognathus*, *Lystrosaurus*, *Mesosaurus*, and *Glossopteris*, have "global" distributions, but their locations can easily be explained by the position of the continents during their existence (see fig. 10.5(*b*)).

Artificial selection (selective breeding)

Through the selective breeding of plants and animals, humans have understood for thousands of years that certain traits can be enhanced or reduced in a particular species. In Darwin's day, it was the fashion to breed pigeons. Amazingly different anatomies, feather colors, and feather patterns emerged via these endeavors (see fig. 10.6(*a*)). Darwin deduced that, if humans could selectively breed certain traits into plants and animals (artificial selection), then a similar process could occur in nature to accomplish change (natural selection). Other examples of artificial selection include the astounding number of dog breeds and the propagation of *Brassica oleracea* to produced broccoli, cabbage, cauliflower, Brussels sprouts, collard greens, kale, and kohlrabi from the same parent plant (see fig. 10.6(*b*)).

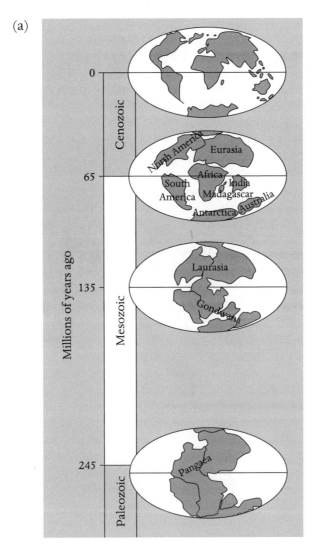

Fig. 10.5 Biogeography. (*a*) Continental drift. The positions of the major land masses at different times in Earth's history are shown. The movement can help explain the distribution of fossils and extant organisms. (*b*) Distribution of fossils and geography at time of existence. Fossil evidence showing the distribution of extinct flora and fauna on different continents is consistent with how the continents fit together during the Permian and Triassic periods (286–213 mya) in the supercontinent Pangaea.

Evolutionary development (developmental genetics)

Darwin's concept of evolution concentrated on changes at the population level, although he did, in *Origin*, indicate that development was the important second part of the evolution equation. However, it is only recently, with our understanding of genetics, that development has provided an important explanatory factor for evolution. Darwin could

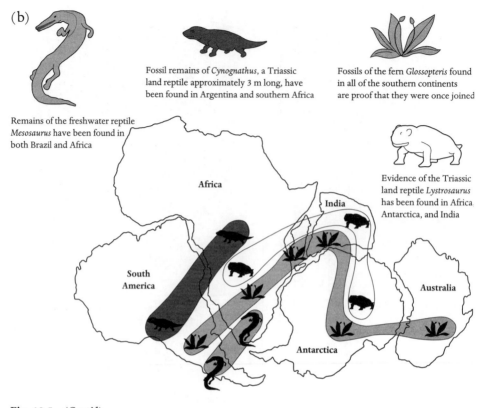

(b)

Remains of the freshwater reptile *Mesosaurus* have been found in both Brazil and Africa

Fossil remains of *Cynognathus*, a Triassic land reptile approximately 3 m long, have been found in Argentina and southern Africa

Fossils of the fern *Glossopteris* found in all of the southern continents are proof that they were once joined

Evidence of the Triassic land reptile *Lystrosaurus* has been found in Africa, Antarctica, and India

Africa

India

South America

Australia

Antarctica

Fig. 10.5   (*Cont'd*)

observe similarities and differences in embryonic development; today we can account for these differences through genetics. The emerging picture is quite extraordinary: many of the differences in organisms result not from different genes, but from how the same genes are expressed during development. Small changes (mutations) affecting the expression of these genes can account for major changes in body structure. Thus, microevolution can explain how new species can evolve (macroevolution).

The genes involved in the development of major body plans are known as homeotic, or homeobox, genes. Many diverse species share these genes. The genetic causes behind dramatic changes in morphology have been uncovered. For example, the development of the eye in species as diverse as fruit flies and mice is controlled in large part by the homeotic gene known as *Pax6*. Although eyes in the animal kingdom are different, this gene is an important player in the development of the organ, and *Drosophila* will form normal eyes under the control of the mouse *Pax6* gene. Although genes may be the same in diverse organisms, differences in gene expression may occur, both in the region where genes are expressed in the embryo and the time at which they are expressed. In addition, each species may have different "targets" for the same developmental gene. These differences in expression patterns and the targets of regulation cause differences in development, resulting in different morphologies. For example, the expression of a gene called *BMP4* in duck and chicken embryos causes cell death. This gene is expressed

Fig. 10.6 (*a*) Artificial selection in animals. The wide variety of body types and feather patterns in pigeons, resulting from selective breeding, shows the incredible diversity possible with artificial selection, which helps support the notion that natural selection can also create this effect. (markku murto/art/Alamy) (*b*) Artificial selection in plants. A wide variety of plants, producing different types of vegetables, is possible with artificial selection.

in certain regions of the feet of these birds, including in between the digits (toes). However, in ducks, another gene, called *Gremlin*, is expressed in the interdigit region. This inhibits the BMP4 protein, and thus the cells in the interdigit region in ducks do not die. Therefore, ducks have webbing in their feet, whereas chickens do not. If the Gremlin protein is applied to the interdigit region in chick embryos before the cell death occurs, the webbing will persist in the chick, and its feet will appear similar to those of a duck. Thus, the expression of a single gene can cause a major morphological change. Other examples like this abound, and we now understand why some insects have two wings and others four, and why some arthropods, such as millipedes and centipedes, have so many legs while insects have only six (in both examples the homeotic gene *Ubx* is involved). The molecular basis for feathers evolving in dinosaurs and the suppression of teeth in birds is also being worked out on a genetic level. Thus, the study of developmental genetics has provided us with much understanding of how massive differences in morphology can result from very minor genetic alterations. This field promises to provide great insights into evolution in the coming years.

(b)

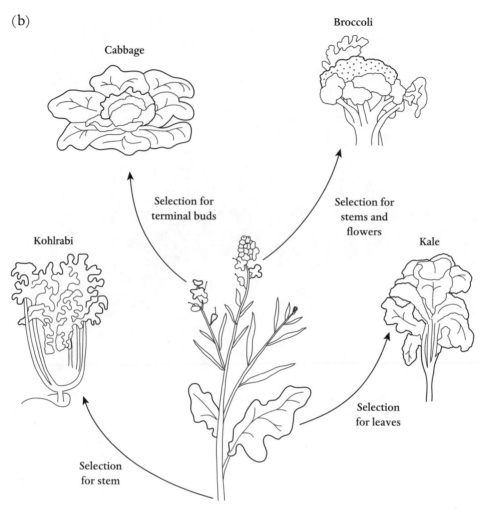

Cabbage

Broccoli

Kohlrabi

Kale

Selection for
terminal buds

Selection for
stems and
flowers

Selection
for leaves

Selection
for stem

Fig. 10.6 (*Cont'd*)

Laboratory experiments

Many investigations have centered on observing evolution in the laboratory, and we will discuss only briefly a few results in one model organism, *Drosophila*. Multiple examples of microevolution have been observed and induced in flies in the lab. Single gene mutations, as we have seen, can dramatically affect the morphology of these organisms. Other mutations have been shown to affect the mating behavior and longevity of flies. By controlling environmental factors, researchers have created instances of macroevolution. For example, *Drosophila* reared on different food sources became reproductively isolated, and hence evolved into different species. Other experiments with *Drosophila* have involved the selective breeding of flies with similar behavioral patterns from a parent population. After many generations of this selection, the resulting flies with different behavior patterns could not mate successfully, another example of speciation. Even without intentional selection or manipulation, lab animals will change from their parent populations. When the descendents of the original lab population are introduced to members of their species recently collected from the wild in the same location as the original population, mating failed to produce viable offspring. This has been observed in species of *Drosophila* and the polychaete worm, *Nereis acuminate*.

Observed examples

The gradual accumulation of changes that Darwin proposed as necessary to produce new species would generally take a long time, and could not be observed by humans. However, there are two caveats: we can observe small changes (microevolution), and we have observed instances of speciation (macroevolution) in natural settings, particularly in plants. Examples of microevolution are numerous. Some of the most famous are the increased antibiotic resistance in bacteria in response to the use of these drugs, and pesticide resistance seen in insects. The idea behind these changes is Darwinian evolution in its purest form: within a population there is variation, so that some individuals in the population are better able to survive in a particular environment. Let's consider the insect example. If a population of insects is exposed to a toxin, most members of the population will die. However, a few will live, as they have a variation that allows them to survive the toxin. These individuals will reproduce, and their offspring will inherit the variation. Therefore, the entire population will be resistant to the poison. Thus, the population has changed. Other examples include:

- increases in the thickness and mass of the shells of marine snails in the Gulf of Maine in response to predation by crabs;
- changes in the morphology of anole lizards when introduced to new environments, over a 10–14 year period, in the Bahamas;
- alterations in developmental time and morphology, including beak length, in soapbugs in Florida, in response to the introduction of a new food source;
- changes in the bill shape of the Hawaiian honeycreeper in response to the extinction of many of its original food plants;
- changes in size and fat content in mosquitofish in Nevada due to changing environmental conditions;
- behavioral, developmental, and genetic changes in the North American apple maggot fly between populations that inhabit its native food source, the hawthorn tree, and apple trees.

These examples of microevolution are complemented by examples of macroevolution:

- *Polyploidy*. Many types of plants, and some animals, can tolerate the duplication of entire sets of chromosomes, a condition known as polyploidy. The polyploid organisms usually cannot reproduce with the parent species, thus the polyploid is a new species. This type of speciation happens within one or a few generations. It has been seen numerous times, for example in the evening primrose. Hybrids created between different species of plants can also result in polyploidy and can produce new species.

- *Cichlids*. The cichlid fish in East Africa are an amazing example of speciation. Currently we know of about 2,500 species. Almost 80 percent of these species can be traced back to a common lineage. The geology of the region is well known, with the formation of lakes such as Lake Malawi and Lake Victoria less than a million years ago, and evidence of drying spells as recently as a few thousand years ago. The diversity of species and the geological history indicate a rapid speciation time for these fish. Molecular data indicate that, in some cases, speciation may have taken place in as short a time as 1,000 years.
- *Green-eyed tree frogs*. Recent studies of the green-eyed tree frog of Australia indicate speciation occurred in under 8,000 years. Climate changes approximately 1 million years ago in a tropical rainforest separated the frog population into northern and southern subsets. The rainforest expanded and the frog populations reconnected about 8,000 years ago. Although the frogs can mate in the laboratory, they do not mate in the wild. The calls of the male frogs are different, and the viability of the offspring between southern and northern frogs is reduced. It is thought that reinforcement of the separation of populations occurred due to female mate choice.

Numerous other examples exist. Table 10.1 provides a brief summary of the main lines of evidence for evolution.

An Example of Falsification?

Recall from our discussion in chapter 2 that Karl Popper stressed the notion of falsifiability, where a theory is scientific if we can figure out a way to prove it false, if we can conceive of an experiment or observation that could disprove the theory. This doesn't mean it will be proven false, only that there is a way to prove it false. Evolution, as with all scientific theories, can be falsified. Many attempts, particularly by creationists (see chapter 11) have been attempted. We will look at one example of a notion that can be falsified, and an attempt to do so. One important tenet of evolution is that DNA mutations, which lead to variation and possible fodder for natural selection, are random. A direction or purpose for change is not part of evolutionary theory; it was, however, an important component of Lamarck's theory. Therefore, if specific mutations could be shown to be driven by a changing environment, if specific mutations were to arise in organisms that allowed them to survive the change, then this aspect of Darwinian evolution could be falsified. In 1988, in the preeminent journal *Nature*, John Cairns (b. 1922) and his colleagues at the Harvard School of Public Health published a paper that falsified the notion of nondirected mutations. Cairns, a well-respected cancer researcher, provided data from experiments with bacteria that indicated evolution could be directed. In these experiments, Cairns began with bacteria containing a mutation which prevented the use of a particular sugar, lactose, as a food source. The bacteria were first grown in a medium with a different sugar, glucose, and then the environment was changed to one in which only lactose was present. Cairns and his colleagues reasoned that some bacteria would randomly mutate, when grown in glucose, and would be able to use lactose. When placed on the lactose medium, these bacteria would survive. Cairns did indeed see this. But he also saw something

Table 10.1 Summary of types of evidence for evolution

Evidence	What it is	What it indicates	Example
Paleontology	Study of fossils: preserved remains of, or impressions from, once living organisms	Organisms change with time; organisms can become extinct	Transitional forms of whales; Burgess Shale
Comparative anatomy: homologous structures	Examination of similarities in anatomy in organisms	Similarities indicate common ancestry	Forelimbs in mammals
Comparative anatomy: analogous (homoplastic) structures	Study of similar structures in distantly related species	Shows convergent evolution: organisms that evolve in similar environments share similar adaptations due to natural selection	Modified leaves in desert plants; wings in birds, bats, and insects
Molecular biology	Comparison of DNA and protein sequences in living organisms	The more similar the sequence, the more recent the last common ancestor; the molecular clock can be used to estimate the date of divergence	Humans and chimps share over 98% of their DNA; time and location of the origin of *Homo sapiens*
Embryology	Examination of the stages of embryonic development; some stages show ancestral forms not used by the organism today, others show similar development to other organisms	Provides insights into the evolutionary history of the organism	Hindlimb buds in marine mammals
Vestigial structures	Degeneration of complex anatomical features; become non-functional or lose their original function	Descent with modification and common ancestry	Pelvic bones in whales; eyes in cave-dwelling animals

Table 10.1 (Cont'd)

Evidence	What it is	What it indicates	Example
Biogeography	Examination of the distribution of organisms extinct and living; takes into account plate tectonics and the movement of land masses	Provides a history of how species evolved	Geographic distribution of marsupials
Artificial selection	The selective breeding of traits in organisms by humans	Human selection is seen as an analogy to how natural selection works; if humans can create such variation, so could nature	Dog breeds; agricultural crops
Evolutionary development	Examination of the genes involved in the development of body plans	Shows how mutations in genes (micro- and macroevolution) can result in speciation	Homeotic genes in diverse organisms
Laboratory experiments	Breeding of laboratory organisms; genetic alteration of organisms	Organisms can change under various circumstances (micro- and macroevolution); alteration of genetics is responsible for changes	Alteration and speciation of *Drosophila*
Observed examples	Observations of naturally occurring changes in wild populations	Show microevolution and, in some instances, macroevolution, in response to environmental changes	Antibiotic resistance in bacteria; pesticide resistance in insects; speciation in plants

else: bacteria that did not grow immediately on lactose began to grow after a few days. This indicated that the "later" growing bacteria were mutating their DNA specifically to allow them to use lactose. Control experiments indicated that these "delayed" mutants did not contain other mutations. If other mutations existed, this would have indicated that the DNA was mutating in multiple places, one of which would have allowed the bacteria to use lactose (which would support the random mutation notion).

This created a buzz in the scientific community. If true, the results indicate that mutations can be directional, which would be a blow to Darwinian concepts. As we have seen, the scientific method is one which tests and retests, and this notion of directed mutations was subjected to much scrutiny. This particular incident provides an excellent example of the scientific method in action. After the Cairns results were published, many researchers took a close look at the data, and attempted to reproduce the work. Cairns was criticized for the particular bacterial strain he chose, as well as for his choice of a control. Some argued that natural biochemical processes, not directed mutation, could account for his results. Some scientists tried to reproduce his results in other systems, to address the criticisms: however, they did not find evidence of directed mutations. Thus, although Cairns's system could have falsified a central tenet of evolution, further investigations did not support his claims.

Although the Cairns data did not falsify random mutations, the work did spur new investigations into how mutations arise. Researchers have since shown that bacteria can increase rates of mutations in response to environmental stress. These increased rates may allow for beneficial mutations to arise, although in a random, not directed, fashion. This could allow for the survival of the bacteria in a changing environment.

Is God Evident in Evolution?

How does all this evidence for evolution affect theology and a Christian understanding of God? Religious reactions to Darwin's ideas included both opposition, as well as attempts at integration. Aubrey Moore (1848–90), an Anglo-Catholic theologian, was one of the integrationists. He contended that evolutionary theory is more Christian than the theory of special creation. Evolution implies the immanence of God in nature: God's creative power is omnipresent. When opponents of evolution cite the intervention of God, Aubrey argued, they implied that God is ordinarily absent. Thus Aubrey saw no reason why there should be any conflict between evolutionary theory and theology.

Karl Rahner (1904–84), a Jesuit priest and theologian, emphasized the oneness of God's creation, and that all things come from God. The history of the cosmos that we know through science is part of the history of matter, life, and humans. There is a single history, which is a history of change and the emergence of new forms. Rahner used this understanding to highlight the connection of matter and spirit.

Arthur Peacocke (1924–2006), a priest in the Church of England and winner of the Templeton Prize in 2001, echoed the sentiments of both Aubrey and Rahner and further developed a Christian theology that incorporated evolution. Through biological and cosmic evolution, we understand the dynamic changing character of nature. This continuous change, Peacocke argued, is God's action as a past and present creator. Evolution is God acting as a creator. God is not a supporting player or an additional factor that intervenes on occasion. Peacocke explained this notion further by incorporating scientific and theological notions, many of which we have already explored. For example, Peacocke emphasized both chance and natural law in the evolutionary processes. The interplay of chance and law allows for creativity and the emergence of new forms. If law alone were at work, there would only be repetitive order, with no variation or creativity. On the other hand, if chance alone governed the cosmos, there would be no forms or patterns, and no organization that could be understood or detected by science. But when chance works within the framework of law, novel possibilities emerge. Peacocke viewed God as the source of both law and chance. God has allocated many potentialities in creation, and chance allows for their actualization.

Peacocke identified four trends or propensities in evolution, which he saw as being inevitable consequences of natural selection:

- *Complexity.* Although the histories of many organisms do not demonstrate an increase in complexity, and indeed some show a decrease, Peacocke contended that evolution permits complexity (but does not necessitate it). The emergence of complexity may certainly contribute to survivability, and may be selected for by nature.
- *Information processing and storage ability.* Organisms that can sense their environment, and that can process and store information, have a distinct advantage for survival in a variety of environments. Thus, Peacocke argued, the evolution of the brain and nervous system would be evolutionarily advantageous. This would eventually lead to the emergence of consciousness.
- *Experience of pain and suffering.* The increased ability to process and store information leads to increased sensitivity and an increase in the ability to feel pain and to suffer. These traits again can enhance survival, as they would force an organism to take action when encountering potentially life-threatening situations.
- *Self-consciousness and language.* The enhanced ability to process and store information provides the basis for communication. Peacocke argued that these traits would be advantageous for survival by allowing organisms to create complex social interactions, including cooperation.

Peacocke saw these propensities as inherently built into the evolutionary process. These trends can be explained by natural selection, as they would allow for enhanced survival and reproduction in a wide range of environments. Thus chance allows for a multitude of potentialities to be realized, and this includes self-conscious entities that would be capable of having a relationship with God. This could be regarded as the intention of God. Chance and law, not any special acts of intervention by God, would have allowed for the emergence of human-like beings.

Conclusions

The importance biologists place on evolution in understanding life cannot be overstated. Every system and relationship studied can be analyzed within the framework of natural selection and other evolutionary forces. This overarching paradigm is not a religion, as some have claimed. It is science: it can be falsified. The discoveries of the twentieth century, particularly in the field of genetics, confirmed what many scientists in the past believed but did not have adequate evidence to support. The independent fields within biology, as well as other natural sciences outside of biology, have presented overwhelming examples of evolution. Evolution is not simply an inference from historical data, as some creationists have contended. Nor do we find only a handful of examples that could be interpreted in different ways. The accumulated evidence, in its entirety, is best explained by evolutionary theory. The theory has been revised in light of new branches of inquiry, as happens in all instances of "good" science. But it is still the best, and indeed the only scientifically testable explanation for the evidence. Many attempts have been made to falsify it but, so far, none have succeeded. Theologically, evolution does not have to pose a problem with our understanding of God, although some insist that it does. Creationists often argue that we have never seen evolution happen, and therefore we should not accept its tenets from circumstantial evidence. This begs the question how much evidence is needed, how much is enough, before we can accept a theory. Darwin had much less evidence, and yet he and many of his contemporaries found it sufficient to accept evolution and the theory of natural selection. Evidence for a round Earth was not conclusive until we sent rockets into space in the middle of the twentieth century. In the next chapter, we will explore the arguments of creationists in more detail.

Primary Literature

Useful primary sources include an article written by Ian Stewart, professor of mathematics at the University of Warwick, in which he applies concepts in mathematics and physics to our understanding of speciation, "How the Species Became," *New Scientist* 180 (2416) (2003), 32–5; and an excerpt from an article by Arthur Peacocke, "Biological Evolution and Christian Theology – Yesterday and Today," in John Durant, ed., *Darwinism and Divinity: Essays on Evolution and Religious Belief* (Oxford: Blackwell, 1985), pp. 121–7.

Questions to Consider

1 Atavisms are the unexpected appearance of traits present in past lineages of an organism. For example, atavistic hindlimbs have been found in living whales, and human babies have been born with tails. How can these atavistic traits be explained using models of evolutionary development?

2 You are a graduate student in the environmental studies program at a major research university. Your advisor is studying different populations of a species of sparrow in Georgia and South Carolina. On one of your many trips to observe these birds, you notice a group of birds in South Carolina that differ dramatically from the population you have just been studying in Georgia. You tell your advisor that this South Carolina population is a new species of sparrow. However, your adviser is skeptical. What evidence could you gather that would indicate the South Carolina

population is indeed a different species, and not just a variant of the Georgia population? Think of several ways to investigate this question.

3   Darwin was interested in the pollination of orchids by insects. One species of orchid in Madagascar (*Angraecum sequipedale*) has an unusual feature: an 11-inch-long nectar receptacle. Darwin reasoned that there must be a moth somewhere in Madagascar that had an 11-inch-long proboscis to harvest the orchid's nectar. Forty years later, *Xanthopan morganii praedicta*, the Madagascan sphinx moth, was discovered with just such a feature. How would Darwin explain the evolution of the unusual anatomical features of the moth and the flower? (Hint: this is an example of what biologists call coevolution.)

4   Some terrestrial plants living today appear to be very similar to species found in the fossil record from 400 million years ago. Identify at least two different ways to interpret this. How could evolution explain these different interpretations?

5   Can you think of a way to falsify the major lines of evidence for evolution? For example, a falsification of the fossil record would be finding a particular fossil, A, during time period 1, no evidence of species A at the successive time periods 2 and 3 (but the presence of fossils B and C, presumed descendents of A, are found in time periods 2 and 3, respectively), but then finding species A again at time period 4. Also, think about the Cairns example discussed in this chapter.

6   Which type or category of evidence for evolution presented in this chapter do you find the most compelling? Why?

7   Consider the idea of punctuated equilibrium. What forces or mechanisms could cause this type of change?

11

Evolution and Design

Overview

The notion of design in nature is paramount in discussions of evolution, and we can trace the history of the different ideas about design since Darwin. Evangelicalism and fundamentalism are important in this history; they both rely on biblical inerrancy but also hold science in high esteem. These doctrines spawned scientific creationism, a movement that refutes evolution. Creationists interpret scientific data using the paradigm that God created the world in the way depicted in the Genesis account, and claim that their conclusions are based in science, not theology. The intelligent design (ID) movement argues that organisms, at the molecular level, are too complex to have evolved via natural selection, and therefore must have been designed. Like creationists, proponents of ID interpret the scientific data from a different viewpoint; unlike creationists, they do not deny evolution occurs, nor do they specifically identify the designer. Various views of theistic evolution embrace evolution as the mechanism for change, and include a role for God within the process itself. Some important topics within these theologies include theodicy, eschatology, and teleology. The debate over what to teach in the public schools regarding evolution, creationism, and ID are ongoing.

Introduction

The order and complexity we see in nature, unsurprisingly, invites us to conclude that a designer planned and constructed the universe and life as we know it. We examined this previously in the light of cosmology. The doctrine of a world created by God from nothing (*creatio ex nihilo*) was, and still is, the Christian worldview. As we have seen, prior to the Enlightenment, the biblical account of the creation of the universe and of all life was not interpreted in a literal fashion. The creation myth was meant to provide meaning and purpose, not a scientific explanation. Nevertheless, as a reaction to the Enlightenment, the Genesis account was taken to be an accurate description of how the cosmos came into being. Prior to Darwin, there were no accepted scientific theories to challenge this notion. Although evidence was accumulating that contradicted a literal interpretation of the biblical account of creation, a theoretical explanation for creation was lacking. Darwin provided evidence to question this interpretation, and presented a theory to explain how and why life changes. The appearance of plants and animals, all specially created "according to their kind," was giving way to a view of gradual change, where the environment is critical, and common descent accounts for all life forms.

Reactions to the idea of natural selection included a renewed fervor for creationism that remains in our society to this day. This chapter traces some of the history of creationism since the publication of *Origin of Species*, the modern incarnation of creationism (intelligent design), and more recent efforts to assimilate theology with the scientific understandings of evolution. A table comparing and contrasting these different positions can be found in table 11.1.

Creationism: Historical Background

The terms "creationism," "fundamentalism," and "evangelicalism" have different meanings in different contexts, and have been used interchangeably, particularly in relation to views about evolution. The evangelical movement began in the 1730s, as an offshoot of Protestant traditions from the English Reformation. A high regard for the Bible, action as an expression of the gospel, and the sacrifice of Christ on the cross are central to evangelicalism. From its inception as a religious movement, evangelicals have embraced and used science. They went beyond a commitment to natural theology, and applied reason and empiricism to the spiritual world. They found cause-and-effect relationships within a theological framework. Evangelicals believe that theologians should use the data and facts in the Bible to understand God, in the same way as scientists use empirical evidence from the world to understand nature, a practice called scientific biblicalism. Scientific language was used to describe what the Bible teaches. Twentieth-century evangelicals continued to view science as a way of glorifying God.

Fundamentalism arose from the evangelical movement in America during and after World War I. The fundamentalist stance, which was anti-modern, emphasized the inerrancy of the Bible, and the miracle-working power and the resurrection of Christ. Fundamentalists did not take a stand on creation, and thus evolution did not pose a theological problem. However, some fundamentalists could not accept the theory of evolution, and began the creationist movement. Some of these were ardent premillennialists, who focused on the return of Jesus Christ (see chapter 7). This new fundamentalist movement called for a literal interpretation of the Bible, and a belief that a single error in the Bible would invalidate it in its entirety. Therefore, these fundamentalists viewed evolution as a threat to the Bible, and rejected the science. We refer to this movement as biblical creationism.

Table 11.1 Comparison of creationism, intelligent design, and theistic evolution[a]

	Creationism	*Intelligent design*	*Theistic evolution*
Basic tenets	God created all living things in their present form less than 10,000 years ago. Evolution does not occur. Creation science allows for an older Earth and some minor changes in species, but not speciation.	Complex, information-rich systems cannot be explained without intelligent causes; Darwinism cannot account for everything we see in nature.	Evolution can be brought together with Christian faith to create a more complete understanding of the natural world.
Source of complexity in nature	God	The designer (God)[b]	Natural forces (natural selection); divine intervention is possible, but does not violate natural laws.
God's role/action	God created everything in special acts of creation.	God designed, altered, and continues to change living things when necessary.	God is the creator, the primary cause; God may continue to intervene through natural laws (secondary causation).
Attitude toward scientific methodology	There is a high regard for science; interpretation of data is the critical difference between those adhering to creation science and evolution.	Methods are basically correct, and evolution is acceptable, but Darwinism is philosophically and scientifically incorrect because it does not allow for purpose or design.	Science generally makes correct conclusions about the natural world which can lead to truth and understanding (in conjunction with theology).
Effect of science on religious doctrine	Science is accepted when it supports doctrine, and rejected when it doesn't; science does not influence or change doctrine.	Science can provide evidence for the existence of God through the argument from design.	Science is accepted, embraced, and incorporated into theology; doctrines may be altered in some cases.

Table 11.1   (*Cont'd*)

	Creationism	*Intelligent design*	*Theistic evolution*
Teleology/*telos*	God designed the universe according to a plan; there is a purpose and goal to everything.	There is design, and therefore there is purpose.	With strict adherence to evolution, there is no *telos*; some view God as intervening without violating natural laws to direct evolution or to nudge it in a particular direction.
Theodicy	Free will, given to humans by God, led to the fall (the cause of evil, suffering, and death).	ID brings God, excluded by Darwin, back into the beauty and horror of nature.	Suffering is an unavoidable part of the creative process.

[a]   Many different viewpoints may exist within each category. The table summarizes the main ideas of each. It is not meant as a comprehensive treatment of all positions.

[b]   For comparison purposes, God is specified as the designer in the intelligent design category, although ID proponents do not insist on God as the designer.

With the evidence from geology mounting to support the notion of an old Earth, many biblical literalists sought to reconcile the six-day creation account in Genesis with the accumulating scientific evidence. Two ideas arose from this:

- *The day-age interpretation* (also called *progressive creationism*), which regards the days of Genesis not as literal 24-hour days, but rather as huge expanses of time that correlate with the natural history of the world. God still creates through special acts, but natural laws are emphasized and divine intervention is considered to be limited.
- *Gap interpretation*, which sees the early chapters of Genesis as representing two different periods of time, separated by perhaps millions or billions of years. According to this view, the first verse of Genesis tells of the creation of the heavens and the Earth, which could have happened long ago. This world was destroyed, and then Genesis 1:2 picks up with the six days of creation, which happened about 4,000 years before the birth of Christ. In this model, the fossil evidence we find today is a relic of the first creation.

Those who adhere to either of these models are often referred to as old Earth creationists: they hold to the doctrine of special creation but do not interpret the Bible in a strictly literal sense.

The biblical creationists are a distinct and separate group from the scientific creationists. For the latter, science takes priority: science is seen as the authority, and it can support the Bible. The Bible is held in high regard, but the scientific creationists see themselves as scientists, arguing on scientific, not theological, grounds. They are often referred to as young Earth creationists. It is this viewpoint that we will focus on in the remainder of this chapter.

In the aftermath of Darwin, the average American still believed in the doctrine of special creation. When the evolution debate began to enter the public forum, particularly with evolution being taught in the public school system, creationists saw a threat to society based on the application of Darwinian notions outside of science (see chapter 12). If evolution were responsible for "creating" humans, then our moral and social values were also a result of this process. Racism, warfare, poverty, and many other social evils could be seen as the perfectly natural, and unavoidable, behavior of a species that is in no way different from its animal cousins. At the heart of this fight was William Jennings Bryan, the former secretary of state under Woodrow Wilson and three-time presidential candidate for the Democratic Party. Today he is best known for his role in the Scopes trial, in which John Scopes was tried for violating the Tennessee law banning the teaching of evolution in 1925 (see chapter 8). Bryan, a fundamentalist, was a social reformer dedicated to preventing war. His views on evolution encompassed both natural science as well as social Darwinism. He was convinced that Darwinian theory had directly impacted society, and ultimately led to World War I. Including evolution in the public school curriculum, he contended, would corrupt the minds of students and be a threat to their faith and to the morals of society. Bryan was not a biblical literalist, and used more of a day–age interpretation of the Bible. He was not necessarily opposed to evolution, but he denied the existence of any evidence to support the evolution of man. Although Bryan's views do not fit a strict definition of creation science, he is considered an icon by the creationist movement for standing up for his beliefs.

Bryan had a large following from all regions of the country and all walks of life. Support was especially strong in the rural south. The anti-evolution movement gained momentum after the victory of the Scopes trial and other trials in Mississippi and Arkansas. However, efforts for legislative reform petered out, and the movement switched its tactics to promote creationism. The momentum did not come from organized churches but from individuals and interdenominational establishments. They were effective at the local level, pressuring school boards, teachers, and publishers not to include evolution in the curriculum. The creationists did not number many in their ranks who were trained in the natural sciences. However, that was soon to change.

In 1923, George McCready Price (1870–1962), a Seventh-Day Adventist, published *The New Geology*, in which he provided scientific evidence to support the biblical flood. He refuted the dating of fossil records according to their order in the geological strata. This theme was reexamined in 1961 in *The Genesis Flood*, by Henry M. Morris (1918–2006) and John C. Whitcomb Jr. (b. 1924). Morris, who had a doctorate in hydraulic engineering, taught engineering at a number of universities, while Whitcomb was an Old Testament theologian at Grace Theological Seminary in Indiana. Their book argues for the recent creation of the universe and a worldwide flood that was responsible for the deposition of the strata over the course of a single year. The book has all the appearances of scientific validity. Its impact was significant, resulting in several societies of scientists with advanced degrees engaging in research and education relating to creationism. Textbooks were also published that were based on creationist principles. Morris established the Institute for Creation Research (ICR) at the Christian Heritage College in San Diego in

1972, which still exists today. In addition, creationist doctrine spread overseas and is now an international movement. A large part of its appeal is its apparent scientific respectability. We will now take a look at the underpinnings of scientific creationism, the claims it has on science, and the theological considerations.

The Science of Scientific Creationism

Scientific creationists consider themselves to be scientists. They claim their motives are not biblically based, rather that the scientific data do not support evolution. The creationists are not rejecting science, and do not oppose it. However, they argue that the interpretation of the scientific data is what needs to be addressed. If the data are interpreted correctly, the tenets of evolutionary biology fall away very quickly, and the biblical accounts of creation are supported.

Although most of the controversy today centers on the ability of natural selection to produce new species, the scope of creationism is not just biology: cosmological evolution is included in a wider worldview. For scientific (young Earth) creationists, the idea of *creatio ex nihilo* (creation from nothing but divine action), excludes the developmental processes of big bang. Time, matter, space, energy, and laws were all created from nothing. *Ex nihilo* creation is a doctrine accepted by most Christians, who see it as a reflection of the power, love, and goodness of God. However, what is unique to the creationist viewpoint is the denial of change in creation over time; everything was created in its final form, as we see it today, about 10,000 years ago.

With regard to the origin of life, creationists believe that life was a special act of creation. In support of their claims, they point to the inability of mutations and natural selection to account for speciation and common descent. Creationists acknowledge that some changes, in the form of genetic variations, can be seen within species (microevolution). However, these changes occur only within the "kinds" expressed in the biblical account in Genesis. The term "kind" is not clearly defined in the Bible, but it is usually interpreted today as the modern scientific concept of a species. Creationists argue the kinds, or species, we have today were created in their present form, and variations may occur through genetic changes. However, organisms are "fixed" and cannot change into other species (macroevolution).

Creationists claim the scientific evidence used to support evolution of this kind is lacking. If natural selection were responsible for macroevolution, we should see transitional forms in the fossil record, but, according to creationists, we don't. Without macroevolution, common descent is also an invalid concept: there could not have been an ancestor for all forms of life given the inability of kinds to change substantially. Humans, therefore, could not have a common ancestor with apes, and were a separate and distinct creation from other animals. This backs up the biblical account and, therefore, science supports the theological notion of the special creation of humans.

In addition to gaps, the fossil record cannot be used to date the age of the Earth or to support evolution. The creationists point to a catastrophic event, the Genesis flood, to account for the Earth's strata. This worldwide deluge caused the deaths of huge numbers of plants and animals within the time span of a year. The remains of the organisms settled and became fossilized in the sedimentary layers. Creationists claim that all life forms, including those found today, can be seen within the same strata, and therefore the fossil record cannot be used to support evolution.

The fossil record is related to the age of the Earth. For evolution to occur, vast expanses of time are necessary. Current scientific estimates of the age of the Earth are at about 4.5 billion years. Creationism can work with the notion of a young or an old Earth; however, the scientific creationists claim the evidence supports a young Earth, less than 10,000 years old. They question the evidence regarding an old Earth using two main scientific principles: the second law of thermodynamics and radiometric dating.

- The *second law of thermodynamics* states that when energy is transformed, some of it is lost. Chaos (entropy) always increases. According to the big bang theory, order emerges from chaos, which is a violation of this law. Currently, we should see organisms "devolving" rather than evolving. Creationists argue this is exactly what is happening and can be seen, for example, through mutations. They claim that the second law of thermodynamics is the result of sin, a consequence of the fall.
- *Radiometric dating* is the use of radioactive decay to date material. Decay occurs when unstable atomic nuclei emit subatomic particles (radiation). The resulting atoms are a different isotope of the element, or a different element altogether. The ratio of the two elements in an object can be used to determine the age of the object. Carbon-14 (which decays to nitrogen-14) is often used to date biological material and has a half-life (the time it takes for half of the material to decay) of 5,730 years. Therefore, by determining the ratio of carbon-14 to nitrogen-14, the age of a substance can be calculated. This isotope is adequate to date material thousands of years old, but cannot be used for older objects. Other radioisotopes have longer half-lives, such as uranium-238 (which decays to lead-206), at 4.5 billion years, and potassium-40 (which decays to argon-40) at 1.25 billion years. These radioisotopes can be used to date material that is much older. Creationists contend that these very long half-lives, in the range of millions and billions of years, cannot be accurately determined. Scientists rely on assumptions regarding the rates of decay and elemental ratios that can't be verified and therefore can't be trusted.

The Earth, creationists propose, may appear to be old, but it really isn't. Different explanations are used to account for this. For example, complex physical and biological processes could have caused the Earth to appear older than it is. Another explanation is divine action: God made the Earth appear to be old, when it really isn't.

Creationists stress that science can only examine what exists today: a picture of the past (or future) is purely speculative because empirical data cannot be gathered, and any extrapolation of events outside of the present time is based on faith. Therefore, science can be said to be based on faith. Where you place your faith will determine whether you are a biblical Christian or a materialistic scientist. This is similar to Kuhn's notions of a paradigm. Two people with different faiths or viewpoints will interpret the same data differently. Scientific creationists claim that what they are doing is science: they are using purely scientific arguments, but starting with a different paradigm from the rest of the scientific community. Today, intelligent design is the new version of creationism. We will discuss this concept in a moment, but first, we will take a brief look at some criticisms of creationism.

Critiques of Creationism

Although creationists regard themselves as scientists, their research is sparse and has not been published in recognized scientific journals. From the creationist viewpoint, it is not necessary to produce new data: most of their arguments center on the interpretation of existing scientific data. And, in the opinion of most scientists, their interpretations are seriously flawed.

With regard to the fossil record, creationists have failed to interpret the data with accuracy or integrity. Flood geology contradicts the scientific evidence, and there are many examples of transitional forms in the fossil record. Creationists often use outdated evidence to refute evolution, and regularly quote scientists out of context.

The basic foundations of the scientific method are ignored by creationists. They cannot make any testable predictions, a concept that is at the heart of the scientific method. And they will not allow their basic premise (their theory), that God created the world in its present form, to be falsified: this cannot be refuted. Their conclusion is known in advance of the research, and therefore what they are doing is not science.

Creationism has many theological problems as well. If God made the Earth to appear older than it is, then God is being deceptive, playing a trick on us. To embrace God, we would need to deny the validity of our empirical observations and to invalidate science. And we would be worshiping a God who misleads us.

Science examines the natural world, the finite causes and temporal reality that can be measured by our senses. Religion tries to grasp the infinite, divine, transcendent order of things. The creationists try to conflate these two realms, and merge these two separate ways of understanding into a single epistemology.

The History of Intelligent Design

Intelligent design (ID) has gained much momentum in recent years, mostly in the debate over what to teach in the science classroom with regard to evolution. Briefly, ID is the notion that complex, information-rich systems cannot be explained without intelligent causes, and that these intelligent causes can be detected empirically. The ID argument is essentially teleological: one or more designers created, and may continue to create, these complex systems for a particular purpose.

We have examined some ideas regarding design of the cosmos, but cosmological and biological design can be viewed on two different levels. Cosmologically, the contingency question pervades the discussion: why is there anything at all? Although we often focus on the fine-tuning of the laws and constants of the universe, the existence of God is supported by design, given the fact that something, anything, exists. Biologically, we look at design pointing to the existence of God based on what does exist. In this realm, we focus particularly on order and the apparent direction of evolution (toward greater complexity). This is the center of the ID argument. Before beginning an in-depth discussion of ID, let's first look at its history.

Complexity in nature is not the debate: the origin, or cause, of this complexity is. With regard to God's action in the universe, we often refer to primary causation and secondary causation. Primary causation is a cosmological cause: the result is the existence of matter, energy, time, natural laws, physical constants, etc. Secondary causation is the cause of the events that we see happening, or that have happened in the past. If God acted to create the cosmos, then God acted as the primary cause. If God also acts to cause the events we see and test for, then God also acts as a secondary cause. However, if natural laws cause the events we test for in science, then these laws are responsible for secondary causation.

We have seen that the argument from design and questions of causation are old topics (yes, we're back to the Greeks again!). Aristotle believed the key to understanding something was to examine the causes that have brought that thing into existence. However, he used the term "cause" differently from how we use it today. All objects had four causes, according to Aristotle:

- *material cause*: the material from which the object is made;
- *formal cause*: the form, shape, or blueprint of the object;
- *efficient cause*: the effort that goes into making the object by the agent, creator, builder, or designer;
- *final cause*: the purpose (*telos*) of the object; the intention of the maker of the object.

A classic example to illustrate these causes is a chair: the material cause is the wood from which it was made; the formal cause is the seat, back, legs, etc. of the chair; the efficient cause is the carpenter who built the chair; and the final cause is its function as an object on which to sit.

If there appears to be a design, does it mean there is a designer? Democritus (c.460–370 BCE) and Lucretius opposed design. They adhered to the idea that the natural world consists of particles that move and collide with each other to form entities which appear to have complexity and order. Lucretius also pointed out that, if there were an intelligent designer, many things have been badly designed.

Thomas Aquinas used some of Aristotle's ideas in his "Five Ways of Knowing God", notably when he argued for cause and for purpose. In the second way, Aquinas argued for the existence of God from first causes: nothing can cause itself, so there must be a first cause. This, he affirmed, must be God. In the fifth way, Aquinas applied Aristotle's final cause to make the teleological argument: purpose is apparent, and things act with *telos*: objects are directed to their end; the purpose of structures, the order of things, points to intelligent causation.

In the seventeenth century, as the scientific method was blossoming, reductionism and determinism gained favor, and mechanical philosophy was popular. In this context, design meant that preexisting matter was formed for a specific purpose by a designer (God acting as secondary causation). With the rise of empiricism, God was eliminated as a cause from the physical world (scientific methodology rejects ideas that cannot be tested empirically). However, we need to take note that not everyone subscribed to this notion. Recall Newton's ideas where God kept the orbits of the planets secure. In this respect, Newton was advocating that God acted both in primary and in secondary causation, although natural laws also accounted for secondary causation.

As we saw in chapter 6, David Hume was deeply critical of natural theology. Not only did he argue that the analogy central to the design argument (that God designs similarly to how humans design) is flawed, but he also concluded that, in an infinite world, all combinations of matter are continuously produced and destroyed; eventually these combinations will be ordered and complex, to give the appearance of design.

Although largely rejected by the physicist, the notion of design lived on in the seventeenth and eighteenth centuries in biology. As we have seen, William Paley was an influential proponent of natural theology. Paley argued that the complexity of organisms could not have arisen through the blind forces of nature, and therefore God must have designed them. He used the example of the eye: how could such a complex structure have arisen without a designer? Darwin's theory of natural selection helped topple natural theology: the eye was not a complex wonder that only a designer could have conceived; it was a structure that could have developed, step by step, through natural selection, over the course of a very long period of time. However, as we saw with cosmology and creation, the notion of design never died. It has now been recast as intelligent design.

It is important to note here that most ID proponents affirm evolution, whereas creationists reject it. These two groups do have one important philosophical idea in common: they both oppose the materialist and mechanistic epistemology of Darwinian evolution. Let's look more closely at the science and theology behind ID.

Intelligent Design Today: Scientific Claims

Current proponents insist that ID is not just a rehash of Paley and others who used natural theology to make the argument from design. They contend that ID can be supported with rigorous scientific demonstrations and empirical evidence. Supporters claim ID is scientific and not philosophical, and maintain the ideas of ID can be falsified. ID rests on the premise that some natural phenomena cannot be explained by natural processes, therefore, necessity cannot account for complexity; and the probability that what we see arose by chance is extremely small. So, we are left with design.

One of the main problems has been the ability to distinguish design from unintelligent cause. What exactly are the criteria for design? William Dembski (b. 1960), research professor of philosophy at Southwestern Baptist Theological Seminary, has written much on design, including his book *No Free Lunch: Why Specified Complexity Cannot Be Purchased without Intelligence* (2002). Dembski created a model to detect design through what he calls specified complexity: if we detect specified complexity in a system, it indicates design. He claims that we cannot explain many biological structures on the basis of natural causes because they show specified complexity. The causal chain for this complexity ends with an intelligent designer. He has formulated an "explanatory filter" which can be used to detect design: if something is designed, it will show contingency, complexity, and specification.

- *Contingency*, as we have seen previously, opposes necessity. It is the notion that nothing has to be the way it is, and, if events or objects cannot be explained by natural processes, then they must be contingent, and therefore they must be designed.
- *Complexity* is essentially a form of probability or chance. If we see high complexity, then there is a low probability of it occurring by chance, and this implies design.
- *Specification* is the notion of a pattern that can be used to explain an event. If we had no knowledge of an event, could we identify or exhibit the pattern that is actually seen in the event? If we cannot identify this pattern, we must conclude it is due to chance, and we must revisit the complexity issue.

Dembski has been criticized on several grounds. Notably, his derivation of probability has been called into question: how can the probability of an event be accurately determined? And his notion of specification is also problematic: he provides different and sometimes contradictory definitions of this concept.

ID proponents claim to work within science and to accept the full validity of scientific inquiry and methodology. Michael Behe (b. 1952), a biochemist at Lehigh University, focuses on irreducible complexity, his version of complex specificity, setting out his ideas in his book, *Darwin's Black Box: The Biochemical Challenge to Evolution* (1996). Behe uses molecular systems to demonstrate irreducible complexity. In an irreducibly complex system, all the component parts fit together and function together as a whole. The parts do not have a function independent of the system and, if any of the parts are missing, the system cannot function. Behe argues that, given these parameters, evolution by means of natural selection (gradual modification) could not have produced these systems. If you take away one of the parts, the system fails. Therefore, the individual parts could not have evolved in a gradual, step-wise fashion, as Darwinian evolution would predict. The parts cannot be refined through natural selection as they have no purpose individually. It is within the whole system that they function, not independently. Therefore, he concludes, an intelligence must have designed the system. Behe uses a mousetrap as an analogy: if just one of the parts is taken away, the trap cannot function (see fig. 11.1). Two of Behe's examples of irreducible complexity are bacterial flagella (a whip-like appendages that allow some bacteria to move: see fig. 11.2(*a*)) and the blood-clotting cascade (a series of biochemical reactions that occurs to stop bleeding in humans and other animals). If one protein of the bacterial flagellum is excluded, or if one of the enzymes in the blood-clotting cascade is removed, then these systems cannot function.

Behe does not deny evolution as a force that acts on living things, and he accepts the theory of common descent. However, he argues that evidence of common descent is not necessarily evidence of natural selection. He contends that Darwinian evolution is not falsifiable, but also accepts that lack of falsifiability does not exclude it as a possible explanation. More proof is required, more specific examples of how complex systems could have arisen by natural selection.

Scientifically, ID poses numerous problems. One of the most outspoken critics of Behe is Kenneth Miller (b. 1948), a cell biologist at Brown University. Addressing Behe's

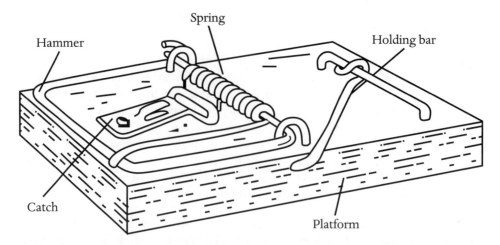

Fig. 11.1 Behe uses the mousetrap as an analogy for irreducible complexity. If any of the parts of the mousetrap were taken away, it would no longer function. Therefore, the system could not have evolved gradually, as there would have been no function for natural selection to work on until all the parts were in their proper place and in working order.

claim that evolutionary explanations for systems are impossible because of irreducible complexity, Miller argues that Behe provides no alternative to irreducible complexity other than design. He refutes Behe's claims by arguing for independent functions of the parts of biochemical systems. The parts have other functions in the cell, and could have evolved independently through natural selection, and then assembled to perform a new function. Then there are the systems which have "missing" parts that still function. Miller uses the bacterial flagellum to support his claims: several of the molecules in the flagellum also function in other cellular processes (see fig. 11.2(b)), and there are examples of flagella in bacterial species that do not have all the parts seen in most flagella, and yet they still function. In addition, many steps in the biochemical pathways that Behe and others point to as examples of irreducible complexity have been shown to function independently of the larger pathway. Miller contends that these and many other examples falsify irreducible complexity and ID.

Another contention of Behe is that the designer did not necessarily act recently. The information for the systems we see today could have been established long ago, passed down through countless generations, and then used later when needed. Scientifically, this presents major problems. The information necessary to establish these complex systems would be encoded in the DNA. We are well aware that mutations are constantly changing the DNA. If regions of the DNA are not used, mutations are not filtered by natural selection. Therefore, these unused regions will acquire multiple mutations which will change the information and render them unusable. And so, the design cannot be ancient, which leaves us with the notion that the designer must be working continuously. If the designer needs to continue to modify what is already here, then what was the purpose of the original design? And if the designer is always creating new organisms, there is no necessity for the homology we see among living things: the designer could

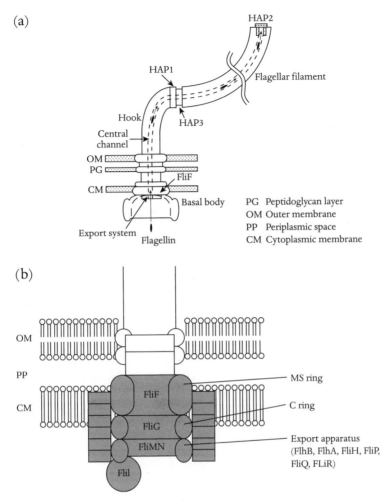

Fig. 11.2 Bacterial flagellum as an irreducibly complex system. (*a*) The eubacterial flagellum: the flagellum is an ion-powered rotary motor, anchored in the membranes surrounding the bacterial cell. This schematic diagram highlights the assembly process of the bacterial flagellar filament and the cap-filament complex. (*b*) A critique of irreducible complexity of the bacterial flagellum. There are extensive homologies between type III secretory proteins and proteins involved in export in the basal region of the bacterial flagellum. These homologies demonstrate that the bacterial flagellum is not "irreducibly complex." In this diagram (redrawn from Heuck 1998), the shaded portions of the basal region indicate proteins in the *E. coli* flagellum homologous to the Type III secretory structure of *Yersinia*.

have invented new and different systems in different organisms. Another issue arises with regard to mutations. If complexity points us to a wise and powerful designer, then we are left to puzzle why the designer did, or does, not repair easily fixable problems. Genetic diseases are a good example of this. Many result from minor mutations in the DNA, such as sickle cell anemia and cystic fibrosis.

Richard Dawkins (b. 1941), the Charles Simonyi Professor of the Public Understanding of Science at Oxford University, is among the most well-known writers of popular science books today. A staunch proponent of evolution, Dawkins denies the necessity of a creator or designer. He borrows Paley's watchmaker analogy and applies it to natural selection, calling it the "blind watchmaker." Dawkins argues there is no purpose or goal to life, and therefore no design. Natural selection does allow for the appearance of design, but it is actually a "random" and "blind" process, without any purpose or goal. He makes two important arguments against design: imperfection and coevolution.

- Imperfectly "designed" forms are abundant in the natural world, which leads one to question why a designer would fashion such faulty entities. Dawkins cites, among other examples, the blind spot in the vertebrate eye. Why would a designer engineer such a strange arrangement? In his view, it must be the result of natural selection, not thoughtful and purposeful design.
- Coevolution is the process whereby a change in one organism necessarily leads to a change in another organism that is dependent on the first. This is also problematic in explaining design: why would God create both cheetahs that are "designed" to catch antelope, and antelope that are "designed" to outrun cheetahs? Dawkins concludes that there cannot be any teleological purpose in this, and that, when natural selection explains the evidence, design does not have to be invoked.

Although ID has tried to distance itself from scientific creationism, and emphasizes its claims can be verified empirically, what we see is the creationist argument all over again. ID proponents do not have empirical evidence to support their claims; instead they rely on the condemnation of a scientific explanation as support for ID. This is exactly what the scientific creationists have done. Scientifically, ID has failed in its attempts to show, through scientific methodology, that design can be detected and demonstrated.

ID and Theology

Generally, modern theologians have rejected the argument from design. Karl Barth famously just said no ("Nein!") to natural theology. Barth stressed knowledge of God through revelation, as recorded in the biblical texts. This is the only way to come to an understanding of God. By examining nature, Barth warned, we may think we see God, but we will actually see a reflection of ourselves and our cultural values.

Proponents claim that ID is limited to the notion of design: they do not use design to provide evidence for the existence of God. The identity of the designer is not specified, and could be God, angels, space/time travelers, mystical forces, etc. Moreover, ID does not make assumptions about the character of the designer(s): whether good or evil, omnipotent or not, competent or not. In the design argument it doesn't matter. Behe acknowledges that many of the conclusions do have theological implications. These reflections emphasize the limits of any design argument: we cannot know the character of a designer from the design. If we wish to get to know God, empirical evidence cannot help us understand the will, love, transcendence, or purpose of God.

What we find in ID, especially in the work of Behe, is a "God of the gaps" theology. Throughout history, when science reached a limit and could not explain a natural phenomenon with the laws and processes known at the time, scientists often invoked God as the causative agent. However, once an explanation was discovered, God was removed from the picture and replaced by a natural cause: God was pushed to the periphery. Is this the only place that God acts, in the phenomena we cannot understand? The German theologian Dietrich Bonhoeffer (1906–45) argued against using the "God of the gaps" argument not only in the sciences, but also in other realms. God is central to our lives, not just in our ignorance or weakness. If we invoke God only in the deficiencies in our lives or in times of distress, we force God from the center of our lives, instead of appreciating that God is the very foundation for existence. Scientific understandings do not, of necessity, exclude God, but to propose God must exist and act in these gaps is theologically problematic and incorrect. We will not find God in nature as a designer who tinkers with biochemical reactions. Instead, the awe and wonder that our world inspires in us can lead us to appreciating the goodness and power of God. We do not find the message of God inside a cell: we find it instead in the Bible, and in the life, death, and resurrection of Jesus Christ.

Theistic Evolution: Finding God in Evolution

So what is the bottom line regarding natural theology and the argument from design? If we see design in nature, we can infer there is a designer. That is all we can do. We could conclude that this designer is God, but the design cannot conclusively prove it is God. And what can the design say about the character of the designer? Our knowledge of God is limited and incomplete if we examine only the natural world. In addition, teleology is not a scientifically valid explanation for the apparent design we see in nature. These arguments are sufficient for most to reject natural theology.

Some modern notions of design center not on specific instances of apparent design in nature, but on the general principles to which life adheres. Frederick Robert Tennant (1866–1957), an English philosophical theologian, looked at some of these general principles that pointed to teleology and design in *Philosophical Theology* (1928–30). He made six important observations:

- The world is intelligible.
- Evolution is progressive.
- Life emerged from inorganic matter and is maintained by it.
- Living organisms adapt to their environments.
- Hardships imposed by the natural environment are responsible for the moral development of humans.
- Nature has aesthetic value.

These observations have been expanded in current discussions of design, notably the intelligibility of the world and the propensity for life.

Faith in God and an acceptance of evolution are not incompatible, and work in the area of theistic evolution has sought to find ways to integrate science and religion. Many different theologies can find their home in this category, with a range of viewpoints. In general, there are three different underlying positions regarding design:

- *Randomness is not real.* God is the cause of all events and directs evolution down a particular path. God is "hands on" and is responsible for secondary causation via natural processes. The questions of waste and suffering are very problematic in this view.
- *Design is not a determined plan,* but more of a general direction guided by natural processes. In this view, both chance and necessity can coexist and contribute to evolution. This implies God acts as a primary cause and not as a secondary cause. It also reveals a God of freedom and patience.
- *Design is both a general process and a plan.* Not only did God set up the conditions as primary cause, but he also introduces novelty into the system. This is not divine coercion. God is seen to interact with and to guide the processes, influencing them to an end.

The viewpoints in theistic evolution are broad, and we will examine only a few ideas here. Specifically, we will look at a theology of nature, process theology, and the ideas of Teilhard, Peacocke, Haught, and Russell.

Theology of Nature

The origin of a theology of nature lies not in biblical texts but in the medieval notions of nature and grace. It is based on the idea of pure nature, and the natural conditions which are required for humans to experience God's grace. In traditional Christian theology, nature is a part of God's grace, and therefore there is no separate, pure, nature. Natural, or general, revelation is the human experience of God through nature (as opposed to special revelation, a personal and life-altering experience that one attributes to God). If we begin, in faith, with the idea that God exists, then we interpret nature as the creation of God. This is a theology of nature. Natural theology is, in essence, the exact opposite: we begin with science and use nature to find evidence for God.

A theology of nature does not deny or oppose science, but instead incorporates scientific findings into a theistic framework. Some, such as Wolfhart Pannenberg, a German theologian who studied under Barth, have taken this idea further. In his maximalist view of a theology of nature, God is constitutive in nature. We cannot understand the natural world through scientific processes alone because science, by definition, leaves out God. Michael Ruse (b. 1940), a professor of philosophy at Florida State University, takes a less extreme approach. He argues that scientific principles, including Darwinism, should be accepted, and that our understanding of nature is enhanced by a belief in the existence, power, and activity of God. Ruse does not accept the notion that Darwinism disproves the existence of God; there are other grounds, outside of science, to support God's existence.

Process Theology

Process theology can be a helpful approach to integrating science and religion, particularly with regard to evolution. Based on the work of Alfred North Whitehead and Charles Hartshorne (1897–2000), process theology contends that both science and religion contribute to our worldview and our complete picture of the universe. A common metaphysics (the concepts that allow for us to interpret reality) is required for both science and religion. Some aspects of this metaphysics, particularly those that can be helpful in understanding evolution, are listed below.

- Relationship and change, not matter, are the fundamentals in this universe. Reductionism is rejected: systems need to be viewed as wholes, not as sums of individual parts. Using these ideas, we see that nature is interconnected, dynamic, and constantly changing.
- God contains the universe but is not identical to it. This is the notion of panentheism, as opposed to pantheism (God is the universe, the material world). Because God contains a changing universe, God is also changing. However, God changes in experience and relationship, not in purpose or character.
- God is the source of novelty and order.
- God is not omnipotent in the sense of a coercive ruler. God is seen as a leader, inspiring and influencing certain events. New events are due to three primary causes: the historical past of the entity, the action of the entity (free will in the case of humans), and God's action. Therefore, God is present in every event but does not exclusively determine the outcome of the event.
- Organisms have inner as well as outer reality. Inner reality exists at different levels, depending on the organism. The ability of an organism to sense the world, to remember and learn from experience, to be aware of the world, and to be self-conscious are different levels of inner reality.

Organisms can create new evolutionary possibilities. Through the choices they make, through learning, and through selection of a territory in which to live, organisms can actively participate in their own evolution. Therefore, genetic and environmental pressures are not the only forces for evolutionary change.

Pierre Teilhard de Chardin

Pierre Teilhard de Chardin (1881–1955), a French Jesuit and eminent paleontologist, entered the dialogue at a critical time in history: the Catholic Church had major reservations about evolution, and was highly suspicious of Darwinism. Teilhard's fascination with evolution began early in his career, and culminated in a somewhat mystical theology which employed evolution as an epistemology and a metaphysics. For Teilhard, evolution not only described biological change, but also integrated cosmological development, what he called cosmogenesis: evolution incorporates the entire history of the universe, its past as well as its future. Subatomic particles formed into atoms, which organized into inorganic matter, which formed organic matter and life. Life proceeded to develop consciousness and, in the human species, the ability to reflect on itself. Teilhard saw evolution as producing increasing consciousness. The next levels will lead to a shared consciousness, which will transcend us. Therefore the path of evolution is always toward complexity and convergence. A "noosphere," analogous to the biosphere, will envelope the planet, and all consciousness will culminate into one supreme consciousness at Point Omega. It is here, at this center of consciousness, that we will see the rise of God. This unity is the eschatological completion of creation. It will create a pantheistic divinity, where everything will be as one, and every entity will be conscious of everything in the universe.

The church's lack of enthusiasm for evolution resulted in Teilhard's theological writings being banned until after his death. The church's position also resulted in his transfer (some would say exile) from France on two occasions. The first was to China, where he was part of the expedition that discovered the 750,000-year-old skull of the *Homo erectus* called Peking Man in 1929, and the second was to New York in 1951. He was also prevented from accepting the chair of paleontology at the Collège de France in 1949. However, once his theological ideas were published, Teilhard gained much notoriety and his work has been a significant influence at the interface between science and religion.

Arthur Peacocke

Arthur Peacocke, a biochemist and theologian, and winner of the Templeton Prize in 2001, shared Teilhard's concept of the epic progressive story of the universe that has led to human consciousness. Consciousness allows humans to be independent of and free from the environment, which initially directed our evolution. This freedom also allows us to be independent of God, which, Peacocke argued, was God's intention. While it means that we can challenge divine purpose, God saw it as a risk worth taking.

Self-organization is a recurrent theme for Peacocke, who saw it as a characteristic of nature. God is the creator: the natural processes are divine creativity, and therefore, as creation is ongoing, God is "active" in this continuing creation. God creates by allowing chance and random events (secondary causation). Peacocke did not argue for teleology *per se*, but he believed in trends, particularly regarding increasing com- plexity, self-consciousness, and language. God is not acting at the micro (quantum) level in Peacocke's understanding, but rather divine direction and purpose can be seen at the macro level, in the process of evolution. Peacocke did not, however, call this divine intervention.

John Haught

We examined some of John Haught's ideas in chapter 9, but a quick review is appropriate at this time. A systematic theologian at Georgetown University, Haught has written many books on science and theology. He believes that nature is autonomous and creative, that it can be so only if the divine is absent, and therefore that God withdraws his power to allow for creative self-organization. However, God's presence is in the guiding or coaxing of the world toward beauty and perfection. Action on a divine level is through the imparting of information. Although self-organization via natural selection is spontaneous, God integrates the parts into wholes. Haught's theology focuses on eschatology in this respect: everything in creation is being called to a future reality. As God is absent from the creative process, a distinct plan is not the objective. Haught sees nature, and natural processes, as a promise. God's vision of the future is of what might be, and is not a specific design.

Robert John Russell

Founder and director of the Center for Theology and the Natural Sciences at the Graduate Theological Union in Berkeley, California, Robert John Russell (b. 1946) has lectured and written extensively on the intersection of science and religion. Russell sees God as actively involved in evolution, as its creator, its guide, and its director. He considers the quantum level in his theology: for him, divine action occurs here. The indeterminacy of quantum mechanics produces random mutations in the DNA, creating genetic variation. God acts as the determiner of indeterminacies, but God does not violate natural laws. It is still valid, and possible, to study the natural world through scientific methodology, but where physics attributes randomness and chance to quantum indeterminacies, faith attributes them to divine action. Russell contends that quantum events can be due to nature or to divine action.

Theodicy

Theodicy remains a sticking point in the whole issue of design. If God did design the world, and if we believe that God is caring, loving, and good, there are difficulties regarding the immense suffering apparent in nature, as reflected in the waste of life in the daily struggle for survival, in death and disease, and in extinction. How do the different views of creationists, ID proponents, and supporters of theistic evolution deal with theodicy?

According to creationism, God created the world and it was good. Suffering, evil, and death did not exist. It was with the original sin of Adam and Eve that the "good" creation changed, physical pain and death being the penalty for sin. This is also an analogy for spiritual death, and the separation of man from God. Redemption, through Jesus Christ, is necessary for our salvation.

Dembski draws on Augustine and Kant in discussing the theodicy problem in relation to ID. Augustine's theodicy permits evil because God will ultimately bring good out of it. Kant focused on how theodicies attempt to correlate the evil in the world to the moral wisdom of God. The problem lies in that we can know evil only through our experience, but the moral wisdom of God cannot be known in this way. Kant looked for a theodicy that would interpret nature and show how God manifests his will through it. For him, the artistic wisdom of nature, including theodicy, elicits a sense of wonder that allows the beauty and horror of nature to coexist. Dembski argues that Darwin took away the sense of wonder, and the artistic wisdom, by imposing natural laws and excluding God. But ID, in finding clear signs of the designer, brings back the artistic wisdom of Kant, and allows for a successful theodicy.

If we accept evolution in neo-Darwinian terms, then we accept that disease, suffering, death, and extinction are natural processes that are necessary within the context of the creative process. As theistic evolution proposes, God creates via evolutionary processes. Therefore, is God responsible for natural evil? How can we have faith in a loving God if this is how the creative process works? These are difficult questions that are not easily answered.

Ruse tackles the theodicy issue by pointing out that evil is often the flip side of good. For example, fire can cause burns, but if God left out this evil, then we could not cook food or warm ourselves. Mutations in DNA cause cancer, but they can also allow for the evolution of new and wonderful species. Good and bad are a package deal: we have to accept both. The good of creation may not be able to occur without the bad.

Russell has addressed these issues in depth, and provides us with several possible ways to explain theodicy in the light of evolution:

- *Evil is natural.* It is the result of biological mechanisms (predator–prey relationships, disease-causing microorganisms, etc.) and it is incorrect to label them as "evil." Therefore, there is no theological question here. Humans are unique in that we experience moral as well as natural evil, and it is not always easy to distinguish between them; thus this viewpoint is simplistic in that all aspects of evil cannot be reconciled with this explanation.
- *Evil is a part of life and is not a result of the fall.* Evil has been around much longer than humans, and is not a result of human sin. Humans did not cause the suffering we see in nature. Augustine rejected the notion that humans are sinful by nature. Sin is within human will. However, he argued that humans cannot overcome sin by will alone: God's grace is required for redemption.
- *God had no choice but to create through Darwinian evolution*: there is no other option except this natural process for creating the beings and the world in which we live. Therefore, suffering is inevitable and cannot be avoided. The problem with this view is that the universe and its laws are contingent. God could have created the universe with any natural principles. Evolution is a choice, by God.
- *God does not remove suffering for a reason.* For example, in the continuing creative process, death and extinction make way for new organisms. Continuing creation is a common theme for many theologians in dealing with theodicy.

Russell's view is that God chose evolution as the creative process. His ideas regarding divine action and indeterminacy highlight a very important question: are God's actions at the quantum level directly responsible for pain and suffering? Russell says no: suffering is the price that must be paid for the evolution of human freedom and moral development. The rationality and morality that resulted from evolution provide the framework for establishing a covenant with God. Free will allows us to choose to accept or to reject faith, and each of us is born with the capacity to make this choice. In addition, rationality confers an adaptive advantage in biological evolution; thus it will be selected for and passed on. Russell rejects sociobiology, the notion that our behavior is almost exclusively controlled by our genes (see chapter 12). If the contingent universe were established to allow for the evolution of rational, intelligent creatures such as ourselves, Russell contends, we cannot understand theodicy in the light of creation alone. God has promised, in the eschaton, a new creation without suffering and evil. We need to examine a bigger picture, which includes redemption as well as creation, to understand theodicy fully.

Process theology looks at the role of freedom in the universe to understand theodicy. If we do not view God as intervening or directing natural forces actively, then the problems of evil and suffering are consistent with, and can be understood in terms of, the context of evolution. And if we conclude that the outcome of events can be seen as good (evolution producing a better-adapted organism, even though suffering and death were necessary to get to that point), then we can argue that the universe was designed to realize these positive events.

Teilhard considered evil to be a temporary condition: it was a barrier to the evolution of complexity, but as we get closer to Point Omega, as the consciousness of the universe increases, evil will be reduced. Teilhard believed evil could be healed by greater consciousness, just as ignorance can be healed by knowledge.

Peacocke saw pain and suffering as beneficial to increasing complexity, within the trends of evolution. Pain is necessary as a warning sign for biological organisms: it signifies danger. And suffering elicits action. These "evils" would provide an advantage for survival, and allow for the evolution of complex life forms, such as humans. Therefore, Peacocke argued, suffering was present long before humans, and cannot be part of the fall. Neither is death, which Peacocke saw as natural, not as a result of sin. For example, death is necessary for nourishment. Predators kill prey so they may live. Ultimately, evil leads to freedom, to free will, and therefore all pain and suffering can be seen as an expression of God's love.

God's self-limitation, which has led to evolution and free will, does not mean that God is absent from the world. Peacocke contended that God is present in suffering, and shares in the pain. This is a form of theology of the cross, a Lutheran theology in which God is revealed in the cross of Jesus Christ: God not only participates in suffering and death, but is a victim of them, and as a victim, God cannot be the perpetrator. If we consider evolution in the light of this theology, we can envision God as present in all suffering in nature. Pain and death are experienced not only by the creation but also by the creator. Haught also uses a theology of the cross to explain the theodicy inherent in evolution. God experiences both the joy and the suffering that come with the creative process of evolution. Haught contends that God will never forget the suffering, but will redeem the world through compassion.

Faceoffs in the Schools and in the Courts

In the early part of the twentieth century the creationist movement brought evolution into the legislature and into the courtroom to keep it out of the classroom. By the end of the 1920s, bills were introduced in at least 15 states to counter the teaching of evolution in schools. In Tennessee, Mississippi, and Arkansas, the teaching of evolution was banned outright in the public schools.

In 1968, the Supreme Court heard the case of *Epperson* v. *Arkansas*, and declared that the ban on teaching evolution was unconstitutional. After this decision, the creationists changed tactics and fought to allow "equal time" in the classroom. They emphasized the role of science in creationism without an appeal to the Bible. They argued creationism was science and should be taught alongside evolution. This is sometimes referred to as the "two model approach" and was adopted by Arkansas and Louisiana. Supreme Court decisions in *McLean* v. *Arkansas Board of Education* (1982) and *Edwards* v. *Aguillard* (1987; regarding Louisiana law) ruled that "equal time" and "balanced treatment" laws were unconstitutional, and that creation science is really religion, not science.

Currently, another change of tactics is reflected in local school board decisions and in the court systems. Intelligent design is the new tool for the creationist movement. With the claim that ID is science, creationists are trying again to refute evolution. In *Kitzmiller* v. *Dover*, parents brought a suit against the Dover, Pennsylvania school board, objecting to the school board's requirement to include ID in the high school science curriculum. In 2005, a federal district court judge ruled that ID was not a scientific alternative to evolution, but that it was a form of creationism and religion, and therefore teaching ID in the science classroom was unconstitutional.

Time will reveal what is next in the fight over what can and cannot be taught in a science class. Although scientific creationism does have some international support, the United States is fairly unique in its emphasis on this debate. For most of the world, evolution is science, creationism is not, and there is no dispute over what should be taught in the schools.

Conclusions

Evolution is the house whose construction began 150 years ago. The foundation was laid by Charles Darwin, with bricks of individual evidence that supported the notion of natural selection. The house has been modified – rooms have been remodeled, with the introduction of punctuated equilibrium to explain gaps in the fossil record; and new rooms have been added, with the advent of new disciplines, such as the field of genetics – but the foundation is firm. From a methodological standpoint, no scientific theory has come along that can better explain the evidence from biology, geology, physics, chemistry, and astronomy that supports evolution. And, as far as it is possible to tell, it will withstand the test of time. A paradigm shift will require the new theory to explain what we already can with evolution, as well as things we still grapple with. And it must have the same or better predictive value. It's a tall order to fill.

Creationists have insisted on a literal interpretation of the Bible, reading modern science into its narrative where it does not, and cannot, exist. The changing tactics that have been adopted in attempts to retain the teaching of creationism in the school system is a sad commentary on the attitudes of some regarding science and religion in the US.

Proponents of theistic evolution must be careful not to embrace science to such an extent that their theology relies on it, as science by its very nature changes. However, these theologies fully embrace the notion that all truth is God's truth. What we discover from science cannot contradict what we know about God. The creationists claim they do not shy away from this, but ultimately they fail even to begin to accept what science tells us about the natural world.

Primary Literature

Useful primary sources include a paper by Richard Dawkins and Richard Milner, "The Illusion of Design," *Natural History* 114 (2005), 35–7; a synopsis of Michael Behe's irreducible complexity argument, "Molecular Machines: Experimental Support for the Design Inference," presented at the 1994 meeting for the C. S. Lewis Society, Cambridge University; and a review of Behe's book by Kenneth Miller, "Review of *Darwin's Black Box*," *Creation/Evolution* 16 (1996), 36–40. John Haught's article from the Primary Literature in Chapter 9 is another good reference for this chapter. It would also be helpful to review the creationists' standpoint as argued by William Jennings Bryan and the first three chapters of Genesis.

Questions to Consider

1 From a theological perspective, is Darwinism a threat to a belief in God? Explain your answer.
2 Falsification is an important concept in science: a scientific theory should be able to be proven false. Can creationism, intelligent design, and/or evolution be falsified? If any of the three can be falsified, explain how this could be done. If any cannot be falsified, what does this mean? Does it matter? Consider in your answer both science and theology.
3 Creationists and ID proponents claim that we should not accept evolution as an explanation of life because the proof for evolution is lacking: evolution is only inferred from the data. Is this a valid point? Why or why not?
4 Compare and contrast the different views of theistic evolution discussed in this chapter (be sure to include theodicies). What do you see as the strengths and weaknesses of each view?

12

Human Evolution

Overview

Comparisons of humans and other animals place us in the order of mammals known as primates. A phylogenetic tree of our ancestry can be drawn up based on fossil evidence and molecular data, whereby we conclude that our most recent common ancestor with chimpanzees lived about 6 million years ago. The hominid lineage is diverse, and appears more like a bush than a tree. Fossil evidence tells us that hominids walked upright before evolving large brains. The *Homo sapiens* line may have out-competed the Neandertals due to symbolic thought spurred on by language. Natural selection has also been applied to human society and used to try to understand the development of human culture and behavior. These ideas have been criticized by many in the scientific and theological communities.

Introduction

Imagine yourself as a member of the scientific community in England, back in 1859, just after the release of Darwin's *Origin of Species*. Think of the conversations and the debates about the validity of natural selection, the arguments for and against it. Imagine the lectures, the letters printed in newspapers, the gossip, and the political cartoons of Darwin as an ape . . . Although Darwin did not address the evolution of humans in his book, as one would anticipate, his ideas were applied to our own species. How could you restrain yourself? Darwin persuasively argued that natural selection is the driving force for evolution, so what of man? Darwin did expound on human evolution in *The Descent of Man* (1871), where he dealt with biological, psychological, and moral issues. Although natural selection seemed to many an obvious road for life to take, the application of evolution to humans was much less palatable. It has often been compared to the demotion of the Earth, and subsequently humankind, from the center of the universe by a heliocentric view of the world. How could the creation of such a complex species, with all our cognitive abilities, our ethics, and our culture, be consigned to a natural process, the same process that shapes the lowest bacteria and slime molds? As we saw in chapter 10, the evidence for evolution is overwhelming, and this includes evidence for the evolution of humans. In this context we are no different from any other living organism on this planet.

With this in mind, we will explore human evolution, focusing on human biology, neurology, and behavior. As part of this exploration, we will also touch on social Darwinism and sociobiology, the applications of Darwinian and biological principles to society. In the next chapter, instead of examining the commonalities we have with other life, we will look more closely at some of the features that separate us from the rest of the animal kingdom.

The Primate Order

A systematic classification scheme, such as what Linnaeus was trying to accomplish, requires a way to group and categorize organisms. Darwin greatly aided this pursuit by helping us to understand that the characteristics we use in classification reflect an organism's evolution. The defining characteristics of a particular classification category (a taxon) are based on common ancestry. All birds have feathers, thus the ancestor of all modern birds must also have had feathers. The field of naming and classifying organisms is known as taxonomy, and cladistics is the use of evolutionary relationships in this classification. Linnaeus grouped humans, orang-utans, and chimpanzees in the same genus (*Homo*), based on their similar traits. Darwin told us that they are related by, and descended from, a common ancestor.

What are the characteristics that put humans in the same taxon as chimps but not pandas? There are hierarchies in the classification scheme we use today. The initial taxa are rather amorphous, and many organisms fit into each taxon. But as we move through the scheme, we use increasingly more specific and detailed criteria, thus fewer organisms fit into each category on each level (see table 12.1). We end at the species level, in which only one organism remains. The scientific name of each organism is its genus and species,

Table 12.1 Taxonomic classification of three different organisms

Category	Cat	Human	White oak
Domain	Eukarya	Eukarya	Eukarya
Kingdom	Animalia	Animalia	Plantae
Phylum	Chordata	Chordata	Anthophyta
Subphylum	Vertebrata	Vertebrata	None
Class	Mammalia	Mammalia	Dicotyledones
Order	Carnivora	Primates	Fagales
Family	Felidae	Hominidae	Fagaceae
Genus and species	*Felis catus*	*Homo sapiens*	*Quercus alba*

Source: Eldra P. Solomon, Linda R. Berg, and Diana W. Martin, *Biology*, 7th edn. Pacific Grove, CA: Thomson Brooks/Cole, 2005

a binomial strategy begun by Linnaeus. Often times the genus is simply abbreviated with the first letter alone, always capitalized.

At the first level of classification are the domains: eukaryotes, eubacteria, and archae-bacteria (see chapter 9). Which of these categories an organism is placed in depends on cell structure. Eukaryotes have a nucleus, so humans, elm trees, sharks and mushrooms all fit into this category. The eubacteria are single-celled organisms that do not contain a nucleus. These bacteria are the ones familiar to most of us: *E. coli*, salmonella, strep-tococcus, etc. The archaebacteria are bacteria that live in what we consider harsh condi-tions: hot sulfur springs, thermal vents at the bottom of the ocean, high-salt environments, etc. The succeeding taxa are kingdom, then phylum, class, order, family, genus, and species. You're probably familiar with some, if not most, of human taxonomy. We belong to the animal kingdom (we do not produce our own food), the phylum chordates (we have backbones), the class of mammals (we have hair, give birth to live young, and nurse our offspring), the primate order, the family hominidae, the genus *Homo* and the species *sapiens*. In this chapter, we will focus on why we are classified in these last four categories. Today, there are many species of primates living on the planet, but only one in the hominidae family, and only one *Homo* species.

Humans and cats and cows are all mammals, but only humans can be classified as primates. What are the features we look for in an organism to classify it as a primate? Two key attributes are vision and the structure of the hands and feet. Primates have a great reliance on their eyesight: they have an enlarged optic region in the brain and three-dimensional (or stereoscopic) vision that allows for depth perception. The structures of the hands and feet allow for grasping (with opposable thumbs and big toes), and at least some digits have nails (instead of claws). This gives us a clue about our most recent common ancestor: these features support an arboreal existence. We conclude the common ancestor of all primates lived in trees. So, we are related to gorillas, chimpanzees, and orang-utans, and more distantly related to the odd-looking tarsiers and lemurs. Based on similarities and differences, we can construct a family tree of sorts, a phylogenetic tree, that shows the relationships among primates and indicates when the split from the most recent common ancestor occurred among the different species that exist today. Figure 12.1 shows such a tree for primates. The branch points represent the time point of the existence of the most recent common ancestor. Cladistics uses taxonomic data to construct evolutionary phylogenetic trees. Fossil evidence, and more recently molecular biology (DNA analysis), have allowed us to determine the time of species divergence. For example, most data point to the last common ancestor for humans and chimps living about 6 million years ago. The lines of a phylogenetic tree represent the evolutionary history of an organism, which include other species that are now extinct. Thus, humans and chimps both evolved and changed after the split from the most recent common ancestor. It is incorrect to say that one living organism is the ancestor of another. Humans are not the descendents of chimps or any other ape. We had a common ancestor, which gave rise to the species that exist today. All species on the path leading to humans, after the split from our most recent common ancestor with chimps, are in the family hominidae, and are known as hominids.

As we shall see in the next section, the identification of hominid fossils often rests on examining features that differentiate humans from apes. Some of the defining characteristics we use to distinguish apes and humans are:

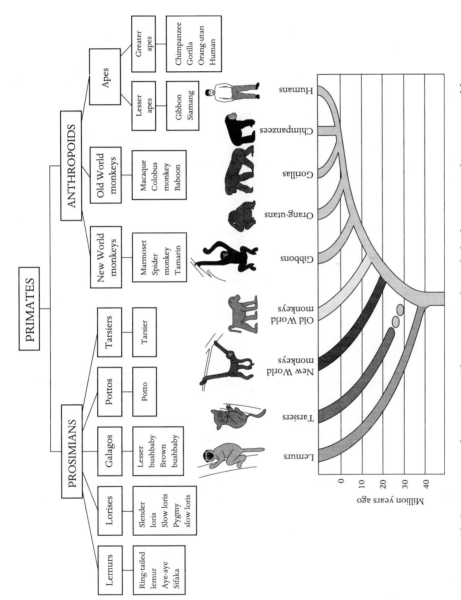

Fig. 12.1 Phylogenetic tree for primates. The primate order includes lemurs, monkeys, apes, and humans. Primates share certain traits, but over millions of years primates have adapted and evolved into the various forms we see today.

- *Bipedalism.* Humans are the only primates that walk upright as a main mode of locomotion. Other primates are known as knuckle walkers – they use their hands when walking. Although other primates have the ability to walk on two legs for short distances, this is not an energetically efficient means of getting from point A to point B, so it is not a primary means of locomotion. Bipedalism requires a different anatomy. Many different features in a skeleton can indicate bipedalism:

    - *The position of the foramen magnum.* The foramen magnum is the hole in the skull where the spinal cord exits. It is found centered at the base of the skull in humans, but at the back of the skull in apes. This anatomy allows humans to see better when walking upright, and so, even with just a fossilized skull, we can predict whether or not an organism walked upright.
    - *A short, broad pelvis.* This allows for attachment of the legs and muscles in a configuration that better supports upright locomotion.
    - *Big toes.* Opposable big toes are useful in climbing trees, but not so good for bipedalism, and the alignment of the big toe with the other toes also aids in upright walking.
    - *A curved spine.* The shape of the spine helps determine balance and weight distribution. Apes have more of a straight spine, whereas human spines are curved.

- *Big brains.* The human brain is substantially larger than that of other primates. We describe brain size as a measurement of volume, determined from the skull (cranium). Modern humans have an average cranial capacity of 1,350 cm^3, whereas a modern chimp's is about 400 cm^3. We'll discuss more about the brain and its evolution later in the chapter.

- *The skull.* Besides the size of the cranium, there are other features of the skull that differ between humans and apes. Apes have a supraorbial ridge (brow ridge) over their eyes, whereas humans don't. They also have a rectangular-shaped jaw with large canine teeth, whereas humans have a more U-shaped jaw and decidedly smaller canines. Other aspects of the teeth are also important in determining ape from human, including the size, shape, amount of enamel, number, and exact placement of the molars. And human faces are flatter, with a more pronounced chin.

These are some of the characteristics paleoanthropologists look for in fossil finds, to try to determine where the organism fits into the evolutionary picture. It has not been easy to classify many fossils. This is one reason why we do not yet have an exact evolutionary tree for our species.

The Human Family Tree or Bush

Darwin's *Descent of Man* was not the first book to be published on human evolution after *Origin.* In 1863, the British biologist Thomas Henry Huxley published *Evidences as to Man's Place in Nature.* In it, Huxley reflects on the apparently ancient origins of humans, and compares the similarities of humans and apes (see fig. 12.2). Huxley predicted that fossils would be found of prehumans, creatures that looked like apes and humans, and that they would be found in Africa. Darwin, in *Descent of Man*, agreed with Huxley that Africa was the cradle of human civilization. He further assumed that humans would be part of the unbroken chain of common descent, extending from the first living beings on Earth. At the time, Huxley's and Darwin's views were quite radical, and brought into question man's uniqueness in the world. By saying that humans were subject to the pressures of natural selection, and that we have evolved, they placed humans on the same level as every other organism on this planet.

Huxley and Darwin were correct about the origin of humans. Fossil evidence has been found to support the origin and descent of modern humans; however, the exact relationship between all these fossils is not yet clear, and the classification of many of them is under contention. Thus a complete picture of human evolution is not yet within our grasp. We will briefly survey some of the fossil finds in this chapter (see table 12.2 and fig. 12.3).

The earliest undisputed ancestor of all primates appears in the fossil record about 60 mya, during the late Paleocene. *Altiatlasius* was a small creature, weighing only about 3 oz. We know this species only from finds of teeth. Not much evidence of primate fossils exists in the Paleocene, but more is found in the Eocene: 40 genra of primates are known from this era. Perhaps the earliest ancestor of Old World monkeys, apes, and humans was *Aegyptopithecus*, a creature that lived about 35 mya. It had teeth similar to apes and early humans but with a skeleton more like a monkey with a long tail. The earliest apes date to the Miocene. One of these was *Kenyapithecus*, from the middle Miocene (about 16 mya), which may be the common ancestor of gorillas, chimps, and humans.

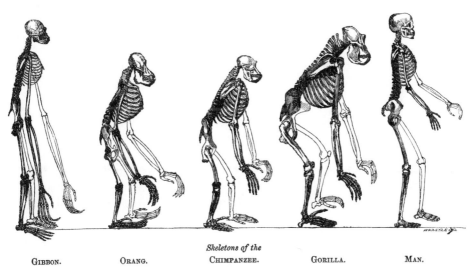

Skeletons of the

GIBBON.   ORANG.   CHIMPANZEE.   GORILLA.   MAN.

Photographically reduced from Diagrams of the natural size (except that of the Gibbon ,which was twice as large as nature), drawn by Mr. Waterhouse Hawkins from specimens in the Museum of the Royal College of Surgeons.

Fig. 12.2 Skeletons of the gibbon, orang-utan, chimpanzee, gorilla, and man. Lithograph by Benjamin Waterhouse Hawkins, from *Evidence as to Man's Place in* Nature (1863), by Thomas H. Huxley. (British Library, London, UK © British Library Board. All Rights Reserved/The Bridgeman Art Library)

Evolution

Table 12.2 Comparison of various hominid species

Species	Dates	Location	Average cranial capacity (cm³)	Distinctive features
Sahelanthropus tchadensis	7.0–5.2 mya	Chad	350	Fairly complete skull; possible bipedalism (based on projected position of foramen magnum); U- shaped jaw; hominid status still in dispute
Orrorin tugenensis	6.0 mya	Kenya	?	Fragments of cranium and other bones; indications of bipedalism; hominid status still in dispute
Ardipithecus ramidus	5.8–4.4 mya	Ethiopia	?	Probably bipedal; large range of variation in anatomy
Australopithecus anamensis	4.2–3.9 mya	Kenya	?	Earliest incontrovertible evidence of bipedalism; U-shaped jaw; lived in forest habitat
Australopithecus afarensis	3.9–2.9 mya	Ethiopia	450	"Lucy": more complete skeleton than other early hominids; bipedal with small brain; apparent sexual dimorphism
Kenyanthropus platyops	3.5–3.3 mya	Kenya	?	Fossil of a crushed cranium; flat face; small molar teeth; status as a separate genus from the australopithecines still questionable
Australopithecus africanus	3.5–2.0 mya	Southern Africa	445	Most fossils found in caves; living in woodland environments; earliest hominids in southern Africa
Australopithecus garhi	2.5 mya	Ethiopia	450	Possible evidence of use of primitive stone tools to butcher prey

Table 12.2   *(Cont'd)*

Species	Dates	Location	Average cranial capacity (cm³)	Distinctive features
Paranthropus aethiopicus, Paranthropus robustus, and Paranthropus boisei	2.6–1.2 mya	Eastern Africa	400–500	"Robust australopithecines"; cranial features indicate consumption of tough food such as nuts and fibrous vegetation; evolutionary dead end
Homo habilis	2.4–1.5 mya	Tanzania	650	Manufactured and used stone tools; may have been capable of speech; large molars, no chin, thick brow ridges
Homo rudolfensis	2.4–1.6 mya	Kenya	750	Controversy over its status as a separate species: could be considered *Homo habilis*
Homo georgicus	1.8 mya	Dmanisi, Georgia	600	Intermediate features of *H. habilis* and *H. erectus*
Homo erectus	1.8–0.3 mya	Africa, China, Indonesia, and Europe	1,000	Wide range of cranial capacities; large molars, no chin, thick brow ridges; may have used fire; stone tools more sophisticated than *H. habilis*
Homo ergaster	1.8–1.0 mya	Eastern Africa	870	A separate classification of *H. erectus* from Africa (some differing cranial features): may not be a separate species
Archaic *Homo sapiens* (*Homo heidelbergensis*)	600,000–200,000 years ago	Africa and Europe	1,200	Features of modern *H. sapiens* and *H. erectus*

Table 12.2 *(Cont'd)*

Species	Dates	Location	Average cranial capacity (cm³)	Distinctive features
Homo neanderthalensis	230,000–30,000 years ago	Europe and Middle East	1,450	Protruding jaw, receding forehead, weak chin; lived mostly in cold climates; short, solid body proportions; powerful; advanced tools and weapons; buried dead
Homo floresiensis	95,000–13,000 years ago	Flores, Indonesia	400	Adults approximately 1 m tall; sophisticated tools and hunting; use of fire
Modern *Homo sapiens* (*Homo sapiens sapiens*)	195,000 years ago–present	Global	1,350	Small brow ridge, prominent chin, gracile skeleton; sophisticated tools; artwork, music, language, complex culture

The earliest hominid may be *Sahelanthropus tchadensis*, nicknamed Toumai, discovered in 2002 in Chad. *S. tchadensis* dates back 7.0–5.2 mya. The skull has features that are characteristic of hominids: small canines, a flat face, and possibly an upright posture. *S. tchadensis* also had a pronounced brow ridge and small brain size. Some contend this was not an ancestor of humans, but should be placed on the ape side of the tree.

Most of the remaining early hominid fossils come from southern Africa and a famous region in east Africa known as the Great Rift Valley (see fig. 12.4). This series of valleys extends from the Red Sea in the north to Mozambique in the south, and cuts through Ethiopia, Kenya, and Tanzania. It is the intersection of two tectonic plates, lined with volcanoes, which have been pulling away from each other for the past 15 million years. Seismic activity in the region has been exposing fossil evidence preserved for millions of years. Now mostly desert, this region was once a very hospitable place for our ancestors to live. The famous Leakey family (Louis and Mary, their son Richard and his wife Maeve, and Richard and Maeve's daughter Louise) have found many hominid fossils in this region. And Donald Johanson discovered Lucy here as well (more on this in a moment).

Orrorin tugenensis (6 mya), discovered in Kenya, and *Ardipithecus ramidus* (5.8–4.4 mya), from Ethiopia, have some characteristics of humans, and possibly walked upright. But their place in the hominid lineage is still not confirmed. In 1995, Maeve Leakey discovered *Australopithecus anamensis* in Kenya. The species dates back to 4.2–3.9 mya. It was bipedal with large canines. The australopithecines are considered hominids, and are not in dispute as to their place in the lineage after the last common ancestor of humans and chimps.

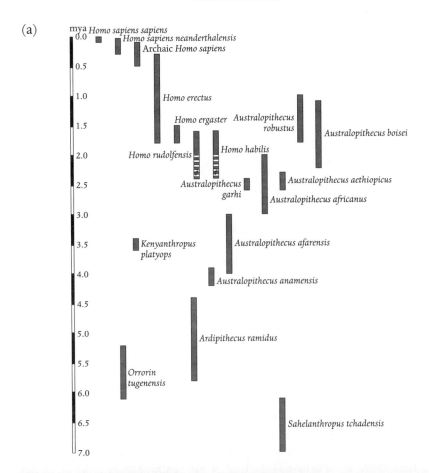

(a)

(b)

Fig. 12.3 (*a*) Timeline of hominids. (*b*) Human ancestor skulls. Seven skulls belonging to some ancestors and relatives of modern humans. From left to right, the skulls are: *Adapis* (a lemur-like animal that lived around 50 mya); *Proconsul* (a primate from 23–15 mya); *Australopithecus africanus* (3–1.8 mya); *Homo habilis* (or *Homo rudolfensis*, 2.1–1.6 mya); *Homo erectus* (or *Homo ergaster*, 1.8–0.3 mya; although the *ergaster* classification is generally recognized to mean the earlier part of this period); a modern human (*Homo sapiens sapiens*) from the Qafzeh site in Israel, which is around 92,000 years old; and a French Cro-Magnon human from around 22,000 years ago. (Pascal Goetgheluck/Science Photo Library)

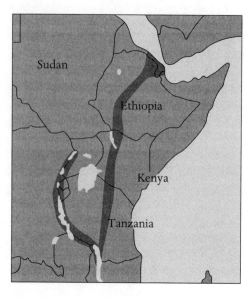

Fig. 12.4 The Great Rift Valley in Africa, where fossil evidence for multiple species of hominids has been found.

We know that our ancestors were walking upright by 4 mya. However, in our historical discovery of fossils, it was an earlier discovery of a later specimen that had everyone talking.

In 1974, Donald Johanson, a paleoanthropologist and then curator of the Cleveland Museum of Natural History, and his team found the remains of a hominid they named Lucy. Lucy and her kind, *Australopithecus afarensis*, lived 3.9–2.9 mya and walked upright. Until this time, there was a debate in the field of paleoanthropology as to which came first in human evolution: bipedalism or a big brain. Lucy is so important because she answered the question for us: she walked upright and had a small brain. In 1978, Mary Leakey and her team found sets of footprints, call the Laetoli tracks, that date back 3.6 mya. This snapshot in time shows three of Lucy's kind, walking, stopping, turning, and continuing their journey over a stretch of about 80 feet. They walked in wet volcanic ash, which preserved the imprints of their human-shaped feet, complete with raised arches and big toes in line with the other toes.

In 2001, Maeve Leakey found *Kenyanthropus platyops*, dating back 3.5–3.3 mya. It was bipedal, with a flat face and small molars. Its position in the hominid family tree is uncertain, but what is interesting to note at this point is that several different species of hominids existed in the same region of Africa (the Great Rift Valley) at the same time (about 4 mya).

Other australopithecines include *Australopithecus africanus* (3.5–2 mya) and *Australopithecus garhi* (2.5 mya). These australopithecines are known as the gracile (slender) australopithecines. Other australopithecines were more full-bodied and powerful than these specimens. The robust australopithecines have heavier skulls and are not considered direct ancestors of modern humans. They are often classified in their own genus, *Paranthropus*. Among these are *Paranthropus aethiopicus* (2.7–2.5 mya), *Paranthropus boisei*

(2.3–1.2 mya, discovered by Mary Leakey in 1959), and *Paranthropus robustus* (2.0–1.5 mya). As we do not think these species were ancestors to any other species, we consider this lineage a dead end.

The earliest hominids in the genus *Homo* date back to 2.4 mya. Louis and Mary Leakey discovered *Homo habilis* in the 1960s. *H. habilis* had a cranial capacity of about 600 cm^3, and lived 2.4–1.5 mya. This species was similar in anatomy to the australopithecines but had a larger brain. *H. habilis* made and used tools. Some paleoanthropologists have further separated this species into others, such as *Homo rudolfensis* (2.4–1.6 mya). By 1.8 mya, advanced hominids appear, and have been found outside of Africa. *Homo georgicus* was found in Dmanisi, Georgia (the former republic of the Soviet Union) and is dated to 1.8 mya. *Homo erectus* (1.8–0.3 mya) has been found in Africa, Asia, and Europe. *H. erectus* had a low forehead and a pronounced brow ridge, with a cranial capacity ranging from 750 to 1,225 cm^3. This species was robust, with greater body strength than modern humans. Their stone tools show more sophistication than those of *H. habilis*, and it is quite possible that *H. erectus* used fire. Some classify the specimens of *H. erectus* found in Africa as a different species, *Homo ergaster*, dating from 1.8–1.0 mya. The skeleton of *H. ergaster* is more similar to that of modern humans. *Homo heidelbergensis* is found in Africa by 600,000 years ago, and in Europe between 500,000 and 200,000 years ago. *H. heidelbergensis* is sometimes referred to as archaic *H. sapiens* and may have given rise to Neandertals in Europe and to modern *H. sapiens* in Africa. In 2003, a discovery on the Indonesian island of Flores surprised the scientific community. Fossils of a new species, *Homo floresiensis*, show a small hominid, 1 meter tall, with a small brain, who walked upright, hunted, and used fire. This species lived 95,000–13,000 years ago. Its small stature is not unexpected: the evolution of a reduced body size is common among animals living on islands, a condition probably resulting from limited resources. It is thought that *H. floresiensis* evolved from *H. erectus* populations living in Indonesia.

Our closest hominid relative is *Homo neanderthalensis*, or the Neandertals. Specimens from this group show large boned, powerful, short individuals with large brains and flat foreheads. They are usually classified as a separate species from *H. erectus*, and date back between 230,000 and 30,000 years ago. They made tools and weapons that were more advanced than *H. erectus*. We know other things about the Neandertal lifestyle: they were good hunters and buried their dead. Neandertal remains are found throughout Europe and in the Middle East. Neandertals coexisted with modern humans for a time.

The first Neandertal specimen was discovered by 1856 in a limestone quarry in the Neander Valley in Germany. Hermann Schaafhausen (1816–95), a physician and anatomist, analyzed the fossils and presented his findings in 1857 (two years before Darwin published *Origin*). He argued that the fossil was from a separate race of men who existed in Europe prior to the Romans or Celts. Many were skeptical about the find, believing it to be the remains of a Cossack who had died during the Russian invasion of Germany in 1814. Huxley examined the evidence in 1864 and concluded that the cranial capacity was within that of modern humans, and so this could not represent a "missing link" in human evolution. Other finds accumulated rapidly, and, although its classification is still some-what controversial, most paleoanthropologists place Neandertals in a separate species from modern humans.

Fossils of modern humans, *H. sapiens*, can be dated to 195,000 years ago in Africa and 40,000 years ago in Europe (the Cro-Magnons). Associated with the fossil evidence are more sophisticated and varied tools, and many forms of art, including cave paintings, body adornments, and musical instruments.

So what can we conclude about the evolution of modern humans with all of this information? There are still many questions left to answer about the exact relationships between these specimens, but some important specifics are known. The australopithecines, and any earlier hominids, evolved and remained in Africa. The first *Homo* species also evolved in Africa (*H. habilis* and *H. rudolfensis*). *H. ergaster* (or *H. erectus*, depending on the classification scheme used) evolved later in Africa, and some populations migrated to other parts of the globe about 1.8 mya. *H. sapiens* also evolved in Africa, less than 200,000 years ago, and spread out, just as *H. erectus* did. *H. sapiens* alone survived. Although there is no doubt in the scientific community that humans evolved, much controversy and many unanswered questions remain as to the exact path hominid evolution followed. See figure 12.3(*a*) and table 12.2 for a summary of what we know about various hominid species.

Some paleoanthrophologists place the hominid fossils into multiple taxa (genus and species), and some into fewer. But it is becoming apparent that there are many hominid species. Our evolution appears not to have been a linear tree branch, but more of a bush, with lots of offshoots and independent evolutionary lines. Multiple hominids existed at the same points in time, in the same regions. How they got along is anyone's guess. With additional fossil finds, we hope to further our understanding and clarify the twisting road that led to our existence.

The evolution of modern humans is also of interest, particularly when we consider the notion of the different races in humans. The physical variations we see are probably due to adaptive responses to different environments. For example, researchers have explained skin color as a response to ultraviolet (UV) radiation from the sun, which affects at least three aspects of human existence: skin damage (cancer), vitamin D synthesis, and folic acid destruction. UV radiation penetrates our skin, and can lead to changes in skin cells and in the metabolism of molecules in the blood. If too much radiation breaches these cells, the DNA will be damaged, potentially leading to skin cancer. However, UV radiation is needed to produce vitamin D, a nutrient necessary for calcium metabolism for teeth and bones. In regions with exposure to high levels of UV radiation, dark skin would be an evolutionary advantage: UV radiation would pass through the skin for vitamin D production but enough would be filtered out to prevent skin cancer. In other regions, where UV radiation is not as strong, lighter skin color would allow more UV light to penetrate, increasing vitamin D production with little risk of skin cancer. Folic acid, a B vitamin, is another part of the story. This vitamin is important during pregnancy: folate deficiencies in the mother can cause neural tube defects in the developing fetus. UV radiation breaks down folic acid in the blood stream. Darker skin would prevent the destruction of folic acid in environments with high UV radiation.

In addition to fossils, we can use molecular evidence (DNA sequence data) to investigate human evolution. Fossil evidence indicates that *H. sapiens* originated in Africa: therefore African populations represent the oldest populations of the species. Populations outside of Africa are evolutionarily younger. What this means is that we would expect to see more changes in the DNA, more mutations, in populations that are older than in recently established groups. These comparisons can be based on the DNA within the nucleus, but more often involve mitochondrial DNA (mtDNA). Mitochondria are organelles that produce the energy our cells need to function. As we have seen, the evolution of mitochondria is one of endosymbiosis: prokaryotic cells lived in a mutually beneficial relationship, with one of the cells eventually evolving into this organelle (see chapter 9). The DNA of the original prokaryotic cell still remains within the mitochondria. This DNA is passed directly from mother to offspring via the egg: no mitochondria are passed through the sperm, and no mtDNA is contributed by the father. Thus, we can trace our human ancestry back via the maternal line with mtDNA. Studies of this kind have shown that the greatest differences in mtDNA are found in African populations, indicating an older origin. With these studies, it has been calculated that modern humans arose in Africa about 200,000 years ago. This population is known as mitochondrial Eve. Y-chromosome analysis, the chromosome that is passed from father to son, has also confirmed the mtDNA analysis, and places the most recent common ancestor of modern humans living about 60,000 years ago in Africa.

Molecular evidence has also placed the most recent common ancestor of humans and chimps at about 6 million years ago. And, in a scenario reminiscent of the film *Jurassic Park*, mtDNA from Neandertal and archaic human specimens has also been recovered and compared with modern humans. The conclusion from these data is that Neandertals were a different species from archaic humans, and were not the direct ancestors of modern humans. Thus, molecular biology is becoming an important tool in paleoanthropology.

Modern Human Evolution

What caused the hominids to evolve the way they did? What environmental changes, what selective pressures could have acted on our ancestors to produce the modern human? Although many possibilities have been proposed, we will focus on only one of them. William R. Leonard, professor of anthropology at Northwestern University, has studied nutrition and energetics in various populations, and contends that these factors played a major role in the emergence of the modern human. Leonard thinks natural selection may have been shaping the dietary quality and foraging efficiency of our ancestors, which resulted in three major events: bipedalism, big brains, and the migration out of Africa.

- *Bipedalism.* Walking upright frees the arms to carry children and forage goods. It also requires less energy than walking on all fours. Many have contended that bipedalism was an evolutionary adaptation that allowed our ancestors to forage food in a changing environment. It has long been proposed that climate change, changing forests to grasslands, applied selective pressure for the evolution of upright walking. This, however, is a contested notion.
- *Big brains.* In 2 million years of australopithecine evolution, the cranial capacity went from an average of 400–500 cm^3. But in only 300,000 years, the cranial capacity in the *Homo* lineage went from 600 cm^3 (*H. habilis*) to over 900 cm^3 (*H. erectus*). Brain tissue consumes 16 times more energy than the same mass of muscle tissue. Compared to those of other primates, modern human brains are three times larger than

what should be expected for our body size. Although it only accounts for 2 percent of body mass, the human brain, at rest, requires about 20 percent of our energy needs. Compare this with 8–10 percent in nonhuman primates, 3–5 percent in other mammals, 11 percent in australopithecines, and 17 percent in *H. erectus*. Our ancestors would need a rich diet to supply the energy needed for big brains – they would have needed high-calorie diets made from at least some animal products. Fruits and foliage alone would not supply enough calories. From the fossil record, skulls and teeth tell us that australopithecines consumed-low quality plant foods, but early humans consumed more animal and less plant foods. The switch may have occurred because of a changing environment: more animals may have been available for our ancestors to exploit. If their consumption of animals increased, the energy necessary for enlargement of the brain would have been available. A synergism may have taken place after this initial step: once the brain started to evolve, more complex social behavior could have emerged that would change foraging and hunting tactics, leading to improved diets and allowing for more brain development.

- *Migration*. A carnivorous diet requires more territory than a diet of fruits and foliage. Early humans would have needed eight to ten times the area than the later australopithecines. Migrating animals may have led early humans out of Africa.

Given the numerous species of hominids, it is natural to wonder why *H. sapiens* are the sole hominid on the planet today, and what allowed our species to survive while all the rest became extinct. Again, there are numerous theories, but we will focus on one idea. Ian Tattersall (b. 1945), curator of the anthropology department at the American Museum of Natural History and author of numerous works on human evolution, approaches these questions from a cognitive vantage point. He identifies some major milestones in human evolution, including the development of the first stone tools about 2.5 mya. These primitive tools were simply sharp flakes that were chipped off rocks. The next major advancement occurred 1 million years later, when we see more sophisticated tools, such as hand axes from *H. ergaster*. Five hundred thousand years ago we see more elaborately prepared and efficient tools from *H. heidelbergensis*. Neandertals also fashioned advanced tools. Interestingly, we see tools of similar quality from caves occupied by Neandertals and *H. sapiens* in the Levant region in Israel, where both species coexisted, beginning 100,000 years ago, and ending about 40,000 years ago with the disappearance of the Neandertals. Neandertals had advanced levels of intuitive reasoning, as is apparent in their sophisticated tools. However, we see little evidence of creativity and complex cognitive thinking. For example, although Neandertals buried their dead, there are few instances of grave goods, the trinkets that indicate ritualized burial or a belief in an afterlife. In a word, there are no symbolic behaviors or objects that can be associated with Neandertals, and this is the hook upon which Tatterall hangs his hat. *H. sapiens*, in addition to sophisticated tools, had art, music, and objects for personal adornment; kept simple records on bone and stone; engaged in elaborate ritualized burials; and had advanced hunting skills. Although Neandertals and *H. sapiens* coexisted for 60,000 years in the Levant, their association in Europe was much shorter. Modern humans appeared in the fossil record about 40,000 years ago, and the Neandertals were gone about 10,000 years later. Thus, the disappearance of Neandertals occurs at roughly the same time in Europe and the Middle East. What happened to end the existence of this species?

Tattersall contends that a technological advancement took place in *H. sapiens* that allowed them to out-compete the Neandertals. In his view, this advancement was symbolic thought, the ability to form abstract concepts of elements of our existence and to represent these concepts with symbols. What was necessary to allow for this type of cognitive behavior? Tattersall argues that it was the invention of language, probably 70,000–60,000 years ago. Language is not just the expression of ideas and experiences but is fundamental to thought processes; we require language to name and categorize objects and to make associations between objects and events. We cannot, today, conceive of thinking without language. If modern humans first appeared in Africa almost 200,000 years ago, why did this innovation of symbolic thought take more than 130,000 years to appear? Did specific physical traits, such as special regions in the brain, have to evolve to allow language to emerge? Tattersall argues that humans had the capacity for symbolic thought from the beginning and supports this with two observations: anatomy and the distribution of species. On the anatomical issue, we see that the brains of early humans and Neandertals are not very different, thus it is unlikely that a gradual development took place in *H. sapiens* to acquire symbolic thought. And the vocal tract in humans could produce sounds for speech by about 500,000 years ago (we see the capability in *H. heidelbergensis*). When we look at the distribution of hominids, we see early modern humans in Africa, Europe, and Asia at the time this symbolic thought appeared. If a biological adaptation was necessary, then the modern human species, already living on three continents, would have to start over again in Africa. A whole new migration would have to ensue. Instead, Tattersall argues, language was invented and spread from culture to culture. This would have occurred very rapidly, much faster than a biological adaptation.

Tattersall contends that language is the result of exaptation, the use of existing structures for something new. The brain is an example of the whole being greater than the sum of its parts. Regions of the brain, already present and functioning for other purposes, were used to allow our ancestors to develop language. Thus, something totally different emerged from the early *H. sapiens* brain, something that could not be predicted based on the parts (anatomy) alone, which allowed *H. sapiens* to survive in their environments better than Neandertals. Did *H. sapiens* just out-compete the Neandertals, or did *H. sapiens* actually destroy them? We don't know at this point, and we may never have a definitive answer. Neandertals may have just faded away, with increasing numbers of *H. sapiens* replacing them in the landscape.

The Brain and Its Evolution

As we have seen, the human brain is an important component in our evolution, as both an entity that evolved, and as a cause for our further evolution. The brain consumes much of our energy intake, and controls so much of how we function. We will take a brief look at the nervous system, and discuss some aspects of how the human brain may have evolved.

Nervous systems work by relaying electrochemical impulses. Our nervous system is composed of the central nervous system (CNS) and the peripheral nervous system. The CNS is made up of the brain and the spinal cord, and receives information from the peripheral nervous system, which responds to internal and external stimuli. The spinal cord is a thick bundle of nerves that passes through the foramen magnum in the skull. The meninges and cerebrospinal fluid surround the brain to help cushion and protect it. Nerve fibers are encased in myelin, making up the "white matter" of our brains. The nerve cell bodies are not covered in myelin and make up our "gray matter." In general, the left side of the brain controls the functions on the right side of the body, and vice versa.

The brain can be divided into multiple regions based on structure and function (see figs. 12.5 and 12.6 and table 12.3). Importantly, the different regions of the brain may have distinguishing functions, but the lobes of the brain do not function alone. We have discovered many complex relationships between regions of the brain. Thus, a particular function cannot usually be located to a single area. We will not be delving into brain

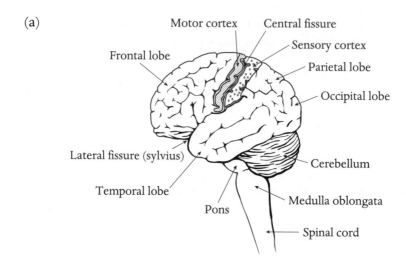

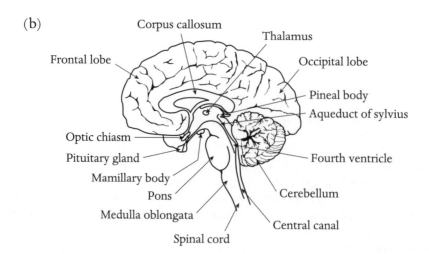

Fig. 12.5 An overview of brain structure. (*a*) Lobes of the brain. (*b*) Structures deep in the brain.

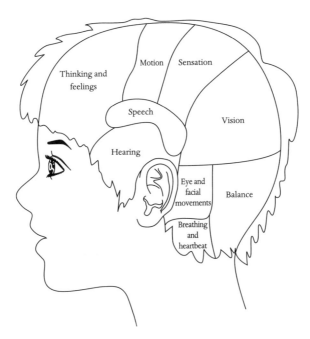

Fig. 12.6 Localization of brain functions.

anatomy in depth, but instead concentrate on comparing the human brain with those of other mammals and primates, and addressing important aspects of its evolution.

The three main parts of the brain are the brain stem, the cerebellum, and the cerebrum (cerebral cortex). It is the cerebrum that has seen the most changes during hominid evolution. The primary cortex defines regions of the cerebrum that are involved directly with motor control and sensory input. The association cortex defines regions where inputs from the primary cortex and the sensory cortices are processed, and where higher-level functions, such as thought and decision making, are found. Most of the human cerebral cortex is association cortex. This region was more likely to increase as primate brain size increased.

Humans share the same basic brain structure with all mammals. Neurotransmitters are responsible for transmitting signals from one nerve cell to the next, the cellular architecture is the same, and the basic functional regions are also the same. One of the key features we usually focus on is brain size. Discussing absolute brain size is usually not very informative, because brain size is significant only when correlated with body size. However, if we look at multiple examples of encephalization (the measure of brain size relative to body size), we can calculate the expected brain size in mammals, and compare this to actual brain size. This gives us an encephalization quotient (EQ). When we take body size into account, humans have a large brain compared to other living primates, based on EQ. EQ estimates show a steady increase from australopithecines through the *Homo* genus.

Other notions have emerged regarding big brains and intelligence: it may not be the size that matters. *H. floresiensis* had a relatively small brain, and yet they used fire,

Table 12.3   The functions of structures in the brain

Structure	Function
Brain stem (midbrain, medulla oblongata, and pons)	Basic life support: breathing, heart rate, blood pressure, digestion; relay station for messages between the body and the cerebral cortex
Cerebellum	Coordination, balance, posture
Cerebrum	
Cerebral cortex ("gray matter")	Conscious thought, perception, voluntary movement, integration of all sensory inputs
Right hemisphere	Spatial relationships, color perception, visual interpretation, musical aptitude
Left hemisphere	Analytical tasks (mathematical computation and logical reasoning)
Corpus callosum	Communication between hemispheres
Frontal lobe	Motor function, highly abstract processes (insight, initiative, concentration, personality and social inhibitions), language functions
Parietal lobe	Receiving and interpreting sensory input from other areas of the brain
Temporal lobe	Hearing, auditory perception and interpretation, storage of memories
Occipital lobe	Perception and interpretation of visual data
Limbic system (includes hypothalamus, thalamus, amygdale, and hippocampus)	Self-preservation: primal urges, powerful emotions (rage, terror, hunger, sexual desire), growth and reproductive cycles
Thalamus	Receives sensory impulses and routes them to appropriate higher centers
Hypothalamus	Regulates heartbeat, body temperature, hunger, sleeping, and fluid balance – sends messages to the pituitary gland
Pituitary gland	Hormonal functions including growth regulation, thyroid functions, adrenal glands, formation of urine
Basal ganglia	Coordination and habitual, acquired skills
Reticular activating system (RAS)	Nerve cells linking various regions of the brain: allows for recognition of important stimuli in a stimulus-rich environment
Pineal gland	Sexual maturation

coordinated hunts, and had tools as sophisticated as those of early *H. sapiens*. It may be the anatomy of the brain that ultimately determines intelligence, not the overall size. Once the wiring is in place, the brain could evolve to be smaller and still maintain the same cognitive properties.

The field of paleoneurobiology depends on endocasts, replicas of the internal surface of the braincase. Endocasts reflect the impressions made by the brain on the cranial walls. These can be made by researchers from a fossilized skull, or they can occur naturally, for example when sediments fill a skull and become fossilized. These endocasts are not perfect, however: recall that fluid and tissues surround the brain and separate it from the skull. Even so, endocasts have been useful in studies of brain evolution.

What can we say about the evolution of the hominid brain? As we have already seen, overall brain size has increased. We also look to reorganization in the brain. Although the anatomical organization in all mammals, including humans, is remarkably similar, some differences can be noted. Three types of reorganization are possible:

- *Change in the size of a region.* The olfactory bulbs, located on the bottom of the frontal lobe, are responsible for interpreting our sense of smell. These regions are smaller in humans than in other mammals. The prefrontal region of the frontal lobe is larger in the primate lineage. This is where higher functions, associated with intelligence, reside.
- *Shift in the functional region.* The primary visual regions, where visual information is processed, are in the occipital lobes. However, we find this processing takes place in slightly different areas in humans versus other primates. In fact, this region is smaller in humans, which may have evolved in conjunction with the expansion of the parietal association cortex for processing sensory information.
- *Supplant or enhance regions.* As discussed earlier, the acquisition of language may have been due to exaptation. Many areas in the brain are involved in language, including the left Sylvian fissure, the frontal lobe, the temporal lobe, and the parietal lobe. Language depends on interactive networks in the brain, and also relies on the movement of the lips, tongue, larynx (voice box), and diaphragm.

It is difficult to trace the evolution of primate, and human, brains, as no fossil evidence exists for these organs. We can use endocasts and look for differences in the craniums of hominids, but it has been difficult to determine the possible events that led to the shaping of our brains.

Evolution of Behavior

We have been able to study our biological evolution through fossil evidence and molecular data. Neuroscience can help us map the regions in our brains, and understand the similarities and differences between our species and other primates and mammals. Thus, we are like all organisms on this planet: we evolved and are continuing to do so. But what about our complex social order and our behavior – are these determined by our biology? Are they subject to natural selection? The concept of natural selection has been applied to humans on many levels since it was introduced. We have used it not only to examine biological evolution, but also to look at our sociological and behavioral attributes.

Darwin's notions of evolution were accepted by many people in his society. Why? We discussed the scientific atmosphere of the time, the discoveries, attitudes, and inevitable conclusions that made natural selection obvious to so many. But another aspect of Darwinism was one step behind: social Darwinism. This notion applied natural selection to society as a whole. According to it, humans in society would survive or perish in line with evolutionary theory: if individuals didn't have the qualities necessary for survival, they would be weeded out by a natural process, and, because it was natural, it was also considered good. At the time, the British Empire was reaping the material rewards of industrialization and was at the height of its imperialist power. Society at large was committed to social progress, the idea that reason can improve our understanding of reality, which in turn leads to the improvement of social conditions for all. The time was ripe for a social theory that would explain why some could climb to the top of the social ladder, while others were destined to remain on its lowest rungs. This idea was not, however, proposed by Darwin himself, but by Herbert Spencer (1820–1903), a philosopher and political theorist. Spencer believed that the evolutionary paradigm was applicable not just to science, but to a universal process that would lead to progressive social change, always for the better. Evolution was working on the organic, social, and cosmological levels. Spencer believed that civilization was not a human construct, but rather a consequence of social evolution. He subscribed to the evolutionary notions of Lamarck, as did many of his contemporaries, and published on how everything, from biology to sociology, obeyed the laws of evolution. Given enough time and progress, the inheritance of acquired characteristics could actually eliminate the struggle for existence. After the publication of *Origin of Species*, Spencer had a paradigm shift, rejecting Lamarck's ideas for Darwin's, and applied natural selection to society. It was Spencer, not Darwin, who coined the adage "survival of the fittest." Spencer regarded society as the sum of individuals. If government stepped back and allowed society to evolve naturally, a greater good would be achieved. If individuals or groups within a society could not compete, then they would not survive. He thought it best if the "less fit" were to die. Spencer's ideas were taken up by those who opposed religion, who saw evolution as a way to consider and implement social policy objectively. Huxley did not agree with Spencer's application of natural selection to moral questions of life and death, arguing that the human mind could overcome evolution and advance the human race beyond where we were.

The notions of social Darwinism gave rise to another movement called eugenics, from the Greek word for "well born." The term was coined by Francis Galton (1822–1911), a cousin of Darwin's, who was also an explorer, geographer, inventor, meteorologist, statistician, criminologist, and knight. A respected member of British society, Galton became interested, after the publication of *Origin*, in human behavior and the question of nature versus nurture (he actually was the first to use this phrase). He believed individuals could improve society, and advocated the reproduction of those individuals with the "best" qualities to advance the society. This positive eugenics, the selective encouragement of certain members of a population to reproduce, may not seem controversial initially. However, there are problems with this approach to social progress. First, how do we decide who is fit, and who has the best qualities? What criteria are to be used? And second, there is a natural progression from positive eugenics to negative eugenics: if reproduction of the fit will make the society stronger, then the prevention of reproduction of the "unfit" will also make it stronger. And what are our criteria to define who is unfit? How do we prevent them from reproducing? Although natural selection, the best science of its day, could be used to "improve" society, it could also be used as a justification of racism and other forms of injustice and lead to negative eugenics.

Great Britain was not the only country to practice eugenics. Two other countries were (in)famous for adopting social Darwinism in their laws and in their culture. One was the United States. From 1910 to 1940, Cold Spring Harbor Laboratory in New York was the center for eugenics in the US, under its director Charles B. Davenport (1866–1944). The Eugenics Record Office collected nearly three-quarters of a million family pedigrees, which it used to determine heritability patterns for insanity, epilepsy, alcoholism, criminality, and "feeblemindedness." Conclusions from these data displayed the overt racism of the researchers. This work resulted in legislation restricting the immigration of specific populations, preventing interracial marriages, and allowing for sterilization of the "unfit." Eugenics laws were still on the books in some states until the Supreme Court declared Virginia's Racial Integrity Act unconstitutional in 1967.

The other country that waved the eugenics flag in the 1930s and 1940s was Germany. Social Darwinism had a long tradition in Germany, going back to 1895 with the physician Alfred Ploetz (1869–1940), who founded the German Society for Racial Hygiene. Ploetz used the notion of survival of the fittest to argue that measures to help the unfit, including medical care, should be avoided, so as to reduce the incidence of reproduction in these unfit individuals. After World War I, the racial hygiene movement grew into an accepted and respectable field in the medical and biological sciences. When Adolf Hitler (1889–1945) came to power, he jumped on the scientific bandwagon, using the ideas of Darwin and Mendel to justify the sterilization and murder of the unfit. Initially, these were defined as the mentally ill, the physically disabled, and criminals, but the term was soon extended to include homosexuals, gypsies, Slavs, and Jews. Hitler's zeal to purify the Aryan race led to the extermination of over 6 million people.

Unfortunately, the underlying issues in eugenics are still alive and well. Today, the terms "ethnic cleansing" and "genocide" ring in our ears, following twentieth-century atrocities in Bangladesh, Cambodia, Yugoslavia, and Rwanda. However, science has nothing to do with these tragedies, whereby a social state, usually in response to a national crisis and led by a powerful totalitarian leader, slowly alters the mindset of the dominant "in-group" so as to blame, exclude, and dehumanize the "out-group." Even with the cries of "never again" after the Holocaust, we continue to face this reality repeatedly.

Another recent advancement in science plays into this scenario: the completion of the human genome project (HGP; see chapter 14). With access to the entire DNA, the complete genetic makeup of human beings, we can now inquire into our biology on a level unprecedented in human history. Many have cautioned that the HGP could give rise to a new eugenics movement. If widespread sequencing of our DNA becomes a reality, how will we be protected from individuals who want to analyze our genetics to see how "fit" we are? Can we keep potential employers and insurance companies from determining if our personalities are right for the job, or seeing the diseases we may develop in our futures? Can we prevent the reductionism that we are what our genes say we are? Will this information be used to create new hierarchies, in addition to race, gender, age, and socioeconomic status that will determine the availability and quality of health care? These are questions that need to be asked, particularly in light of our past mistakes of allowing political groups to wield science as a weapon in the interest of their own ends.

Recent Thoughts on Biology and Behavior

Social Darwinism came to a crashing halt with World War II. However, the desire to understand behavior did not. Research on animal behavior, particularly in the context of social behavior, came to the forefront with the publication in 1975 of *Sociobiology: The New Synthesis* by Edward O. Wilson (b. 1929), professor emeritus of entomology at Harvard University and an expert in the behavior of social insects, particularly ants. Most of *Sociobiology* focuses on the biological basis of social behavior in animals, and how evolution and natural selection could have shaped these behaviors. In the last chapter of the book, Wilson applies this model to humans. At the time, there was little dispute that animals relied on their genes for behavior, but the paradigm for humans was different. The prevailing view came from the social sciences, that human behavior is entirely cultural, and that genetics plays a role only in shaping the capacity for intellectual thought and emotions. Wilson argued that genetics plays a large role, and that human behavior cannot be understood except in the context of evolution. This represents a reductionistic approach, in that behaviors are mainly, if not exclusively, biologically determined traits. Behaviors were "selected" because they allowed individuals to reproduce. Therefore, everything in our culture serves to increase reproductive fitness, including values, ethics, and religion. In this discussion the important concept is spelled out in the title of Richard Dawkins's book, *The Selfish Gene* (1976). A popular science writer who holds the Charles Simonyi Chair in the Public Understanding of Science at Oxford University, Dawkins defines fitness as the ability of the gene, not the individual, to survive. Social structures and individuals are the "creation" of the DNA in its efforts to continue on to the next generation.

According to sociobiology, morality developed from behaviors in our human ancestors that contributed to the survival of their genes. However, if behavior, including morality, is defined by our "selfish" genes, it is difficult to understand why a behavior such as altruism would have evolved. Why would individuals engage in behaviors that could potentially cost them their lives? Isn't this counter to the survival and the continuation of our genes? For sociobiologists, altruistic behavior can be explained in terms of kin selection. Here's how it works. You inherit your genes from your parents, and the same goes for your siblings. Therefore, your genes are not only in you, but in members of your immediate family: you share your genes with your kin. Therefore, if an altruistic act on your part helps your relatives to survive, even at the expense of your life, then your genes will also survive and get passed on to the next generation. Because of this, you engage in kin preference: you take care of, and care more for, your closely related family members than for those outside your family group. However, this does not explain altruism toward individuals who are not related to you. This is called reciprocal altruism, and sociobiologists contend that you engage in this type of behavior because you are betting that your altruistic act will be reciprocated at some point in the future. These models of altruism have been supported by many examples in the animal kingdom and by other disciplines such as game theory. However, they are still in contention when applied to human behavior.

Evolutionary psychology is another recent notion in this discussion. The focus here is on the design of the human mind. Evolutionary psychologists see the mind as a computer, devised by natural selection to solve problems. They emphasize brain adaptation rather than behavioral adaptation. The complexities of the brain go beyond the genes: therefore, evolutionary psychologists contend that their ideas cannot be seen as reductionism, and the selfish gene idea does not apply. However, the brain could be considered an adaptation that increases reproductive fitness, and therefore the complex brain could still be viewed as a product of the selfish gene.

Another interesting viewpoint regarding evolution and behavior is proposed by Daniel C. Dennett (b. 1942), professor of philosophy and director of the Center for Cognitive Studies at Tufts University. Dennett believes that natural selection accounts for the complexity of the brain, denying any divine interference to shape the human mind, and that culture has also been shaped by evolutionary processes. He uses the concept of memes, complex ideas that, on the societal level, are analogous to genes on the biological level. Memes include things such as arithmetic, writing, music, myths, clothing, ethics, etc. Dennett likens them to viruses infecting our brains. Memes have allowed for a behavioral complexity in humans that is unseen in other animals. Dennett argues that patterns in cultural evolution cannot be explained by genetic factors, or Darwinian fitness, but by the evolution of memes. Memes are subject to a type of natural selection. Useful and beneficial ideas survive and are transmitted from one generation to the next, and are improved upon in an evolutionary fashion. However, memes that are not so useful, even ones that are detrimental, can also survive and reproduce. Consider the propensity of humans to consume fats and sweets in our diets. Our culture has created industries to feed off our genetic composition which persuades us the taste of fat and sugar is pleasant. Will these memes increase our fitness from a Darwinian point of view? Not in the long run: we see the cost of this behavior in obesity, diabetes, coronary artery disease, cancer, and other health problems. Thus, memes can become ingrained in our culture even though they may not be advantageous for survival.

Overall, Dennett takes a reductionistic and materialistic approach to the brain, and contends that belief in God is irrational. This belief may, however, serve a useful function in society, and Dennett considers this an example of a meme.

Theological Responses to Sociobiology

An evolutionary approach to understanding human behavior poses many theological problems. A completely biological explanation of human behavior, based on "blind" natural selection, does not fit in with a Christian understanding of morality. The notion of the selfish gene and reciprocal altruism cannot explain why we would sacrifice our lives, either in a single act (such as saving a child from a burning building) or over a lifetime of service (such as Mother Teresa's dedication of her life to helping the poor and sick of Calcutta). How can we explain these acts in terms of ways to increase our genetic fitness? Critics of Wilson argue that he places too much emphasis on the evolution of ethics, that his justification of behavior requires more philosophical, even theological, explanation. If ethics is truly inherent in our genes, then we would have to go the route of eugenics, and we would find ourselves following in Hitler's footsteps. And can we really buy into the notion that the human species evolved to be as complex as we are just to provide a vessel for the replication of our genes? Are we here only to survive and reproduce? As we have seen, science cannot provide purpose and meaning to our lives, and to argue for a purpose for our existence, no matter what that purpose is, is not possible within the realm of science.

Some have argued that we can use sociobiology to aid our understanding of human behavior, and thus contribute to Christian ethics. Sociobiology may shed light on our predispositions. This approach means acknowledging that human behavior is influenced by innate proclivities. For example, kin preference may not be simply a product of our culture – it may have evolved as a human trait because it helped the survival of our species – but the innate tendency to prefer your kin over others is by no means absolute, and culture can certainly alter this inclination. Sociobiology can be used to provide insights into our behavior, and to help us reflect on theological and ethical issues, but it cannot be used to explain our behavior in its entirety. In this sense, sociobiology oversteps its boundaries as a science.

Some have looked at sociobiology in a different light, pointing to the similarities and consistencies found between Darwinian and Christian ethics. Michael Ruse, professor of philosophy at Florida State University, argues that the ethics of natural selection can be reconciled with Christian ethics. However, Christian ethics require us to go beyond what evolution has provided. Using the example of kin preference again, we find that morality tends to be high in small social groups, such as the family unit, but tends to dissipate the further away from this group we go. Christianity stretches us to see beyond our immediate group, to look to other societies in crisis, and to reach out to them. Our obligation, in sociobiological terms, is to our family, that is, our genes. But Christ taught us to extend those obligations to our neighbors and beyond. If God works through evolution, then the evolution of morality may be a product of natural selection. At the same time, Ruse contends, this evolution should not take away from the nature of God, or from God's will.

Conclusions

Evolution is a powerful tool that can explain much about our humanity. To deny human evolution is to deny the myriad of evidence, from anatomy, paleoanthropology, molecular biology, neuroscience, genetics, and scores of other fields. There is no dissent between scientists in these fields that humans did indeed evolve. But as we have seen, it is not easy to paint the whole picture from the evidence we have. We cannot yet draw a nice phylogenetic tree, starting with one fossil and tracing our lineage to the present day. There are lots of question marks, lots of uncertain connections. We could think of these data as pieces that belong to a very large puzzle. Every new fossil find, every DNA sequence comparison, adds to the puzzle. However, we don't know what the exact picture is, because so many pieces are missing. With time and patience, the picture will become clearer.

The application of evolutionary theory to society and human behavior is a natural intellectual progression. However, we must never lose sight of what science is, or of the limitations of its methods. When disciplines such as sociobiology and evolutionary psychology, and individuals like Dennett, attempt to explain all of human existence using science, they step beyond the boundaries and ignore the limitations of the methodology. We have seen time and again that reductionism, determinism, and materialism work only up to a point. We are more than the sum of our parts. The physical sciences have accepted this, and the biological sciences are beginning to as well. The emerging field of systemic biology is looking at how components, such as genes and proteins, are integrated into the larger picture of systems and networks, and how that big picture functions. Although still contained within the scientific method, this approach may reverse the trend of reductionism and help us to understand that we are not simply the sum of our genes.

Primary Literature

Useful primary sources include an article by Ian Tattersall, "Will We Keep Evolving?" *Time* 155 (14) (2000), 96; a summary of the Piltdown Man hoax, Anita Frullani, "The Piltdown Man Forgery," *British Heritage* 19 (4) (1998), 16; and an Op-Ed piece by Cardinal Christoph Schönborn, "Finding Design in Nature," *New York Times* (July 7, 2005); and a response by John Haught, "Darwin and the Cardinal," *Commonweal* 132 (14) (2005), 39.

Questions to Consider

1 What is the difference between placing our species in the same taxon as other primates based on common characteristics (as Linnaeus did) and the idea of common descent? Think about this from a scientific viewpoint and also consider the impact on the wider community.

2 From a theological standpoint, it is interesting to consider the cognitive capacities of our ancestors and to speculate on their understanding of the world. Ritualized burial of the dead has led many to conclude that early humans held a belief in an afterlife. If this is true, what does it say, if anything, about their understanding of God? As a species, did we need first to evolve biologically and/or culturally before entering into a relationship with God? Could other hominid species have known God? If they did, what does this mean for our special position as having been created in the divine image?

3 A parallel can be noted between the application of Darwin's theory of natural selection to human evolution and the application of Wilson's sociobiology to human behavior. Wilson claimed that much of the initial opposition to his ideas was ideologically based, with many objections from those who were Marxists. What similarities and differences do you see between these two cases? Do you think Wilson's ideas will eventually be accepted by scientists, just as Darwin's ideas are today? What about acceptance by other disciplines and by the public at large?

4 The notion that behavior has a biological basis, and the application of evolutionary theory to behavior, has been used to explain and even justify certain types of behavior. For example, alcoholism used to be viewed as a defect of the will or in the moral character of an individual. Now we consider it to be a disease, a defect in a biochemical pathway, with a genetic component. How has the identification of a biological basis for certain behaviors helped our society? How has it hurt us?

Part IV

Ethics in an Age of Science

13

What It Means to be Human

Overview

An understanding of what it means to be human combines the fields of neuroscience, evolution, and theology and focuses on characteristics such as the soul and personhood. Dualism (body–mind and body–soul) is not supported biblically, theologically, philosophically, or scientifically. The functioning of our brains can explain many of the human characteristics once attributed to the soul, and the cerebral cortex has been identified as the region responsible for higher-order cognitive skills. However, minimalism and reductionism cannot be applied to the concept of personhood and soul. The complex interactions of our neurons, our experiences in life, and our relationship with God and other members of our community define who we are.

Introduction

In chapter 12, we considered some biological principles regarding human evolution. We examined this evolution from the perspective of a common process: all life has changed over the course of millions and billions of years, and humans are no exception. We peered into the structure and function of the brain, an entity that controls so much of what we are. Yet, for all the effort we devote to understanding it, the brain still mystifies us. And we considered how natural selection could account for human behavior, as exemplified in the fields of sociobiology and evolutionary psychology. These investigations remind us that we are no different from other life forms, in that we are a product of our genes and our evolution.

In this chapter we will try to understand what makes humans unique, and what sets us apart from other living creatures. What are the distinctive features of humanity that define us? How did these features arise? Is there a difference between the "brain" and the "mind"? In wrestling with our humanity, we must also consider the notion of personhood, and when a human acquires (and loses) this quality. And we must address the concepts of morality, sin, and soul, which are so important to human identity. We cannot attempt to cover all of these topics fully, or even to scratch the surface here: humans have been grappling with these issues for thousands of years. We will, however, begin to explore some thoughts, and to reflect on our humanness through the lenses of theology and science.

What Sets Us Apart from Other Animals?

We saw in the last chapter that humans have evolved, just like every other creature on this planet. We share so much of our biology and behavior with other living things. Then why do we also consider ourselves unique? Why are we special? A short list of suggested answers is given below. It is by no means comprehensive, but we will use these characteristics in our discussions in this chapter.

- *We are aware of our existence and our mortality, and we have hope.* Our awareness gives rise to some very abstract thoughts. We ask about the meaning of life. We are aware of our mental processes: we can think about thinking. We can conceive of time, and have an understanding of the past, the present, and the future. We are aware of ourselves; in essence we have a relationship with ourselves and we practice self-direction. Our selfhood is not given to us; it is not ready-made as with other organisms, controlled only by genetics and environmental influences. We are born with potentialities that may or may not be fulfilled in our lifetime. But all this is juxtaposed with our mortality: we are aware that someday we will die. The apparent futility of our efforts, in the light that it is ultimately for naught, is counterbalanced by hope. We recognize our own mortality, and yet we have hope that our existence will be worthwhile.
- *Humans are rational creatures who have responsibility.* Our rationality allows us to judge our actions, discriminate between and sift through choices, understand the consequences of our actions, and interpret the world around us. Even though these can be countered by our irrational, emotional side (we never fully understand our motives for things, we do not always choose the rational path), rationality is a uniquely distinguishing human trait. Responsibility is a type of consciousness, a self-understanding that demands decisions and actions in the face of events. Responsibility also lies in the failure or success of actualizing potential in the self. Humans uniquely realize this responsibility. We have free will. What results is a system of ethics and morals.
- *Humans have a unique social structure in which language plays an integral role.* Although other animals live in societies, humans are different in that the structures of our societies are not fixed in genetics. We can move through and change our social order. We create societal institutions for the betterment of the population. Language allows for the communication of complex and abstract ideas and the continuation and accumulation of knowledge. Although other animals can communicate with each other, and some primates have been taught aspects of our language through symbols and sign language, there is nothing that even approaches the level we display in the exchange, expression, and inheritance of ideas.

- *Humans have faith.* Not all humans believe and have faith in God, but the existence of faith is uniquely human. We pursue theology to understand our faith. The codes of ethics and morals we live by are largely based on our faith traditions, and sin is often defined in these traditions as the violation of these codes. For Christians, forgiveness comes from God: redemption from sin and salvation were made possible through the death and resurrection of Jesus Christ. Faith is not just belief, but an existential attitude. In looking beyond ourselves, we find God, who provides meaning for our existence. No other living creature can do this.

The remainder of this chapter will focus on these qualities. We will examine them in more detail, and try to come to some understanding of how they arose in the human species.

The Historical and Biblical Soul

Most of the qualities we associate with being human, such as consciousness, thought, feeling, free will, emotions, and morality, have been attributed to the soul at various times in history. So much of our understanding of what it means to be human rests on this concept. We briefly touched on some aspects of this in chapters 1 and 7, but we will take a closer look here at historical and recent understandings of the soul.

Plato believed in the immortality of the soul, that it enters the human body and survives after death. For Aristotle, the soul was a principle of life, inseparable from the body. Aristotle recognized three different kinds of souls: the vegetative soul, responsible for growth and reproduction; the sensitive soul, responsible for movement and sensation; and the rational soul, which resides in the heart. Plants had only a vegetative soul, animals also had a sensitive soul, and humans also had a rational soul. In humans, the three souls unify to form a single soul containing an active and passive intellect. Thoughts are formed by the active intellect and are transferred to the passive intellect as concepts. When we die, the soul dies with us, but the active intellect is immortal.

The concept of the soul has changed in Christianity. For early Christians, the biblical view of the soul was not as a separate, unique entity found only in humans. The word for the soul in the Old Testament is *nephesh*, and in the New Testament *psyche*. Both words convey life, or a principle of life. In neither case is the soul portrayed as an immortal entity exclusive to humans. Examples include:

- the creation story in Genesis, where *nephesh* is used in relation to both animals ("everything that has the breath of *life*," 1:30) and humans ("and breathed into his nostrils the breath of *life*," 2:7);
- the biblical tradition of healing, which centers on a holistic approach whereby restoration of health to the body accompanies the return of the individual to family and community, emphasizing the notion that humans cannot be separated into distinct parts of body and spirit, nor can they be separated from the community;
- the concept of resurrection, which the New Testament views as a resurrection of the whole person, not just of the soul.

Thus, in early Christianity, there was no notion of dualism of body and soul. Humans were considered in a holistic manner. The body was not a source of evil from which the soul needed to escape. There was a positive acceptance of the material world, including the body.

It was only after the revival of the Greek philosophers that this view changed. The Platonic notion of the separation of the material, mortal body and the immaterial, immortal soul greatly influenced the thinking of the church. Aristotle's concept of an immortal active intellect was integrated with the later Christian belief of the soul as an immortal entity separate from the body. Thomas Aquinas accepted the Aristotelian concept of the soul, and concluded that God created a soul for each individual a few weeks after conception. The notion of the immortal soul became a dividing line between animals and humans. With this understanding, we can examine some biblical texts and find support for dualism:

> And as her soul was departing (for she died) ... (Genesis 35:18)

> And do not fear those who kill the body but cannot kill the soul; rather fear him who can destroy both soul and body in hell. (Matthew 10:28)

> Then Jesus, crying with a loud voice, said, "Father, into thy hands I commit my spirit!" And having said this he breathed his last. (Luke 23:46)

In the New Testament, we are told that resurrection occurs in three stages: death of the body is followed by a temporary disembodied existence, with judgment on the last day. The intermediate state that follows death has been viewed as support for dualism of body and soul. Paul's words in his second letter to the Corinthians can also be read in support of this interpretation.

> We are of good courage, and we would rather be away from the body and at home with the Lord. (2 Corinthians 5:8)

However, it is the preconceived assumption of dualism that causes us to read this notion into the texts; these readings in themselves do not necessarily support dualism. This is an inaccurate interpretation, which is clearly shown in Paul's first letter to the Corinthians, where he discusses the resurrection of Christ and of humans and clearly states that there is nothing immortal in the human body. Resurrection requires transformation. Thus, immortality is not a preparation for resurrection, but a consequence of it.

> So is it with the resurrection of the dead. What is sown is perishable, what is raised is imperishable. (1 Corinthians 15:42)

Taken as a whole, the Bible does not affirm a duality of body and soul, but establishes humans as a bio-psycho-spiritual unity. Therefore, if it is not a separate, immortal soul that sets us apart from other animals, what does?

Only humans are created in God's image. In this respect, humanity is defined in terms of relationships. The most important of these relationships is our relationship with God. But we also see that social relationships define the individual, and the individual contributes to the integrity of the community. No other creature can be defined in these terms. In addition to relationships, humans have been promised resurrection after death. From an eschatological perspective, resurrection can be defined in terms of our relationship with God. Thus, from a biblical outlook, our uniqueness is due to our relationship with God, not to the possession of an immaterial and immortal soul. The notion of the soul as relationship is an important concept in modern theology, as we shall see in a moment.

With the concept of biological evolution, as applied to humans, contemporaries of Darwin examined the concept of the soul in this light. Many argued the soul was not a product of biological evolution, but rather a divine creation. As we noted in chapter 8, St. George Jackson Mivart upheld this view, which became the official doctrine of the Catholic Church.

Modern Concepts of the Soul

The body–soul dualism of later Christianity assigned personhood to the soul, whereby the soul determines our uniqueness, consciousness, intelligence, and free will and is the source of our thinking and feeling and our moral center. As we have seen, there is no biblical support for this dualism. In addition, the body–soul dualism has been criticized on philosophical grounds. The continued existence of the soul apart from the body after death was problematic: since we can only experience the world and others within a body, we cannot be a "self" without a body. We cannot maintain our individuality, our own uniqueness, without a body.

Dualism has also been questioned by science. It is difficult to imagine how a nonmaterial soul could interact with the material (physical) brain. In addition, neuroscience has shown us that we do not need a separate immaterial soul to explain many aspects of our humanity. Warren Brown (b. 1944), a professor of psychology at the Graduate School of Psychology at Fuller Theological Seminary has written much on neuropsychology, neurobiology, and the soul. He cites several examples of brain damage that can affect aspects of the "soul." The following are some examples:

- *Sin, guilt and morality.* Damage to the frontal lobes (orbital frontal cortex) can result in a loss of morality. The intellect of the individual may be intact, and the person may be able to describe appropriate moral behavior if provided with an abstract example. But he or she will not display this type of behavior in life. For a person with this type of injury, relationships suffer, employment may be difficult, and even social and legal standings in the community may be at risk.
- *Spiritual experiences.* Revelation is an important event, recognized as critical in helping us come to know God. But are these events due to the soul or to something else? Feelings of transcendence, divine presence, awe, and religious ecstasy have resulted from epileptic seizures centered in the temporal lobe.
- *Love.* Our ability to experience and express love has also been attributed to the soul. However, we can separate our visual perceptions of loved ones with our feelings for them. Those who suffer from a rare disease called Capgras syndrome believe their

friends and relatives have been replaced by exact duplicates. They acknowledge that these people are similar to their loved ones in every respect, but insist that they are imposters. The dissociation of the physical appearance of a person from feelings about them shows that love is an activity of our physical selves, not of an immaterial soul.

"Replacing" the soul with the brain still leaves us with many questions. Humans are not the only animals with a brain, so what makes us unique and special? What does it mean to be created in God's image? If our humanity is reduced to the activity of neurons in the brain, what of free will? How can we understand life after death? How do we develop systems of ethics? It does, on the surface, appear to be problematic. However, there are many ways of looking at our uniqueness without the traditional concept of the soul now that neuroscience has helped to dispel the notion of the dualism of body and soul, and the monism found in the Bible is reemerging. Our soul is an aspect of our physical existence. We are now looking more to neuroscience to explain the "functioning" of the soul.

Brown stresses that the concept of monism should not necessarily imply reductive materialism or determinism. Our behavior is not caused by a collection of neurons that obey physical laws in a predetermined fashion. We have free will and we make conscious decisions. During evolution, the increasing complexity of the brain allowed for new forms of information processing and behavioral regulation. These top-down influences allow us to process data from our senses in various ways. Brown calls this nonreductive physicalism. As an example, consider the visual system. The images we perceive are a representation of what is actually formed on our retina. We choose to focus our attention on something, and this alters how we see the object. Looking for a book on a crowded bookshelf is made easier if you know to look for a red book. Brown cites other examples of top-down influences in biology, where we actually have some control over biological processes. Perhaps the most noteworthy example is the placebo effect. A placebo, or ineffective drug substitute, is administered to a control group in a medical study. The data from this group are compared with the data from another group that received the real drug. Each individual in the study does not know if he/she received the real drug or the placebo (this experimental setup is called a blind study). An effect is often found in the placebo group even though these individuals were not exposed to the drug. If the individuals in the placebo group believed they were getting the drug, they may have actually enhanced some aspect of their metabolism, for example the activity of their immune systems, leading to an improvement in their condition.

Brown looks at theological questions regarding nonreductive physicalism. What has become of the soul? What is the nature of spirituality? Brown contends that the function of soul, or the property he calls "soulishness," is the capacity for relationships: a relationship with God and with other members of the community. But what of individuals who have diminished capacities to form relationships (for example, infants, people with dementia, and those with autism)? Do they still have soulishness? Brown's answer is yes, they do. They may not be able to form relationships, but members of the community can form relationships with them. Thus, other people, and indeed the entire community, are critical in this capacity.

Much of Jürgen Moltmann's theology, as we saw in chapter 7, centers on hope; his understanding of the soul is similar to Brown's. Moltmann believes that the soul is the relationship between the whole person and the immortal God. God experiences our lives as we live them. In this way, our lives become immortal: they are in the mind of God. Nothing is lost when we die, for we are within God.

And what of spirituality? Brown defines spirituality as the recognition of the nonmaterial and the divine by a physical being. It is, by its nature, subjective. As mentioned earlier, physical processes in the brain can result in experiences of transcendence and awe, which suggests that a nonmaterial soul separate from the physical body is not required for spiritual experience. However, an individual views a spiritual experience differently from an epileptic seizure: true spiritual experiences occur during religious practice and have a strong manifestation of the divine. Thus, although many aspects of spirituality can be explained by neuroscience, a relationship with God is also necessary.

The Mind and Personhood

Personhood has been attributed to the soul, but it has also been defined in terms of the mind. We have already seen that there is no evidence for the separation of soul and body, nor is there any for a mind–body dualism. However, we contend that the mind is different from the brain, although the mind may be a manifestation of the brain. At the very least, an intimate relationship exists between the two. What do the mind and brain provide that define our humanness? And what criteria do we use in determining this humanness, this personhood?

In defining the concept of the mind, we apply certain properties to it, such as consciousness, personality, and even soul. These attributes were not always associated with the brain: it was only toward the end of the nineteenth century that abnormal thoughts, behaviors, and beliefs were linked to the brain via disease and trauma. But if our personhood is a manifestation of our brain, can/are we just a product of neural wiring? Do we really have any control over our actions, or do we just react to electrical and chemical impulses that are initiated by our environment? There are many examples that show we do not have as much control as we may believe.

- A "clock" exists within the hypothalamus that regulates our bodies according to a circadian rhythm. It responds to the rotation of the Earth via the cycles of light and dark, day and night. The hypothalamus controls body temperature, sleep, growth, reproduction, and even water balance. It plays an important role in the functioning of the heart, lungs, intestines, and kidneys. If the hypothalamus does not develop correctly, as in the genetic disease Prader Willi syndrome, eating impulses and emotions are not under proper control. If the hypothalamus is damaged in adulthood, as with sleeping sickness (von Economo's encephalitis), day–night rhythms can be reversed or lost, changes in appetite and body temperature may occur, and sudden violent behavior and death may also result. Thus, some of our most basic behaviors can be traced to this one region of the brain.
- Conditions such as Parkinson's disease, Huntington's chorea, and Tourette syndrome show organic causes for behavior and movement that were once considered free will. Diseases of the brain affect free will. Therefore, is free will real, or are all our choices dictated by our neurons?

- In addition to the idea of free will being brought into question by movement disorders, the role of emotions can also be scrutinized. We often recognize that our rational mind can be overwhelmed and overridden by our "irrational" emotions. Surely this must be an example of free will and choice. Again, we find neurological diseases that contradict this notion. Interactions of the frontal and temporal lobes of the brain with the limbic system are important in emotions. The rage often seen with Prader Willi syndrome and sleeping sickness results from damage to the hypothalamus. Sexual gratification originates in the central regions of the brain, and damage can produce abnormal and psychopathic behavior. Damage to the frontal, temporal, and limbic systems, as seen in multiple sclerosis, causes emotional instability, resulting in exaggerated expressions of sadness, happiness, or despair.

Thus, much of our "humanness" is determined by the brain, the same biological unit we all share. It allows for the automatic control of functions essential to life, the "voluntary" movement of our muscles, and expression of emotions that can override our rationality. Although we all share the same brain, and so many human qualities appear to be under automatic control, we recognize that the brain is the seat of our personhood. If we damage any other organ, the personhood of the individual remains intact. But if we damage the brain, the person may change beyond all recognition. The personality may change, but our essence – who we are – is separate from the brain in that it cannot be defined merely by the matter that makes up the brain. In other words, we cannot reduce the whole to the sum of its parts. Neurobiology can help us to consider what it means to be a person, but it cannot provide all the answers.

And just where in this amazing brain do we find our individuality, our personality, and our freedom? The frontal lobes are the seat of the highest intellectual functions, such as judgment, consciousness, and reasoning. When these regions are damaged, we lose our humility, wisdom, moral values, and relationships. But it is important to stress that personhood is not simply a product of the genes. The basic structure of the nervous system is found in our genetics, but the specific neural connections are shaped by our environment and our experiences. During development, many more nerve cells are produced then are actually needed. There is competition, and only half will survive. Some connections will persist and some will not. Which remain is determined by experience and use. For example, external visual stimulation is necessary at critical developmental times to fine-tune the visual region of the cerebral cortex. Environmental factors, such as alcohol consumption by a pregnant woman, can affect the development of the brain in the fetus. We can also see the effects of environment with identical twins: even though their DNA is the same, they have different personalities and different brains.

The brain is considered "plastic," in that it is affected by the environment. This allows us to learn and to adapt to our environment. And neuroscience can also change our brains, as in the development of treatments to repair damage caused by disease and trauma. If we change our brains in this way, does it also change our personhood? Experiments done with the transplantation of healthy brain tissue into those who suffer from Parkinson's disease, and the implantation of cochlear and retinal devices that aid hearing and vision, do not alter personhood. Brain chips that may someday alleviate physical disabilities are not expected to affect our personalities. But future therapies that may affect cognitive abilities, such as enhancing memory and increasing sensory perception, have the potential to affect our personalities, and we need to consider the consequences of these technologies carefully.

Thus, although so much of who we are is determined by the brain which we all have, our personhood is not defined by our genetics or by our neurobiology. Our experiences help to shape the functioning of the brain, which influences our personality.

When Are We Persons?

One important area of investigation in both science and religion is the understanding of when we become, and when we cease to be, a person. Perspectives that focus on the brain as central to our personhood force us to look to neuroscience to help us understand when personhood begins, and when it ends. We will look first at some considerations of when personhood ceases, and then discuss when personhood emerges (a topic we will come back to in chapter 14).

We are familiar in the Western world with the concept of brain death, which we distinguish from biological death. Brain death can be defined as the permanent loss of cognitive functions, including consciousness, memory, and thought, and can be classified on two different levels: whole-brain death and cerebral death. Whole-brain death involves the brain stem. The ability of the brain to maintain bodily functions, such as heartbeat and breathing, are permanently lost. In cerebral death, the cerebral cortex is damaged, but not the brain stem. Higher-order functions, such as judgment, reasoning, memory, and consciousness are lost. It is in cerebral death that personhood is lost. Whole-brain death, if no medical intervention is available, will lead to biological death. Cerebral death will not. And so we need to ask, if the cerebral cortex is damaged and personhood is lost, is the person still alive in a meaningful sense? The body may still function, but the person we once knew is no longer there. We refer to this state, where there is no mental activity, as a persistent vegetative state (PVS). The impact of this situation on the family and friends of the individual is devastating: the body is a constant reminder of who the person was, but the continuation of biological life is in no way related to the continuation of the person. Should we consider those in a PVS, who have biological life but no personhood, as having the same status as those with cognitive abilities?

Diseases and injuries may not result in brain death, but may result in decreased cognitive abilities. Alzheimer's disease is one condition with which most of us are too familiar. Those who suffer from Alzheimer's disease experience progressive, irreversible dementia. Some of the common symptoms are memory loss, personality changes, deterioration of cognitive abilities, and a progressive dependence on others for all aspects of daily life. Self-awareness, rational thinking, and morality also degrade and are eventually lost. The question we are faced with in this and similar situations is: does the loss of personhood affect the value of that life? Even with a loss of personhood, the relationships that person has – as a spouse, parent, sibling, friend – still remain. The patient is still part of the community. But does this life have less value? With regard to medical resources, how much should we devote to those with these conditions? Of course basic care should be provided, but many would argue against any type of extraordinary life-extending treatment.

From the perspective of neuroscience, the loss of these higher-level cognitive abilities represents a loss of personhood. The ethics of how we treat these individuals, and of what medical care is administered to them, is not for science to decide. But the conclusions we draw from this viewpoint can be useful in these deliberations.

Emergence of personhood, or brain birth, can be defined differently from the perspective of neuroscience. Some argue that a functioning brain, which occurs at about eight weeks of gestation, is when personhood emerges. Others contend that personhood centers on awareness and consciousness. This requires integration of peripheral nerves, the spinal cord, brain stem, thalamus, and cerebral cortex. The emergence of awareness and consciousness has been placed anywhere from 22 to 36 weeks of gestation. If we see brain birth as the opposite of whole-brain death, then brain birth would take place at six to eight weeks' gestation. But the higher brain functions that we define as being lost in cerebral death emerge between 24 and 36 weeks.

Some viewpoints totally exclude neurobiology and use criteria other than the brain to define personhood. However, even in these paradigms, neuroscience should not be totally excluded.

- *Personhood as a social construct.* According to this view, the nervous system allows for physical and intellectual activity. It is a tool that humans use: simply possessing the tool does not ensure or determine personhood. In this view, we look to society to shape the thoughts and behaviors of the individual. Although this view denies the innate capacity of the brain to form our personality, it does acknowledge its importance. Thus an understanding of neuroscience will ultimately help us understand the social and cultural influences on personhood.

- *Personhood from conception.* The notion that personhood begins at conception is an argument that has been used in the abortion debate and, more recently, in discussions of the use of embryonic stem cells for research purposes (see chapter 14). In this view, characteristics of personhood, such as self-awareness, choice, and creativity are present as potentials that may be realized later. These qualities are not "added" at a later point in development, but are there from the beginning, and thus personhood does not require the actualization of these potentials. Although this view excludes neurobiology in defining personhood, science is still useful as a way to provide insight into what shapes our essence.

- *Personhood is present throughout our history.* At certain times in our lives (in infancy and childhood), and as the result of illness (such as dementia) or injury, we may lack certain capacities that define personhood. Individuals in these situations are considered the weakest members of our community and are given special attention and consideration. In some cases, the missing cognitive capabilities will emerge or be restored. In other cases, they will not. The treatment and care provided to these individuals can often present us with ethical dilemmas. Although this viewpoint does not appeal to neuroscience in determining personhood, the biological perspective may help us resolve some of the ethical issues. For example, do we provide the same treatment to an infant as an elderly person to keep the individual alive? Should we go to extraordinary lengths to save the life of person in a coma? Science cannot find solutions to these problems, but it can provide information that can be used in decision making.

What can we conclude from neuroscience regarding personhood? Although we cannot use science exclusively to define a person, we can use the knowledge gained from neuroscience to help in decision making, and to aid our understanding of the functioning of the brain and the prospects for the future of an individual. Regardless of the criteria we use to define personhood, neuroscience must be part of the discussion. This approach rejects the dualism of body and mind, and instead offers an integrated understanding more consistent with Christian theology. It helps us to consider the wholeness of an individual and not to fragment a person into separate, unrelated compartments.

Morality and Free Will: Philosophical Understandings before Darwin

Philosophers have grappled with the notion of free will and morality for thousands of years. Prior to Darwin, a dualistic approach was popular among philosophers. Reason and emotion were seen as two contradictory and competing attributes. Emotions had to be brought under control for good to prevail.

According to Kant, morality was the purview of religion, and nature the domain of science. Nature is governed by causal laws; therefore free will cannot exist in nature. For Kant, reason played no role in the natural functioning of animals. Reasoning would require the animal to keep the end goal in mind. Kant argued that instinct is a better, more efficient, way for behavior to be determined. Therefore, reason does not play a role in our natural functioning. However, moral law transcends nature (and therefore cannot be understood by science). Kant thought that reason functions to produce a moral will. Free will is important, and necessary, in this understanding, because humans can choose to obey or disobey moral laws. Humans transcend their nature through free will. Thus, free will cannot be derived from nature, and science cannot help us understand morality. Our nature causes us to be selfish and asocial, and the goal of emotional behavior is the happiness of the individual. We can exist as social beings only when we transcend our nature and take on moral laws. The center of morality lies in duty, not in individual well-being. Moral dignity means that we act on our principles, which have been derived not from nature and emotion but from pure reason.

Hume was not a dualist in his analysis of morality. For Hume, morals were based on both pure reason and a moral sense. Moral judgments are not totally objective and based only on reason; they depend partly on circumstances. Therefore, moral judgments are subjective to some extent. If emotions lead us to false judgments, reason can help us to correct the mistakes. According to Hume, reason is capable of directing action, but emotion is necessary to motivate it. Hume recognized the necessity of society in morality: if humans were solitary creatures, and selfish in behavior, we would have no need of morals. Thus, morality is rooted in human behavior. The root of sociality and morality for Hume was the parent–child bond. The long-term care required for raising offspring binds families together, and can lead humans to form bonds within the larger social group. This creates interdependence between members of a society. We become concerned with the welfare of others in the group, and this leads to morality. For Hume, pure reason by itself could not lead to morality because it cannot elicit emotions, but reason does play a role in morality because it is necessary to direct and organize emotions. Our cognitive capacity to reflect on our feelings in the present, and to place them in the perspective of our past and in anticipation of our future, is what makes human behavior unique among animals.

Morality and Free Will: Scientific Notions after Darwin

In examining biological, psychological, and moral aspects of human evolution in *The Descent of Man* (1871), Darwin took a decidedly Humean approach to understanding the evolution of morality. He focused on the issue of child care, and concluded that the time and effort necessary for raising offspring require strong attachments within kin groups, and therefore humans must be social creatures. The parent–child bond is the foundation of social structure and moral responsibility. Natural selection would favor cooperation as well as emotions such as benevolence. The extension of these attitudes beyond one's family group, to the larger society and humanity as a whole, helps to unite humans into a larger community. Darwin saw the cause of our morality in our cognitive capacities. We can judge our desires and prioritize them, and feel concern for others. Morality may appear to contradict natural selection, especially when we consider altruistic acts. However, Darwin was studying selection at a group level: the fitness of an entire society would be enhanced if, for example, individual courageous acts allowed for the success of one group over another. For Hume and Darwin, free will was not a transcendental property apart from nature, but rather a natural ability to reflect on, and deliberate over, our feelings and desires.

Henry Drummond (1851–97), a popular theological writer and lecturer in his day, proposed in his book *Ascent of Man* (1894), that the highest moral value, altruism, was actually the cause of evolutionary progress in humans. He contended that evolution was not based on competition, but rather on cooperation. Humans represented the culmination of this cooperation. Drummond's views are supported by sociobiology. As we have seen, altruistic behavior increases inclusive fitness: caring not only for ourselves and our offspring but also for our closely related kin allows for the survival of our genes. Thus, the sacrifice of ourselves for those who share our DNA is a type of natural selection. But we also see altruistic behavior between individuals who are not closely related: if we make a sacrifice for someone now, we hope that they will return the favor in the future. This is known as reciprocal altruism.

Not everyone agreed with the notion that morality is based in evolution. As we have seen, Mivart held a dualistic view with regard to the evolution of the human body and the supernatural development of the soul. He contended that the soul allowed humans to transcend their nature, and that morality was uniquely human in that it was not a result of natural causes. Thomas Henry Huxley, who was known as "Darwin's bulldog" for his strong support of biological evolution, held a Kantian view on this topic. He argued that human nature was selfish and asocial, and that morality was a denial of our natural state. Therefore morality could not be derived from our nature. Evolutionary adaptations lead humans away from morality, and thus morality lies in opposing evolution.

In the light of evolution, philosophers and scientists have come to understand that emotions are necessary for human life, and that they play an important role in reasoning. Therefore a dualistic view is no longer tenable. Examining the evolution of emotion and reason has helped to bring the concept of morality into a naturalistic framework.

Why did emotions evolve? The answer may be found in the social nature of humans. To get along in society, emotions appear to be necessary. Sociality is not unique to humans, but is found in many mammalian species. And we find some emotional capabilities in other species, especially those closely related to humans. Sociality would foster the evolution of emotions to provide the ability to care, understand, and relate to other members of the group. Social structures that require memory of past events, predictions of the behavior of others, and coordinated actions among individuals also require a complex cerebral cortex. As we have seen, the cerebral cortex is the seat of higher-order thinking, the region of our "intelligence." Thus intelligence may have evolved as a result of complex sociality. Emotion, not reason, holds social groups together. Reason comes from our capacity to think, from our intelligence. Therefore, the evolution of much of what makes us human probably began with sociality, which led to the evolution of emotion, then intelligence, and then rationality. Thus the evolution of morals can be understood in the context of the evolution of our emotions and our cognitive (intellectual and reasoning) properties. These aspects of our humanity are not separate and distinct, but come together to help us deal with the problems we encounter in our existence. Evidence from many fields, including neuroscience, behavioral genetics, and the social sciences, supports the interplay between reason and emotion in morality.

The nature versus nurture argument is also important in this discussion. If, as Hume and Darwin thought, our nature is biological, then morality is not determined by nurture (culture). However, many social scientists do not think biology plays a large role in morality. More recent research has shown that the nature versus nurture debate is more of a cooperation between nature and nurture. Our innate traits, those programmed in our genes, are not fixed at birth. Rather, they are potentials that can be molded and shaped by our environment. If a trait, such as parental care, is innate, our cultural experience will further refine our behavior. Our innate behavior is not invariant; it can be modified through learning. And we can change our behavior when the circumstances change.

We can identify several problems in ascribing so much of moral behavior to evolution. For example, this type of reasoning assumes there is a progressive nature to evolution, which allows for the emergence of complexity in humans. This view of evolution is not necessarily supported by the evidence. There is no fundamental principle in evolutionary theory that requires complexity to emerge. Indeed, we do see examples of many life forms that have not made this type of "progress." George Gaylord Simpson (1902–84), a paleontologist and professor of zoology at Columbia University, cautioned against reading progressivism into the evolutionary record, but stressed that evolution was indeed important in ethics: our faculties to understand, implement, and conform to moral codes are a product of evolution. We need to keep this in mind when considering morality, but we should not look to evolution for its justification.

Another problem with focusing on the evolution of morality is that we have failed to incorporate any theological understanding into this view. So it would be prudent to examine ideas that take into account scientific evolution, but also offer a more complete picture and include notions apart from science.

Morality and Free Will: A Theological Response

The concept of free will is one of the defining characteristics of humanity. God has given us freedom, and it is for us to decide how to live our lives and how to respond to the events and people around us. Biblical texts have provided guidance for our morality. The Ten Commandments, the Sermon on the Mount, and the great commandment to "Love your neighbor as yourself" are the principal moral codes of Christianity. Jesus provided continuity with the laws of the Old Testament, but also helped us to see a new depth in them. He was obedient to the law, all the way to the cross, but he also called for greater understanding, stressing the primacy of love and rejecting narrow legalism. Paul associated natural law with the conscience. Faith, hope, and love are the foundations of existence, and laws act as guidelines for this existence. Paul believed, not that moral behavior would lead to salvation, but that the path to salvation would be the foundation for the development of morality which would be part of the new creation.

Christianity does not deny that human behavior has been shaped by evolution, or that moral laws arose from our nature to guide our behavior. Rather, Christian theology looks at the divine presence in determining ethics. God glorifies the morality that is already there. Humans were created in God's image: we are co-creators. We have the ability to transcend our nature. Through revelation we can see more deeply into our nature. There is flexibility in these natural moral laws. Christian theology helps us understand the tendencies, aspirations, and obligations that are already inherent in the natural laws. In most religions, there are only a few defining moral principles, and these tend to be common to very different traditions. Three of the most prominent are love, compassion, and altruism. Thomas Aquinas provided the basics of morality when he wrote, "Good is to be done and promoted, and evil is to be avoided."

Faith and hope are integral in morality. We must have faith that creation is good and that it is moving toward good. Hope calls for action that helps to spur on moral endeavors, to move us toward the consummation. We can acknowledge two categories of ethics: aspiration and obligation. It is in human nature to pursue good: it is the fulfillment of our existence. It is our aspiration. However, our sinfulness prevents us from always pursuing good and makes an ethics of obligation necessary. This obligation minimizes our deviation from the path of good. Obligations are usually enforced by the state through laws, and these laws are based on natural laws that help to protect and encourage the good. Thus, the New Testament stresses obedience to civil authority, which provides order and justice.

Sin

Sin can be viewed in a number of different ways. Many early Christian philosophers believed that free will allows humans to make unnatural choices, and that humans are the only beings that can be corrupted. Sin is universal among humans, and it came into the world through human agency. This idea supports the fall from grace and the doctrine of original sin. The story of the fall in Genesis tells us that death is the punishment for original sin. But we realize that death is part of the natural world: it is the cost of creation. Another cost is human nature, specifically free will, which makes sin possible. As humans are rational creatures, we may see sin as a defect of reason. But it is not: it is rather a defect of will. God calls us to be responsible agents, and not just "thinkers."

From an evolutionary perspective, sin has been seen as the conflict that occurs between the two components most necessary for our survival: our genes and our society. Typically, we view our genes as giving rise to selfish behavior, in order to increase our chances for survival as individuals. This focus on our individual needs has often been interpreted as evil. Our social interactions require cooperation and altruism, usually seen as good qualities. The problem with this view is that genes and societies are neither good nor evil. It is difficult to get past this polarization to try to understand the contributions of nature and nurture to our evolution and existence.

We can define sin as the violation of moral and ethical laws. The conscious decision to violate a code of conduct in society is not unique to humans. Other animals, particularly other primates, can be said to sin as well. However, in humans, sin produces feelings of guilt and wrongdoing. The act of sin is not uniquely human, but the need for redemption and forgiveness is. Therefore sin is more than just an act: sin is a turning away from God. We become alienated and separated from God, and our relationship with God is damaged. This alienation is not just with God, but with others as well. All of our relationships can be tainted by sin. In this respect, sin is self-centeredness. Sin can also be seen as disorder and imbalance in life which can alienate us from God, from other people, from the world, and even from ourselves. In this light, redemption, as forgiveness of sins, can be seen as a restoration of relationships.

Conclusions

What does it mean to be human? In answering this question, many would discuss the aspects of the mind and the soul. We could divide the duties: subscribe the mind to science and the soul to theology. But we could also ask how the two disciplines can inform each other to create a holistic picture of what it means to be human. Dualistic approaches do not work anymore.

We can look at many of the unique properties of humanity and argue that reason, intellect, language, and consciousness, among others, set us apart. And many of these can be attributed to the function of the brain. But we cannot reduce our humanity to our neurons, even if we acknowledge that top-down information processing is occurring. We need to include evolution and neuroscience in our discussions of humanness. But foremost in all of this, at least for Christians, is the understanding of our relationship with God. This connection is unique in all life on this planet. Humans participate in a special relationship with our creator. This relationship is our soul. Sin is damage to this relationship. God maintains this relationship: indeed, we cannot sever this connection, only God can, and God never will. Therefore, through God's grace and redemption, we always have hope that we can repair the damage we cause in this relationship by our free will. And we know that our soul will always be present in God, even when disease and injury rob us of our personhood.

Primary Literature

Useful primary sources include a passage from the first letter of Paul to the Corinthians (15:1–58), emphasizing monism; an excerpt from Darwin's *The Descent of Man* (Chapter V) on human morality; and an article by John Polkinghorne, "Beyond Darwin," *Christian Century* 122 (2005), 25–8, regarding the ability of natural selection to explain human behavior.

Questions to Consider

1 In your opinion, what makes humans unique? Which of the characteristics discussed in this chapter would you consider important in this definition? What other characteristics not discussed in the chapter would you add to this list?

2 How would you define soul, personhood, and mind? How do they relate to the body? Do you see yourself as having a dualistic or a monistic perspective?

3 Think about how we have treated those who suffer from mental illness. Consider cases from different periods of history. For example, we can infer from historical accounts that many individuals persecuted as witches were suffering from mental illnesses and infections that affected the brain. How were these individuals viewed by society? What treatments were used to "cure" them? Now consider the present-day situation. What attitudes do we have toward those who are mentally ill in our society? What attitudes do you see in the health-care system? A dualism is evident in our health-care system (if you have a headache, you go to a neurologist; if you are depressed, you go to a psychologist). Research how health-care companies fund treatments for a mental illness, such as depression, and a physical illness, such as cancer. Do you see a dualism? Is this an adequate way to deal with these health-care issues?

4 Would you consider an individual with cerebral brain death to still be a person, having personhood? Does this individual still have a soul? What about an individual who has whole-brain death? Support your answers. In both types of brain death, would you argue for or against medical intervention (including a feeding tube) that would sustain the person's life? Explain your answer.

5 Consider a court case involving a mother who has killed her infant son. The mother admits killing the baby, but claims she was suffering from post-partum depression. Use the ideas of Kant and/or Hume to argue (*a*) for the prosecution that this woman should be sentenced to life in prison, and (*b*) for the defense that the court should show leniency and allow the woman to undergo psychological counseling, with no prison time.

14

Modern-Day Marvels: Biotechnology and Medicine

Overview

Part of the human condition is the constant struggle to improve our existence. This includes the basic human needs of food and good health. Modern technologies addressing these issues include biotechnology and medical science. Today, we can alter the genetics of organisms in order to produce better food, manufacture improved drugs, clean up the environment, and create animal models to research human diseases. Medical advances have enabled infertile couples to conceive children, provided diagnoses and treatments for a greater number of diseases, and extended life. But many concerns prevail. Critics question the safety of genetic manipulation and the ethics of patenting life. Religious debates highlight the status of the embryo and our responsibility to our fellow humans. In today's society, with many new advancements being made so rapidly, it is not easy to assess whether the use of this technology is always appropriate. Theological issues that address intrinsic value and help us to understand our role as created co-creators may help us in our deliberations.

Introduction

Science so often promises a better life for us. And in many instances, it has made good on this promise. Think of all the technology you use each day, from cell phones to clean water, from electricity to automobiles, from aspirin to laundry detergent. We don't normally think of where our food comes from, other than the grocery store. And we can't imagine the devastation that a disease such as polio could have on our population. We are fortunate, blessed, that we live in the culture we do, where so many basic needs have been addressed through technology. However, we also face staggering problems that science cannot solve, particularly in the use of these technologies. As our understanding of life and our ability to manipulate it grow, the ethical and theological dilemmas increase. In this chapter, we will look at recent advances involving biotechnology, and consider some controversial issues in medicine. We will also discuss the interplay between technology and theology.

Biotechnology can be broadly defined as the use of living organisms to manufacture products. Many traditional human endeavors that have been practiced for thousands of years fall into this category, including the production of wine and cheese, and the selective breeding of plants and animals in agriculture. However, today, we can enhance these endeavors: the term "biotechnology" implies an organism has been specifically modified within its genetic makeup to perform a task. These modifications, also known as genetic engineering or recombinant DNA technology, can be made in all organisms, from bacteria to plants to animals. In some cases, the function of the endogenous DNA is altered, either to improve or to prevent the expression of specific genes. In other cases, new pieces of DNA can be added to an organism: usually this DNA is from another species. Through recombinant DNA, plants can become resistant to pests, agricultural animals can grow bigger, medicines can be manufactured in bacteria...the list goes on and on. Genetic engineering is staggering in its reach, and the possibilities are extensive. But it is not without controversy. The manipulation of organisms calls into question notions of safety, ethical responsibility, and intrinsic value.

The science, and indeed the art, of medicine is another attempt at improving human lives. We desperately want to reduce human suffering: modern technologies have produced amazing advances, but they bring with them new ethical and theological questions. Reproductive technologies that allow infertile couples to have a child force us to contemplate how we view disabilities in the drive to produce "perfect" children. Stem cells can be used to treat and cure diseases today, and their use will undoubtedly expand in the future, but controversy surrounds the source of these cells, requiring us to consider the status of the embryo. Life-sustaining technology can be employed following severe accidents, or devastating and debilitating illness, but it brings with it some difficult end-of-life questions. We have the ability to analyze DNA and to alter the genome of an individual, but we must determine which conditions to look for in the genetic code, who has access to this information, and which diseases should be treated with gene therapy. In the quest to better our health, we need to balance our desire to help each other with our hubris and our status as imperfect beings.

We begin this chapter with some background on how we came to understand inheritance and how we manipulate DNA, and look at what has been done using these techniques. We will then examine the opposition to genetic engineering, and consider how the use of biotechnology can be viewed from ethical and theological perspectives. The remainder of the chapter will focus on some modern medical technologies, many of which rely heavily on biotechnology, and examine some important ethical and theological concerns.

The Beginnings of Modern Biotechnology

Humans comprehend basic biological inheritance from a very early age: we know we resemble our relatives more than our neighbors down the street, and we know that a pregnant woman will give birth to a human baby, not a litter of puppies. Observations by our ancestors allowed them to increase the quality and quantity of their food supply by breeding specific plants and animals, based on the observation that a parent will pass on its traits to its offspring. If you want a cow that can produce a lot of milk, you choose a good milking cow to breed. But just how do traits get passed on from one generation to the next? Although there were lots of ideas, the modern answers began to emerge in the middle of the nineteenth century, with Gregor Mendel. An ordained priest who had studied at the University of Vienna, Mendel researched the transmission of characteristics through multiple generations in St. Thomas's Abbey, an Augustinian monastery in Brno, now part of the Czech Republic. By breeding pea plants and examining the inheritance pattern of different traits, Mendel established that each trait is determined by two "elements" found in each individual, one "element" from each parent; the combination of the two determines the appearance of the offspring.

Today we know the identity of these "elements": they are in the DNA. A region of the DNA that codes for a certain trait is called a gene. A variation of the gene is called an allele. The combination of alleles (the genotype) of an organism determines its appearance (the phenotype). Although Mendel's work was not appreciated in his lifetime, it was rediscovered in the early twentieth century. The replication of his work and the application of his ideas to other species soon gave birth to the field of genetics. Although we have discovered much more about genetics than Mendel could ever have imagined, his basic principles are still considered the foundation of modern genetics.

With regard to biotechnology, Mendel's understanding of inheritance is only half the story: we still did not know the identity of the hereditary material. The discovery of the exact nature of the "elements" came in the twentieth century. Microscopic observations of the behavior of chromosomes during cell division, specifically in egg and sperm cells, was found to correspond to the behavior of Mendel's "elements." This led to the understanding that the genetic material resides on the chromosomes. Biochemical analysis of chromosomes determined that they are made up of two components: proteins and DNA. By the 1940s, experiments had confirmed that the hereditary material was DNA.

How Modern Biotechnology is Done

In 1953, Watson and Crick determined the structure of DNA and, by the late 1960s, researchers had made amazing headway into understanding its role in the cell (see chapter 9). Much of this work was done with bacteria, as these organisms are relatively easy to grow and use. Soon after, researchers began to focus on manipulating DNA. Paul Berg (b. 1926) and Stanley Cohen (b. 1922), at Stanford University, and Herbert Boyer (b. 1936), at the University of California, were the pioneers in this field in the early 1970s. A class of enzymes, called restriction enzymes, was discovered in bacteria. These enzymes cut the sugar–phosphate backbone of the DNA at very specific base sequences, and can be purified and used to cut up DNA in the lab. Restriction enzymes generate what are known as "sticky ends." Specifically, when these enzymes cut the DNA backbone on both strands, and the strands separate, the DNA pieces have small

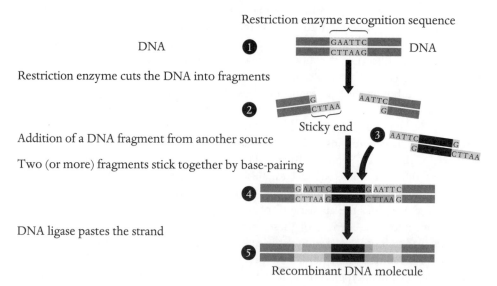

Fig. 14.1   Cutting and joining DNA using restriction enzymes. Each restriction enzyme recognizes a specific base sequence in the DNA (in this example, GAATTC) and will cut only at that sequence. This creates single-stranded regions on the ends of the DNA (sticky ends) which can then base-pair with another molecule of DNA cut by the same enzyme. Ligase seals the cuts in the DNA to make the association permanent.

single-stranded regions on the ends of the molecule. This is important because, as we have seen, the bases in DNA can pair up, A with T and G with C (complementary base-pairing). If two different molecules of DNA are cut with the same restriction enzyme, they will have complementary single-stranded ends. This means that, if the two preparations of DNA were mixed together, the bases at the end of one DNA will pair with the bases at the end of the other (see fig. 14.1). The association becomes permanent when we repair the sugar phosphate backbone with an enzyme called DNA ligase. Typically, the DNA of interest (perhaps human DNA) is joined with a vector that is useful for propagating the DNA in a cell. Then the recombinant DNA molecule is placed back into a cell (transformation; see fig. 14.2). Vectors can be small circular pieces of DNA (plasmids) or viruses. In modern molecular biology, this process is often referred to as cloning (as opposed to the colloquial use of the term, which we will discuss below).

Cloning and biotechnology involve the analysis, synthesis, and manipulation of DNA. Some techniques important for this work include:

• *Gel electrophoresis.* DNA cannot be analyzed by examining it under a microscope. Instead it is visualize by gel electrophoresis, a process whereby DNA fragments are separated by their size in a gel via an electric current. The different fragments of DNA appear as lines or bands on the gel, and the patterns of these bands are then interpreted (see fig. 14.3).

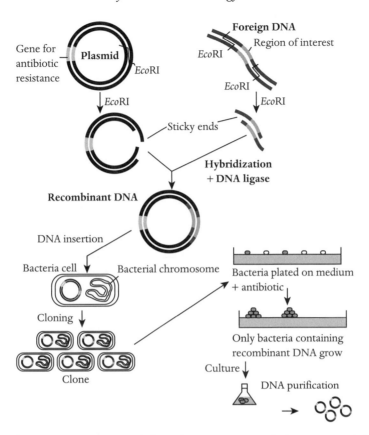

Fig. 14.2 Cloning DNA. Foreign and plasmid DNA are cut with the same restriction enzyme, creating the same sticky ends, which can then join (hybridize) together. The association is made permanent with ligase. The recombinant plasmid is transformed into bacterial cells and grown in the laboratory.

- *Restriction fragment length polymorphisms (RFLP)*. Species have different genetic codes, and individuals within a species have slight variations in their DNA. These can be detected through the use of restriction enzymes: as the DNA sequences are different, the enzymes will not recognize the same cut sites in each DNA molecule. This will result in different banding patterns on an electrophoresis gel. Using this technique, we can develop DNA profiles of individuals, which are useful in many applications, from diagnosis of genetic diseases to criminal investigations to paternity cases.
- *Polymerase chain reaction (PCR)*. In 1983, Kary Mullis (b. 1944), a biochemist working for the Cetus Corporation, developed a technique that would copy specific regions of the DNA. By exploiting the normal cellular methods that copy (replicate) the DNA prior to cellular division, Mullis was able to amplify the number of copies of specific regions or genes for analysis. DNA from a single cell can provide results. The PCR products are analyzed via gel electrophoresis, and DNA profiles can be ascertained, just as with RFLP. Mullis was awarded the Nobel Prize in Chemistry in 1993 for the development of PCR.

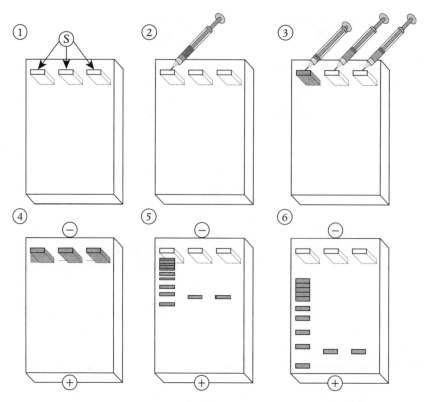

Fig. 14.3   Gel electrophoresis: schematic diagram of a gel. The semi-solid gel (1) contains wells where DNA samples (S) are placed (2 and 3). An electric current is added (4) which forces the DNA to move through the gel (5). The gel allows for separation of fragments of DNA based on their size (6).

- *Transgenics*. Transformation of bacteria with recombinant DNA was only the beginning: other cell types, and multicellular organisms (including plants and animals) can be genetically engineered. Once altered, these organisms are referred to as transgenic organisms, genetically engineered organisms, or genetically modified organisms (GMOs). Transgenes allow the cell to produce a product (usually a protein) it naturally could not. This can alter the way the organism functions.

Applications of Biotechnology

The analysis of genetic material and the creation of recombinant genes, altered sequences, and transgenic organisms have many far-ranging applications and economic impacts. According to the Biotechnology Industry Organization, there were 1,452 biotechnology companies in the US in 2006. The value of publicly traded biotechnology companies was estimated at $360 billion in 2008. Health-care biotechnology revenues increased from $8 billion in 1992 to $58.8 billion in 2006. Some of the applications and products of biotechnology include:

- *Biopharmaceuticals* (the production of drugs by living organisms). The cloning of human insulin by Cohen and Boyer is the first example of this application. Prior to this, insulin was obtained from the pancreas of animals, which caused negative reactions in many patients. Human insulin was cloned into bacterial cells, and today the insulin used by diabetics is purified from these recombinant cells. Other biopharmaceutical products include vaccines and antibodies (used to treat different forms of cancer, arthritis, and allergies, and to help prevent rejection of transplanted organs). Transgenic animals that produce pharmaceuticals in their milk allow for unlimited production of the drug. The use of plants in this realm is increasing: cost, efficiency, and safety factors favor the use of plants over animals and microorganisms. As of 2006, 254 biopharmaceutical drugs had been approved for use in treating 392 conditions. Research spending by pharmaceutical and biotechnology companies in the US totaled $55.2 billion in 2006. More than 400 biotechnology drugs and vaccines are currently in clinical trials. And biopharmaceuticals are made for animals other than humans. For example, one product in widespread use in the agricultural industry is recombinant bovine somatotropin (rBST). When injected into cows, rBST increases milk production by 10–15 percent. Currently this protein is administered to approximately one-third of US dairy cows.
- *Detection.* The use of biotechnology for detection purposes has exploded in recent years. In many cases, medical diagnosis no longer has to be done exclusively in a lab: many tests are now portable and easy to interpret, and can be done in the field or at a patient's bedside. These techniques are cheaper, more accurate, and quicker, and detection can occur much earlier in the progression of the condition. Examples include home pregnancy tests, blood screening kits for HIV and hepatitis, cholesterol tests, and diagnosis of prostate and ovarian cancers. Identification of DNA sequences with RFLP and PCR can be used in forensic analysis, to track genes in plant and animal breeding, to determine paternity (in humans and other species), to assess the compatibility of tissue types for organ transplants, to detect and identify pathogens in the environment or in an organism, to estimate the genetic diversity of captive and wild animal populations, and to identify mutations causing genetic diseases.
- *Agriculture.* Through better farming practices and improved technology, farmers have been able to increase crop yields, reduce chemical use, and allow for a stable food supply for the US and around the world. Part of this has come from the use of biotechnology. In 2008, 309 million acres of biotechnology crops were grown in 25 countries. In the US in 2007, 91 percent of soybeans, 87 percent of cotton, and 73 percent of corn were genetically engineered. Most genetic engineering has focused on pest (insects, bacteria, fungi, viruses) and herbicide resistance, but other modifications are in development, including increasing yields, better utilization of resources in the environment (to reduce the need for fertilizers), improvements in taste and nutritional quality, and better responses to environmental stresses such as drought. Some potential applications of genetically engineered farm animals include faster growth, increased resistance to diseases, leaner meat, lower cholesterol, and reduced feed requirements. To date, no transgenic animals, or products from them, have

been approved for human consumption in the United States. A few transgenic organisms are currently being evaluated, such as salmon that grow four to six times faster than standard salmon, and pigs that generate manure with lower levels of phosphorous.

- *Animal models.* In some cases, the cause or progression of a disease can be difficult to study in humans, and testing of potential treatments may not be ethical. To address these concerns, transgenic organisms have been created that mimic human conditions. Animals, mainly mice, have been developed to model conditions such as diabetes, cystic fibrosis, Alzheimer's disease, sickle cell anemia, AIDS, arthritis, depression, and many forms of cancer. Animals such as pigs are also being engineered to provide compatible organs for transplant into humans.
- *Bioremediation.* Bioremediation is the use of biological agents to remove toxic wastes, including herbicides, pesticides, refrigerants, and solvents, from the environment. Many types of naturally existing microorganisms can live off, and thereby degrade, hazardous organic substances. These chemicals are broken down into nontoxic substances, mainly CO_2 and H_2O. Naturally occurring bioremediation has been documented in cases of crude oil spills, sewage disposal sites, and contaminated water sources. Genetic manipulation can enhance the natural abilities of microbes: additional metabolic pathways can be engineered in a species so one microbe can process multiple toxins, and growth requirements can be altered so microbes can live and function in different environments. Other organisms, such as plants, can aid in the cleanup of the environment by the uptake of contaminants from soil and water through their roots, a process known as phytoremediation. These abilities can also be enhanced through genetic engineering.
- *Improvements in manufacturing processes.* Biotechnology has allowed for large-scale manufacturing that is cheaper, faster, and cleaner than other methods. Biotechnology can help to lower the amount of pollutants in fossil fuels, allowing them to burn more cleanly. And we can reduce the use of petroleum through biomass-based feedstock technology. This process uses agricultural waste as a food source for the growth of microbes. The microbes convert natural sugars in the plant material into compounds that can be used in manufacturing processes. An example of this is "green plastics," such as the biopolymer polylactic acid (PLA) used in packaging material, clothing, and bedding. Large-scale manufacturing often uses harsh chemicals that pollute the environment, such as the chlorine bleach and dioxin used in paper manufacturing. Biotechnology can reduce this pollution through products that work better than their chemical alternatives, require less petroleum in the manufacturing process, and produce wastes that are biodegradable.

Opposition to Biotechnology

Biotechnology has not been without controversy, and there are many who question its use. Opposition has centered on the safety of genetically engineered organisms to humans and the environment, on the commercialization of genetically modified products with regard to economic and legal issues, and on ethical and theological questions regarding the alteration and use of living things, the patenting of life, and the analysis of DNA. One of the staunchest critics of biotechnology is Jeremy Rifkin (b. 1945), the founder and president of the Foundation on Economic Trends (FOET). Rifkin criticizes those in the scientific and business communities, the government, and the media for failing to examine the environmental, cultural, economic, and ethical implications of biotechnology. He asks questions about the potentially negative effects of biotechnology, and is often criticized by the scientific community for being alarmist and for misusing and exaggerating the facts. In this section, we will examine some of the specific concerns voiced by Rifkin and other opponents of biotechnology.

Critics claim that few credible studies have been conducted regarding the safety of genetically modified (GM) foods, and that regulatory procedures for risk assessment are flawed. In the US, the regulation and oversight of biotechnology, including GM foods, is the responsibility of the US Department of Agriculture (USDA), the Environmental Protection Agency (EPA), and the Food and Drug Administration (FDA). Despite regulations on GM foods, critics claim that companies are not required to do rigorous, detailed testing of the composition of GM foods, which could be different from their nontransgenic counterparts. Environmental assessment is often confidential, in the name of trade secrets; thus the testing processes and results are not available for review by the scientific community or the public. Critics claim that the safety tests that have been done on GM foods have been inadequate. There is very little published data, and the quality of the existing reports is not good. Animal trials are lacking, and some experiments that have been done show adverse effects on animals fed on GM foods. Critics claim that a naturally occurring bacterial toxin from *Bacillus thuringiensis* (Bt), once bioengineered into plants as a pesticide, is hazardous to nontarget insects and laboratory animals, and has caused allergic sensitization of the skin in field workers. The vectors used to create GMOs could allow for the transfer of genes to other plants, potentially creating herbicide-resistant weeds, and to other organisms, which could lead to the creation of new pathogenic bacteria and viruses. And viral vectors could spread to human cells and cause diseases, including cancer. Herbicides are regarded by critics as unsafe, and the increased use of these herbicides, with the development of herbicide-resistant GM crops, will have detrimental effects on the environment and human health.

The need for GMOs is also questioned by critics. Problems in the global food supply can be solved by proven sustainable agricultural techniques and better distribution practices. Critics see the biotechnology industry not as a benevolent producer of crops that will save the starving and improve the health of humans, but as a greedy industry making profits by selling seeds resistant to the herbicides it also produces.

Proponents of biotechnology find flaws with the experimental protocols that lead to the conclusion that GM foods are dangerous, most notably, anecdotal evidence is often treated with the same credibility as peer-reviewed scientific studies. Proponents point out that critics emphasize what could happen, even when there is no evidence to support the realization of these fears; for example, the unfettered transfer of genes from GMOs to wild species has not occurred. Proponents criticize the approach that opponents have taken under the guise of "informing" the public of credible health risks: comparisons of transgenes, or the vectors used to carry them, with hazardous toxins and pathogenic viruses are meant to scare the public, not to inform communities of likely problems. Supporters of biotechnology point to multiple examples of where the industry has improved and saved lives, and where it has impacted the production of food to increase quality and quantity while at the same time protecting the environment.

Patenting

The invention of any commercial product requires investments of time and money. The patent system was designed to protect these efforts from competitors while encouraging industrial innovation. A patent does not confer ownership to the holder, just the exclusive right to use the invention. Traditionally, one of the requirements for a product or process to be patentable is that it cannot be a product of nature. Nature is considered to belong to the public and to be for the common good. Someone could, however, patent a process for extracting, purifying, or utilizing a product from nature, just not the product itself. For example, Cohen and Boyer received a patent in 1980 for the use of viral and plasmid vectors in recombinant DNA technology and the cloning of genes. However, in the same year, another patent application was granted which caused much controversy. The first patent ever awarded for a living organism was given to Ananda Mohan Chakrabarty (b. 1938) for a genetically modified bacterial strain. Chakrabarty, working for General Electric, did not use genetic engineering to create the bacteria: instead, he relied on a process of genetic exchange (conjugation) that occurs naturally in bacteria. He isolated a strain that could degrade multiple components in crude oil. Since bacteria are part of nature, the US Patent Office denied his application. Eventually the case went to the US Supreme Court, where it was determined, on the basis of the manipulation of the organism, that the bacterial strain was indeed made by a human, and was not a product of nature. Therefore, the court ruled that human-made microbes are patentable. In a similar case in 1987, the US Patent Office decided that nonnaturally occurring multicellular organisms (including animals) could be patented. Today patents can also be awarded for organisms produced by conventional breeding techniques. DNA sequences can also be patented.

Patents are sources of revenue for many companies and universities. Critics question the ethics of making money from patents, and claim that patenting can hinder research by preventing the sharing of information. However, the income is used for research and development, and proponents point to rapid advances even in fields with patents, so scientific progress has not been hampered. To date, thousands of patents have been granted for DNA sequences, cell lines, and transgenic animals.

Although patents have been described as temporary legal monopolies with no moral or theological implications, the patenting of life has raised many questions. Is life a commodity? Should someone really have exclusive rights over a DNA sequence or a living thing? Have we lost our reverence for life, our understanding of its sacredness, by awarding patents for it? Some religious groups have opposed the granting of patents to DNA sequences, cells, and organisms by arguing that God is the designer of life. Therefore God has a "prior claim" on whatever "intellectual property rights" could be issued on living things. Some theologians, such as Ted Peters, have called for the patent policy to make clear distinctions between discovery and invention, to distinguish what already exists in nature from what humans create. Most theologians regard the human genome as already existing in nature and think it should not be subject to patenting. Some also consider transgenic animals to be a product of nature. Regardless of the patenting issue, most theologians, including Pope John Paul II, have been supportive of genetic discoveries, biotechnology, and even genetic engineering. In a 1994 speech to the Pontifical Academy of Sciences, the pope stressed the benefits of this research for therapeutic uses.

Intrinsic Value

Some ethical controversies surrounding the use of GMOs for food, or the creation of animal models for research into human diseases, focus specifically on the integrity and intrinsic value of all life. Brewster Kneen, a widely published author and critic of genetically engineered agriculture, considers most uses of biotechnology unethical, on the basis that many of the problems could be solved by conventional methods, including better farming practices and lifestyle changes. Kneen admits that some uses of biotechnology are beneficial and ethically responsible, for example the production of new and safer methods of human and nonhuman birth control and the genetic engineering of plants with vaccines. However he is opposed to the genetic modification of animals, because animals possess feelings and consciousness, can suffer, and have intrinsic value. Kneen believes animals, like humans, need to be treated with respect and compassion.

Proponents of genetic engineering point to the benefits of this technology in the rapid advancement of medicine and agriculture. The creation of transgenic organisms is necessary to understand, fight, and cure numerous diseases. Animals, particularly mice, have been engineered to mimic human diseases. If we don't use transgenic animals as disease models, we would have to use humans or give up on the research entirely. Both of these options are ethically problematic. In agriculture, proponents argue that modern techniques used to create GMOs are not fundamentally different from the breeding procedures we have been using for thousands of years. In the past, our ancestors selected plants and animals with particular qualities to breed to enhance these attributes in the next generation. Today, through the use of recombinant techniques, we can be more precise in this venture. We can select specific genes to insert into plants and animals, and we do not need to rely on the chance that the trait we want will be inherited. In addition, the undesirable traits that may be passed on with conventional breeding can be avoided. The techniques are also much faster: we can engineer an organism in a relatively short amount of time, rather than breeding strains for multiple generations.

However, critics argue that genetic engineering is not the same as conventional breeding. Today, we can cross species boundaries, for example by placing a gene from an animal into a plant, a task that is not possible without recombinant DNA technology. For Kneen, genetic engineering is an unethical approach, which does not respect the integrity of organisms and species. Kneen believes that our attitude toward, and acceptance of, the genetic manipulation of living things reveals the fundamental principle that we consider living things to be tools for our survival, that plants and animals are a means to an end.

This end does not focus on the well-being of nature and the flourishing of creation, but on the economic benefit of an elite few.

Social Justice

Kneen questions the operation and motives behind the biotechnology companies. He criticizes corporations that spend vast amounts of money lobbying government officials, supporting political candidates and university research programs, and "brainwashing" the public. Biotechnology corporations force their products on the third world to make a profit at the expense of indigenous peoples and the environment. Kneen argues that biotechnology companies are causing and reinforcing a reliance on technology and Western culture to solve problems. Others have echoed these sentiments, adding genetic modification to other aspects of colonialism and domination. Biotechnology is viewed as just another way for Western society to control nations.

There are indeed problems with food production in many nations, and most recognize that Western societies could help. However aid needs to focus on improving agriculture in ways that respect the indigenous cultures and the land, maintain diversity, and address the real needs of the local population. Along with "food security" we also need "food sovereignty," the ability of people to have control over their food, and the authority to decide what is right for them. For Western cultures to truly help, local farmers, scientists, and governing officials need to be involved in developing solutions that will work in these regions. Biotechnology may indeed be a part of the solution, but it cannot, and should not, be touted as the only solution.

Some Theological Perspectives

Many have argued that genetic modification intrudes on God's domain. We often hear the phrase "playing God" used with reference to genetic engineering. In a theological framework, we must ask ourselves how we should use this technology. Overall, we need to see the big picture: objections to biotechnology are not specific to genetic engineering, but instead are recurring concerns that surround all types of technology. To understand how we should address biotechnology, we need to examine the relationship between technology and our concept of God. Since many of our ideas about God rest on what God is able to do, our own understanding of what we as humans can do directly impacts our understanding of God.

Technology is how we act. The anxiety that some religions have toward technology is predicated on the advancement of technology. As we progress, humans begin to do things that only God could do before. The audacity that we, as humans, have in using technology to achieve something that only God can do is usually associated with hubris (pride, arrogance, and ambition). Hubris is a recurring theme in the downfall of humans, especially in Greek myths. But we also find it in the Bible. We are warned:

Pride goes before destruction, and a haughty spirit before a fall. (Proverbs 16:18)

Hubris is highlighted in the stories of the Garden of Eden (Genesis 3) and the Tower of Babel (Genesis 11:1–9). In the Garden of Eden, Adam and Eve sought to become like God, to know good and evil, even though God had told them not to eat the fruit of the tree. The arrogance and disobedience of Adam and Eve caused the fall of humanity. In the Tower of Babel story we see the use of technology (the construction of the tower to reach Heaven) as an arrogant act. Humans wanted to be like God, and tried to reach God under their own power. Hubris again is the sin: through the use of technology, humans believed nothing was impossible, and God prevented further advances by causing them all to speak different languages, and by scattering the population across the Earth. In all stories of hubris, there is no threat to God. Sin is the motivation. The folly is that humans waste their efforts, energies, and talents trying to become like God, something they can never do.

Although the use of biotechnology may be considered hubris, there is another aspect to it. As Patrick D. Hopkins, a philosopher at Millsaps College, notes, many opposed to biotechnology no longer focus on the futility, but rather emphasize the fact that our efforts are not fruitless: we have developed technology that can allow us to act. With regard to biotechnology, we have the ability to alter life on a fundamental level. And we may actually be able to create life. We have gained a power that makes us like God. We are no longer attempting: we are actually doing. By doing, we may be exceeding the authority God gave us. Critics no longer focus on our hubris, but talk more of our newly acquired power. We can threaten God because we have acquired some of God's powers. Therefore, many have called for the regulation of biotechnology through legislation. They believe that we cannot allow humans to "play God," and therefore certain uses of science should be banned or limited because they seem to rival the power of God.

However, this argument is not theologically valid. As Hopkins notes, neither biotechnology nor any other technology will make us God. But as long as critics see humans, absurdly, as a threat to God, as posssessing the ability to rival God, we will try to legislate our technology to protect God. Hopkins argues that what is needed is a change in our theological framework to accommodate the new possibilities of technology. Under the old theological framework, calls to limit our use of technology actually diminish God: what does it mean theologically when we think God needs our protection? What type of understanding do we have of God if we think we can, or even need to, provide protection through human rules and laws? In actuality, we are only protecting religious views of God.

Science and technology have allowed humans to understand nature and have provided ways to harness from nature what we want or need. We are not helpless. This challenges some religious views of our dependence on God. Therefore, in some religious traditions, our understanding and reliance on God may be undermined by technological advances. Other objections hearken back to the "God of the gaps" idea: if we "play God," we are encroaching on the boundaries between human knowledge and ignorance, the realm that God occupies. Laws restraining the use of technology can be seen as a political play over jurisdiction, relegating humans to certain areas that don't overlap with God's domain. As we have seen, the "God of the gaps" idea is problematic. From a scientific perspective, as soon as we understand another piece of the puzzle, God must be shifted somewhere else. From a theological perspective, each time technology advances, we have to reevaluate God. According to this view, God is constantly relinquished to the next gap, and we are left trying to determine once again what separates humans from God. The notion of humans as rivals to God anthropomorphizes God. If we focus on God as being more powerful than humans, we must ask what kind of power makes God God, and what happens when humans acquire power through science and technology. This view of God as a being who is similar to us, different only in degree of power, limits our understanding of God.

Hopkins argues that this constant reevaluation of God and power should not be the task of theologians and religious believers. Instead, we need to shift our theological framework from one that centers on the power of God (which humans can steal) to one that emphasizes the care of God's creation. This will deemphasize our view of God as a "superhuman" and bring us back to concepts such as meaning, purpose, and transcendence. God can be present with and through technology. We have already discussed the role of humans as created co-creators, and biotechnology can be thought of as one way in which humans share in God's plan for the universe. We have been invited by God to participate in creation and redemption, to take responsibility for ourselves, and to use our technologies for the good of all creation. If we approach our understandings in this vein, then, Hopkins states, technology can be Godly.

Biotheology is a theological framework that allows for reflection on all levels of life from ethical and theological positions. Brian Edgar, professor of theological studies at Asbury Theological Seminary, has identified six important principles at the heart of biotheology. Although there are no pat answers regarding the ethical and theologically sound uses of biotechnology, these principles can be used to steer our efforts. When we ask questions regarding genetic manipulation, we can use these principles as a framework to guide our discussions and to ensure that critical issues are addressed. Edgar advocates that each of the following principles be considered:

- *Respect for the intrinsic value of all life.* The world is a divine creation and has value because God judged it to be good. We often do not place importance on this, because of our tendency to use the reductionist approach of science, and our emphasis on the significance of humans in God's creation. Edgar argues that anthropocentric thinking is shifting as we are beginning to stress Trinitarian theology, which emphasizes relationships and the concept that all of creation is intimately tied together. Nature is not a means to an end.
- *Value of human uniqueness.* Humans were created in the image of God (*imago Dei*). We are different from the rest of creation in that we can enter into a relationship with God, while other life forms cannot. *Imago Dei* could imply that we are part of the creation, albeit one that has the responsibilities of dominion and stewardship, and that we should not change God's creation. Therefore, in this view, biotechnology would be inappropriate. On the other hand, if we focus on the relationship aspect of *imago Dei*, we can see a more dynamic situation where change is important for teleology. Theologically we should focus on redemption, and, in this case, humans may be justified in altering life through genetic engineering.

- *Preservation of organismal integrity.* Organisms cannot be reduced to their genes alone – the whole is more than the sum of its parts. We need to understand life at the organismal level. We need to ask what effects genetic modification may have for people, and we need to focus on the effects engineering has on the intrinsic value of the organism. In our role as created co-creators, we must care for and respect the integrity of organisms. This does not rule out genetic engineering, but it is another principle to consider.
- *Recognition of ecological holism.* All life is connected, and anything done to isolate or alter the value of a life form should be opposed. All life is connected by DNA (on a biological level) and by God. The interaction of life means that, if one form is altered, it could affect all life. The parts exist for the whole.
- *Minimization of future liability.* What our world becomes tomorrow depends on our actions today. We have a responsibility to the future, and, if we can identify a possible threat to the environment, we should do what we can to stop it. Unintended consequences of genetic engineering, for example the horizontal transfer of genes from genetically modified crops to wild plants, need to be considered and assessed.
- *Production of a social benefit.* We should develop biotechnological innovations for the good of society, not for trivial purposes or economic gains.

Edgar stresses that these principles need to be considered together: one is not more important than any other. For example, the social benefit may not be clear, but this principle should not be given precedence over any of the other principles. This could greatly enhance our decisions regarding the appropriate uses of biotechnology.

Cloning

As we have seen, some of our modern medical advances involve biotechnology, specifically the production of biopharmaceuticals and diagnostic testing. We will now turn our attention to other issues related to medicine, beginning with cloning.

As defined above, cloning refers to the isolation and propagation of a region of DNA. Another use of the term is more familiar in the public sphere, where cloning can also refer to the production of an embryo, and potentially an organism, with the same genetic material as an adult donor. Two uses of the term must be distinguished: *reproductive* cloning is the production of another individual, whereas *therapeutic* cloning produces cells that can be used to treat a condition. The first animals to be cloned were frogs in the 1950s and 1960s. This involved the transfer of a nucleus from an undifferentiated embryonic cell (a cell that has not yet developed into a specific cell type) into an enucleated egg (a fertilized egg that has had its nucleus removed). These eggs went through normal embryonic development to produce animals that contained the exact same genetic code as the nuclear donor animals. The first mammal to be cloned was the famous sheep, Dolly, born in 1996. The process used to create Dolly was similar to the one just described: however, the nucleus was not taken from an undifferentiated cell, but from a cell that already had a fate. This process is known as somatic cell nuclear

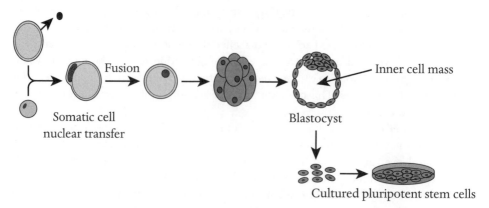

Fig. 14.4 Somatic cell nuclear transfer. A nucleus from a cell (*lower*) is fused to an enucleated egg (*top*), which develops into a blastocyst. Cells from the inner cell mass of the blastocyst are cultured to make stem cells.

transfer (see fig. 14.4). Ian Wilmut (b. 1944) and colleagues at the Roslin Institute in Edinburgh, UK fused nuclei from adult mammary cells from a 6-year-old sheep to enucleated fertilized egg cells. Out of 277 attempts, 29 embryos developed to the point where they could be transferred into surrogate mothers. Of those, only one survived (see fig. 14.5).

Dolly was genetically identical to the adult donor and was able to reproduce. However, she was not entirely normal. She was euthanized in 2003 after contracting a progressive and lethal lung disease. At 6 years old, Dolly was middle-aged, but she was developing conditions normally seen in older sheep, such as arthritis and obesity. Other mammals, including cats, mice, and cows, have been cloned since Dolly's birth. Many clones die early in life or develop abnormalities and unanticipated diseases as they mature. Although we don't know why this happens, many think it is because the clones are already "old" when they are born: the nuclei and chromosomes used in the cloning process are from adult cells. As we age, our chromosomes change.

Dolly made the possibility of human cloning a reality. Is reproductive cloning in humans ethical? To answer this question, it may be helpful, first, to consider the reasons why humans might be cloned. Cloning would allow:

- infertile individuals to have biologically related offspring;
- healthy children to be born from parents who both carry a recessive genetic condition;
- organs and tissues to be produced by the clone that could then be transplanted to the donor;
- a loved one who died to be replaced;
- the "best" members of our society to be reproduced.

Many of the potential uses of human reproductive cloning can be accomplished through other means. For example, children have been conceived naturally to act as

Fig. 14.5 Dolly the sheep, the world's first cloned adult animal, developed by a team at Edinburgh's Roslin Institute. (PA/PA Archive/Press Association Images)

organ donors for siblings, and tissue donation through therapeutic cloning may soon be realized. Healthy children can be conceived by parents who carry genetic conditions through artificial reproductive technologies and embryo screening (see below). Some uses of reproductive cloning are not possible: environmental effects will confer a unique identity to individuals who share the same DNA. Therefore, replacing a loved one or cloning the "best" members of our society will not necessarily culminate in the desired result.

Currently, the technology to produce a human embryo is not effective, and hundreds of attempts are needed to produce one viable embryo. Even with that one embryo, the possibility of its developing to term is very slim, and the potential health problems after birth are staggering. If these scientific limitations can be overcome, we face many ethical questions: should children be conceived as a means to an end, or for the end itself? What types of psychological problems will these children have, knowing they were conceived for a particular purpose? And what will happen to these children emotionally if they do not succeed in the task? Will clones feel unique and will they have distinct identities? Will they be under intense pressure to achieve the same success as the donors, and will the clones be judged and evaluated based on the donors?

Many feel that reproductive cloning is ethically wrong, but therapeutic cloning could have tremendous benefits. Others oppose therapeutic cloning because of the fear that it could lead to reproductive cloning. Thirty countries have banned human reproductive cloning and, in 2005, the United Nations adopted a nonbinding resolution that banned both therapeutic and reproductive cloning. The National Academy of Sciences and 66 other scientific societies have recommended that reproductive cloning be banned but that therapeutic cloning be permitted. No federal laws have yet been passed on this issue in the US. Religious views regarding human cloning are varied. The Catholic Church objects to both reproductive and therapeutic cloning. Most mainstream Protestant denominations have no inherent objections to reproductive cloning, but have recommended a moratorium on cloning until ethical considerations can be addressed. To better understand these views, we must examine how different religions view the status of the embryo, a topic to which we will now turn.

The Status of the Embryo

The status of the embryo has been debated for thousands of years. Aristotle condoned the termination of a pregnancy before "animation," or the point of ensoulment at day 40 after conception. Thomas Aquinas and other Catholic theologians also espoused this view. English common law, originating in the twelfth century, placed the beginning of human life at the quickening, when a fetus can be felt moving. This occurs about 120 days (4 months) after conception. In 1973, the Supreme Court used this common law definition in *Roe* v. *Wade* to make abortion legal in the US.

From a scientific point of view, the question "When does life begin?" is moot: life is always there. The egg and sperm cells are alive. The question that must actually be addressed is, "When does personhood begin?" (Recall that we also addressed this question in chapter 13.) Scientifically, this question cannot be answered, but science can provide information about human development, when critical events take place in the growth of an embryo into a fetus and infant. Fertilization, the fusion of egg and sperm, occurs in the oviduct (fallopian tube) in the female. By about the fifth day, the embryo has developed into a ball of cells, called a blastocyst, containing an inner cell mass (see fig. 14.4). Cells within the inner cell mass have the potential to develop into all types of cells in the body. Identical twins result from the splitting of the inner cell mass, and embryonic stem cells (see below) can be generated from this. About seven days after fertilization, the blastocyst implants into the uterine wall. By day 14, gastrulation occurs, whereby cells begin to acquire a specific fate. The neural tube is the first organ to form in the third week of gestation: it will eventually become the brain and spinal cord. The heart and limb buds form at four weeks, the eyes begin to form during week 5, and by the end of the first trimester, all the major anatomical parts are present in the fetus, although most will continue to develop further. Electroencephalograph (EEG) patterns, an important indicator of brain function, can be detected at week 25. Birth occurs when the lungs are fully mature at about 40 weeks.

Thus, based on science, we can recognize several key developmental stages where one could argue personhood begins:

- *At the moment of conception.* When egg and sperm fuse together, a unique genome is created, and this can be used as the definition of a human being. However, if a unique genome is all that is required for personhood, then any human cells cultured in the lab (skin cells, muscle cells, white blood cells, etc.) would by definition be a human being. We don't give these cells the rights or status of personhood. There is typically a notion not only of a unique genome, but also of the potential to develop into a fetus or infant, which distinguishes the status of a fertilized egg from other cell types.
- *At gastrulation.* As we saw, by day 14 after conception, cells begin to take on a determined fate. It is about this time that the precursor to the nervous system appears. Some consider this to be the time when an embryo acquires a unique identity. This viewpoint is important in embryonic stem cell discussions, as these stem cells are cultured from the blastula stage, prior to gastrulation.
- *When the brain becomes active.* Recall from chapter 13 that brain death, where the cognitive abilities of an individual are no longer functioning, is an important consideration at the end of life. The acquisition of these functions can also be used to determine the beginning of personhood. When EEG patterns are detected at about 25 weeks, the fetus has the capacity to be aware of its surroundings.
- *At or near birth.* Some consider a fetus a human being when it has the ability to survive on its own, outside of the womb. The lower limit for this, without medical intervention, is when the lungs are formed and functional (at about 28 weeks). With medical technology, we have pushed this limit back (the youngest babies to have been delivered and survived were 21 weeks old). Although infants born prematurely may survive, they are at high risk for physical and mental disabilities.

Science cannot determine when the developing embryo should acquire the rights, privileges, respect, and status afforded to human beings. Religious views could guide us in this: however, these views vary and have changed over the years. In the Jewish faith, Talmudic law recognizes that the fetus is potential life, but its status is not equal to that of the mother until its head can be seen coming through the birth canal. Although abortion is not typically permitted under traditional Jewish law, it is accepted when the mother's life is in danger. Some cultures wait until a period of time after the birth before personhood is conferred (from days to weeks, months, or even years). This, presumably, is due to high rates of infant mortality. Some Jewish writings advocate that humanness be conferred 13 days after birth.

In early Christian history, a distinction arose between an unformed and a formed (or animated) fetus. A formed fetus had full human status, and abortion or purposeful miscarriage was considered murder. In 197 CE, Tertullian denounced contraception and abortion, citing that destroying a fetus is murder. This represents one of the earliest statements that personhood begins at conception. However, Tertullian did condone abortion to save the life of the mother. Aquinas considered termination of a pregnancy before ensoulment to be a sin (a form of contraception). However, he did not consider termination of the pregnancy at this stage to be abortion. Views changed over the centuries, but the official Roman Catholic view of the modern era dates back to 1869 with Pope Pius IX: since we do not know the exact moment that life begins (the exact moment of ensoulment), the fetus should be protected from the very earliest possible time (conception). Pius IX declared that anyone performing an abortion would be excommunicated. Later theologians argued that ensoulment occurs at conception, a view which is officially held in Catholic doctrine today. The *Donum Vitae* (1987) states that a fetus is a human being from conception, and has the same rights as a person from this moment on. Therefore, therapeutic cloning is rejected by the Catholic Church: the destruction of an embryo is regarded as the killing of a human being.

Biblical passages have been used to determine the status of the embryo. Of course, notions such as cloning and stem cells are not addressed in scripture, but many look to the text for guidance on when personhood begins and how an embryo should be regarded. When examining these texts, we must be careful not to apply contemporary scientific concepts: when biblical writers talked of a woman conceiving a child, they did not know of egg and sperm fusion, early divisions, implantation into the uterus, and other developmental stages. Conception usually refers to the time a woman was aware she was pregnant. Some have used certain passages to support the position that personhood begins at conception:

> Thy hands fashioned and made me; and now thou dost turn about and destroy me. Remember that thou hast made me of clay; and wilt thou turn me to dust again? Didst thou not pour me out like milk and curdle me like cheese? Thou didst clothe me with skin and flesh, and knit me together with bones and sinews. Thou hast granted me life and steadfast love; and thy care has preserved my spirit. (Job 10:8–12)

> For thou didst form my inward parts, thou didst knit me together in my mother's womb. I praise thee, for thou art fearful and wonderful. Wonderful are thy works! Thou knowest me right well; my frame was not hidden from thee, when I was being made in secret, intricately wrought in the depths of the earth. Thy eyes beheld my unformed substance; in thy book were written, every one of them, the days that were formed for me, when as yet there was none of them. (Psalm 139:13–16)

> "Before I formed you in the womb I knew you, and before you were born I consecrated you; I appointed you a prophet to the nations." (Jeremiah 1:5)

These passages show that, just as God cared for these individuals in adulthood, God was also caring for them as embryos, indeed even "fashioning" them. Thus, one interpretation applies these notions to all embryos, that is: there is a relationship between God and all embryos, all embryos are the potential children of God, and God cares for all embryos.

Others argue that these passages must be considered in context. They are specific reflections, do not apply to a general assessment of all embryos, and say nothing of when personhood begins. For example, in Psalm 139, God created the psalmist, but there is no specific mention of when he attains human personhood. In Jeremiah 1:5, the verse describes the plan that God has for Jeremiah before his birth. It says nothing about human development. Some passages have been interpreted to indicate that a fetus has a lower status, for example Exodus:

> "When men strive together, and hurt a woman with child, so that there is a miscarriage, and yet no harm follows, the one who hurt her shall be fined, according as the woman's husband shall lay upon him; and he shall pay as the judges determine. If any harm follows, then you shall give life for life, eye for eye, tooth for tooth, hand for hand, foot for foot, burn for burn, wound for wound, stripe for stripe." (Exodus 21: 22–5)

The death of an unborn child requires punishment in the form of compensation. But if "harm" comes to the woman (if she dies), then death is an appropriate punishment. Thus, the fetus does not have the same status as an adult.

So what does the Bible tell us about the status of the embryo? It tells us that God cares for all humans, including those in the womb. But, for many, it does not tell us when a person is present in the womb. This ambiguity has led to many disagreements regarding cloning and the use of embryonic stem cells.

Stem Cells

Stem cells are unspecialized cells that have the ability to differentiate, or develop into, different cell types. Two main types of stem cells exist: embryonic stem cells and adult stem cells. Embryonic stem (ES) cells come from the inner cell mass of the blastocyst (see fig. 14.4). They are pluripotent, meaning they can differentiate into any cell type. Adult stem cells can be found in different tissues in the body. These cells do not have the same potential as ES cells, but can differentiate into multiple types of cells. For example, hematopoietic stem cells can develop into the cells in the blood and immune systems. In fact, we have been using adult stem cells for decades through bone marrow transplants. These stem cells are rare, found less than once in 15,000 bone marrow cells. In the body, stem cells are induced to differentiate through hormones and other molecules which regulate the expression of specific genes. The goal of research with both adult and ES cells is to culture these undifferentiated cells in the lab and induce them to develop into a specific cell type which can be used to replace cells, tissues, and maybe even organs in the human body. Conditions that could benefit from stem cell therapy are those that involve the destruction of cells that the body cannot repair or replace, including Parkinson's disease, Alzheimer's disease, diabetes, and spinal cord injuries. Currently, stem cells are being used in the treatment of some diseases, such as cancer, and thousands of clinical trials are underway.

Scientifically, there are challenges in the use of stem cells. One of the problems with using ES cells is the rejection of the cells by the immune system. The donor ES cells have a different genetic composition from the recipient, and the body may recognize these cells as being foreign, leading to an immune response. The use of adult stem cells, isolated from the patient and induced in a lab to differentiate into the needed cell type, would avoid this situation. However, if it is not feasible to use adult stem cells, therapeutic cloning (through somatic cell nuclear transfer: see fig. 14.4) can be used. Nuclei from the patient can be fused to human enucleated eggs, creating embryos, and ES cells can then be isolated, induced, and transferred to the patient. ES cells derived through therapeutic cloning are not recognized as foreign and have been successfully used to treat Parkinson's disease in mice and monkeys. Researchers in South Korea have created ES cell lines from 11 humans suffering from spinal cord injuries or type 1 diabetes, through therapeutic cloning. Work is ongoing to try to induce these cells to become neurons or pancreatic cells.

The ethical and theological considerations focus on ES cells, not adult stem cells. Proponents argue that the use of ES cells is justified on moral grounds: the potential benefits for the individual and for society are immense. Cures for diseases and injuries can be developed from research into and the use of ES cells. And these diseases are some of the most hideous imaginable: conditions that cause suffering from the loss of physical, mental, and spiritual abilities. They are diseases that dehumanize the patient. The use of ES cells becomes a question of compassion. Ted Peters has been involved in discussions regarding stem cells, cloning, and other bioethical issues. He argues that the potential good resulting from the use of ES cells is enormous, and our charge to emulate Jesus as healer, to contribute to God's healing work on Earth, makes the use of ES cells ethical. Peters does not deny the embryo has potential, or that it should be treated with dignity. He does not advocate the creation of new embryos for research purposes but rather argues for utilizing "excess" embryos resulting from *in vitro* fertilization (IVF, see below). These embryos are frozen, and controversy surrounds what should be done with them when they are no longer wanted or needed. There are estimates that more than 500,000 frozen embryos are in storage in fertility clinics in the US, and this number is increasing by 20,000 a year. Most of these will be destroyed. Peters believes the use of these embryos as stem cells constitutes beneficence, a generous gift, to help relieve the suffering of many. He does not see the use of embryos as the killing of a human person. Peters supports the use of adult stem cells, but acknowledges that they may not have the same potential as ES cells. In his view, research with both should be encouraged.

Opponents of research using ES cells focus on the destruction of the embryo and not on the potential benefits. Whether the blastocyst was obtained via IVF procedures or created by somatic cell nuclear transfer is irrelevant. For those who believe that embryos are persons from the very beginning, the generation and use of ES cells is immoral because it results from the killing of a human being.

No matter what the view, everyone in the discussion understands that the human embryo has value, and that it should be treated with respect, and not as a commodity. This brings us to an ethical issue regarding the intention when the embryos were created. Ethical review committees, including those from the National Institutes of Health (NIH), are against the selling of embryos resulting from IVF. If a couple decides to discard extra embryos, they should be given the option of donating them for research purposes. For many, the ethics of this approach is acceptable: the embryos were created for reproduction, not commercial purposes, and their use in ES cell research is ethical. However, the ethical issue with regard to therapeutic cloning is different, for its purpose is the creation of embryos for destruction and the harvesting of ES cells. Some consider therapeutic cloning to be unethical because it regards the embryos as a product to be used however someone sees fit. The embryos are not respected. Others argue that it is actually less ethically problematic than using embryos from IVF because the intention of therapeutic cloning is to generate an ES cell line, not, as with IVF, to produce a child. Another consideration is the potential of these embryos to develop normally. Embryos generated from IVF result from the natural process of fertilization of egg and sperm. IVF has a relatively high probability of producing a viable embryo that could develop into a fetus. Embryos generated for therapeutic cloning result from the transfer of a nucleus from an adult cell into an enucleated egg. The vast majority of these cloned embryos, as we have seen, do not have the potential to develop fully into a fetus.

Some countries have banned the use of human ES cells, while others have allowed research, with restrictions. In the United States, no laws prohibit research on ES cells, but federal funding for this research has changed due to shifts in the political climate. In 2001, President George W. Bush issued an executive order that federal funding could be used only for cell lines created before August 9, 2001. Private and state funding were made available to establish and work with new ES cells. However, many feared that this situation would put the US far behind other countries that fully supported ES cell research, and that any research done with private funding would not be fully communicated to the rest of the scientific community, further limiting progress in the field. When Barack Obama took office in 2009, he reversed the Bush ruling and reinstated federal funding to support work with these cells.

Reproductive Technologies

In the US, approximately one in every 10 couples is infertile, as a result of hormonal imbalances, abnormalities in the reproductive system, sexually transmitted diseases, or other causes. Many approaches to help infertile couples conceive are available, from hormonal therapies (to release more eggs) to artificial insemination (where sperm are transferred into the uterus and do not have to travel through the cervix, a point where many sperm die). Assisted reproductive technologies (ART) are based on the manipulation of the egg outside of the women's body, such as with *in vitro* fertilization (IVF).

IVF was first successfully used in 1978. The process involves hormonal stimulation in the female, causing the release of multiple oocytes. These are harvested by a physician through aspiration and the eggs are placed in a sterile Petri dish. A semen sample is collected from the male partner, and active, live sperm can be selected and further treated to prepare them for fertilization. A single egg is typically incubated with 50,000 to 100,000 sperm for 12–18 hours, and fertilization rates range from 50 to 70 percent. Several embryos are transferred into the uterus three days after fertilization. The embryos must implant into the uterus for pregnancy to begin. Embryos not transferred can be frozen and later thawed for another attempt.

Success rates vary. Approximately 31 percent of couples will achieve pregnancy and delivery with one round of IVF, but that number decreases as the age of the woman increases. Frozen embryos have a reduced rate of implantation (10 percent). Multiple births are not uncommon with IVF, depending on the age of the woman and how many embryos were transferred into the uterus. Younger women are at a higher risk for multiple births even when fewer eggs are transferred.

About 1 million women use infertility services in the US each year. By 2005, more than 177,000 children were born in the US using IVF. Many questions surround the safety and ethics of ART, including health risks to the woman, mistakes in laboratory practices, and multiple births (which may result in physical and mental handicaps, or death, to the infants). Cost is also a major issue. For a single pregnancy, couples spend $44,000 to $200,000 for IVF procedures. Infertility is a $2 billion a year industry.

Theologically, some have questioned the use of ART based on the notions of *imago Dei*, co-creation and stewardship. At the center of this argument is a passage in Genesis:

> So God created man in his own image, in the image of God he created him; male and female he created them. And God blessed them, and God said to them, "Be fruitful and multiply, and fill the earth and subdue it; and have dominion over the fish of the sea and over the birds of the air and over every living thing that moves upon the earth." (Genesis 1:27–8)

God created humans, bid them procreate, and gave them dominion over other living things. Adam and Eve were created in the image of God, and therefore, as co-creators, their children are also made in the image of God. Consequently, children should be respected and treated with dignity. Children are a gift from God, equal to their parents in the eyes of God: they cannot be regarded as property or products. Parents have a responsibility to their children, and this stewardship was conferred in the context of marriage, with responsibility falling on both parents.

Some claim that ART violates these important precepts. Artificial reproduction is a way to produce children as a means to an end, where children are a product rather than a gift from God. The importance of the marital relationship (the act of intercourse) is absent in ART. The techniques used (IVF) are by their nature manipulative and encourage a disrespectful attitude toward the child. Donations of egg and sperm, and surrogate parenting, are also problematic, because they treat the child as a commodity (even if no money is being exchanged), violate the notion that a child should result from the union of loving parents (the genetic material is not from one or both parents, and a surrogate mother will not fulfill the stewardship role), and rejects the notion that a child is a gift from God (instead it is donated or fashioned by a human). All of this hinges on the notion that the embryo is a person from the moment of conception. Reproductive cloning can also be condemned on the basis that a cloned person is made in the image of another person, not in the image of God. It is not a unique gift from God.

The Catholic Church adheres to this line of reasoning. The conjugal act has two meanings: it represents the marital union and procreation. The church condemns the use of ART because these technologies separate the physical union from the act of procreation. The church uses the same reasoning in its condemnation of contraception.

Genetic Testing

In 1990, the Human Genome Project (HGP) officially began (we looked at this briefly in chapter 9). Its goal was to sequence the DNA in the human genome, to determine the order of the 3 billion nucleotides that make up our species. The project was essentially completed in 2003. With this information, our ability to diagnose, treat, and cure diseases, and to understand the myriad cellular processes that go on in our bodies, will advance. Many other genomes have also been sequenced, from important species of bacteria and plants to animals such as mice and fruit flies. By comparing human DNA sequences with those from another species, we can gain some insight into how a gene may act. By analyzing sequences and comparing which regions of the genome are expressed in different cell types, we can identify the genes that are involved in disease processes, leading to diagnosis and potential treatments. A goal has been set to develop technologies to sequence individual genomes for $1,000. This will allow us to determine an individual's susceptibility to various diseases and identify which drugs will be most effective for each person (individualized medicine). We will now consider two important issues surrounding the Human Genome Project: genetic testing and gene therapy.

Today we can test an individual's DNA for specific genetic diseases, such as cystic fibrosis and sickle cell anemia. We can determine if an individual has a disease-causing allele, while not expressing the disease, that can be passed on to offspring (a carrier). We can look at specific DNA regions that will indicate predispositions (risk assessment) for conditions that may appear later in life, such as heart disease, diabetes, cancer, Alzheimer's disease, and a host of other "common" ailments. The results from the Human Genome Project will greatly increase the number of conditions that can be detected. The decision of when (or even if) to have a test done, and what to do with the results, are complex issues that are not easily sorted out.

Prenatal diagnosis for particular genetic conditions can be done via amniocentesis or chorionic villus sampling (CVS), both of which involve obtaining and analyzing cells from a fetus. Prenatal results may indicate the child will be born with a disease, in some cases, a lethal disease. In other cases, the condition may cause severe limitations, but will not necessarily be fatal in childhood. How do we determine which, if any, of these conditions warrant the termination of a pregnancy? And is there any value in performing these tests, even if the couple has decided to continue the pregnancy, no matter the results?

For couples who know they are at high risk of conceiving a child with a genetic condition (for example, if both carry a lethal allele for the condition), ART can allow for the screening of embryos for specific genetic disorders before the embryos are transferred into the uterus. This is known as preimplantation genetic diagnosis. Recall that, with IVF, embryos are transferred about three days after fertilization, after they have gone through several rounds of cell division. A single cell from an embryo at the eight-cell stage can be removed and tested. If it is free from the mutation, the embryo can be transferred to the uterus. As we learn more about the human genome, we will be able to test for more conditions. Although this will be advantageous for debilitating conditions, we will quickly encounter gray areas. For many genetic conditions, the severity of the disease cannot be predicted. In some cases, for example with Down syndrome, individuals may lead very full and rewarding lives even with the genetic condition. We must also ask ourselves about late-onset diseases such as Alzheimer's: should we deny a person existence if we know that a terrible disease will manifest itself later in their life? Should we fail to transfer embryos that will develop diseases we can treat with some success, such as diabetes? What about susceptibility to conditions such as cancer and heart disease? What about personality or lifestyle traits, such as homosexuality? What about autism, schizophrenia, bipolar disorder, and alcoholism?

The fear with preimplantation or prenatal diagnosis is that, in the future, we may pick and choose the traits we want in our children. The issue of eugenics emerges once again (see chapter 12). The potential for discrimination looms heavily: if we can "perfect" a human, how do we treat those who are "imperfect"? The first thing we need to understand is that not everything is written in our genes, and we cannot test for everything. So the scenario of "perfection" will never be realized. But we still encounter problems with our "limited" abilities. In creating or designing a child with preferred traits, we have to ask if we have the right to treat a person as a means to an end and not an end in itself. If all humans are created in the image of God, then all human life is valued, and all human life is equal. Compassion and the sanctity of life are important concepts that are voiced by religious traditions in times of prenatal decisions. The Catholic Church forbids abortion but permits prenatal testing when the benefits are greater than the risks. With all cases of testing, a diagnosis of a genetic disorder does not mean the pregnancy has to be terminated. Instead, the results may allow the couple time to plan for the special needs of the child.

Other forms of genetic testing include postnatal testing and carrier screening. Postnatal testing can detect alleles associated with diseases and provide risk assessment for conditions that usually occur later in life, such as cancer and heart disease. If an individual is presymptomatic, then lifestyle changes and close monitoring by health-care professionals may reduce the risk of their developing the disease, or lessen its severity. Some argue that, with conditions for which there is no treatment, very little is to be gained from genetic testing. But, where there is a chance of passing on the condition, this information may influence an individual's decision whether or not to have children.

Reproductive decisions are at the heart of carrier screening, which is used to determine if an individual who does not express a disease carries an allele that can cause the disease. If a couple knows they are both carriers for a condition such as sickle cell anemia, any children they conceive will have a 25 percent chance of being born with the disease. Some couples in this situation have opted for IVF and preimplantation diagnosis, or forgo having children and choose adoption. In other cases, especially in societies with arranged marriages, a match will not be approved if both individuals are carriers. This can address the objections to IVF in some religious traditions while greatly reducing the incidence of children born with a genetic condition. This approach has been used successfully in the Ashkenazi Jewish population to decrease the incidence of Tay–Sachs and other diseases.

Privacy issues need to be addressed with regard to genetic testing. Carrier screening can prevent the birth of children with debilitating diseases, but the carriers themselves could be stigmatized because of their genetic status. Presymptomatic testing can be used to prevent diseases or diagnose them earlier, but insurance companies could deny coverage to people with potential illnesses to save money, and potential employers could refuse to hire them, to reduce problems of low productivity in the workplace. Genetic discrimination is similar to discrimination based on age, ethnicity, or gender: we do not choose, and cannot change, our genetics. After 13 years of debate in congress, the Genetic Information Nondiscrimination Act was finally signed into law by President Bush in 2008. This law protects individuals against discrimination based on their genetic information when it comes to health insurance and employment.

Gene Therapy

We have the ability to create transgenic organisms, so do we also have the ability to fix mutations in humans that lead to genetic diseases? Gene therapy focuses on replacing the defective gene with a normal copy of the gene, allowing the patient's body to produce the normal protein. In *ex vivo* gene therapy, cells are removed from the body and cultured in a laboratory. The cells are genetically altered, grown, and reintroduced to the patient. For example, hematopoietic stem cells can be engineered to treat defects involving the blood and immune systems. When injected back into the patient, they have a fairly long life and can give rise to other cells that will also contain the alteration. The very first gene therapy trial utilized this approach. In 1990, white blood cells from Ashanti DeSilva, a 4-year-old girl suffering from a form of severe combined immune deficiency (SCID) were collected and altered to include a functional copy of the gene for adenosine deaminase (ADA). Ashanti had a mutation in this gene which prevented her immune system from functioning correctly. Patients with SCID cannot fight off many ordinary pathogens, and common diseases can prove fatal to them. When the altered cells were injected back into Ashanti, her immune system improved. This was not a permanent cure, and today Ashanti must periodically receive new cells and take a drug containing ADA.

For cell types that cannot be easily obtained and cultured, *in vivo* gene therapy is needed. In most cases a virus is used to deliver DNA to a cell. The virus is engineered to contain a functional copy of the affected gene and is also disabled so it will not cause a disease (see fig. 14.6). Problems with *in vivo* approaches include determining exactly how to regulate the gene, targeting the gene to the correct cell type, and the immune reaction that is often elicited due to the viral vector. Cystic fibrosis (CF) was one of the first candidate diseases for *in vivo* gene therapy. In CF patients, a faulty chloride channel in respiratory cells causes a buildup of mucous in the lungs. This results in severe bacterial infections, breathing difficulties, and a greatly reduced life span. Delivery of a functional copy of the gene to the respiratory cells would restore the ion channel. However, only limited success has been achieved and therapeutic results have been very disappointing.

Currently, gene therapy carries very high risks with uncertain outcomes. Nevertheless, more than 500 gene therapy protocols have been approved, most of them for the treatment of cancer. As with any other pharmaceutical agents, gene therapy must go through a series of clinical trials to ascertain the safety and efficacy of the agent. Unfortunately, we have seen some tragedies with these trials. In 1999, 18-year-old Jesse Gelsinger died while involved in a gene therapy trial at the University of Pennsylvania. It is suspected that his body mounted a massive immune response to the viral vector used in the trial. Another gene therapy trial, begun in 2000 in France, involved 11 patients with SCID. Nine of the recipients were apparently cured of the condition. However, two of the patients developed leukemia after the trial began. Apparently the therapy activated a cancer-causing gene (an oncogene) in these patients. Both trials were halted after these tragedies.

Ethically, some questions need to be addressed regarding gene therapy:

- What are the financial costs of research, development, and delivery of these therapies?
- Should the government establish the medical research priorities?

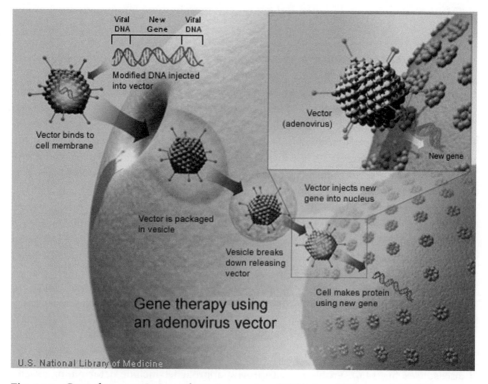

Viral   New   Viral
DNA   Gene   DNA

Modified DNA injected
into vector

Vector binds to
cell membrane

Vector
(adenovirus)

New gene

Vector injects new
gene into nucleus

Vector is packaged
in vesicle

Vesicle breaks
down releasing
vector

Cell makes protein
using new gene

Gene therapy using
an adenovirus vector

U.S. National Library of Medicine

Fig. 14.6   Gene therapy using an adenovirus vector. (US National Library of Medicine
http://ghr.nlm.nih.gov/handbook/therapy/procedures)

- Will our focus on gene therapy discourage the development of conventional treatments that might be effective and more cost-efficient?
- Will it be possible to provide successful gene therapy to all who need it?
- Will therapies be patented? Will one company or individual have exclusive rights to a certain therapy?

There is a distinction between somatic (body cell) gene therapy and germ-line (gamete, or reproductive cell) gene therapy. If somatic cells are altered, then only the patient is affected by the genetic changes. Altering the germ line affects future genera-tions: they will inherit the altered genotype. If proven to be safe, germ-line therapy could be a powerful tool to eliminate devastating diseases from the human population, alleviating much suffering in future generations. This type of healing can be viewed as a reflection of God's redemption and could be considered acceptable from a theo-logical perspective. Germ-line gene therapy also presents problems, among which are eugenics and choice. Altering germ cells to affect traits, such as intelligence, brings us back to the eugenics argument. With regard to choice, all medical procedures require informed consent, and some ethicists point out that future generations will not have the opportunity to have a say in the manipulation of their genome. For the moment at least, our techniques are still in their infancy, and so we may begin to think and make some decisions before this technology is a viable option. Today, only somatic cell therapy is permitted.

End-of-Life Issues

End-of-life issues, involving life-saving and life-extending technologies, are becoming more common and more complex with each passing day. Questions surrounding death and dying have always been difficult to address, but we now have the additional complication that the focus of medicine is on curing the patient. This has led to a culture which defies suffering and death, where the prevailing attitude is that we are always entitled to good health. Because our society is focused on acute care, and economic considerations determine the course of much of our health care, the long-term needs of the elderly have not always been addressed and adequate end-of-life care has been slow to develop. We need more support for families and better long-term health care. We cannot prevent death, but careful reflection and management can help all involved in the process. Considerations must include:

- *The dignity of individuals.* The wishes of patients must be assessed. How can we respect their desires and best address their needs?
- *Extraordinary medical procedures versus basic care.* Extraordinary treatments, such as the use of respirators, dialysis machines, and medication, may be necessary for life to continue. Other procedures and equipment, for example feeding tubes, are considered basic care. It is usually regarded as ethical to withdraw extraordinary treatments but not basic care. What is acceptable at the point where basic care becomes extraordinary? And who determines whether a treatment is extraordinary or basic?
- *Quality-of-life questions.* Quality of life centers on the ability of patients to engage in physical, mental, and spiritual pursuits. If a treatment to extend life decreases the quality of life, should it be used?

One institution in our society that addresses end-of-life issues well is hospice care. Patients are treated with dignity and provided with companionship and medical (especially palliative, or pain-reducing) care. The financial burdens on these individuals and their families are greatly reduced. Hospice care, which is underutilized in the United States, is well supported by theologians specializing in bioethics.

End-of-life discussions often include debates centering on physician-assisted suicide (PAS) and euthanasia ("mercy-killing," or medically assisted killing). Advocates for PAS focus on the terrible suffering that patients endure: the diminishing physical, mental, and spiritual abilities individuals must deal with is seen as an evil, and ethically there is no solution to this ordeal. When the end is near, and there is no treatment to relieve suffering, proponents argue that mercy should be shown, and physicians honor the wishes of a dying patient. Oregon legalized PAS in 1997, and Belgium and the Netherlands legalized euthanasia in 2002.

The consensus in the theological community is that euthanasia and PAS are unethical. We disregard the sanctity of human life when we allow these options, and we open the floodgates for potential abuse. Consider some of the possibilities that could result.

- PAS and euthanasia may be used to avoid distressing medical treatments.
- The category of patients "eligible" for euthanasia may be expanded to include conditions where death is not imminent.
- Conflicting priorities may cause crises with health-care professionals, who are responsible for the relief of suffering but must not do any harm to a patient.
- The pressure placed by society or the family on health-care professionals may result in the taking of a life when it is not the wish or in the best interest of the patient.

In many instances, alternatives to these drastic measures exist, often unbeknownst to the patient and the family. Some more ethical possibilities include the use of "do not resuscitate" orders, the cessation of extraordinary treatment, and the use of palliative care. It is the duty of the medical community to relieve pain and of the religious communities to provide spiritual care for those who are chronically ill and those facing death. This ensures social justice, human dignity, and personal respect. The spiritual community must be there for others, to help in their care, to be compassionate. Despite all our efforts, suffering cannot be prevented: although we must always try to fight it, we also need to find ways to accept and deal with it.

The Catholic Church does not advocate the use of extraordinary or disproportionate means of life support, and is very supportive of palliative care. However, in both these cases, there can still be ethical problems. Do we use high doses of pain medication or terminate treatment even if these actions are likely to hasten death, that is, do we accept the inevitable and take an action that will eventually cause death? The patient or family must make this decision, based on the condition of the patient, how useful or taxing the treatment is, and, to a lesser degree, the cost of the treatment. The church grants that treatment can be refused or withdrawn if its use is disproportionate to the anticipated results, or if it will impose suffering that does not coincide with the benefit gained. This is not considered suicide or euthanasia, but an acceptance of the human condition and the avoidance of excessive expense on the family or community. Medication can be used in dosages to relieve pain, even if this may shorten the life span of the individual. The notion of extraordinary procedures and basic care has also been addressed by the Catholic Church. In 2004, Pope John Paul II stated that artificial nutrition and hydration (ANH) were not medical procedures, but natural means of preserving life. Therefore these procedures are morally obligatory, particularly in cases of permanently comatose patients (those in a persistent vegetative state or PVS: see chapter 13). This is based on the argument that all human life has value and each person has inherent dignity. Even if the patient is not conscious and cannot have spiritual or personal experiences, there is a duty to preserve life. The quality of that life is not an issue.

Critics argue that, when a person has lost any potential to engage meaningfully in relationships with others, the removal of a medical device, such as a respirator or feeding tube should not be seen as suffocation or starvation but as the removal of a technology that does not contribute to the total well-being of the patient. The physical condition of the patient should not be the only consideration in these decisions: the intellect and will, the overall condition and prospects, indeed the quality of life, must be part of any decision made.

The Art of Medicine

Western medicine is based on many traditions originating from the ancient Greeks. Hippocrates is a legend in the establishment of Western medicine, and his name is identified with the pledge traditionally taken by physicians at the beginning of their career. Although the Hippocratic oath was written long after Hippocrates' death, it is believed to reflect his ethics. According to the oath, the physician's primary concern is to be for the patient, and no harm should come to them. Abortion is forbidden. The physician pledges not to practice beyond his or her competencies, and must be a consummate professional, with no separation or distinction between life and art. The physician should not engage in sexual misconduct and is to keep information confidential. The Hippocratic oath was taken in the name of the gods, which reflected the understanding that there are many things beyond our physical realm. Today, medical schools that require an oath use a modified version of the oath: the Greek gods are replaced or omitted, and, in most cases, the clauses regarding abortion and sexual misconduct are omitted. Some see this as a departure from Christian tradition.

Medicine has three underlying or core values that are consistent with Christian faith: healing, relief of suffering, and compassion. If these core values are honored in the treatment of individuals, we may be able to overcome some of the ethical problems we encounter, especially with new technologies involving genetics and biotechnology. The ability we possess to influence life cannot overshadow the teachings of Jesus and the message of the Bible. We must understand that there are limits to what we, as humans, can do. The apostle Paul wanted to transcend pain and suffering, not through his own hand, but through God's power of redemption:

> But we have this treasure in earthen vessels, to show that the transcendent power belongs to God and not to us. We are afflicted in every way, but not crushed; perplexed, but not driven to despair; persecuted, but not forsaken; struck down, but not destroyed; always carrying in the body the death of Jesus, so that the life of Jesus may also be manifested in our bodies. For while we live we are always being given up to death for Jesus' sake, so that the life of Jesus may be manifested in our mortal flesh. So death is at work in us, but life in you. (2 Corinthians 4:7–12)

> So we do not lose heart. Though our outer nature is wasting away, our inner nature is being renewed every day. For this slight momentary affliction is preparing for us an eternal weight of glory beyond all comparison, because we look not to the things that are seen but to the things that are unseen; for the things that are seen are transient, but the things that are unseen are eternal. (2 Corinthians 4:16–18)

> For we know that if the earthly tent we live in is destroyed, we have a building from God, a house not made with hands, eternal in the heavens. Here indeed we groan, and long to

put on our heavenly dwelling, so that by putting it on we may not be found naked. For while we are still in this tent, we sigh with anxiety; not that we would be unclothed, but that we would be further clothed, so that what is mortal may be swallowed up by life. He who has prepared us for this very thing is God, who has given us the Spirit as a guarantee. (2 Corinthians 5:1–5)

Theological and religious understanding can and should play a role in shaping bioethics, and in helping to formulate policies that will guide physicians in the best practices to "do no harm."

Conclusions

Both the promise and perils of biotechnology and advanced medical procedures are the luxury of Western societies. We need to weigh the benefits and risks in the applications of these technologies, but we must not lose perspective. Most people on this planet have limited access to food and clean water, and will never have the opportunity to be treated with the expensive medical procedures discussed in this chapter. Many will die of diseases that can be treated and cured in Western societies. Should we focus our resources on high-tech efforts to relieve the suffering of those with Alzheimer's disease, Parkinson's disease, multiple sclerosis, and other debilitating diseases, or should we pay more attention to the millions who are suffering because they don't have adequate basic medical care? Should we concentrate on eliminating poverty on a global scale or on eliminating genetic diseases through gene therapy? Do we save those who are already here, or do we fight for the rights of those who are not yet born? Can we alleviate the crises caused by war and injustice to allow the global population to prosper, or can we hope to improve only our corner of the world? There are no easy answers. Instead of worrying about technology being a threat to God, we should be asking how technology can help to relieve suffering and to carry out God's will for the whole of humanity.

We need to consider aspects of the intrinsic value of living things, respect for all life, and justice for the people who will be affected by the use of these technologies. We should always keep in mind our role as stewards of this planet, and the directive from God to care for one another.

Primary Literature

Useful primary sources include an article by the chair of the Department of Nutrition and Food Studies at New York University, Marion Nestle, "Food Biotechnology: Whose Values, Whose Decisions?" *Witness* 84 (5) (2001), 14–17; an editorial article by Jeremy Rifkin, "Beyond Genetically Modified Crops," *Washington Post* (July 4, 2006), A15, and a response, Erik Stokstad, "A Kinder, Gentler Jeremy Rifkin Endorses Biotech, or Does He?" *Science* 312 (5780) (2006), 1586–7; an article by Ted Peters, "In Search of the Perfect Child: Genetic Testing and Selective Abortion," *Christian Century* 113 (1996), 1034–7; and an article by the founder and president of a Christian ministry addressing the needs of people with disabilities, Joni Eareckson Tada, "The Threat of Biotech," *Christianity Today* 47 (3) (2003), 60–2.

Questions to Consider

1 We have seen in this chapter that both opponents and proponents of biotechnology have convincing arguments supporting their respective sides. Both have scientific, economic, and ethical arguments to sway the public.

  (a) How can you gage the validity of the arguments on each side? What type of evidence is most convincing? Research one or two of the issues discussed in this chapter and list what you find to be most convincing on each side of the argument.

  (b) Is the implementation of biotechnology an all-or-nothing issue (either we use it or we don't), or should we look at each use on a case-by-case basis? How much expense (in time and money) is feasible to assess the effects (to human health, to the environment, to society and our future) of each use of biotechnology? When can we, if ever, assume that a new genetically engineered organism is safe?

2 Use Edgar's six principles to analyze the following applications of biotechnology. According to this strategy, which are ethical?

  (a) A strain of zebrafish has been genetically engineered to contain a gene that makes the fish florescent. In a black light, the fish glow an intense red color. Although they are sold only as pets, California banned the sale of them, fearing that if they ever were released into the environment, they could spread the transgene to wild species.

  (b) One application of biotechnology in the textile industry is the creation of a microbe that has been genetically engineered to produce stonewashed jeans. Previous treatments of tough denim fabric relied on acid or pumice (volcanic rock mined from open pits). An enzyme produced by GM bacterium can now fade and soften the material without the environmental damage caused by acid or mining and with reduced energy consumption.

  (c) A biotechnology company is in the process of developing an anti-obesity agent. The Centers for Disease Control, based on 2003–4 statistics, estimates that 66 percent of US adults are overweight or obese. A transgenic line of plants may someday be able to produce a protein that will block the ability of our digestive systems to uptake specific fats we consume in our diet. The products of the plant (fruit, seeds, etc.) could be eaten directly by the consumer, or the protein could be purified and sold as a nutritional supplement.

3 In 2006, SemBioSys, a Canadian biotechnology company, applied for a permit to grow genetically altered safflower in Washington state. The plant has been engineered to produce a carp growth hormone in its seeds. The seeds will be tested as a supplement for aquaculture meal. In 2007, the EPA asked for public comments on the field trial. Write a letter addressed to the EPA, and provide a recommendation as to whether or not the field trial should be permitted. Be sure to support your opinion.

4 Germ-line gene therapy raises ethical questions about informed consent: future generations cannot provide consent for the manipulation of their genome, and

therefore it may not be ethical to perform this type of procedure. However, with many medical procedures today, advocates make decisions for those who are not in a position to provide consent (for example, parents make choices for their children, family members make decisions for patients who are in comas or mentally incapacitated). Would a decision in favor of germ-line gene therapy just be an extension of this practice? What about couples who know that their children have a high probability of being born with a genetic condition – do they violate the principle of informed consent when they choose to have children?

5   We have examined several views on the ethics of reproductive and therapeutic cloning. Outline the arguments for and against each. Some contend that reproductive cloning is more ethical; some argue that therapeutic cloning is more ethical. Which do you think has more support? Consider your answer from biblical, theological, scientific, and societal perspectives.

6   Many new medical technologies have given rise to intense debates, both ethical and theological. In the past, some medical advances, including vaccinations and surgery, were seen as obstructing God's will. The first organ transplant, the donation of a kidney from a man to his sick identical twin, was debated because surgery was to be performed on an individual who didn't need it and the potential consequences on the health of the donor twin might violate the principle of doing no harm. Most of these objections seem rather silly to us today. Do you think we will come to a point in the future where the use of gene therapy, stem cells, cloning, and end-of-life technologies will be agreed on and accepted by the majority of society? Can you envision a future where we will look back at this time in history and regard these discussions as "silly"?

7   Medical advancements improve and extend our lives. For those of us in affluent societies, a new paradigm is emerging: we assume we are entitled to good health; if something goes wrong, I (or my insurance company) can pay someone to fix it. Think about this with regard to both individuals and society as a whole. How does this attitude affect our sense of self-responsibility? How does it impact our view of God's grace in our lives? How does it change our notion of suffering?

8   Research other religious views of the embryo. What do the Jewish, Islamic, Hindu, and Buddhist faiths have to say about the status of the embryo and whether or not it should be used in research and medical treatments? Can these views help to inform our current discussions?

15

Stewardship and the Environment

Overview

Human activity is responsible for many of the environmental problems we face today, and has contributed to global warming, the destruction of habitats, and the extinction of species. The rapid growth of the human population, in conjunction with our attitudes toward nature, many of which are based on the view that humans are separate and distinct from nature, are the main causes of these ecological crises. An understanding of the interconnectedness we have with nature, and the biblical calls for stewardship, can help change our attitudes and our behavior. Viable solutions, from reducing population growth to the use of alternative fuels, may allow for a reversal of current trends.

Introduction

There is no doubt that human activity has greatly altered the Earth's ecosystems. Exactly how much damage has been done, and what the future holds, is open to debate. Our current environmental problems challenge us to think about our actions not only on a local scale, but also globally. We need to ask ourselves how we can best conserve the environment and preserve species, while developing natural resources and still taking what we need. Discussions regarding these issues must include a complex mix of biological, societal, economic, political, and ethical voices. The many problems that exist have relatively few easy answers. As with most multifaceted issues, there are extreme views at both ends of the spectrum: some see the eminent and impending collapse of "nature," while others believe that nature will take care of itself, regardless of what we humans do. The truth probably lies somewhere in between.

In this chapter, we will take a look at some present concerns and then consider ideas on how we should view humanity in relation to the environment. We will conclude the chapter with a brief survey of some solutions.

The Problems

A short list of existing environmental concerns includes global warming, overpopulation, habitat destruction, extinction of species, and pollution of the air and water. Many of these issues are global in scale, and we may feel our efforts to recycle plastic containers and turn off unneeded lights cannot impact the state of affairs. It seems an impossible task to accomplish anything that requires worldwide effort. Yet local initiatives and individual efforts can and do make a difference. And, using the right approaches, large-scale (even global) efforts can succeed.

Although numerous issues confront us, we can only consider a few in this chapter. We will start with an example of an event that had a sudden and devastating impact on a local environment (the *Exxon Valdez* oil spill). We will also consider the population crisis, greenhouse gas emissions, and extinction rates.

The *Exxon Valdez* Oil Spill

Ecological problems can take place gradually over a long period of time, or abruptly because of a catastrophe that threatens the environment in a matter of days or weeks. These catastrophes can be felt globally, as with massive volcanic eruptions that release tons of dust into the atmosphere, or on a much smaller, local scale, as often happens with accidents caused by humans. We will examine one of these accidents, the *Exxon Valdez* oil spill, and look at the immediate and long-term consequences of this environmental disaster.

On March 24, 1989, the oil tanker *Exxon Valdez* ran aground on Bligh Reef in Prince William Sound, Alaska. In all, approximately 42 million liters (11 million gallons) of oil were released into the bay, contaminating the water and 1,990 km of the shoreline. Clean-up efforts included burning the oil, using booms and skimmers to trap and contain the oil, applying dispersants, enhancing bioremediation to degrade the oil, and using high-pressure washing on the shorelines. A high mortality of wildlife was seen immediately after the spill: it was estimated that up to 2,800 sea otters, 250,000 seabirds, and 302 harbor seals were killed. Populations of microalgae and invertebrates on the shore were devastated. Not all of the oil was removed from the environment, and some remains even today on intertidal beaches. Decay rates for the degradation of the remaining oil are slowing down, meaning the oil will persist for longer than initially anticipated. Research and continued monitoring of the area have shown that recovery is taking place, but wildlife still suffer from the effects of the spill, and may continue to do so for a long time.

Ecosystems are complex, and the relationships between organisms form an interconnected web (see fig. 15.1). If only one or two species are affected by an accident, many others, and even the entire ecosystem, could suffer due to cascade events. Research in Prince William Sound has found examples of cascade events and long-term effects from the oil spill. Chronic exposure to "weathered oil," or oil that has been partially degraded, was implicated in the elevated mortality of incubating pink salmon eggs four years after the spill. Abnormal development was seen in salmon after the spill, and subsequent laboratory tests have shown that even small amounts of polycyclic aromatic

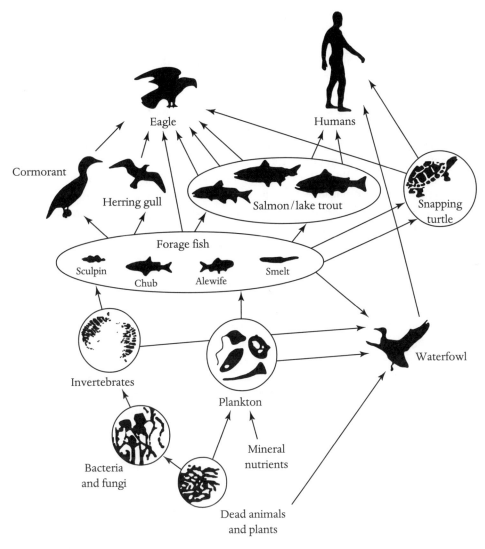

Fig. 15.1 A typical food web. The interconnectedness of organisms in the ecosystem is exemplified by the food web.

hydrocarbons (PAHs) from oil can stunt the growth and affect the survivability of these fish. Sea otter populations have not recovered to their estimated prespill levels, even as populations in unaffected nearby areas doubled in the late 1990s. The survival rate of sea otters born after the spill is lower than that of other populations: chronic exposure to residual petroleum hydrocarbons during foraging in sediments, and the consumption of mussels and other bivalves that are also contaminated, are blamed for this. Harlequin ducks are also experiencing long-term consequences of the spill. They prey on intertidal invertebrates, and biochemical analyses showed increased levels of CYPIA, a detoxification enzyme, in the ducks even nine years after the spill. Female survival rates declined in the years after the spill, in contrast to harlequins in nonoiled environments. Barrow's goldeneye birds also show continued effects. Chicks, which are fed only fish, show no ongoing exposure to toxins, but adult birds, which consume invertebrates from intertidal areas, have elevated levels of CYPIA in their liver.

The *Exxon Valdez* incident has taught us much about these types of environmental disasters, and has changed our paradigm regarding oil spills and the recovery of ecosystems. We now understand that oil degrades at varying rates and that contamination can continue for years. Concentrations of PAHs do not have to be high to cause effects in fish: parts per billion can cause growth problems, deformities, and reproductive difficulties for many years. For marine mammals and seabirds chronic exposure to oil has lasting effects. And the clean-up efforts themselves can damage the environment, as was seen with the power washing along the shoreline, which disrupted vegetation. Learning from these incidences can lead to safer methods of transportation of oil, and better ways to clean and preserve the environment after an accident. But perhaps the biggest lesson is that effects from an oil spill may still be felt decades after the initial event.

The Population Crisis

A population is defined as a group of organisms that interbreed. Populations will grow exponentially if there are no constraints. Some limiting factors that can curb growth rates include availability of food, water, and physical space, and predation. The carrying capacity is the maximum number of individuals that can be sustained by the environment. If this value is exceeded, there will be a rapid decrease in the population as resources are depleted. Currently, the worldwide human population is growing exponentially (see fig. 15.2). The

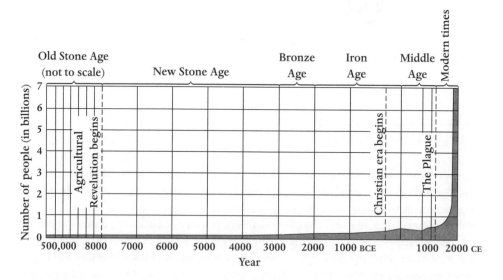

Fig. 15.2 Human population growth. Although, from this graph, exponential growth is not apparent until the modern era, many date its beginning to the agricultural revolution, about 10,000 years ago.

development of agriculture approximately 10,000 years ago allowed the human species to begin this population explosion. It took from the beginning of human history to the early nineteenth century for the human population to reach 1 billion. It now takes 13–14 years to add another billion people to the planet. In 2006, the population reached 6.5 billion. Factors other than agriculture, such as urbanization, sanitation, and medical advancements, have contributed to this rapid increase. The more people there are, the more resources are needed. Overfishing, erosion of farmland, increasing pollution, destruction of ecosystems, and depletion of energy resources are but a few of the environmental consequences of overpopulation. As with all biological organisms, our exponential growth cannot be sustained indefinitely. However, scientists do not agree on the maximum number of humans that can be sustained by the planet.

Growth rates fluctuate over time. Globally, the human growth rate peaked between 1965 and 1970, at 2.1 percent per year. Currently it is about 1.2 percent per year. Individual countries experience different rates of growth, determined by two key factors: the birth rate and the death rate. In nonindustrialized countries, death rates tend to be high, mainly due to elevated infant mortality. Birth rates are also high: couples tend to have large families because many children do not survive to adulthood. In this case, the growth rate is usually low. When a country begins moving toward a more affluent status, where people have dependable access to nutritious food, clean water, and health care, infant mortality rates drop and people tend to live longer. Thus, the death rate goes down. However, the culture has traditionally encouraged large families, which means that the birth rate stays high. This results in an increase in the growth rate, and the size, of the population. After a few generations, however, the birth rate decreases, as does population growth. This period of growth, due to decreased death rates and high birth rates, is known as demographic transition (see fig. 15.3). Industrialized nations tend to have near-zero growth rates, and in some cases even negative growth rates, whereas the growth rates of developing nations are still increasing (see fig. 15.4). Current trends indicate that the human population will reach about 9.1 billion in 2050, and that it will begin a slow decline after that.

Growth rate not only affects the size of a population, but it also affects its age structure. Rapidly growing populations show a pyramid shape, with younger cohorts larger than their predecessors (see fig. 15.5). Populations with low or zero growth show roughly equal numbers of individuals in all age cohorts. Populations are said to be aging when a significant portion occupies the older cohorts. Industrialized nations have seen a dramatic increase in average life span in the twentieth century, from 30 years at its beginning to 65 years at its end. After the year 2000, the "old" outnumbered the "young." The graying of a population will require changes in social and health-care systems. In the United States, we have already seen the need to act because of this phenomenon: our social security system, where younger workers support retirees financially, is becoming stressed. Each younger worker is now supporting an increasing proportion of the older population, and there are predictions that the system will go bankrupt in the near future. After 2010, there will be a sharp acceleration in the size of the aging population in most countries.

Besides the graying of populations, the shift in the ratio of rural versus urban individuals is also a cause for concern. In 2007, urban populations outnumbered rural ones. Agriculture in rural areas provides the vast majority of food for city populations. Globally, there is one agricultural worker for every urbanite. By 2050, the global urban

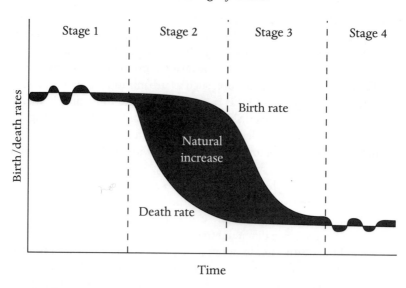

Fig. 15.3 The classic stages of demographic transition. In stage 1, birth and death rates are high, allowing for a stable population size. When death rates decline but birth rates stay high, as in stage 2, the population experiences growth. Eventually, birth rates decline (stage 3), and the population again levels off with little overall growth (stage 4).

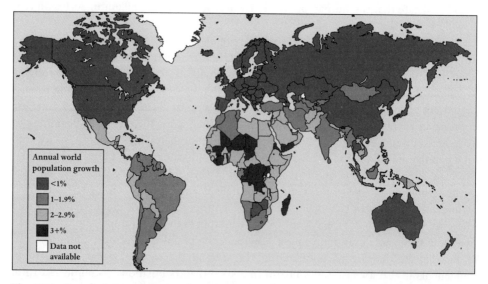

Fig. 15.4 Population growth rates by country.

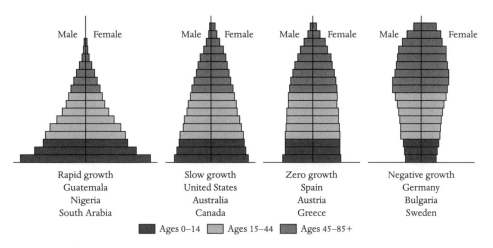

Fig. 15.5 Age structure histograms of selected populations.

population size will increase from the current 3 billion to 6 billion, without a significant increase in rural populations. This means that each agricultural worker will need to produce enough to feed two urbanites. Technological innovations will be necessary to increase food production. In addition, expanding cities may take over valuable arable land that could be used for agriculture. Increased density in urban areas may cause other problems unless adequate infrastructure is available. For example, the risk of outbreaks of epidemic diseases will be high unless proper sanitation systems and health care are made available. The growth of urban populations, and the lure of the rural young to these centers, means that social bonds will change. Cities provide more opportunities for the young, including education. However, this move tends to sever family ties, which is not good for the aging.

Greenhouse Gases

For many, global warming tops the list of environmental concerns. Certain gases in the atmosphere, notably carbon dioxide (CO_2) and methane (CH_4), trap the Sun's radiation, much as the glass of a greenhouse traps this heat inside. These gases occur naturally, from the decay of plant materials, the burning of forests by natural fires, and the biological processes of living organisms. But certain human activities have increased the concentrations of CO_2 and methane in the atmosphere. More of these gases means that more heat will be trapped, and this causes an increase in temperature. The main sources of CO_2 from human activity include the burning of fossil fuels (mainly coal) for energy in factories (beginning with the industrial revolution in the eighteenth century) and gasoline-based transportation. The CO_2 in the atmosphere can be absorbed through the oceans, soil, and photosynthesis. However, we are currently expending three times more CO_2 than can be absorbed, and hence it remains in the atmosphere. In the US, about 6.6 tons of greenhouse gases are emitted per person every year, the highest of any nation.

In the seas, much of the absorbed carbon dioxide reacts with water to form carbonic acid (H_2CO_3), and much of the carbonic acid releases hydrogen ions (H^+) into solution, forming bicarbonate ions (HCO_3^{1-}) and carbonate ions (CO_3^{2-}):

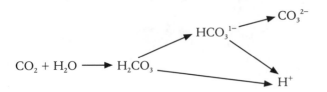

The amount of H^+ in a solution is expressed as pH, an indication of acidity. With increasing amounts of carbon dioxide, hydrogen ion levels increase, which inversely affects the pH. In other words, the more hydrogen ions, the lower the pH, and the more acidic the solution is. Pristine sea water has a pH between 8 and 8.3. Today, pH levels have dropped by about 0.1, compared to preindustrial times. It is predicted that the level will fall an additional 0.3 by 2100. Even small changes in pH can dramatically affect biological functions on many levels, including the ability of organisms to build shells and other hard body parts. This will endanger individual species as well as the construction of coral reef ecosystems, where we find incredible biodiversity.

Accumulation of greenhouse gases in the atmosphere has been correlated with trends in global warming (see fig. 15.6). In the past century, the average global temperature has increased by 0.6 °C. This may not seem like much, but as we shall see, such a "minor" change can have a major impact on the global ecosystem. Melting glaciers and decreased snow cover have been attributed to global warming. Greenhouse gases are expected to increase to at least mid-century and probably beyond. The exact impact this will have on our planet is difficult to predict. Average global temperature may increase 1.4–5.8 °C by the year 2100. This will change precipitation patterns, affecting agriculture on a widespread basis. Sea levels will rise, with devastating impacts on coastal and island communities. Hurricanes and other storms may be more intense owing to warmer waters. Human diseases, especially those found in the tropics, may become more prevalent. Computer models can be used to predict the effects of global warming, and as they become better at integrating information, we will get a clearer picture of the likely scenario. But the large number of variables that influence environmental change prevents us from being certain about what will happen.

Some have argued that global temperatures have fluctuated throughout Earth's history, and the global warming we are experiencing is just part of a natural cycle. How do we know whether or not the current trend is due to human activity? Researchers look for geological and astronomical patterns that can tell us what the Earth should be experiencing today. This is done by determining greenhouse gas concentrations from air bubbles trapped in ice samples collected in the Antarctic and Greenland. These ice cores date back thousands of years, and the levels of CO_2 and methane can be compared with estimates of global temperatures at different periods. Variations in the Earth's orbit are also critical to global climate changes. Astronomical data for the past 3 million years

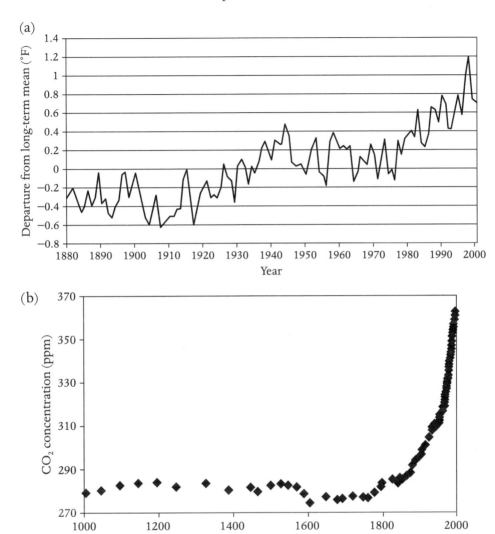

Fig. 15.6 (*a*) Global changes in temperature, 1880–2000. (US National Climatic Data Center, 2001) (*b*) Global changes in carbon dioxide concentrations, 1000–2000.

has allowed researchers to correlate the occurrence of ice ages with these orbital variations. The basic pattern has been long ice ages followed by shorter, warm, interglacial periods. Increases and decreases in CO_2 and methane levels follow particular patterns during glacial and interglacial periods. The most recent interglacial period began about 11,000 years ago. CO_2 concentrations peaked about 10,500 years ago, and began to decline. Methane concentrations also began to decrease at this time, consistent with the patterns observed during other interglacial periods. However, about 8,000 years ago, the CO_2 trend reversed, and about 5,000 years ago the methane levels also began to increase. Based on historical patterns, both of these greenhouse gases should still be declining today, and current global temperatures should be 2 °C cooler than they are, cold enough for another ice age.

William F. Ruddiman, a marine geologist and professor emeritus of environmental sciences at the University of Virginia, explains this trend in the light of human activity. It was presumed that human civilization developed during a period of interglacial warmth, but Ruddiman contends that human activity actually extended this period, and that global warming did not begin with the industrial revolution, but rather with the agricultural revolution.

Humans began farming in the eastern Mediterranean about 11,000 years ago, and a bit later in China and the Americas. Trees cleared for farming purposes were burned or left to rot: either of these methods would cause CO_2 to be released into the atmosphere. Intensive deforestation for agricultural purposes began about 8,000 years ago in Europe and China. The cultivation of rice requires large amounts of water and causes massive decomposition of plant material. This in turn releases methane. Irrigation of rice paddies began in Asia about 5,000 years ago. Ruddiman contends that human agricultural practices began emitting CO_2 and methane into the atmosphere long before industrialization, and reversed the trends normally seen during interglacial periods. Temperatures may have increased by 0.8 °C prior to the eighteenth century, enough to have actually prevented another ice age.

In more recent history, our observations of climate change, documented through yearly measurements of global and local temperatures, CO_2 and methane levels, sea levels, glacier size, water vapor in the atmosphere, snow cover, ocean salinity, and precipitation have all been correlated with human action. The Intergovernmental Panel on Climate Change (IPCC) is an international committee established in 1988 to assess the scientific and technical information on climate change. More than 600 scientists from around the globe contributed comments and information to a working group for the IPCC, which issued a report published in 2007 documenting these changes and assessing the likelihood that humans are responsible for them. Their conclusion was that changes in the global parameters we have measured are, with 90 percent probability, due to human activity.

Extinction Rates

As we have considered in our discussions of evolution, extinctions are common events that have occurred throughout the history of life on Earth. Although individual species come and go continuously in the fossil record, five mass extinctions have been identified (see table 9.2). According to some estimates, extinction rates have accelerated in the past 100 years and are now 1,000 times what they were before modern humans evolved. E. O. Wilson, whose ideas about sociobiology were discussed in chapter 12, argues that between 1 and 10 percent of all species are extinguished every decade, with at least 27,000 extinction events each year. This rate may be increasing, and the sixth mass extinction in Earth's history may be in progress. The cause? Human activity. Our actions are directly responsible for the extinction of some species, and the stress that is being placed on ecosystems is causing the extinction of many others. Not all of these effects are recent: multiple extinction events have been correlated with the arrival of humans into various habitats over the course of thousands of years. These extinctions were probably the result of overhunting and destruction of habitats for agriculture. The introduction of invasive (nonnative) species is another cause of endangerment and extinction.

Although most biologists believe a mass extinction event is in progress, there is considerable debate as to how fast this is occurring. Estimates of the extinction rate range from 0.15 to 10 percent of species annually, and, as noted above, some consider these rates to be much higher than the "natural" rate. However, two main difficulties prevent us from confirming this:

- *Estimating the natural (or background) extinction rate.* Only about 4 percent of all species are represented in the fossil record. Thus, it is difficult to determine how long the "average" life span of a species is.
- *Determining the number of actual extinction events in our present time.* It can be very difficult to conclude that a species has gone extinct. Even if an organism has not been seen for many years, populations may still exist in the wild. The predictions that thousands of species are being lost each year cannot be verified, and indeed does not appear to be valid. Thus it is difficult to determine how different the current extinction rate may be from the background extinction rate.

Regardless of the exact numbers, it is clear that humans have greatly impacted the global environment. It is estimated that half of all species live in approximately 25 "hot spots" (see fig. 15.7). Humans have removed more that 70 percent of the vegetation in these areas. Once 90 percent of a habitat is lost, half the species are also lost. We need

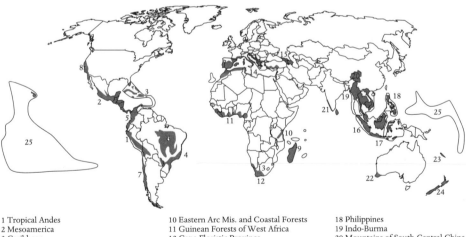

1 Tropical Andes	10 Eastern Arc Mis. and Coastal Forests	18 Philippines
2 Mesoamerica	11 Guinean Forests of West Africa	19 Indo-Burma
3 Caribbean	12 Cape Floristic Province	20 Mountains of South-Central China
4 Atlantic Forest Region	13 Succulent Karoo	21 Western Ghats and Sri Lanka
5 Chcó–Darién–Western Ecuador	14 Mediterranean Basin	22 Southwest Australia
6 Brazilian Cerrado	15 Caucasus	23 New Caledonia
7 Central Chile	16 Sundaland	24 New Zealand
8 California Floristic Province	17 Wallacea	25 Polynesia/Micronesia
9 Madagascar and Indian Ocean Islands		

Fig. 15.7 Biodiversity hotspots. These 25 sites have been identified as particularly important in maintaining biodiversity.

to take a long look at our actions and consider how they can be changed to secure biodiversity on this planet.

Attitudes toward Nature: Ecology and Stewardship

The state of the global environment has been attributed by some to the exploits of science, and by others to the anthropocentrism of Christianity. Those who blame science argue that science denies any goal or purpose for the universe and does not recognize a divine hand in the operation of nature. Science is perceived to be uncaring when it comes to nature, content to use technology for human good without regard for other living beings. According to this paradigm, humans are free to use nature in any way we desire, and to believe that any problem we encounter can be solved by science and technology.

Those who view religion as the culprit focus on the creation story in Genesis, where humans were given dominion over the Earth. According to this view, the Judeo-Christian tradition provides justification for humans doing whatever we please with regard to the environment. In addition, religious beliefs focus on the coming world: this world will eventually be destroyed, and thus we do not need to concern ourselves with preserving what exists today.

However, these myopic arguments fail to take into account important factors. Science has come to understand the interconnectedness of all species, including humans, and the importance of the environment for the well-being of all living things. The use of science has caused much of the destruction we see, but it is not science itself that is to blame. The dominion (not domination) that is granted to humans, according to the Bible, is tempered with stewardship, the responsibility we have of respecting and caring for God's creation. And the Bible tells us that all of creation, not just humanity, will be included in the coming kingdom. Suffice it to say that science and religion can influence our attitudes in positive as well as negative ways. However, politics and economics may actually be more influential in determining the state of the global environment than either science or religion. We'll look first at a bit of history, and then examine some of the various attitudes and arguments about the current ecological crisis.

The Enlightenment introduced the idea of a mechanical universe, whereby nature was seen as a machine, to science. This idea was formulated during a time when the Western world was converting from farm economics to market capitalism, and science was influenced by this societal change. The "economy of nature" (later replaced by the term "ecology") reflected the notion that nature could be studied in similar ways to human economic systems. Scientists used terms such as "nations," "budgets," and "factories" to describe the workings of the natural world. Within this view, God was seen as a divine economist, similar to a housekeeper watching over a well-run house. Human involvement in nature was justified by the biblical notions of *imago Dei* and our role as stewards of the creation. As we saw in the Genesis creation account, humans are created in God's image and given dominion over nature:

> Then God said, "Let us make man in our image, after our likeness; and let them have dominion over the fish of the sea, and over the birds of the air, and over the cattle, and over all the earth, and over every creeping thing that creeps upon the earth." (Genesis 1:26)

And God directs man to use and care for nature:

> The Lord God took the man and put him in the garden of Eden to till it and keep it. (Genesis 2:15)

The story of Noah also provides examples of stewardship and care, and of the power humans were given over nature:

> And of every living thing of all flesh, you shall bring two of every sort into the ark, to keep them alive with you; they shall be male and female. Of the birds according to their kinds, and of the animals according to their kinds, of every creeping thing of the ground according to its kind, two of every sort shall come in to you, to keep them alive. (Genesis 6:19–20)

> And God blessed Noah and his sons, and said to them, "Be fruitful and multiply, and fill the earth. The fear of you and the dread of you shall be upon every beast of the earth, and upon every bird of the air, upon everything that creeps on the ground and all the fish of the sea; into your hand they are delivered. Every moving thing that lives shall be food for you; and as I gave you the green plants, I give you everything." (Genesis 9:1–3)

Other texts praise God while reminding us of the themes in Genesis:

> When I look at thy heavens, the work of thy fingers, the moon and the stars which thou hast established; what is man that thou art mindful of him, and the son of man that thou dost care for him? Yet thou hast made him little less than God, and dost crown him with glory and honor. Thou hast given him dominion over the works of thy hands; thou hast put all things under his feet, all sheep and oxen, and also the beasts of the field, the birds of the air, and the fish of the sea, whatever passes along the paths of the sea. (Psalm 8:3–8)

These passages have been interpreted to mean that humans should act as managers, and, given the mechanical nature of the world, science would be the best way to determine how to manage nature. These notions ultimately led to our current ideas of cost–benefit analysis, sustainable development, and environmental-impact assessments.

Theologically, there have been two hermeneutical approaches to these texts. God giving humans dominion over nature can be interpreted to mean that we have the right to exploit nature and do what we please with it. However, the texts also support an interpretation whereby humans are to act as stewards of the creation, which belongs to God. Other texts reveal the love that God has for all creation, strengthening the notion that humans, created in God's image, are responsible for its care:

> Then God said to Noah and to his sons with him, "Behold, I establish my covenant with you and your descendants after you, and with every living creature that is with you, the birds, the cattle, and every beast of the earth with you, as many as came out of the ark. I establish my covenant with you, that never again shall all flesh be cut off by the waters of a flood, and never again shall there be a flood to destroy the earth." And God said, "This is the sign of the covenant which I make between me and you and every living creature that is with you, for all future generations: I set my bow in the cloud, and it shall be a sign

of the covenant between me and the earth. When I bring clouds over the earth and the bow is seen in the clouds, I will remember my covenant which is between me and you and every living creature of all flesh; and the waters shall never again become a flood to destroy all flesh. When the bow is in the clouds, I will look upon it and remember the everlasting covenant between God and every living creature of all flesh that is upon the earth." God said to Noah, "This is the sign of the covenant which I have established between me and all flesh that is upon the earth." (Genesis 9:8–17)

There are many instances in the Christian tradition of the importance of stewardship and human interaction with nature. One of the most notable was St. Francis of Assisi (c.1182–1226), the founder of the Franciscan order. Well known for his treatment of all objects in nature as his brothers and sisters, Francis believed that all creatures had the ability and the duty to praise God in their own way. Stories are told of how he communicated with animals. He preached to birds who rejoiced by singing and flapping their wings to praise God. When a wolf terrorized a town, Francis found the animal and persuaded it to stop behaving in that way.

The Roots of the Crisis

Notwithstanding the call to stewardship in biblical texts and the idea of management through the "economy of nature," human actions have had devastating effects on the environment. Why and how did this happen? In 1967, Lynn White (1907–87), professor of medieval literature at the University of California, Los Angeles published a paper in *Science*, entitled "Historical Roots of Our Ecological Crisis," which addressed this question. White asserted that two key developments in the history of Western culture are to blame for our current crisis. The first was the Christian conquest of paganism, which led to Christian beliefs permeating Western civilization. According to his argument, Christianity is the most anthropocentric religion the world has ever seen: pagan and Eastern religions revere nature and see humans as part of it, whereas Christianity regards humans as separate and distinct from other beings. The second development was the union between science and technology. During the mid nineteenth century, the spread of democratic cultures brought the scientifically literate upper classes together with the technologically savvy lower classes. Through this union, humans developed the means to manipulate and control nature. Thus, the Christian beliefs that had led us to see ourselves as different from nature, coupled with science and technology, provided us with the justification and the means to exploit the environment. If we want to reverse the condition of the environment, White argued, small acts are not going to do it. We need a change in attitude: a new religion, or a reformulation of the old one.

While some agreed with White's assessment, others have argued that there were many factors contributing to our detachment from nature and mistreatment of the environment, including private ownership of property and the switch to a money economy. Critics also pointed out that other religions may revere the environment, but their proponents are just as likely to exploit it.

On the heels of White's essay, ecologist Garrett Hardin (1915–2003) published "The Tragedy of the Commons," also in *Science*, in 1968. Hardin asserted that our attitudes regarding the environment are based on individual use of public resources ("the commons"). We consider only our individual benefit, not the importance of sustainability, when we exploit the commons. Thus, we, as individuals, benefit from catching more fish, but ignore the fact that overfishing is causing the destruction of ecosystems and the extinction of species. We add more cattle to a herd, regardless of the erosion and weed dominance that result from overgrazing. Our individual pollution is more easily and economically dumped into "the commons" than if we were to clean it up ourselves.

Hardin blamed current ecological problems on the growing human population. So many people using common resources, each caring only about their individual needs, bring ruin to the environment and to society. Our "welfare state" contributes to this: couples have more children than they can support through their own resources, because they expect the state to take care of them. This "freedom to breed" results in overpopulation. Hardin argued that technology cannot solve the environmental crisis, nor would an appeal to each individual conscience to refrain from destructive behavior for the general good. The only way to reverse our ecological problems is to relinquish the "freedom to breed." Only a change in morality, enforced through the legal system, can put an end to these disastrous situations.

Current Notions

Perhaps the most important voice in the modern environmental movement is that of Rachel Carson (1907–64). In 1962, Carson published *Silent Spring*, a book documenting the effects of human activities on ecosystems. It became a bestselling book and inspired many to work to clean up the environment. Carson documented the scientific evidence for how agricultural and industrial chemicals were affecting the environment, and advocated their limited use and safe disposal. Her efforts led to environmental protection legislation, such as the Clean Air Act, and the banning of the pesticide DDT in the US and other countries. Throughout her life, Carson advocated protection of human health, moral consideration of nonhumans, and the importance of human efforts in preserving nature. By taking care of the environment, we are taking care of ourselves. The release of chemicals such as DDT into the ecosystem affects not only the target organism (mosquitoes), but also other life forms through the food chain. Carson documented the thinning of eggshells from DDT, and the decline of bald eagles was blamed on its use. Recent studies have shown that DDT can persist in the environment for more than 30 years, potentially affecting species for decades after its use.

Carson argued that we should see ourselves as affected by, and therefore part of, the environment. We should respect nature, know nature, and know our place in nature. We have an emotional attachment to, and an aesthetic appreciation of, the environment. These allow us to have a connection with nature which, together with science, will help us understand our world. The artificial environments that humans create pull us further away from nature and blind us to the destructive effects we are having on the world.

Prior to the paradigm of nature as a mechanical entity, an organic view of the Earth was popular. In the Middle Ages, nature was seen as a living being. This notion was revitalized in the 1970s by James Lovelock (b. 1919), a scientist at NASA. While working on the Viking project and contemplating the existence of life on Mars, Lovelock proposed the Earth is a single living organism made up of the atmosphere, ecosystems, oceans, and organisms. He called this the Gaia hypothesis, named for the earth-mother goddess of Greek mythology. Gaia is self-regulating and self-sustaining, and changes its environment to promote life. This idea was further expanded by Lynn Margulis, who, as we have seen, formulated the endosymbiont theory of the evolution of eukaryotic cells. Recall that symbiosis, the close relationship and dependence of two organisms, is central to Margulis's ideas. Expanded to a global level, she contended that all life exists in symbiosis, with each organism helping others to survive. Cooperation is central to evolution, in contrast to the competition that underlies Darwinian evolution. These ideas have been criticized on the basis that not all symbiotic relationships are mutually beneficial. Indeed, many relationships that we know of are parasitic: one organism benefits at the expense (injury or death) of the other. But those who support the Gaia hypothesis see cooperation within competition: survival of the fittest does not favor an individual, but rather is a coopera-tive affair that eliminates species for the benefit of the single Gaia organism.

Notions of an organic Earth place humans within nature, not apart from it. Lovelock contends that humans are just one species on the planet, and whatever we do will not ultimately affect Gaia: it will recover from any damage. Pollution, overpopulation, even nuclear war, will not affect Gaia dramatically, although these acts may be detrimental to and even cause the extinction of the human species.

Philosophically, some have argued that the role of humans in the Gaian context is to accept that we are not special and that our existence may be only one transitory phase in Earth's history. We are in no position to "manage" the environment if we are just a part of it. However, we may be able to empathize with Gaia and act to lessen our destructive tendencies.

Theological responses to the Gaia hypothesis have concentrated on the opportunity this notion provides. Rethinking our place in this world and how we relate to other living things is important in addressing our stewardship role and in reversing injustices, such as poverty and sexism, experienced by our fellow humans. This new view of the Earth may encourage us to empathize with the suffering of others and to find ways to interact that are mutually beneficial and life-enhancing for all. However, it is an agnostic viewpoint and does not appreciate the power that humans do have over the environment. Although we are a part of nature, we are also separate from it: we are not just another species.

Christian Viewpoints

Today's environmental movement has often been referred to as a secular religion and has parallels with some Christian beliefs and traditions. For example, the trappings of modern life are seen to contribute both to the corruption of humans as well as to the destruction of nature. The accumulation of wealth and material objects, the separation of humans from the environment as a result of urbanization, and the overuse of reason (science) leading us further away from our true selves are rejected by Christians and environmentalists. The "back to nature" theme is common, but the call to return to a natural state has a different meaning. In the Christian tradition, the natural state refers to a time before sin, a time before the fall. For environmentalists, the natural state is a time before humans had influence over the environment; thus, a change in attitude (that is, seeing ourselves as part of nature) and a radical reduction in the size of the human population are necessary to reverse the trend. This view is problematic from a theological perspective, and is difficult to reconcile with a Christian viewpoint. For example, if humans are just another animal species, why are we held morally accountable for our actions and our responsibilities when other creatures are not?

Some Christian thinkers question mainstream science and the exact impact humans are having on the environment. Many of these viewpoints are also wrapped up in political and economic ideologies. Groups, such as the Interfaith Council for Environmental Stewardship and the Acton Institute for the Study of Religion and Liberty, deny the extent of our environmental problems and see the actions of environmentalists as being detrimental to the human species. Some common themes include:

- *An emphasis on the value of humanity.* God has given humans a special place in nature as co-creators and we have dominion over creation. The view of humans as destroying the environment is contrasted with the notion that humans have added to the Earth's abundance. As humans, we were created in the image of God: we must rule over nature as God does, allowing for the common good of humanity while respecting creation. We need to act responsibly to use and develop the resources God has provided. We are participating in the development of creation, toward an end we do not yet understand. We can bring nature to a higher state of perfection through our actions. For this reason, we should not strive to go back to a primitive state, prior to human attempts at dominating nature.
- *Unfounded environmental concerns.* Some environmental issues are without adequate foundation, such as global warming, overpopulation, and the high rate of species extinction. Other concerns have been greatly exaggerated, such as pollution, limited resources, the disposal of hazardous waste, and health issues in developing countries. Some data indicate that carbon dioxide in the atmosphere is actually decreasing, America's forests are regrowing, and pollution is on the decline. More natural resources can be made available through technology.
- *The necessity of economic growth.* By devoting our effort to solving problems that have been exaggerated, we are preventing economic development that is necessary to improve human life as well as to protect the environment. The Christian view has been called anthropocentric, but the biocentric view of most environmentalists negates the idea of stewardship by humans. Thus, we need to have a theocentric view, where God's moral laws are central to the actions of humans, with a small government and decisions occuring at a local level, and virtuous human action in the marketplace. This will allow for economic growth and the protection of the environment. We need to use creation and to care for it wisely, to use reason in stewardship decisions, and to have economic freedom which will make it easier for us to fulfill our role as stewards. The government and economics of different countries are the cause of poverty, not overpopulation.
- *Contradictions between the basic tenets of the environmental movement and church doctrine.* God is no longer seen as separate from creation, humans are not afforded their proper place in the created order, and nature is being given values that belong to humans alone.

- *Optimism.* Agriculture and industrialization, in the short term, have impacted negatively on the environment. But technological advances have decreased these effects, and human life has been improved. Economic growth, moral restraint in consumption of goods, and decentralized governance can solve most environmental problems and are alternatives to population control programs. Human innovation and creativity, particularly advances in science and technology, are the keys to the developments necessary for our continued well-being.
- *Imposition of cultural biases.* Before humans can consider environmental issues, they need to feel secure that their basic needs are being met. The reason the Western world is so concerned with environmental protection is because of our wealth and prosperity. By imposing ecological ideas on developing countries, we are actually imposing our cultural sensibilities on these nations. This may delay their development, resulting in continued poverty and disease, and hinder rather than help their efforts at stewardship.

Christian thinkers who accept the mainstream views of our environmental problems argue that the Judeo-Christian values can be used to form the foundations for a responsible environmental ethic. We can find guidance for the protection of our planet and ways to approach sustainability of resources for our use. We do not need to reject what civilization has brought, nor do we need to abandon reason and science. If we act as stewards, we can achieve the balance we need.

The theologian John Haught, who has expressed many different ideas on the environment, some of which we have looked at, has weighed in on this issue. The science of cosmology tells us that the universe had a beginning and is constantly changing and evolving. We are part of this universe. Our existence is a product of evolution, and we are changing with our world. Haught believes that our place in this world is therefore, out of necessity, a dynamic one. The universe, our world, and our species will one day come to an end. Theologically, we believe that we should not hold onto nature or any material objects that can lead us away from our relationship with God. But we are part of nature, and we cannot ignore this fact. Therefore, we need to care for the environment, as we need to understand and respect our place in the evolving universe that will one day be transformed into a new kingdom. The destinies of all of humanity and nature are linked, and indeed, are the same.

Haught contends that hope is an important consideration in this discussion. If we have no hope for the future, then we have no reason to take care of the environment. Thus, the eschatological notion of a coming kingdom, whereby there is continuity between this world and the next, calls for us to take care of what we have now. Nature is part of God's promise. It is limited, and we need to realize that we cannot use it as though it were infinite. And the notion of hope also helps us to understand the suffering and indifference that we see in nature. The promise, not perfection, of nature underlies hope.

Haught also regards nature as important to religion in relation to the sacraments. He considers any object, event, or experience that brings us in touch with God as a sacrament. Nature, as objects and means of experience, functions in the role of sacraments. If we view nature only as the source of raw materials for our existence, then we lose this important route to a fuller relationship with God. This notion can help us in making moral decisions about how to use our limited resources. Therefore, the intrinsic value of nature as a sacramental entity can help us protect the environment and understand the value of nature to religion.

Holmes Rolston III (b. 1932), professor of philosophy at Colorado State University and 2003 Templeton Prize laureate, also stresses the notion of intrinsic value. There is an observable trend in evolution, a tendency toward increasing numbers of species and increasing complexity. This can be interpreted as a type of progress, reflecting the creativity of natural selection. However, evolutionary theory denies any increase in the worth of a species: the only mechanism for change is survival. Neo-Darwinian theory cannot explain this increase in complexity. As we contemplate this problem in the sciences, we also need to examine how Christianity regards nature. We need to appreciate all forms of life as parts of a whole that is collectively good, as we are told in the creation story in Genesis. All life has value in this context. All life is intrinsically good.

However, the classical theological notion of design does not mesh with evolutionary theory. Therefore, a paradigm shift is needed, both in theology and in evolutionary theory. Rolston finds God in the creative, dynamic process that is life. God coaxes changes in life via the process of natural selection. Therefore, we need to respect the creativity inherent in life. If we view nature as something to be used, we will manipulate it, sometimes to the detriment of our own species. But if we view life as having intrinsic value, and if we respect the creative process that has resulted in the biodiversity we have, we will revere and appreciate it. By respecting nature, we can turn the secular visions of the world into the sacred. Rolston talks of the sacred as the creativity we find on Earth; the spirit of God is this wonderful, ever-changing world.

Anna Case-Winters, a professor of theology at McCormick Theological Seminary, argues that we need to rethink our creation in the image of God. Two interpretations of *imago Dei* are common. One emphasizes that we are like God in our freedom, and in our capacity to think and reason. The other focuses on how we live our life and how we maintain our relationship with God: our image, in the likeness of God, is distorted or lost if we turn away from the mirror, that is, if we don't live a life that reflects God. Case-Winters argues that the emphasis we have placed on the first Genesis creation story, where humans are made in the image of God, separates us from nature and causes us to ask how and why we are different. This results in anthropocentrism, which leads to ecological problems. We do not give the same attention to the second account, where humans are created from the dust of the ground and given the role of a farmer, tilling the soil. This view places us much more within nature.

God considers all of creation special, not just humans, and will restore all things in the new creation. Case-Winters asks why we have not focused on these ideas as much as the *imago Dei* notion. If we view nature as a set of resources that we must sustain so that we can continue to use them, we ignore the intrinsic value of nature and strengthen the separation between humans and the rest of creation. Instead, we need to understand our connectedness with nature. We were created, and we evolved, just like every other organism. Our similarities to other creatures, and our appearance rather late in the grand scheme of things, should caution us against anthropocentric thinking. The species that lived and thrived for millions of years before we evolved had value and were important. We are a small part of the whole, a single species on a single planet in a vast cosmos.

In contrast to setting ourselves apart from nature, Case-Winters calls us to focus on what we have to offer nature, and what we can do for nature as created co-creators. We have been given qualities that other beings do not have, and we are called to reflect the image of God. If we are to cultivate our relationship with God, and if sin is viewed as a turning away from God, then we must act as stewards of the environment. Our natural origins, our connectedness with nature, our rationality, and our freedom require us to be responsible for nature.

Solutions

Our environmental problems did not happen overnight, and the solutions will also not come rapidly. The key points in approaching the situation are:

- We need to have a good understanding of the elements and trends that are contributing to current circumstances, of how society, governments, and industries are contributing to our current problems, and what the future may hold.
- We need to finds ways to preserve natural habitats while still respecting the people who need to live off the land.
- The reduction, and possible elimination, of our use of fossil fuels is important, as these fuels are nonrenewable and cause so much damage to the global ecosystem.
- By helping individuals and nations develop in environmentally friendly ways, we can increase standards of living and eliminate poverty, which in turn may increase the awareness of ecological problems in these regions, reducing the crisis even further.

The last point needs to be considered in more detail. When we, in the West, think about the destruction of the rainforests, we wonder why people would slash and burn these amazing treasures of diversity that are so important to our world. However, the 1 billion people living in deep poverty are not thinking about the state of the planet, but rather about how they will feed themselves and their family today. If we can lift people out of poverty, if they can meet their basic daily needs of food, clean water, and shelter, if they have access to medical care, sanitation, and education, they will be able to focus on other priorities, such as the environment. If the economy of a country becomes dependable, then the government will stabilize. And it may then become apparent that protecting the environment is not only feasible but also beneficial and profitable. Thus, many feel that if we help developing countries, if we can alleviate and even eliminate poverty, the global environment will benefit in the long run.

However, this transition can be difficult, and the growing pains may appear to be more detrimental than helpful. Just as countries go through demographic transitions, where populations increase before they stabilize (and even decrease), so too the problems with pollution and the environment may worsen before they improve. For a country like India to develop, it may need, first, to increase its contribution to global ecological problems: as Indian citizens gain more wealth, they will buy more cars, which will increase the consumption of oil and contribute to the emission of greenhouse gases. But if wealthy nations can assist and provide developing countries with the latest technology, the effects of this pollution transition can be reduced.

Population Control

As we have seen, populations in many regions continue to increase. The struggle to stabilize this growth has resulted in different measures to curb reproduction. China's efforts have attracted worldwide attention and much criticism. Its population officially stands at 1.3 billion, and it is estimated that it will reach a peak of 1.46 billion in the 2030s. This slowing of growth has been attributed to a controversial program begun in 1979, the one-child policy, which includes restricting family size, marrying and bearing children later in life, and (where more than one child is allowed) spacing between children. By restricting the number of children per couple, China could dramatically reduce its population size in a relatively short period of time. Some estimates say that it could be as low as 700 million by the end of this century. Advocates say the policy is good for China in many ways. There will be less stress on natural resources, from agriculture to fossil fuel consumption; more time and money to devote to a single child, with the result that each child will have a better education and quality of life; and women will be able to have careers as well as families, giving them a larger role in the economy and society. Some estimates claim that the policy has prevented 300 million births, and the mean number of children born per woman has decreased from 2.9 in 1979 to 1.7 in 2004. Officials further claim that the policy has averted food shortages and the starvation of countless people.

But there are many problems with this policy. As we discussed above, changes in growth rate also cause changes in population structure. In China's case, there are two prevailing problems. First, the population is aging, as in the United States. By 2050, it is estimated that about one-quarter of the population, or 430 million people, will be over the age of 60. There will be stress on resources to support such an elderly population. Most elderly people are taken care of by their adult sons. With the one-child policy, two sets of elderly parents must be taken care of by one married adult couple. This creates what is known as the 4:2:1 phenomenon, whereby four elderly parents are being supported by two working adult children, who are also supporting their one child.

The second major problem with the policy is the sex ratio. Chinese culture values male children, because sons carry on the family name and support their aging parents. Therefore, if a couple is allowed to have only one child, they prefer the child to be male. This has led to the killing of female babies and the selective abortion of female fetuses. The result is a skewed sex ratio. In industrialized countries, the live male to female birth ratio varies from 1.03 to 1.07, in other words, for every 100 females born, there are 103 to 107 males. In China, the ratio was 1.06 in 1979, 1.11 in 1988, and 1.17 in 2001. The consequences of this trend could have a devastating impact on Chinese society: some estimate that there will be 30 million more men than women by the year 2020. Fewer possibilities will exist for men to marry and have families. There appear to be increases in the kidnapping and trafficking of women for marriage purposes, and there has also been a rise in the number of female sex workers, which may lead to more cases of HIV and other sexually transmitted diseases.

Many have questioned the need for the one-child policy. During the inception of this plan, certain trends in Chinese society were ignored, specifically the fact that birth rates were already declining: between 1970 and 1979, the fertility rate decreased from 5.9 to

2.9. Many argue that no policy was needed in China, that the fertility rate would have continued to drop.

Implementation of the one-child policy has occurred on different levels, and has also been the focus of much scrutiny and global outrage. Contraception is widely available. Among married couples, 87 percent use contraception, and most of them use long-term methods, such as intrauterine devices (IUDs) and sterilization. Abortions are also widely available: 25 percent of women of reproductive age have had at least one abortion (the comparison with US statistics is interesting: only one-third of married couples use contraception, and 43 percent of women have had abortions). For many Chinese couples, the method of contraception is not a choice. The implantation of IUDs is standard practice for women with only one child, and sterilization (usually of the female) is the norm if a couple have two children.

Tremendous pressure is placed on a woman to abort a second pregnancy, and there are no time limits to when the abortion can occur (eight- and nine-month-old fetuses can be aborted). As a response to the skewed sex ratio and the number of female infanticides, the government allows rural couples to have two children if the first child is female. However, a time delay must be observed between births: the first child must be 4 years old before a second pregnancy occurs. If the interval is too short, the pregnancy must be terminated. Women are forbidden to marry until the age of 23, and if they marry earlier, the union is not recognized. A woman who is married younger and becomes pregnant must have an abortion, even if it is her first child. This has led to women hiding their pregnancies, and then usually giving birth without any trained medical help. This increases the risk of maternal and infant mortality: a 1990 report showed that women who had unapproved pregnancies were twice as likely to die as those who had government-sanctioned pregnancies.

These policies are not voluntary: they are the law and are enforced through coercion. Sometimes this enforcement comes as pressure from local authorities or the local community (who are in turn rewarded or punished for the behavior of individuals). Couples and members of their family may be imprisoned, or forced to pay heavy fines. Local officials, under intense pressure to meet quotas set by the government, may even destroy the home of a couple who do not comply. Propaganda is also used, which blames all of China's problems on population growth.

Initially, there was much support for population reduction in China from the world-wide community, including the United Nations, and various aspects of China's policies have been exported to other countries, including Peru and Vietnam. But investigations into human rights abuses have caused the United States to withdrawal its support of the UN-funded program promoting China's one-child policy, although the UN has not cut off its support.

Is there still a need for the one-child policy? Certainly, the human rights abuses consequent upon this policy would argue that it needs to be changed or abandoned. The skewed sex ratio and the growing proportion of the aging population would also argue for change. But a recent survey shows some interesting trends: it appears that the social mindset has been altered in China. Most women surveyed would be satisfied with one or two children, regardless of government regulations. Thus, if the one-child policy were abandoned, it is unlikely that any sort of baby boom would result. In 2001 it was announced that the fundamental policy would not change, but that the implementation of it would be relaxed. Couples now have more choice in the method of contraception used, and they no longer need to obtain permission to have their first child, a practice that was used to delay pregnancy in accordance with local birth quotas.

Many have argued that it is not necessary to place controls on population growth. Other factors, such as democratic governments and sound economic policies, can manage and reduce the problems usually associated with large populations. We have already seen the concept of demographic transition, and we need to keep in mind that population growth usually declines as a natural result of industrialization. And the education of women can also reduce birth rates: as women become more educated, they tend to marry later, have children later, and also place more emphasis on the education of their children. There are many ways to reduce the birth rate without legislation, propaganda, coercion, or human rights violations.

Sustainable Use of Energy

Reducing greenhouse gas emission, specifically carbon dioxide, is necessary to curb global warming. New technologies have made it possible, and affordable, to do this. In many cases, costs actually go down. For example, DuPont increased production by 30 percent while cutting energy use by 7 percent and greenhouse gas emissions by 72 percent. This saved the company more than $2 billion. Within a five-year time span, Procter & Gamble increased production in a factory in Germany by 45 percent with only a 12 percent rise in energy needs and no increase in carbon emissions. Today, buildings are constructed in Germany, Switzerland, Austria, and Scandinavia that require only one-sixth of the energy needed in comparable buildings in the US. The construction of environmentally friendly power plants, office buildings, houses, and vehicles, focused on fuel efficiency and the utilization of alternative fuels, can reduce greenhouse gases and prevent the gloom and doom scenarios some have proposed. This is not science fiction: we have the ability to begin this transition today. Some examples include:

- *Carbon capture and storage.* We can reduce the CO_2 emitted from power plants or prevent it from entering the atmosphere. Methods include pumping emissions underground and capturing CO_2 that can then be injected into oil fields to help produce more oil.
- *Alternative power sources.* Utility plants that use coal emit the most CO_2, and 37 percent of global carbon emissions in 2002 were from coal. Oil (43 percent of 2002 emissions) and natural gas (20 percent of emissions) plants are cleaner, but they still produce the greenhouse gas. Renewable sources of energy, such as solar, wind, water, and biofuels, are environmentally friendly alternatives. Worldwide, there is a doubling of wind power every three years, and a doubling of solar power every two years. Currently, one-fifth of Denmark's power, and one-tenth of Germany's, is obtained from wind turbines (compared with 0.5 percent of US power). In countries where the infrastructure is not well developed, solar power offers a way for people to have

electricity without connecting to a grid. Much of Kenya and other African countries gain power from small solar power systems. Two projects in California are currently underway to use solar-thermal power to produce electricity. Biofuels, such as ethanol made from switchgrass or poplar, could reduce greenhouse gas emissions by over 90 percent.

- *Preventing energy loss.* Most of the energy used in human activities comes from fossil fuels. This energy is converted from the original source (coal, oil, natural gas) into a carrier (electricity) and eventually into the energy that is used (in lights, TVs, washing machines, engines, etc.). The conversion process is very inefficient: two-thirds of all energy is lost from the original source to its final use. Averting this loss is perhaps the quickest and most cost-effective way to cut down on CO_2 emissions. The energy required by buildings and houses contributes more than one-third of CO_2 emissions. Better insulation, double-paned windows, more efficient appliances, and fluorescent light bulbs make substantial contributions to energy savings. For example, new models of household refrigerators use only about one-quarter of the power of earlier models. It is estimated that there are 150 million refrigerators in the US: the savings in energy between 1974 and 2001 models is approximately equal to the generation of 40 gigawatts at power plants (this is 40 billion watts – think of a 100-watt light bulb). New buildings can be constructed to improve energy efficiency greatly. In the past, buildings have been designed to minimize construction costs, with the notion that energy efficiency is too expensive. However, over the long term, the costs of fuel-efficient buildings decrease. Some important design features include roof overhangs and balconies that reflect heat, solar panels to capture energy, and open floor plans and central stairwells to promote ventilation.

- *Alternative transportation.* Half of the 43 percent of carbon emissions from oil in 2002 was from transportation. In the US 70 percent of oil is used by transportation. China and India are increasing their use of cars dramatically. The problem of energy conversion is exemplified in the use of gasoline and internal combustion engines: only 13 percent of the fuel energy ever actually reaches the wheels of a car. The rest is lost to heat, idling, or accessories such as air conditioning. More than half of the energy that reaches the tires is lost to heat. Only 6 percent of fuel energy actually makes the car go. And, considering that the driver represents only about 5 percent of the mass of the car, less than 1 percent of the fuel energy used actually makes you move! Production of more fuel-efficient vehicles, and ones that run on alternative fuels such as hydrogen, biofuels, and low-carbon electricity, will have a dramatic effect on greenhouse gases. In addition, reducing the weight of vehicles would reduce energy needs. Today, new metal alloys and polymer composites are lightweight yet strong, and smaller engines can provide plenty of power but reduce mass. These engines are also cheaper to make. And all these changes still maintain the safety, power, and comfort we have come to expect in our cars. By implementing existing technologies, the United States could completely phase out oil consumption for vehicles by 2050, saving $70 billion per year.

The European Union and Japan are already far ahead of the US in terms of efficient fuel use. But we are far ahead of developing countries. If we can help to build fuel-efficient infrastructures in these countries, the need for power would be dramatically reduced, and thus the greenhouse gas emissions from fossil fuels would also be reduced. China is taking steps in the right direction by increasing its use of natural gas and renewable energy.

Cleaning Up

Preventing further environmental problems is juxtaposed with reducing the damage that has already been done. There are two interesting approaches to cleaning up the environment: bioremediation and cap-and-trade systems.

We described bioremediation in chapter 14 as the use of biological agents to remove toxic wastes from the environment, and discussed how genetic engineering can enhance the ability of an organism to clean up these wastes. This technology has been used at many Superfund sites, at sites where organic explosives, such as TNT, have migrated into the soil during manufacturing and storage, and also during the *Exxon Valdez* oil spill in Prince William Sound in Alaska (which was discussed at the beginning of the chapter).

One particularly amazing use of bioremediation occurred at a service station on Andrews Air Force Base in Maryland. Seven large underground gasoline and oil storage tanks had been removed, with contamination of the surrounding soil and groundwater covering approximately five acres. Several attempts to clean up the high concentrations of petroleum hydrocarbons had failed, and the next step was excavation and treatment, estimated to take 28 years and to cost over $1.5 million. Instead, bioremediation was used. In December 2003, 2,180 tons of soil was excavated and disposed of off-site. A bioremediation formula was applied at the site which encouraged the growth of endogenous microbes. By the following November, levels of toxins had been dramatically reduced, in some areas by 100 percent. The Maryland Department of the Environment was satisfied that the pollution concerns had been addressed. The final cost of the clean-up was approximately $500,000 and took 11 months to accomplish, substantially below the original estimates using conventional technologies.

Microorganisms have specifically evolved to process human-made pollutants. In 1997, a bacterial species, *Dehalococcoides ethenogenes*, was isolated from sewage sludge. This microbe consumes tetrachloroethene (PCE) and trichloroethene (TCE), chemicals used by dry cleaners, electronics companies, and the military. Amazingly, PCE and TCE did not exist before World War II: thus, this species evolved in a relatively short period of time to live off these xenobiotics. Analysis of the genome of *D. ethenogenes* revealed a series of 17 genes that allows the bacteria to consume PCE and TCE. This organism may be useful in cleaning up contaminated aquifers: PCE and TCE sink in water, and it is difficult, if not impossible, to remove them with conventional methods.

Other organisms, such as plants, can aid in the clean-up of the environment. The growth of vegetation in polluted areas helps prevent the spread of contaminated materials through wind and water erosion. Many plants can take up contaminants from soil and water through their roots, a process known as phytoremediation. The harmful substances can either be internalized (stored) in the plant or broken down into nontoxic compounds. Research is currently focused on the phytoremediation of mercury, zinc, selenium, arsenic, cadmium, and other toxic substances. Cottonwood trees have been engineered to contain genes from the bacterium *E. coli* that allow the trees to live in mercury-contaminated soil. These trees are currently being grown in Danbury, Connecticut, and will be cut down and incinerated after several years. The poplar, a fast-growing tree that produces large quantities of biomass, is also being engineered to increase its capacity to live in and to absorb heavy metal contaminants.

In addition to cleaning up the environment, we need to focus on reducing our pollution of it. One solution is the cap-and-trade system, which has its roots in the Clean Air Act of 1970, whose goal was to improve the quality of our air and reduce pollution. Over the next 20 years, emissions of lead, sulfur dioxide, and particulates dropped, but ozone, carbon monoxide, and nitrogen oxides had grown owing to increased use of automobiles. The Act was amended in 1990 to further reduce sulfur dioxide (SO_2) emissions, the culprit in creating acid rain. Sulfur dioxide is released by the burning of fossil fuels, largely in power plants, metal smelting, and other industrial processes. The plan was to create what is now known as a cap-and-trade system. The government puts a limit on how much SO_2 can be released nationally each year, and the Environmental Protection Agency (EPA) holds annual auctions for permits to release SO_2. The program was designed to persuade the worst polluters to make affordable upgrades to reduce their emissions, and then sell their excess permits at a profit to cleaner plants, where upgrades were too expensive. The EPA monitors smokestack emissions to ensure compliance. Some ways of reducing emissions include the burning of coal with lower sulfur content and the use of scrubbers in smokestacks (the increased demand for these scrubbers made them more affordable and increased their efficiency). By 2010, the cost for these improvements is estimated to be approximately $1 billion. The government emission standards have so far been met, and acid rain has been reduced. The real buzz about this program has not focused on its success so much as its approach: the EPA did not specify how plants should reduce emissions. By letting the industries determine the best way, the total cost will be 30–50 percent less than if the EPA had enforced particular procedures in a "command and control" situation.

In 1997, following this success, the Kyoto Treaty called for the implementation of a similar cap-and-trade system on an international scale to cut greenhouse gas emissions. This set up a "carbon market," which went into full operation in the European Union in 2005. Governments hand out permits to emit greenhouse gasses to power plants, and these can be traded. Offsets also exist, whereby the establishment of an environmentally friendly project in a developing country would be considered a curtailment of pollution, and the industrial nation supporting the project would receive an offset. This allows poorer economies to grow more quickly while the industrial nation meets the Kyoto obligations without all the necessary reductions. Some examples of these offset projects include harvesting methane from landfills in Brazil, the construction of wind farms in China, and hydroelectric projects in Honduras.

Another example of a cap-and-trade system is in the fishing industry in the US and New Zealand. In 1995, the US arranged for tradable quotas in the Alaskan halibut fishery. At the time, overfishing had resulted in a season that was only 48 hours long for the entire year. Fishermen were given property rights to catch a certain number of fish, and could retire by selling these quotas. This reduced gluts in the market, raised the price of fish, increased the income of the fishermen, and allowed the halibut population to recover. The 2005 season was 258 days long. The New Zealand system works in a similar fashion and now covers 93 species of fish.

Cap-and-trade systems are by no means foolproof. In the case of the Kyoto Treaty, the UN has been slow to approve offset projects, and there are questions of cheating and corruption in some countries. In addition, the US does not participate in the treaty. And although sulfur dioxide emissions in 2001 were 50 percent of the 1982 emissions, acidity in lakes and streams is still a problem. But the use of government caps, with markets for trading permits, credits, and quotas, and the freedom for industries to decide how they can best meet government goals, has proved successful. This model could help in other situations where conservation, protection, and clean-up are necessary.

Protecting Environments and Reducing Poverty

All organisms use the resources available to them in the environment. Humans are no different in this respect. No matter what view we subscribe to, whether it is our right to take what we want or to let nature be, we must still survive. And this means using the land, air, water, and living organisms. If we want to continue to survive, we need to find a balance whereby we take what we need without destroying or damaging the ecosystem. This balance is known as sustainable use. In most, if not all, cases, where the development of land and the harvesting of resources have been planned with sustainable use in mind, the outcomes have been more beneficial than without the planning. We saw an example of this above: the fisheries in the US, New Zealand, and other regions around the globe have been overharvested. However, proper planning and control have increased the fish population and helped the fishermen, the economy, and tourism, and has had a positive impact on local communities all around.

An important issue in sustainability is the plight of those in poverty. Limited resources are often harvested in an uncontrolled manner, just so a population can survive for another day. The impact of such practices on the environment can be devastating (the notion behind the "tragedy of the commons"). With some effort, many of these situations can be alleviated, with a benefit to all, including the preservation of habitats and an increase in the living standards and wealth of individuals. A key factor to making this work is democratic governance. When political systems make decisions that take into account the rights and needs of its citizens, resources can be used in appropriate, sustainable ways.

Democratic governments, ecological management, and poverty reduction are linked. An estimated 1.3 billion people worldwide rely directly on the environment for their employment – almost half of all jobs. Activities include fishing, farming, mining, logging, and hunting. Seven out of 10 poor people in rural Africa rely on environmental resources, and the gross domestic product of many African nations is substantially made up of these small-scale activities. But many of the poorest countries are not democratic, and individuals do not have a say in decision making regarding the natural resources on which they rely. Economic growth, along with improvements in equality and distribution of wealth, are also needed to help reduce poverty. Many poor people depend on the commons for their income, and the use of these resources must be regulated, or they will likely become overused. Therefore, the management of the ecosystem needs to be a priority. Developing niche markets (for example, the harvesting of bamboo, mushrooms, and herbs, instead of timber, from forests), and the cultivation of recreational activities (particularly tourism), encourages the preservation of ecosystems while increasing the income of the local people. Private ownership of land may also lead to beneficial outcomes, as owners will often invest for long-term improvements, such as reduction in soil erosion, planting trees, and restricting hunting and fishing to keep populations optimal.

One example of sustainable use is in Mexico's community-managed forest program. As a result of the Mexican Revolution, much of Mexico's forest was placed in the hands of local communities early in the twentieth century. Today, over half of all forests are on community lands. Many of these communities are actually involved in international markets, and are taking measures to maintain the biodiversity and productivity of the forests. The money stays in the community, generating employment and building assets that benefit the local population. These include health-care services, educational opportunities, clean drinking water, and even pensions for the elderly. Another benefit has been a reduction in the violence associated with drug trafficking. Several communities have been successful in stabilizing, and even expanding, the natural forests. These communities have gone beyond the environmental laws put in place by the Mexican government to protect the habitats. Along with these great accomplishments, problems still exist. Overexploitation is still a concern, not enough employment opportunities exist for all the local people who need them, and some communities are not managed as well as others. Still, Mexico offers a unique example of how local regulation can succeed in helping the people and the environment.

Conclusions

Environmental groups often argue that if we just leave nature alone, everything will be fine. However, these views do not take into account that nature is not the cooperative, beneficial entity we would like it to be. Massive environmental changes in Earth's history have been caused by ice ages and other natural events, without any humans on the scene. There is immense suffering, waste and death in the natural world, apart from anything in which humans have a hand. Nature is not a loving goddess, but rather an impersonal, dog-eat-dog survival boot camp. Humans worked, suffered, and died for thousands of years to get to a point where nature does not necessarily have the huge impact on our lives as it used to. Why would we have done this if nature had been the benevolent caregiver it is often made out to be? On the other hand, we have also squandered many natural resources for little human benefit, and been careless and destructive in many of our actions. We do have the power to affect the environment greatly, and we have mostly used this power in a destructive manner. Our quest should be not one of going back to nature, but of determining the best way to treat nature. How can we as humans take what we need and want without destroying the beauty, productivity, and intrinsic value of creation? How can we best fulfill our role as God's created co-creators, and watch over this wonderful creation? How can we maintain our image in the likeness of God and utilize the resources at hand without destroying ourselves and the planet? How can the life-sustaining abilities of this planet be used by all, in a fair and just manner? If we keep these questions in mind as we make environmental decisions, we will be the stewards and caretakers of all creation.

Changing our attitude is the key to caring for the planet. The environment and the human species can both flourish, as long as we make the effort to allow it to happen. This requires listening to all voices in the mix, from religion and science, economics and politics, the wealthy and the poor, the urban and the rural, the industrialized and the developing. By considering the needs of all and all the options available, and by incorporating a moral code into our decision making, we can sustain, and thrive on, our limited resources. There are no easy answers or quick solutions. But there is hope, and there is opportunity: these are not limited. They are ours for the taking.

Primary Literature

Useful primary sources include a passage from the book of Leviticus (25:1–12) and an opinion piece by Gregg Easterbrook regarding the reduction of greenhouse gas emissions, "Some Convenient Truths," *Atlantic* 298 (2) (2006), 29–30.

Questions to Consider

1   Do some additional research on the *Exxon Valdez* oil spill. What is the current view of ExxonMobil regarding the status of Prince William Sound? Is this view supported by science? What is the history of litigation surrounding the incident? What additional lessons can we learn?

2   Consider the ideas of William Ruddiman and a "what if" scenario. If humans had not developed agriculture, how might civilization have been different, considering that global temperatures would now be well into the range of a typical ice age? In other words, did human activity, by altering the global climate, allow for the establishment of civilization and all its consequences?

3   The Gaia hypothesis and other organic Earth notions place humans as just another species on the planet. If the ideas of Margulis and others are correct in that cooperation between species characterizes life, what is our role? Can this be justified on theological grounds? Many have argued that the Gaia hypothesis is scientific. Do you think the ideas as presented by Lovelock are falsifiable? Justify your answer.

4   Consider the problem of energy conversion: so little of the energy in the source actually becomes available for human use, and the waste contributes to greenhouse gas emissions. Does turning off a light in your room when it's not in use really make a difference? Do more efficient appliances really make a difference? Where do you think we could do better, on an individual, a local, and a societal level, in reducing the waste caused by energy conversion?

5   Many theologians have stressed the concept of justice with regard to stewardship. How might the idea of justice, applied to all people and to nonhumans as well, help to protect the environment?

6   When a toxin is released into the environment and, for example, contaminates water sources, even a small amount can pose a great threat. Consider the concept of a food web (see fig. 15.1). Fresh water invertebrates and fish exposed to the toxin may ingest and retain it in their tissues. What happens when these organisms are consumed by others? What happens when the predators become the prey (this concept is known as bioaccumulation)?

7   What role should worldwide organizations, such as the UN and the Catholic Church, play in helping solve environmental crises? What are some advantages and dis-advantages in using such organizations to help solve these problems? Do other or-ganizations exist that could help? What role should local groups play?

Further Reading

Chapter 1   Learning from the Past

Desroches, Dennis (2004) Figuring Science: Revisiting Nature in Bacon's *Novum Organum. Midwest Quarterly: A Journal of Contemporary Thought* 45 (3), 304–18.

Downie, Robin (2001) Science and the Imagination in the Age of Reason. *Journal of Medical Ethics: Medical Humanities* 27, 58–63.

Ferngren, Gary B., ed. (2002) *Science and Religion: A Historical Introduction.* Baltimore: Johns Hopkins University Press.

Lindberg, David C., and Ronald L. Numbers (1987) Beyond War and Peace: A Reappraisal of the Encounter between Christianity and Science. *Perspectives on Science and Christian Faith*, 39, 140–9.

Pannenberg, Wolfhart (2006) Problems between Science and Theology in the Course of Their Modern History. *Zygon* 41(1), 105–12.

Chapter 2   How We Know What We Know

Chalmers, A. F. (1976) *What is This Thing Called Science? An Assessment of the Nature and Status of Science and Its Methods.* St. Lucia: University of Queensland Press.

Dowey, Edward A. Jr. (1958) Tillich, Barth, and the Criteria of Theology. *Theology Today* 15, 43–58.

John Paul II. (1998) *Fides et Ratio.* Available at www.vatican.va/holy_father/john_paul_ii/encyclicals/documents/hf_jp-ii_enc_15101998_fides-et-ratio_en.html (accessed September 11, 2009).

Johnson, Elizabeth A. (1993) A Theological Case for God-She: Expanding the Treasury of Metaphor. *Commonweal*, 120 (2), Jan. 29.

Keller, Evelyn Fox (1987) The Gender/Science System; or, Is Sex to Gender as Nature is to Science? *Hypatia* 2 (3), 37–49.

Migliore, Daniel L. (1991) *Faith Seeking Understanding: An Introduction to Christian Theology.* Grand Rapids, MI: Eerdmans.

Chapter 3   Common Threads and Ultimate Truths

Barbor, Ian G. (1997) *Religion and Science: Historical and Contemporary Issues*. San Francisco: HarperCollins.

Case-Winters, Anna (1997) The Question of God in an Age of Science: Constructions of Reality and Ultimate Reality in Theology and Science. *Zygon* 32 (3), 351–75.

Deane-Drummond, Celia (2001) Wisdom: A Voice for Theology at the Boundary with Science? *Ecotheology: Journal of Religion, Nature & the Environment* 5 (10), 23–39.

Pannenberg, Wolfhart (2006) Problems between Science and Theology in the Course of Their Modern History. *Zygon* 41 (1), 105–12.

Polkinghorne, John (2000) Science and Theology in the Twenty-First Century. *Zygon* 35 (4), 941–53.

Chapter 4   Scientific Explanations of the Cosmos

Barker, Peter, and Bernard R. Goldstein (2001) Theological Foundations of Kepler's Astronomy. *Osiris* 16, 88–113.

Finocchiaro, Maurice A. (2001) Science, Religion, and the Historiography of the Galileo Affair: On the Undesirability of Oversimplification. *Osiris* 16, 114–32.

North, John (1995) *The Norton History of Astronomy and Cosmology*. New York: Norton.

Russell, John L. (1995) What was the Crime of Galileo? *Annals of Science* 52, 403–10.

Shapin, Steven (1996) *The Scientific Revolution*. Chicago: University of Chicago Press.

Chapter 5   Creation Myths

Broadie, Sarah, and Anthony Kenny (2004) The Creation of the World I: Plato's Intelligible World? And The Creation of the World II: Seven Concepts of Creation. *Aristotelian Society Supplementary Volume* 78, 65–79; 81–92.

Freund, Philip (1965) *Myths of Creation*. New York: Washington Square Press.

Knitter, Paul F. (2000) A Common Creation Story? Interreligious Dialogue and Ecology. *Journal of Ecumenical Studies* 37, 285–300.

Sarna, Nahum M. (1966) *Understanding Genesis: The Heritage of Biblical Israel*. New York: Schocken.

Welker, Michael (1995) Creation: Big Bang or the Work of Seven Days? *Theology Today* 52, 173–87.

Chapter 6   Current Understandings of the Universe

Brooke, John Hedley (1991) *Science and Religion: Some Historical Perspectives*. Cambridge: Cambridge University Press.

Hodgson, Peter E. (2000) God's Action in the World: The Relevance of Quantum Mechanics. *Zygon* 35, 505–16.

Mason, Neil A., ed. (2003) *God and Design: The Teleological Argument and Modern Science*. London: Routledge.

Stix, Gary (2004) The Patent Clerk's Legacy. *Scientific American* 291 (3), 44–9.

Tegmark, Max, and John Archibald Wheeler (2001) 100 Years of Quantum Mysteries. *Scientific American* 284 (2), 68–75.

Chapter 7   Eschatology

Battersby, Stephen (2005) The Unraveling. *New Scientist*, 185, 30–7.

Pannenberg, Wolfhart (2000) Eternity, Time and the Trinitarian God. *Dialog: A Journal of Theology* 39 (1), 9–14.

Peters, Ted (2001) Eschatology: Eternal Now or Cosmic Future? *Zygon*, 36, 349–56.

Polkinghorne, John, and Michael Welker, eds. (2000) *The End of the World and the Ends of God*. Harrisburg, PA: Trinity Press International.

Russell, Robert John (2000) Time in Eternity: Special Relativity and Eschatology. *Dialog: A Journal of Theology* 39 (1), 46–55.

Chapter 8   Darwin Changes Everything

Magner, Lois N. (1994) *A History of the Life Sciences*. New York: Marcel Dekker.

McComas, William F. (1997) The Discovery and Nature of Evolution by Natural Selection: Misconceptions and Lessons from the History of Science. *American Biology Teacher* 59, 492–500.

Miles, Sara Joan (2001) Charles Darwin and Asa Gray Discuss Teleology and Design. *Perspectives on Science and Christian Faith* 53, 196–201.

Ormseth, Dennis (1984) Darwin's Theory and Christian Orthodoxy. *Word & World* 4 (4), 401–9.

Understanding Evolution. Available at http://evolution.berkeley.edu/evolibrary/home.php (accessed September 14, 2009).

Chapter 9   Scientific Explanations of the Origin of Life

Clowes, Chris (2006) Major Events in the History of Life and the Cambrian Explosion. Available at www.peripatus.gen.nz/paleontology/ (accessed September 15, 2009).

Ingber, Donald E. (2000) The Origin of Cellular Life. *BioEssays* 22 (12), 1160–70.

Peretó, Juli (2005) Controversies on the Origin of Life. *International Microbiology* 8, 23–31.

Rolston, Holmes III (2005) Inevitable Humans: Simon Conway Morris's Evolutionary Paleontology. *Zygon* 40 (1), 221–9.

Shapiro, Robert (2007) A Simpler Origin for Life. *Scientific American* 296 (6), 46–53.

Chapter 10   Evidence for Evolution

Colby, Chris (1997) Evidence for Evolution: An Eclectic Survey. Available at www.talkorigins.org/faqs/evolution-research.html (accessed September 23, 2009).

Durant, John, ed. (1985) *Darwinism and Divinity: Essays on Evolution and Religious Belief*. Oxford: Blackwell.

Gilbert, Scott F. (2003) Opening Darwin's Black Box: Teaching Evolution through Developmental Genetics. *Nature Reviews Genetics* 4 (9), 735–41.

Miller, James B., ed. (2001) *An Evolving Dialogue: Theological and Scientific Perspectives on Evolution*. Harrisburg, PA: Trinity Press International.

Prothero, Donald R. (2005) The Fossils Say Yes. *Natural History* 114 (9), 52–6.

Chapter 11   Evolution and Design

Case-Winters, Anna (2000) The Argument from Design: What is at Stake Theologically? *Zygon* 35, 69–81.

Cunningham, Mary Kathleen, ed. (2007) *God and Evolution: A Reader*. London: Routledge.

Manson, Neil A., ed. (2003) *God and Design: The Teleological Argument and Modern Science*. London: Routledge.

Moore, Randy (2000) *In the Light of Evolution: Science Education on Trial*. Reston, VA: National Association of Biology Teachers.

Padgett, Alan G. (2003) Crucified Creator: The God of Evolution and Luther's Theology of the Cross. *Dialog: A Journal of Theology* 42, 300–4.

Peters, Ted, and Martinez Hewlett (2003) *Evolution from Creation to New Creation: Conflict, Conversation, and Convergence*. Nashville, TN: Abingdon Press.

Russell, Robert John (2003) Is Evil Evolving? *Dialog: A Journal of Theology* 42, 309–15.

Chapter 12   Human Evolution

Dennett, Daniel C. (2001) The Evolution of Culture. *Monist* 84 (3), 305–24.

Martin, Robert A. (2004) *Missing Links: Evolutionary Concepts and Transitions through Time*. Sudbury, MA: Jones & Bartlett.

Ruse, Michael (2000) Can a Darwinian be a Christian? Sociobiological Issues. *Zygon* 35 (2), 299–316.

Stanford, Craig, John S. Allen, and Susan C. Anton (2006) *Biological Anthropology*. Upper Saddle River, NJ: Pearson Prentice Hall.

Wilson, Edward O. (1995) Science and Ideology. *Academic Questions* 8 (3), 73–81.

Chapter 13   What It Means to be Human

Arnhart, Larry (1998) The New Darwinian Naturalism in Political Theory. *Zygon* 33, 369–93.

Jeeves, Malcolm, ed. (2004) *From Souls to Cells – and Beyond: Changing Portraits of Human Nature*. Grand Rapids, MI: Eerdmans.

Macquarrie, John (1977) *Principles of Christian Theology*, 2nd edn. New York: Scribner's.

Ruse, Michael (1999) Evolutionary Ethics: What Can We Learn from the Past? *Zygon* 34, 435–51.

Sussman, Robert W. (1999) The Myth of Man the Hunter, Man the Killer and the Evolution of Human Morality. *Zygon* 34, 453–71.

Chapter 14   Modern-Day Marvels: Biotechnology and Medicine

Biotechnology Industry Organization. Available at http://bio.org/ (accessed October 1, 2009).

Burley, Justine, and John Harris, eds. (2002) *A Companion to Genethics*. Malden, MA: Blackwell.

Edgar, Brian (2006) Biotheology: Theology, Ethics and the New Biotechnologies. *Evangelical Review of Theology* 30 (3), 219–36.

Glick, Bernard R., and Jack J. Pasternak (1998) *Molecular Biotechnology: Principles and Applications of Recombinant DNA*. 2nd edn. Washington, DC: ASM.

Jones, D. Gareth (2005) Responses to the Human Embryo and Embryonic Stem Cells: Scientific and Theological Assessments. *Science & Christian Belief* 17 (2), 199–222.

Kilner, John D., and C. Ben Mitchell (2003) *Does God Need Our Help? Cloning, Assisted Suicide, and Other Challenges in Bioethics*. Wheaton, IL: Tyndale House.

Modell, Stephen M. (2007) Genetic and Reproductive Technologies in the Light of Religious Dialogue. *Zygon* 42 (1), 163–82.

Chapter 15   Stewardship and the Environment

Collins, William, Robert Colman, James Haywood, Martin R. Manning, and Philip Mote (2007) The Physical Science behind Climate Change. *Scientific American* 297 (2), 64–73.

Deane-Drummond, Celia (2003) Wisdom, Justice and Environmental Decision-Making in a Biotechnological Age. *Ecotheology: Journal of Religion, Nature & the Environment* 8.2, 173–92.

Mock, Greg, and Paul Steele (2006).Power to the Poor. *Environment* 48 (1), 8–23.

Nelson, Robert H. (1990) Unoriginal Sin. *Policy Review* 53, 52–9.

Pimm, Stuart L., and Clinton Jenkins (2005) Sustaining the Variety of Life. *Scientific American* 293 (3), 66–73.

Rolston III, Holmes. (2004). Caring for Nature: From Fact to Value, from Respect to Reverence. *Zygon* 39 (2), 277–302.

Source Acknowledgments

At points throughout the text, extracts from the Revised Standard Version of the Bible have been used. Revised Standard Version of the Bible, copyright 1952 [2nd edition, 1971] by the Division of Christian Education of the National Council of the Churches of Christ in the United States of America. Used by permission. All rights reserved.

The editor and publisher wish to thank the following for permission to use copyright material for the below figures:

4.1a	© The Print Collector/Heritage-Images
4.1b	© Royal Astronomical Society/Science Photo Library
4.3	Galleria Palatina, Palazzo Pitti, Florence, Italy/The Bridgeman Art Library
4.7	akg-images
6.2	akg-images
8.1	Down House, Kent, UK/The Bridgeman Art Library
8.2(a)	© Bettmann/Corbis
10.6(a)	markku murto/art/Alamy
12.2	British Library, London, UK/© British Library Board. All Rights Reserved/ The Bridgeman Art Library
12.3(b)	PASCAL GOETGHELUCK/SCIENCE PHOTO LIBRARY
14.5	PA/PA Archive/Press Association Images
14.6	U.S. National Library of Medicine http://ghr.nlm.nih.gov/handbook/therapy/procedures

Every effort has been made to trace copyright holders and to obtain their permission for the use of copyright material. The editor and publisher will gladly receive any information enabling them to rectify any error or omission in subsequent editions.

Index

Note: page numbers in italics refer to Figures; those in bold to Tables.